THE
SCIENCE FICTION
SOURCE BOOK

THE
SCIENCE FICTION
SOURCE BOOK

edited by
David Wingrove

Longman

For John, Lorraine, Christian, Rory and Luke

Longman Group Limited,
Longman House, Burnt Mill, Harlow,
Essex CM20 2JE, England
and Associated Companies throughout the world.

Produced by Shuckburgh Reynolds Ltd,
8 Northumberland Place,
London W2 5BS

First published 1984

British Library Cataloguing in Publication Data

Wingrove, David
  Science fiction source book.
  1. Science fiction/–/History and criticism
  I. Title
  808.3'876   PN3433.5

  ISBN 0-582-55592-2

Set in Ehrhardt by SX Composing Ltd, Rayleigh, Essex

Printed and bound in Spain by Printer Industria Grafica SA
D.L.B. 96-1984
Design by Roger Pring and Associates
Illustrations by Graham Rosewarne, Elizabeth Hankins
and Sylvia Kwan

Pictures kindly supplied by: Arrow Books Ltd, Barrington Bayley, Sandy Brown, Jonathan Cape Ltd,
Corgi Books Ltd, Faber & Faber Ltd, Fontana Books Ltd, Granada Books Ltd, Victor Gollancz Ltd,
Robert Holdstock, Macdonald & Co Ltd, New English Library Ltd, Penguin Books Ltd, Peter Owen
Ltd, Christopher Priest, Sphere Books Ltd, David Wingrove. Shuckburgh Reynolds Ltd would also
like to thank those artists and companies who could not be traced in the course of preparing this book
for publication.

Contents

continues overleaf

Contents continued

Contributors

EDITOR

David Wingrove is a full-time writer and editor and was formerly editor of *Vector*, the critical journal of the British Science Fiction Association. His previous publications include *The Immortals Of Science Fiction* and *Apertures: A Study Of The Writings Of Brian W. Aldiss* (co-authored with Brian Griffin). He is currently working on a full-length study of Philip K. Dick and preparing a doctoral thesis in English Literature on Thomas Hardy, D. H. Lawrence and William Golding. In his spare time he actually writes science fiction.

CONTRIBUTORS

Brian W. Aldiss is one of science fiction's leading writers, critics and editors, and his history of the field, *Billion Year Spree* is highly acclaimed and widely used. His most recent work has been on the best-selling *Helliconia* trilogy, the final volume of which is due in 1985.

Kingsley Amis is a respected English novelist and critic, best known perhaps for his *Lucky Jim*. Within the science fiction field he has produced four fine novels (*The Alteration* amongst them) and an affectionate study of the genre, *New Maps Of Hell*.

Malcolm Edwards is science fiction editor for Victor Gollancz Ltd and was formerly editor of *Vector* as well as Administrator of the Science Fiction Foundation and editor of their journal, *Foundation*. He is co-author, with Maxim Jakubowski of *The Complete Book Of Science Fiction And Fantasy Lists*.

Frederik Pohl has been a stalwart of the genre for more than 40 years, as writer, editor, critic and agent. Two of his 1970s novels, *Man Plus* and *Gateway* won Hugo Awards. With Brian Aldiss he is a prime mover in making science fiction an international phenomenon, founding World Sf.

Brian Stableford is a prolific writer and critic within the genre. He is also a Lecturer in Social Sciences at Reading University and holds a Doctorate in the Sociology of Literature. Science fiction fans may know him for his intelligent 'Hooded Swan' adventures.

CONTRIBUTORS TO SCIENCE FICTION WRITERS: A CONSUMER'S GUIDE

Robert Allen is a freelance journalist and founder of the Northern Irish science fiction magazine, *Extro*. He has done editing work for the BBC and for a number of British weekly newspapers.

Colin Greenland holds a D.Phil from Oxford. His doctoral thesis was polished and published as *The Entropy Exhibition*. A first novel, *Daybreak On A Different Mountain* is to be published in 1984. His reviews have appeared in *Foundation* and *The Times Literary Supplement*.

Brian Griffin is author of two science fiction novels, *The Nucleation* and *The Omega Project*. He is also co-author (with David Wingrove) of *Apertures: A Study Of The Writings Of Brian W. Aldiss*. His criticism – sf and general – has been published widely in the UK.

Maxim Jakubowski is the English Language's foremost exporter of science fiction to France. As editor, anthologist, writer and commentator on rock music, he has produced more than two dozen books. He currently manages a London publishing house.

Roz Kaveney has reviewed science fiction for a number of journals, including *Vector, Foundation* and *Books and Bookmen*. She is currently a reader for Chatto & Windus and for the BBC.

Tony Richards is a freelance writer whose short stories (many sf) have appeared in *Isaac Asimov's Science Fiction Magazine, The Magazine Of Fantasy & Science Fiction* and a number of horror anthologies.

Andrew Sawyer has reviewed for *Vector* and *Arena* and is currently preparing a thesis on Thomas Dekker, the Jacobean dramatist.

Cyril Simsa is a graduate of Cambridge, a short-story writer and reviewer. He was also keyboards-player for the short-lived *Somewhere A Voice*.

Ritchie Smith is a teacher and freelance writer. His short stories have appeared in *New Writings In SF*.

Other contributors to Consumers' Guide: **Brian W. Aldiss, Brian Stableford** and **David Wingrove**.

Foreword
Brian W. Aldiss

SCIENCE FICTION: still for some of us the most marvellous subject – or at least the second most marvellous subject. 'The glory, jest, and riddle of the world' – at once abominable and abysmal in so many of its manifestations, and yet, in its best, the voice nearest to our inner voice.

Presumably many people would admit that science fiction has shaped their lives: not only scientists, not only astronauts and experts at NASA, but ordinary earthbound mortals who know little of science but crave glimpses of realities less prosaic than their own. It has never been determined exactly who reads SF, or even what SF is. Within its mode, it is many conflicting things, and therein lies its strength. It is a trifle, a hot-air balloon, a penetrating survey of our troubled time, a conceit, a dancing bear, a blueprint for the future, a safety valve, a commercial package . . . what you will.

So to formularize the whole circus in a book is a brave endeavour on David Wingrove's part. We do need to know a great deal more about science fiction. In particular, we need to understand the relationship between the traditional written literature and the recent overwhelming iconography of film, TV and video. The immense popularity of SF in visual media is not necessarily good for the written word. So often, the visual element is the enemy of the intellectual one, while, as we know, any product seeking wide popularity, in whatever medium, reverts to the formulaic. The formulaic is, quite simply, the enemy of good science fiction – or indeed of anything which sharpens the imagination and the critical faculties or tries to widen our range of experience.

At the present moment, we have a situation of crisis: on the one hand, elaborate popular films like *Blade Runner*, choked with weirdo sets and hardware, grounded in dubious morality; and on the other hand a fiction where its writers are either in financial straits or growing rich by plagiarism. Whether this crisis is one inherent in SF itself, in the gradual erosion of genre material, as a coin is defaced by constant use, or a more transitional phase, remains to be seen. The hopeful signs that the latter is the case may perhaps be seen in the writings of authors such as Gene Wolfe, Stephen Donaldson, and Doris Lessing, who have the courage to pursue grand and intricate themes over several volumes, deepening – rather than diluting – those themes as they go. Whatever the outcome of the crisis, we need such discussion books as this to guide us.

If the weather is so stormy, why continue to write science fiction? This is a question writers are often asked. But one does not lightly abandon what one does best. I have even managed to enjoy (for some of the time) the short-sighted prejudice against science fiction; at least it gives one a cause to fight for.

In the end, there can be only a personal response to that multi-coloured beast, science fiction. I love SF for its surrealist verve, its looney non-reality, its piercing truths, its surprises, its wit, its masked melancholy, its nose for damnation, its bunkum, its traditionalism, its contempt for home comforts, its stranglehold on first causes, its slewed astronomy, its xenophilia, its hip, its classlessness, its mysterious machines, its allegorical figures, its gaudy backdrops, its subversion, its tragic insecurity. Long may its obsessions flourish!

A BRIEF HISTORY
Brian W. Aldiss

SO FAR, science fiction has earned itself little history and much rigmarole. Anything that can be regarded as marvellous, or as scientifically likely (or, on the other hand, as scientifically unlikely) has been press-ganged to serve under that rather amorphous term "science fiction".

This is hardly surprising, since the mode has achieved recognition only in recent times. Such histories or overviews as exist have been written by people involved, often science-fiction writers themselves. Dispassion has yet to enter the discussion.

SF has a voracious appetite and shows a protean capacity for change. Credit enough is never given for its diversity. A common mistake is to classify it as a genre, like thrillers, spy stories, romances, and so on; SF includes many genres, such as the catastrophe novel, space opera, etc, and thus by definition cannot itself be a genre. It is more correct to consider SF a mode of expression. Use of this term helps to remind us that SF is rather more amorphous than is generally thought to be the case.

The early days of science fiction

In my history of science fiction,[1] I argued for an acceptance of Mary Shelley's *Frankenstein: or, The Modern Prometheus* (1818) as a convenient starting point for the texts which can be fruitfully considered within the science-fiction canon. Since then, I have further extended this argument,[2] which seems to have been generally accepted.[3] Mary Shelley reinforces her position as first science-fiction writer by a second novel, *The Last Man* (1826), which takes up the now familiar theme of world-wide catastrophe.

No clear progression presents itself after these publications, for two reasons. In the first place, Mrs. Shelley's personal situation was unusual, and even today we can savour the unusual qualities of her Frankenstein, which is not easily imitated. In the second place, the tradition in the ur-SF of her time lay not in romantic agony but rather in a classical optimism still in vogue on the continent of Europe, of which Louis Sébastien Mercier's *L'An 2440* (first published anonymously in Paris in 1786) is a noteworthy example.

Mercier's novel, a utopian discourse which was translated into several European languages, remains a speculation firmly based in the anticipations of the Enlightenment. It represents the triumph of Reason, or at least of reason-ableness, as Kurd Lasswitz's *Auf Zwei Planeten* (On Two Planets; 1897) – a story of Martians and Earthmen establishing a world state – was to do over a century later. Both the French and the German novel represent a European tradition which has never entirely merged with the Anglo-American, the latter at its most characteristic carrying a vein of dark romanticism. In this brief essay, emphasis must remain on the SF written in the English language.

A rigorous history of SF would include the enormous contribution made by European movements this century, such as Marinetti and the Futurists, the Symbolists, many architects, and writers. Here there is room only for a mention of that remarkable earlier French writer, Jules Verne (1828-1905), whose tide of

1. *Billion Year Spree. The History of Science Fiction.* Brian W. Aldiss. London, 1973.

2. See "Mary Wollstonecraft Shelley" in *Science Fiction Writers*, edited by E. F. Bleiler. New York, 1982.

3. For instance – without acknowledgement – by Scholes Robert and Eric S. Rabkin in their *Science Fiction: History. Science. Vision.* New York, 1977.

novels covers some four decades. Verne's best liked novels, such as *Journey to the Centre of the Earth* (1864), *Twenty Thousand Leagues under the Sea* (1870), *From the Earth to the Moon* (1873), and *Hector Servadac* (also known as *Off on a Comet*; 1877) are all early and optimistic works, showing individualists working in harmony with their machines. The writings of Verne's old age, *Master of the World* (1904) and so on, paint a darker picture.

To find a way through the maze of titles which begin to accumulate before the nineteenth century is dead, it is necessary to ask if there is some kind of philosophy behind the majority of SF writings. Anthony Burgess[4] concludes that positivism is behind it all. "Without positivism there would be no Mill, Darwin, Spencer, Engels or Marx and, in literature genuine or sub, no science fiction. Certainly no Jules Verne or H. G. Wells."

This may apply to Verne, with his passion for observable phenomena. It seems less applicable to the dark vision of Wells's *The Time Machine* (1895). A more cautious view would discern two main and often warring impulses, the positivism we associated with Comte and the Enlightenment, and the romanticism which abandons any steady-state model of reality in favour of more dramatic and inward events. These, in other words, are the utopianists and the catastrophists.

Burgess's dictum also ignores another feature of a mode which is on the whole sturdily atheist, its preoccupation with religious motifs, and with apocalypses of ingeniously varied kinds.

Nevertheless, the force of Burgess's remark underlines the way so many SF works aspire to cloak their romantic or personal natures within the formality of positivism, particularly the kind of scientific positivism suggested by the very term science fiction. Even Mary Shelley employs this tactic, as is shown by the opening words of the preface to Frankenstein: "The event on which this fiction is founded has been supposed, by Dr. Darwin and some of the physiological writers of Germany, as of not impossible occurrence".

Possibility, in fact, hardly enters the matter; Mary Shelley received her seminal idea in a nightmare, not a treatise. Ever since her time a kind of plea of positivism has been entered by SF writers. Many a nightmare has been given credibility by being draped in scientific or pseudo-scientific theories. "It could happen" is always a good excuse for a flight of fancy.

H. G. Wells enters the plea of posivitism by calling his imaginative novels "scientific romances". His is one of the greatest names in SF, and his greatest SF novels remain in currency today. They are *The Time Machine, The Island of Dr Moreau* (1896), *The Invisible Man* (1897), *The War of the Worlds* (1898), and *The First Men in the Moon* (1901). All had far-reaching influence, while if we include with them Wells's various and beautiful short stories, they constitute together a striking anthology of SF themes which have been constantly reworked since Wells's day – rarely to such good effect as in their originals.

What time-travel story has the power of *The Time Machine*?

When Wells's great creative powers flagged, he produced more polemical work, also set in the future, of which perhaps the most important is the rarely read *A Modern Utopia* (1905). Increasingly, preachments entered into his work, a tendency noticeable in the works of more recent writers such as Mack Reynolds,

4. Anthony Burgess, "The Apocalypse and After" in *Times Literary Supplement*. London, 18 March 1983.

Frank Herbert, Robert A. Heinlein, and Julian May. The controversial nature of SF, particularly when it deals with extrapolated societies, leads easily to didacticism; nor do readers on the whole appear to be averse to a little preaching.

Wells was once said to be the most widely read author in the world. He certainly focused attention on the challenges opened up by new technology, and popularized a fiction which, while using realism as its tool, trafficked in unreality. In particular, his exciting prognostications of new men and new forms of government fell on receptive ears among the technician and engineer class in Europe and the New World. It was this class who formed both the originators and readers of the first magazines devoted purely to science fiction.

Popular culture: the SF magazines

Certainly the covers of the early magazines did not differ greatly from the covers of such magazines as "Popular Mechanics", both displaying enticingly unlikely machines running amok in primary colours. Hugo Gernsback published the first issue of his "Amazing Stories" in April 1926, relying heavily on the writings of Wells, Verne, and Edgar Allan Poe, as well as on numerous European writers, to fill his pages. It is significant that "Amazing" was in many respects an extension of Gernsback's "Science and Invention", which helped to promote the radios in which he dealt – and in which his own attempt at "scienti-fiction", *Ralph 124C41+*, first appeared. This atrocious piece of writing is indeed imbued with the spirit of positivism and utilitarianism.

Edgar Rice Burroughs was the first American writer of any stature to contribute to the SF magazines. He reinforced an enjoyable tradition for funny alien animals which, as the Star Wars films demonstrate, is far from dead. Burroughs has a strong visual sense, although his powers of invention desert him when it comes to plots, which are of a roughneck variety. His Mars, Barsoom, has genuine moments of magic, which set readers imagining.

Many of Burroughs's successors succeeded only in trivializing the subject-matter with which they dealt. Astronomy was reduced to high jinks. However, the situation improved as a generation of writers arrived on the scene who had been brought up within the SF mould.

Such names as Murray Leinster, E. E. Smith, and Jack Williamson are recalled with pleasure. Leinster wrote a fluent workaday prose and is honoured as the originator of the theme of parallel worlds (in the short story, "Sidewise in Time"). Williamson's prose glints with good reflective touches, most particularly in his novel, *Darker Than You Think* (1948), which first appeared in the magazines. Both Williamson and Leinster belong in part to the American tradition of writing about the outdoors, from which they derive a strength lacking in some of their rivals.

One perplexity confronting critics of SF is the way in which the most popular writers exhibit glaring faults to which their readers are either blind or indifferent. E. E. Smith, known to his charmed audience as "Doc" Smith (he had a Ph.D. which conferred status in the 1920s), wrote dialogue of a sophistication somewhere between Frank Richards and Daisy Ashford. Yet the public is always right, if only in the short run. For what Doc Smith did well was to unravel an escalating tale of interstellar evil and its defeat, in the architecturally complex "Lensman" series, from *Triplanetary*, a serial in 1934, to *Children of the Lens*, a serial in

1947-48. Smith invented space opera. He took his writing seriously. The six novels in the series became best-sellers during the 1970s; when one might have thought his 1920s slang ridiculously dated, the Gray Lensman rode again.

These three writers – and many others of lesser rank – wrote for and were in part ruined by the insensitive commercialism which governed the magazines. Williamson, for instance, has gone on record rather touchingly regarding his short story, "With Folded Hands", in which small black utilitarian robots, representatives of dominant technology, come to undermine the value in men's lives by supervising their every action. The story was successful, and Williamson's editor, John W. Campbell, persuaded him to write a sequel. This Williamson did, against his better judgement: "And Searching Mind" resulted. Williamson's judgement was not at fault. The later story was published in novel form as *The Humanoids* (1949). The SF virus of elephantiasis is contained in its sequels.

The secret of the success of the pulp magazines, and a possible cause of their ultimate demise, was that each title specialized narrowly in one type of story: cowboy, detective, romance, maritime, etc, within a narrow code of ethics. Readers knew what to expect before they opened each new issue. SF, as a late category, suffered less from this handicap.

Writers such as Clark Ashton Smith, A. Merritt, and Henry Kuttner might be found in fantasy, horror, or SF magazines. But the best-remembered name here is that of Howard P. Lovecraft, who moved from "Weird Tales" to become one of the ikons of SF. Much of Lovecraft's work, such as *The Dulwich Horror* and the stories of the Cthulhu mythos, reflect the morbid world of Edgar Allan Poe (who, as one of the early exponents of the short story, developed a form in which SF has shown great strengths). Since his death in 1937, Lovecraft has become the subject of a cult – another feature of the enthusiasms which SF engenders.

Magazine SF provided intense pleasure for those who were insensitive to its literary shortcomings. It was hastily written for the most part, and that perhaps helped give an edge to the plot or to the surprise denouement which was *de rigueur* in the pulps. If there was one symptom which marked this body of writing off from less commercial kinds, it was the emphasis on plot at the expense of character and scene. The anxiety to press on with the story without embodying it convincingly in scenes which further action and meaning remains typical of the lower orders of SF to this day.

Serious culture: Huxley, Stapledon, and their successors

While the SF magazines were beginning to proliferate, and to spread from New York to other countries, another kind of science fiction was being written which came from an older tradition, the tradition developed by Wells, which had at its centre a stronger interest in people and societies than in machines. One sees this immediately in the three most important SF works of the 1930s, Aldous Huxley's *Brave New World* and the two related novels of W. Olaf Stapledon, *Last and First Men* and *Star Maker*.

Aldous Huxley made his name as one of the Bright Young Novelists of the 1920s, with pranksome novels like *Antic Hay* and *Crome Yellow*. *Brave New World* (1932) opens without compromise in the future, in the Year After Ford 632, and the reader is then treated to a society where babies are graded and moulded according to the job that awaits them. Culture is abolished; in its place is casual promiscuity. With a lightness and wit uncharacteristic of dystopias, Huxley defines his morally crippling social structure through the character of The Savage, who dares claim the right to be unhappy.

That problems of large societies dramatized in *Brave New World* remain central to us in the 1980s, half a century later, probably accounts for the way in which the novel is still eagerly read, as well as studied.

Some of the ideas in *Brave New World* may have derived from the disturbing chapters in *First Men in the Moon*, in which Wells outlines the basis of Selenite Society. Critics have also detected the influence of the expatriate Russian, Yevgeny Zamyatin, who, in *We* (1920), outlined an even more faceless and rigid hierarchy, a satirical paradigm of the Soviet state then under construction, from which Zamyatin had retreated to Paris. It certainly seems likely that Huxley, who read everything, including science fiction, may have absorbed this dystopia (which in its turn owes something to Wells: traders in utopian fiction are always well-read in each others' works).

Late in life, Huxley turned his utopia upside down in *Island* (1962). Here, the drugs and free love he once anathematized have become good medicine in his threatened island paradise. The novel itself is laboriously written, lacking the wit which informs its predecessor; but the aspects of human nature with which Huxley deals remain ones with which any masters of society will have to deal.

Compared with the various and well-documented life of Aldous Huxley, Olaf Stapledon remains a shadowy and rather numb figure, defined by negatives. Like Huxley, he went up to Balliol College, Oxford, but there similarities end.

From Stapledon's study came forth ten works of fiction, among them two ambitious and related master-works, *Last and First Men* (1930) and *Star Maker* (1937). *Last and First Men* seeks to tell the whole future of mankind as it spreads over the solar system. After its poor and laboured opening chapters, it turns into true myth, reinforcing its authenticity with time scales which emphasize the grandeur of time. *Star Maker* even more impressively tells the history of our universe, of what preceded it and of what will follow. The prose, as far as prose can, matches the theme. Textually, *Star Maker* is as rich as it is astonishing.

It is hard to see SF going beyond Stapledon. But the current fashion in the 1980s for long series of books centred in the same universe includes Jean M. Aule's *Earth's Children*, *The Book of the New Sun* by Gene Wolf, Philip José Farmer's *Riverworld Saga*, Herbert's *Dune* series, Doris Lessing's *Canopus in Argos: Archives*, Aldiss's *Helliconia*, and Stephen Donaldson's immense *Chronicles of Thomas Covenant*, not forgetting Moorcock's inter-related series within series. Some or all of these represent a Stapledonian impulse to conjure up the whole world, or, at least, "seize this sorry state of things entire".

Not that a fashion for the immense is particularly new. Smith's grandiose Lensman series was once published bound in leather, boxed, and labelled *The History of Civilization* . . .

Slowly, over the years, the gap between the serious culture, as represented by Stapledon, and the popular culture as represented by the magazines, has diminished. World War II helped greatly in this respect, presenting everyone – including authors – with a great drama of complex issues which involved the whole planet in turmoil, the results of which are still with us.

It is necessary, therefore, in limited space, to leap ahead to see how science fiction has developed into its present diverse state, rather than to spend time on such acknowledged and amply discussed works as C. S. Lewis's *Out of the Silent Planet* (1938) and its linked successors, *Perelandra* (1943) and *That Hideous Strength* (1945), or George Orwell's *Nineteen Eighty-Four* (1949).

The acculturization of the magazines

Praise for the SF magazines has so far been cautious. But from the early 1940s onwards, the whole field showed a remarkable and continuous development which is still by no means spent. It is worth emphasizing that this development, this acculturization, was accomplished by those within the field. They felt, rightly, spurned by those outside. When hardcover publishing came along, when successful paperback publishing came along, the impetus derived from within the field. Indeed, when what is now an impressive critical and academic industry began, its seeds also were sown by writers or fans.

The first spear to glitter in the dawn of acculturization was editor John W. Campbell's "Astounding". From the late 1930s, for over a decade, it was where one went to find the best authors at their best.

From the strictly literary point of view, the contents of the magazines were sometimes negligible. The attractions of the magazines, however, outweighed their blemishes. Each issue, at least in prospect, offered new astonishments (it was not for nothing that their first publishers seized on such tempting titles as "Amazing", "Astounding", "Wonder", "Marvel"), and the landscape of an issue offered a menu of disorientations. One could not tell, when embarking upon a new story, whether it was to be in the far or near future, on another planet, in another dimension, or inside a spaceship; one could not tell if the eyes through whom the events were seen were those of a human, a robot, an alien, or even a god. One could not tell what sacred cows were to be overturned, what shibboleths blasted.

Some authors presented a view of unremitting progress towards technical perfection; others – and by no means the least popular – presented a view of mankind as doomed always to suffer. In a famous story, F. L. Wallace postulated that mankind had developed from a kind of rat escaped from an interstellar ship. Another favourite theme at one time was the view of mankind as representing all that remained of a once great inter-galactic race which had been defeated many thousands of years ago in a mighty space war.

Optimists and pessimists alike believed that mankind would one day take flight from Earth and visit other planets. Tame though this may sound now, it remained an extremely heterodox opinion until the late 1950s and even beyond. When the space race came and changed everything, only SF readers were prepared for the event; just as, some two decades earlier, they were among the least surprised by the invention of the A-bomb (which also changed everything).

The magazines, in fact, as experienced month by month, formed a sort of pleasurable debating club, an in-group for whom their year's subscription gave access, as was once said of Romanticism, to "... a chaos from which a new certainty must necessarily develop".[5] A ton of *Brave New Worlds* could not offer the similar continuity of experience.

5. Ludwig Tieck in a letter to Frederick Schlegel, March 1801. Quoted in Alexander Gode von Aesch's*Natural Science in German Romanticism.* New York, 1966.

This continuity worked in two ways. On the one hand, readers, astute students of form, could follow the development of a new author or a new idea bandied among authors. Some authors, like Poul Anderson and Robert Silverberg, took root and rampaged like weeds over all the magazines. (In the English magazines, the great suppliers were E. C. Tubb, John Brunner, and Kenneth Bulmer.) Others were more frugal, like William Tenn, and had to be sought out. A Cold War idea, such as the concept of an alien which could imitate almost precisely a human being, took on conflicting nuances under different hands. Among the best-remembered interpretations of this theme are Ray Bradbury's Martians and the sinister pods in the movie *Invasion of the Body-Snatchers*.

On the other hand, one author could develop his ideas over a number of years, remaining sure of an audience quick to catch on and to empathize. Isaac Asimov's celebrated Foundation Trilogy developed in this way, from an initial short story in 1942 (entitled "Foundation") to a three-part serial some seven years later. Similar cases are Asimov's robot stories and James Blish's stories of *Cities in Flight*, among many others. Smith's unfolding Lensman series has already been mentioned.

The magazines were designedly ephemeral. Devotees turned collector hoarded them. Anthologists were to pillage them for stories, for "classics". Entire issues of magazines were later reprinted in hardcover on acid-free paper, or transferred to microfiche. The fans of the future proved vigilant preservers of their past.

Similarly, another group of fans was to raise the ephemeral and relatively unsuccessful TV series, *Star Trek*, into a cult which is still playing all over the world and has boldly spawned a movie and paperback industry where no man spawned before.

The theme of telepathy
A theme given almost equal prominence with space travel is telepathy. Whereas interplanetary and interstellar voyages have a technological and scientific basis, telepathy is almost as clearly anti-scientific. No rational reasons can be conjured as to why humanity should develop an ability to communicate directly, mind to mind, without speech in this or any future generation.

The idea of telepathy is ancient, but was given new impetus by the discovery of wireless waves and the development of radio at the beginning of this century: if unseen messages can be directed from crystal, why not from head to head? This false analogy has taken root in the popular mind. Any charlatan coming along and claiming to bend spoons or read print with his or her fingertips finds ready credence among the gullible.

Yet psi powers have deservedly found their way from the various quack psychic phenomena investigated so solemnly at the end of the last century into the pages of science-fiction stories. For SF readers wish to see the world change, to see that new certainty which must necessarily develop, and telepathy would change the world even more effectively than the A-bomb or space travel.

Telepathy would banish privacy of thought. It might usher in a new era of intimacy, understanding, and peace as in Stapledon's *Odd John* (1935) – the colonists on his island "expand their 'now' to embrace hours, days" – or, of course, it might usher in a new form of terror and oppression. On the whole, SF writers have opted for the latter.

Again, we can see the concept bandied about among authors. Henry Kuttner's interesting series of stories about the Baldies (later gathered into book-form as *Mutant* (1953), depicts a post-atomic world where telepaths are persecuted, and easy to spot because they are bald – an acute if unsubtle stigma. John Wyndham's handling of the same theme is presented in *The Chrysalids* (1955) in completely different terms from Kuttner's. Wyndham's little girl who utters a "deafening" telepathic scream may derive from the almost limbless crofter's infant in the aforementioned *Odd John*, who opens its telepathic mind to disclose "the bottomless black pit of Hell".

The misfits who inhabit Stapledon's island may be recalled again when we read Theodore Sturgeon's *More Than Human* (1953), where a group of six of society's rejects constitutes a self-help psi-gestalt. Sturgeon may never have read *Odd John*; the idea of a strongly bonded community of outcasts occurs naturally to a compassionate mind. Hippie communities would soon arise to act out the sexual freedoms of which Stapledon, Sturgeon, and others wrote.

The most brilliant portrayal of telepaths living within an almost unchanged society occurs in the wayward Alfred Bester's gaudy novel, *The Demolished Man* (1953), which, together with Bester's *Tiger Tiger* (also published as *The Stars My Destination*; 1956), stands foremost among the brilliant novels of the 1950s. Its anti-hero, Ben Reich, has committed a crime; how is he to keep the knowledge from the "peepers" who surround him? The book owes – as do all good novels – a debt to what went before, but the hard-edged baroque is Bester's own.

The 1950s: an SF heyday

If things may be measured in decades, then perhaps the 1950s was the perfect decade for science fiction. It remained inbred, inter-related. The magazines still survived, not yet overtaken by the paperback revolution. Television was scarcely a

Billion Year Spree In this history-cum-guide to SF Brian Aldiss, *left*, was the first to argue that science fiction began with Mary Shelley's *Frankenstein*.

potent force. The few SF movies which were made lagged behind the sophistication of the written word.

Stars of the 1950s included Ray Bradbury, whose *Fahrenheit 451* (1953) and many pellucid short stories helped make him for a while the most famous SF writer in the world; and Frederik Pohl and C. M. Kornbluth, whose satirical overviews of society included *Gladiator-at-Law* (1955) and the much reprinted *The Space Merchants* (1953), a palpable hit against advertising agencies and the decay of human dignity.

John Wyndham, with *The Day of the Triffids* (1951) and *The Kraken Wakes* (1953), neither of which took genteel English destruction further than Wells had done, reached a wide public.

Several novels have already been mentioned as having a book publication date of 1953. To that *annus mirabilis* also belongs the most remarkable novel of Arthur C. Clarke, *Childhood's End*. Clarke's name was already noted when this story of mankind's transcendence of its own limitations appeared. Clarke went on to greater success with the script for the film he wrote with Stanley Kubrick, *2001: A Space Odyssey*, but it is doubtful if he was ever to write a better novel than *Childhood's End*.

Hal Clement's remarkable conjuration of another world, the high-gravity planet of Mesklin, was published in 1954: *Mission of Gravity*. Other already well-known authors reinforced their reputations at this time. Robert Heinlein's modestly-scaled novel, *Double Star*, one of his most lucid, with a likeable central figure, appeared in 1956, as did Asimov's tightly knit robot detective mystery, *The Naked Sun*, currently under-rated.

At the same time, many lively short-story writers were active, among them Damon Knight, Theodore Sturgeon, William Tenn, Algis Budrys, Richard Matheson, Fredric Brown, Robert Sheckley, and others almost as noteworthy.

Careers commencing in the 1950s included many of whom more would be heard later: Frank Herbert, James Blish, Harry Harrison, Gordon Dickson (whose continuing "Childe" cycle awaits better attention), the energetic Harlan Ellison, Bob Shaw, J. G. Ballard, Michael Moorcock, Brian Aldiss, and the near-genius, Philip K. Dick. Not to mention the phenomenal Oxford philologist, J. R. R. Tolkien, whose *Lord of the Rings* trilogy (1954-55) became an irresistible world-wide fashion in the 1960s.

The 1960s: the "New Wave"

Great changes took place in the 1960s, among which the ongoing paperback and L.P. revolutions were aspects of spreading popular culture. The race was on for the Moon. The West started adopting new lifestyles. Dope was in the air and the Pill was in vogue. The rigours of the Cold War abated. TV-viewing became universal for those who failed to Drop Out. Youth Culture reigned. The one magazine to respond to the new epoch was the hitherto staid *New Worlds*.

The *New Worlds* writers rejected not only the old subject-matter but some of the old stale tropes of SF, particularly as practised by minor British authors. There was strenuous and rather silly talk about banishing linear narrative, as if story-telling itself was suddenly old hat. The future was abdicated in favour of the here-and-now. Spiky sensitivity replaced plodding philistinism. Style ruled. Life began in Shepperton and the Portobello Road.

J. G. Ballard was God and Michael Moorcock was the prophet of God. Fortunately for this exciting time, Ballard was a genuinely talented writer – perhaps the greatest short-story writer after Wells – whose enthusiasm for SF was real enough. Of some of the lesser members of the movement, soon dubbed the "New Wave", the same could not be said. Nevertheless, there were authors associated with the New Wave during this period who developed formidable new talents.

Michael Moorcock himself has become a cult figure, creator of the somewhat apocryphal figure of Jerry Cornelius and an abundant and various *oeuvre*. His editorship has obscured, as these things will, his real stature as writer, creator of such novels as *Gloriana* and *Byzantium Endures*. Norman Spinrad, Thomas Disch, Samuel Delaney, John Sladek – a satirist of note – and Christopher Priest all found individual voices within the group.

The New Wave idea soon spread to the States, where, mainly under the aegis of the rebellious Harlan Ellison, it underwent a metamorphosis, eventually incorporating itself into Ellison's gigantic, celebrated, record-breaking, loquacious anthology, *Dangerous Visions* (1967) and its successors. On the whole the American version proved to bear about as much resemblance to the original as the Monkees did to the Beatles.

Although the New Wave suffered much criticism from an older audience, as is always the case, it revolutionized the techniques available to writers as well as widening the audience for SF. Among those to learn and profit from it was a multi-talented writer who had long shown himself more capable of diagnosing the traffics of the here-and-now than many of his colleagues, Frederik Pohl. Such recent novels as *Man-Plus* (1976) and *Jem* (1979) show a highly impacted narrative which marks an advance over the looser textures of even the celebrated *Space Merchants* (1953).

As the 1960s zipped along from trend to trend, the SF scene became more diverse, and from then onwards often seemed to be about to lose its old corporate identity entirely. This has never happened. Even today, old loyalties prevail, and science fiction fan activity has become, in some instances, big business: but the sense of a small industrious *umwelt*, cosy for some, stifling for others, where everyone at least knows of everyone else, is far from dead.

Among the major writers of the 1960s must be ranked Philip K. Dick. There is no room here to examine his genius adequately. Dick's pages flow with a dark but never lugubrious invention; his glittering eye sees the future dying in the ash-cans of present-day California, and his findings are conveyed with a sharp relish. He died in 1982. There is no writer remotely like him. Always prolific, even in a field of stakhanovites, he produced three memorable novels in the mid-1960s alone: *The Man in the High Castle* (1962), *The Three Stigmata of Palmer Eldrich* (1964), and *Martian Time-slip* (also 1964).

In Dick's work is a true voice speaking for the individual – just as it speaks, perhaps more monstrously, in the voices of Philip José Farmer, Harlan Ellison and Michael Moorcock. What they have to say is a long way from Burgess's dry attempts at classification. The glory of the SF field lies in such rebellious voices.

Whispers came from afar, like news from a distant battlefield, that the old master, Robert Heinlein, had won an unprecedented victory. His novel, *Stranger in a Strange Land* (1961) had become a cult novel on the campus, and could be ranked as a best-seller beside ordinary or so-called "mundane" fiction. More and more people were *grokking* SF.

More distant bugles! Frank Herbert's *Dune* (1965) was out-selling Heinlein. The space-age world had become weird enough to accept SF on its own terms. The breakthrough the fans had long desired had happened. Now it is nothing to find one or more SF titles on the ordinary best-seller lists.

Recent developments in SF

Much has happened in SF in the 1970s and since, which can scarcely be more than noted here. The startling rise of Ursula LeGuin, who followed her *Earthsea* trilogy (1968-72) with such successes as *Left Hand of Darkness* (1969) and *The Dispossessed* (1974), was the signal for other women writers to enter the fray, perhaps most notably Marion Zimmer Bradley – creator of the Darkover novels – and Anne McCaffrey, who founded a commercial trade in dragons, starting with *Dragonflight* (1968) and *Dragonquest* (1971). The weight of praise heaped on LeGuin was too great: but neglect and fashion are the Scylla and Charybdis between which writers sail their frail reputations.

With the 1970s, the entertainment media changed their attitude to SF. The Stanley Kubrick/Arthur Clarke movie, *2001: A Space Odyssey* (1968), had shown that science fiction could be box office if done with care (and sufficient expenditure). In 1977 came both *Star Wars* and *Close Encounters of the Third Kind*. Each was almost phenomenally successful. Television became jammed with sci-fi and semi-sci-fi, like the series *The Billion Dollar Man*; it invaded cartoons, it got into the commercials. What had been almost a secret movement in the 1940s and 1950s became the most public of·property.

Writers like Heinlein, Herbert, Bradley, Alan Dean Foster, Clarke, McCaffrey, Niven, Pournelle, Harrison, Asimov, and others, have joined the ranks of best-sellers. The stormy bride of obscurity has turned into the fawning courtesan of fame.

There is another change. A change that may, with time, act as counterbalance to the increasing commercialism of SF. SF began to be studied academically, and to be taught in schools and universities. In the 1970s, SF criticism swelled in volume, to become a major growth industry in the 1980s.

Science fiction itself was always a massive self-help area. The criticism it engendered grew by the same rule, and expertise is coming to match enthusiasm. One hopeful sign for the advancement of science fiction is that academic wisdom may counterbalance prevailing exploitation. SF will become a full literature only if it nourishes a lively critical wing, allowing it real meat to feed on.

It has been possible to give only an outline of the growth of science fiction. I have not placed emphasis on the roles of the editors; although such names as Hugo Gernsback, John W. Campbell, Michael Moorcock, H. L. Gold, Frederik Pohl, Harlan Ellison, and others are rightly praised, too much has been made of their roles. The heroes of science fiction are the ordinary artists and the writers, working often for miserable pay, often against crassly insensitive editors and publishers. Of those heroes, too few have been mentioned here. To them, my apologies.

THE SF SUB-GENRES
Brian Stableford

Introduction

SCIENCE FICTION HAS DEVELOPED its various characteristic themes for many different reasons. Some concerns it has taken over from earlier kinds of imaginative fiction, others it has developed from scratch. Some themes have attracted the attention of SF writers because of their perennial relevance, others because of momentary topicality. Some recommend themselves for serious attention because they relate to real human problems, others simply because they have an aesthetic appeal in the way of intellectual game-playing.

Science fiction is first and foremost a literature exploring future possibility. The word "possibility" can be construed in two different ways – as a licence for imaginative adventurousness permitting writers to test the limits of the-imaginable, or as a constraint requiring writers to be scrupulous in avoiding pure flights of fancy. Science-fiction writers have always tried to have it both ways.

People have always been interested in the future, but in ancient times everyone assumed that the world would go on pretty much as it always had. In terms of their personal horizons, they were usually right. In contrast, it is the characteristic of modern times that within the span of a single lifetime the world is likely to be transformed by technological advancement. Most of the themes of science fiction arise out of that realization. Science fiction was a necessary invention in the last years of the nineteenth century. It had a task to perform in helping to alert people to the reality of change and the precariousness of their cultural situations. Its proponents once hoped that it might provide actual maps of the future, by

anticipating discoveries and demonstrating by logical extrapolation the manner in which they would change the world. From this ambition flowed an abundance of representations of future society, catalogues of mechanical gadgets, and promises of the conquest of space.

The notion that history treads a predestined path is, however, untenable. The future cannot be mapped because there is a multitude of possible futures so great and so various that it defies any attempt at accurate speculative navigation. Science fiction has had to help in making this clear to us as well, with its thousands of conflicting accounts of other worlds and its painstaking exercises in historical alternatives. Although science fiction cannot navigate us through the wilderness of *if* it can attempt to characterize that wilderness; it can juxtapose triumphant accounts of human success in great historical projects with images of the holocaust. It can remind us, too, that the path we actually take through the wilderness of *if* is one that we choose by the exercise of our collective will – and that we must therefore be careful in that exercise.

Even these functions do not require science fiction to be entirely serious; they permit frivolity and comedy – but another function which science fiction has is to demonstrate the sheer delight which can be had from playing with ideas. It participates in the joys of wish-fulfilment, and provides a means for us to take a holiday from the strain and tedium of reality. Thus, science fiction has become one medium for the telling of new folk-tales and for the playing of imaginative games. If this role does not fit too well with the others, it hardly matters – science fiction is a thing of threads and patches, in which a number of things are mixed up together. So, too, is that pattern of needs and desires which we look to fiction to serve.

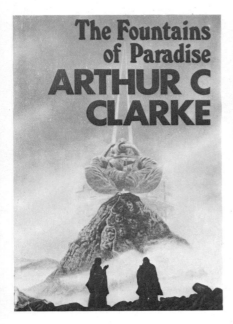

The Fountains of Paradise
ARTHUR C CLARKE

Science Fiction as an international phenomenon Whilst the category "science fiction" was formulated in the American pulp magazines in the 1920s, the field has a long history in many countries, often pre-dating the pulps. As a result each country has developed its own science fictional characteristics. The Strugatski brothers from Russia blend intellectualism and wit. Edgar Pangborn typifies American lyricism and optimism in the face of disaster, and Arthur C. Clarke provides English technical ingenuity and care for characterization.

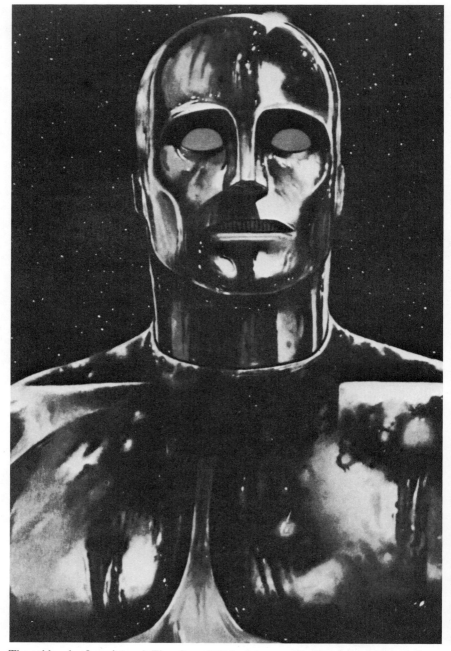

The noble robot Isaac Asimov's Three Laws Of Robotics opposed the "Frankenstein" breed of machine and created the robot as dependable servant to Man.

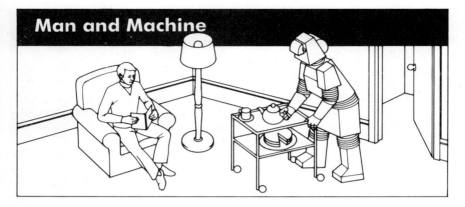

Man and Machine

THE RELATIONSHIP BETWEEN MAN AND HIS MACHINES is, necessarily, one of the main preoccupations of SF. It is through our machines that we expect to remake tomorrow so that it will be different from today. Much speculative thought has been devoted to the task of trying to foresee the social changes forced or permitted by new machines.

In Romantic fiction of the early 19th century there was a reaction against technology, a horror of mechanical artifice illustrated by E. T. A. Hoffmann's story "The Sandman" (1814), whose hero falls in love with an animated doll made by an evil "mechanician". Later, however, this horror was largely displaced by awed enthusiasm for the wonders of technology, exemplified by such fabulous machines as Captain Nemo's *Nautilus* in Jules Verne's *Twenty Thousand Leagues Under The Sea* (1873). The most prolific of the Victorian futuristic writers, H. G. Wells, hoped that technology would give us the means to solve all the social and political problems we face, but he was also aware of a darker side to future possibility. In *The Time Machine* (1894) machine-production allows some people to live a lotus-eater existence, but makes monsters of the rest. In *The War In The Air* (1908) the use of advanced technology in war precipitates a new Dark Age.

Modern science-fiction writers have inherited both the enthusiasms and anxieties of their forerunners. The wonders of future technology are extravagantly featured in many early pulp stories, following the example of Hugo Gernsback's *Ralph 124C41+* (1911); but one can also find images of men become decadent, heading for extinction because of over-reliance on machines, as in John W. Campbell Jr.'s "Twilight" (1934) and "Night" (1935).

European writers frequently became bitterly pessimistic about the ultimate results of mechanical progress – a pessimism reflected in such works as *The Absolute At Large* (1922) by Karel Capek and *Brave New World* (1932) by Aldous Huxley. Even in America, where such despairing *angst* was less fashionable, fearful stories about menacing machines and societies dehumanized in being mechanized did appear – for example, "Killdozer!" (1944) by Theodore Sturgeon and *Player Piano* (1952) by Kurt Vonnegut. These were balanced, however, by stories in which Earthly problems were solved by mechanical inventiveness and starships opened the way to the conquest of the universe.

There is one kind of machine that is crucial to SF's analysis of man/machine relationships: the intelligent machine, which is a hybrid of human and mechanical attributes. Because of their ambiguous nature, the attempts of writers to characterize intelligent machines can be very revealing. Some intelligent machines are talking computers, but many are endowed with human form.

The creation of artificial men was once held to be blasphemous; by the time that SF writers began to use the idea it was considered merely dangerous. Capek's play *R. U. R.* (1921), which gave us the word "robot", is a satire in which artificial men are gradually made more competent, until they rebel and replace mankind. In American SF, however, the menacing aspects of robots were soon set aside in favour of a more even-handed approach. In Lester del Rey's sickly "Helen O'Loy" (1938) the artificial woman with whom the hero falls in love has all the qualities desirable in the perfect wife.

In contemporary SF robots are frequently portrayed as cute, childlike beings, as in *Star Wars* (1977). In more sophisticated work, particularly the novels of Philip K. Dick, they are enigmatic, requiring the human protagonists to ask how different people and androids really are. Dick always concludes that it is the moral differences between benevolent and malevolent beings which matter, not the differences between flesh and metal.

The writer who has played a central role in developing this argument through-out the history of American pulp SF is Isaac Asimov, whose series of robot stories extends through three collections: *I, Robot* (1950), *The Rest Of The Robots* (1964), and *The Bicentennial Man* (1977). These stories are built on the premise that robots are equipped with an unbreakable code of inbuilt ethics, the three laws of robotics:
1. A robot may not injure a human being, or, through inaction, allow a human being to come to harm;
2. A robot must obey the orders given it by human beings except where such orders would conflict with the First Law;
3. A robot must protect its own existence as long as such protection does not conflict with the First or Second Law.

Almost all of Asimov's robot stories are puzzles in which robots appear to be behaving perversely until analysis (often by "robopsychologist" Susan Calvin) shows that their actions are logically in accordance with the three laws. As the series progresses from early stories like "Reason" (1941), which is a comedy of misapplied logic, to "Evidence" (1946), an argumentative undercurrent begins to suggest that because of their inbuilt ethics and cool logicality robots are actually nicer and more competent than people. In "The Evitable Conflict" (1950) intelligent machines run the world better than people ever could. Eventually, in the most recent stories in the series, robot philosophers decide that robots are entitled to be thought of as "human beings", and are better human beings than men are. In "The Bicentennial Man" (1976) a robot wants to become a man, and succeeds in spite of the petty jealousies of humankind, gracefully and condescendingly surrendering his own innate superiority in order to put on frail flesh and die.

Asimov has declared that in these stories he set out to oppose the "Franken-stein syndrome," whereby people sometimes exhibit a neurotic fear that their creations will destroy them. He set out to allay anxiety, and in so doing called in question the philosophical basis for our attitudes to machines. Like Philip Dick,

Asimov arrives at the position that there is no reason why intelligent machines should not be considered *good people*, because it is their capacity to be good rather than the happenstance of their fleshiness, that entitles beings to call themselves human. The stories also argue the further point that if and when our machines do harm us, or disappoint us, then we must look for the fault in ourselves, because it is we who have designed them and we who are responsible for what they are. Whatever our machines do to our society, we are doing to ourselves.

Forbidden Planet (1956) which introduced the loveable Robby the Robot.

Utopia and Dystopia

"UTOPIA" MEANS "NOWHERE", but the term has come to imply an imaginary state whose society has been perfected, where men live happy and fulfilled lives. One of the literary genres ancestral to science fiction was the kind of story which imagined that the perfect society would be discovered at some future time, when the plot of history had reached its denouement. Edward Bellamy's best-selling *Looking Backward 2000-1887* (1888) is a typical example. Unfortunately, writers could not agree on the nature of such an ideal state, and in the confusion they could not help but lose faith in the probability that the tide of history would inevitably carry them to their favourite destination.

H. G. Wells was the last of the great utopian designers, drawing up a whole series of blueprints for the ideal state in *A Modern Utopia* (1905), *Men Like Gods* (1923), and *The Shape Of Things To Come* (1933). Even he despaired, in the end, of our ability to build a society based on common sense and justice. Twentieth-century fiction has been dominated instead by images of Dystopia: evil futures where men have lost everything that they hold dear, either through recklessness and moral weakness or because the many have no way to fight the scientifically supported tyranny of their rulers. The classics of this new genre include *We* (1924) by Yevgeny Zamyatin, *Brave New World* (1932) by Aldous Huxley, and *Nineteen Eighty-Four* (1949) by George Orwell.

Few writers can take much satisfaction in unrelenting pessimism, and only the most embittered have been content to paint the future utterly black. Hardly anyone has been able to rediscover faith in the future Utopia, but many people have tried to map escape-routes from Dystopia.

One common argument suggests that happiness and fulfilment can be sought by means of a partial retreat from modern technology. This line of argument runs from Samuel Butler's *Erewhon* (1872) and William Morris's *News From Nowhere* (1890) to Ernest Callenbach's *Ecotopia* (1975). Another tradition, particularly strong in American SF, suggests that an escape from Earth into the wider universe, where we may become perpetual pioneers, is the answer. This case is put in such novels as *The Space Merchants* (1953) by Frederik Pohl and Cyril M. Kornbluth and *The End Of Eternity* (1955) by Isaac Asimov. A third common proposition is that we might escape from our predicament by transcending our present mental limitations, either by the development of abilities we are already presumed to have, or by evolving new ones. This is the argument of *Island* (1962) by Aldous Huxley and *More Than Human* (1953) by Theodore Sturgeon. This third argument, involving a retreat toward magical solutions, testifies to the magnitude of the problem. Only in Soviet SF can one find recent novels which assume that political planning can create a better world; examples include Ivan Yefremov's *Andromeda* (1957) and Vadim Shefner's *Kovrigin's Chronicles* (1971).

The debate about the likely shape of future society is complicated by the

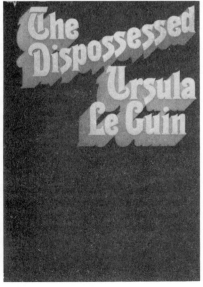

Dystopian Visions Yevgeny Zamyatin's *We* (1920) prefigures both Huxley's *Brave New World* and Orwell's *1984* and perhaps influenced them. Influenced in their turn are two modern dystopias, Ursula K. LeGuin's *The Dispossessed* (1974) and Brian W. Aldiss's *Enemies Of The System* (1978). One thing all these works have in common is a melding of things political and philosophical.

frequent allegation that it is our relentless desire to live a life of ease and to seek fulfilment in idle pleasure which will result in Dystopia. This paradox is central to *We* and *Brave New World*, and is further exemplified by such novels as *Player Piano* (1952) by Kurt Vonnegut and *The Joy Makers* (1961) by James E. Gunn. Images of Utopia and images of Dystopia are much more similar than one would have supposed.

Almost all Western SF writers seem to have settled for the view that there never could be an ideal state, and that the best possible social order is one which allows people freedom to select whatever idiosyncratic lifestyles will temporarily please them. An example is *Commune 2000 A.D.* (1974) by Mack Reynolds. Many writers have lost all interest in examining the politics of imaginary states or describing the social systems of future society in any detail. One of the most notable exceptions is Ursula K. LeGuin, who has written one of the most careful and conscientious of political SF novels in *The Dispossessed* (1974).

In the story a physicist named Shevek leaves his own world of Anarres, where he has grown up in an egalitarian anarchist society without private property, to visit Urras, where he finds a capitalist society committed to individualistic ideals. Anarres is hardly a Utopia, nor is Urras a Dystopia, although the one is the product of noble ideals and the other is a world which has expelled its idealists in order to maintain the unchallenged hegemony of vulgar pragmatism. Anarres is a desperately poor world, Urras a richer one, and the contrast sanctions the common belief that it is only when people have very little, leaving greed no scope for ambition, that real equality can be sustained. The problem set by the story is whether any kind of reconciliation between the two cultures can ever be attained. At a personal level, this is represented in Shevek's attempts to adapt himself to the alien society; at a more general level the question is asked as to how the history of the two worlds will unfold if they are allowed to interact.

The Dispossessed offers no solution to the problems which it poses; it would be unreasonable to expect one. Its virtues as a speculative novel are to be found in the fact that it is prepared to confront the problems, to recognize their importance, and to estimate their form and dimensions. The difficulty of doing even this much is reflected in the desperation of Shevek's plight as he tries to work through his project. In the end, the reader is left with the impression that LeGuin has opened Pandora's Box, exposing all the ugly troubles of the world and finding nothing left in the cavity but unfocused hope. In the end, Shevek's "solution" is a private one, which will serve him alone if it will serve at all; thus the story veers back to the prevailing orthodoxy that the only answers that *can* be found are personal ones. LeGuin recognizes well enough, however, that this still leaves all the practical political questions unsolved; she is not content to leave us with the illusion that everything would be fine if only people were allowed to do their own thing.

The Dispossessed is an open-ended novel, which offers the reader food for thought without attempting to preach a particular message with evangelical fervour. If there is one insistent point which it does make, it is that only Utopians can live in Utopia, and that if we are doomed to live in an undesirable society, it is because we cling to undesirable desires and methods of fulfilling them. It seems probable that literary works of this kind can do no more than make sure that we do not forget this.

Time Travel

IN ANCIENT MYTHOLOGY it was widely assumed that information could travel through time – that people might occasionally catch glimpses of the future. This is one of those beliefs that people have tried hard to hold on to, and it has remained everpresent in imaginative fiction. Writers of early futuristic fiction found it convenient, as a literary device, to move their characters through time as information-gatherers. Sometimes they journeyed only in their dreams, but it became increasingly common in the 19th century for them to fall asleep for a few hundred years. Such a method was useful for visiting the future, but not well-adapted to visiting the past, although Mark Twain's Connecticut Yankee used it to visit King Arthur's Court in 1889. The whole business of time travel was streamlined, however, when H. G. Wells converted the literary device into a mechanical device in *The Time Machine* (1895). This fortunate invention opened up the entire past and future to imaginary tourism.

With the establishment of the time machine as a literary convention journeys into the far future became simpler, but the logical corollaries of the ability to hop back and forth in time quickly revealed paradoxes. If a man from the present interfered with the past, he could presumably obliterate the present from which he came, thus making his initial interference impossible.... The aesthetic possibilities of this kind of juggling with ideas were irresistible to SF writers.

The first novel to play with time paradoxes was F. Anstey's comedy *Tourmalin's Time Cheques* (1891), and writers have exploited the farcical potential of such knotted plots ever since. A good recent example is Bob Shaw's *Who Goes Here?* (1977). Most SF writers, however, have approached the matter more earnestly. There are many seriously minded stories in which journeys into the past divert history into a new track – accidentally, as in Ray Bradbury's "A Sound Of Thunder" (1952), or deliberately, as in L. Sprague de Camp's *Lest Darkness Fall* (1941). In some stories the "original" present is simply wiped out, but in many stories all the variant time-tracks remain, somehow co-existing side by side. Several writers have imagined networks of time-tracks patrolled by policemen whose task it is to prevent promiscuous reality-changing. Others have imagined armies from different time-tracks fighting to preserve the past events that created them. Such wars are fought in *The Legion Of Time* (1938) by Jack Williamson and in *The Big Time* (1958) by Fritz Leiber, while in Isaac Asimov's *The End Of*

Eternity (1955) a political dictatorship jealously preserves its own everlasting hegemony by controlling history.

The chaotic shifting of the timeline in Leiber's stories of the "Change War" can be contrasted with what happens in time-paradox stories of a different stripe, which set up closed causal loops in time. In such stories time travellers, far from obliterating the world from which they came, unwittingly perform exactly those actions which will eventually create it. Two classic stories of this kind by Robert Heinlein are "By His Bootstraps" (1941) and "All You Zombies . . ." (1959). In the latter story a man travels back and forth in time to become his own father and mother. A compendium of time-paradox themes can be found in *The Man Who Folded Himself* (1973) by David Gerrold.

There are, of course, many time-travel stories which are simply devoted to imaginary tourism, where paradoxes never become an issue. Favourite tourist-traps in the past are the age of the dinosaurs and the crucifixion of Christ – but in the latter case the temptation to set up ironic closed loops, as in Michael Moorcock's *Behold The Man* (1969) or Garry Kilworth's "Let's Go To Golgotha" (1975) is often irresistible. Also worthy of note are the many "timeslip romances" in which people unhappy in the present find true love by time-travelling, usually to the past. Examples include "The Demoiselle d'Ys" (1895) by Robert W. Chambers and *Time And Again* (1970) by Jack Finney.

The outstanding time-travel novel of recent years is Gregory Benford's *Timescape* (1980), one of the very few SF novels which tries to provide a convincing scientific basis for time travel. Here, as in the earliest stories, it is only information which is transmitted through time, via tachyons (particles which travel faster than light). The story contains an elaborate account of the transmission of the message (from 1998) in parallel with an equally elaborate account of its receipt (in 1962). The analysis of the consequences of its being received (incomplete and

Sphere Science Fiction

MICHAEL BISHOP

NO ENEMY BUT TIME

A masterly journey to the dawn of time –
'marvellous' *The Times*

Time Travel Since H. G. Wells' *The Time Machine* made time travel a popular theme, each generation of science-fiction writers has re-fashioned its ideas about time and the paradoxes of time travel. The idea of policing time to prevent (or create) changes in the structure of reality was made popular in the 1950s in novels like Fritz Leiber's *The Big Time* (1958). In the 1960s drugs were seen as a means of changing perception and warping time, as in Philip K. Dick's *Now Wait For Last year* (1966). In recent years a more philosophical approach to the actual physics of time has resulted in fine novels like Michael Bishop's *No Enemy But Time* (1982).

partly garbled) is subtle and suggestive, deliberately undetailed so as to leave in the balance until the last possible moment the question of whether the message can divert the course of events and thus create a paradox.

Timescape is an important novel because it argues cleverly that the universe may actually be organized so as to *permit* paradoxes, if our current understanding of physics is correct. It asks us to take this seriously, not merely with the seriousness appropriate to the playing of an intellectual game, but with the seriousness due to the recognition of something which bears upon our real existence. Benford's aim is to create a very peculiar sense of existential insecurity, to make us accept the possibility of our lives being reconstructed or cancelled out. It is perhaps good for us to be led to think such thoughts occasionally, and one of the merits of science fiction is that it can help us to think what were once unthinkable thoughts, if only we have the imagination.

If the message dispatched from Benford's 1998 does not have the desired effect, then the world will end. The issue of communication across time is dramatized by hanging the fate of the world upon it. In one sense, therefore, *Timescape* is an apocalyptic fantasy which demands a miraculous solution. It suggests that the abstruse world of theoretical physics may provide the means by which mankind might be redeemed from destruction. There is an element of special pleading here (Benford is a physicist by profession), and there is also a kinship between the novel and the timeslip romances, which play on our emotions to make us *want* to believe that the barrier of time can be breached if only our need is great enough. This may be wishful thinking, but it does have some kind of substantial core. We will, of course, continue to believe in the impossibility of time travel, but just for a moment *Timescape* lets us into that conceptual world where such things *can* be done. It is an interesting place to visit, and – after all – we cannot be *absolutely* sure that it is not the place we live.

Aliens

THE EVOLUTIONISTS OF THE 19TH CENTURY, having abandoned the idea that God created every natural species independently, realized that the vast profusion of living organisms represented many different ways in which creatures could be adapted to follow particular ways of life in particular physical circumstances. Even before Darwin explained how this gradual adaptation happened, therefore, it was possible to see that on other worlds, where conditions were very different, different kinds of organisms would have developed.

The first writer to develop this hypothesis, in fiction and in non-fiction, was Camille Flammarion, who describes several alien life-systems in *Lumen* (1872). Another French writer, J. H. Rosny the elder, followed this example in "The Shapes" (1887) and other stories. In these stories humans and aliens are part of a great cosmic scheme planned by God – a notion later developed by Olaf

Stapledon in *Star Maker* (1937). In English SF, however, alien beings made a more spectacular debut, as the Martian invaders of Earth in *The War Of The Worlds* (1898) by H. G. Wells. This story presumes that alien beings must be our deadly enemies, competitors in a struggle for existence in which only the fittest will survive. Wells later produced the first account of an alien society, modelled on an ant-hive, in *The First Men In The Moon* (1901). The idea of aliens as loathsome invaders remained dominant in English and American SF for many years, and persisted in Hollywood monster movies even longer. It was so commonplace by the 1930s that it was possible for Orson Welles's radio version of *The War Of The Worlds* in 1938 to provoke a panic. Raymond Z. Gallun felt it appropriate to offer an ideological reply to Wells's novel in "Old Faithful" (1934), where human and Martian recognize their intellectual kinship despite their biological differences.

Early pulp SF writers took a playful delight in populating other worlds with all manner of bizarre creatures, often without the least regard for evolutionary or ecological plausibility. Stanley Weinbaum, whose "A Martian Odyssey" (1934) remains a favourite among such stories, was one of the few writers to pay any attention at all to the logic of his creations in the 1930s. In subsequent years, though, it was gradually realized that there was a special aesthetic pleasure to be derived from constructing peculiar alien life-systems which actually made sense. As a consequence, most science fiction writers of the post-war period have been more conscientious in this matter.

The confrontation between human and alien provides an opportunity for writers to imagine mankind as others might see it, and hence to weigh ourselves in the cosmic balance against all kinds of standards. Alien beings have often been used as points of contrast in order to examine all kinds of human traits: our propensity for emotion; our tendency to racial and sexual prejudices; our

Little Green Men Not all of science fiction's aliens are small, green or even vaguely man-like. Willy Ley's part-constructed Extra-terrestrial with its ill-matched anatomical bits and pieces typifies many of the field's early aliens. From the 1940s onward, however, writers took greater pains to make their aliens more credible, if no less colourful. The May 1969 cover of *If* magazine captures the sense of a variously-populated and teeming galaxy, whereas the July 1975 cover of *Analog* reflects a gradual interest in depicting alien psychologies and sociologies.

aggressiveness. The colonial history of the Western world is harshly judged in many stories which project a similar pattern into the conquest of the universe. A surprisingly large number of stories use hypothetical aliens to examine religious questions. The central question, however, always remains: can we actually learn to get along with the aliens when we meet them, or must there be conflict?

Early pulp writers like Edward E. Smith and Edmond Hamilton exulted in tales of interplanetary war. World War II, however, helped to make such stories less fashionable, and generated many new stories where the objective was to create a stable and peaceful relationship rather than to commit genocide. Stories like Murray Leinster's "First Contact" (1945) and "The Ethical Equations" (1945) suggested that this might not be easy, but could be done. In recent times, though the alien menace story has not disappeared, the dominant view seems to be that it would be very nice to know that we are not alone in the universe. The meeting of minds between human and alien is now seen to be a potentially wonderful event – a watershed in human affairs. It is still assumed that this will be difficult to achieve, but even Hollywood has gone to extremes in this regard with films like *Close Encounters Of The Third Kind* (1977) and *E.T.* (1982).

One of the classic works in which first contact between human and alien proves to be of tremendous import is *The Black Cloud* (1957) by Fred Hoyle, which is one of the few novels to feature a truly extraordinary alien intelligence. *The Black Cloud* begins as a catastrophe story, with a cosmic dust cloud entering the solar system and blocking off the light of the sun. Earth is plunged into cold and darkness for a while, but the cloud adjusts itself so the damage done is not too great. Scientists on Earth, realizing that the behaviour of the cloud implies intelligence, attempt to communicate with it via radio.

There is an immense physical difference between the "brain" of the cloud and the human brain, but the two life-forms nevertheless have one important thing in common: the scientific method of inquiry and its fruits. The scientists therefore manage to set up a way of exchanging communication. The cloud rapidly learns English and absorbs the contents of the *Encyclopedia Britannica*, but the human brains which try to take in the knowledge possessed by the cloud are overloaded and destroyed.

The Black Cloud is partly propaganda for science and scientific research, attempting to dramatize the importance of science by emphasizing its universality. It is our knowledge of mathematics and the nature of matter which will provide us not only with the means to make contact with alien intelligences, but also with the motive for doing so. Contact with aliens is nowadays seen as a way to learn more – an enlightening experience.

It is interesting to note that Hoyle, in collaboration with Chandra Wickramasinghe, went on to develop an idea similar to that employed in *The Black Cloud* in his non-fiction book *Lifecloud* (1978), which hypothesizes that life-bearing clouds really do exist in deep space, and are in fact the seed-bed from which planetary life comes. This kind of transference of an idea back from imaginative fiction into scientific speculation is further reflected in the projects which are part of SETI (Search for Extra-Terrestrial Intelligence), which involve using radio-telescopes to search the sky in the hope of picking up messages from distant stars. It is widely assumed that the aliens *are* out there somewhere, and that it may not be impossible to open channels of communication.

Space Travel

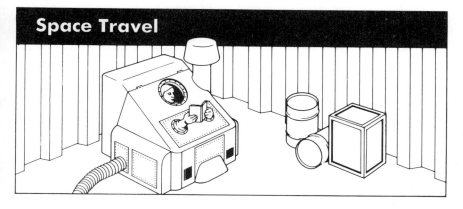

IN THE EYES OF MANY PEOPLE, space travel is *the* classic theme of science fiction. Modern SF writers inherited a tradition of imaginary lunar voyages that began with Lucian of Samosata's "True History" (*ca.* 160 A.D.) and extended through such works as Cyrano de Bergerac's *Voyage To The Moon* (1657) and Daniel Defoe's *The Consolidator* (1705). Edgar Allan Poe, in a foreword to "The Unparalleled Adventure Of One Hans Pfaall" (1835), complained that earlier writers had paid too little attention to the practicalities of such a voyage, though Pfaall's balloon hardly strikes modern readers as a plausible conveyance. Jules Verne tried to do better in *From The Earth To The Moon* (1865) and *Round The Moon* (1870), but his space-gun would have killed the people inside its shell. The gravity screens used by H. G. Wells in *The First Men In The Moon* (1901) are an unashamed literary device.

Konstantin Tsiolkovsky was the first man to realize that men might get outside the atmosphere by means of rockets, and popularized his ideas in the novel *Beyond The Planet Earth* (1920). Rocket ships eventually became part of the standard apparatus of SF, featured in a host of stories. Attempts at realism were constantly updated, from the German film *The Girl In The Moon* (1929), on which rocket experts Herman Oberth and Willy Ley were technical advisers, through Robert Heinlein's "The Man Who Sold The Moon" (1950) and Arthur C. Clarke's *Prelude To Space* (1951), to stories actually contemporary with the Apollo programme.

SF writers were quick to send their rocket ships to the other planets of the solar system, and were quite prepared to imagine new devices that would take them to the stars. Most early fantasies in this vein, pioneered by Edward E. Smith's *The Skylark Of Space* (1928), blithely ignored the theory of relativity which forbade travelling faster than light and hence set time-limits on interstellar journeys. Some writers, however, have produced interesting stories based on the premise that a journey to another star might take many generations; examples include Robert Heinlein's "Universe" (1941) and Brian Aldiss's *Non-Stop* (1958). Others have constructed a special jargon which has become a conventional way of side-stepping the logic of relativity, usually by means of "hyper-space" or "space-warps"; the trend appears to have been instituted by John W. Campbell Jr. in *The Mightiest Machine* (1934). A very few writers have ingeniously used the relativistic effects of approaching the velocity of light as the basis for stories, most notably Poul Anderson in *Tau Zero* (1967), which features odd time-dilation effects.

Allegations have frequently been made about the supposed phallic symbolism of SF's spaceships, but in fact their symbolic potential is not nearly so narrow. Space travel is the ultimate escape – the gateway to unlimited adventure and infinite experience. In many SF novels, especially of the 1950s, the spaceship is the symbol of fugitive hope in a hopelessly corrupt world.

The advent of real space travel has made surprisingly little difference to science fiction. By the time the minor gulf between the Earth and the moon was crossed, attention had long since shifted to the much greater gulf separating our solar system from other stars. It was accepted before the 1960s that our planetary neighbours would be of very limited interest compared to the possibilities offered by the whole galaxy. It now seems that if we want to move away from Earth in our immediate locality we will have to build our own habitats from scratch; only in other solar systems might we find hospitable worlds already waiting for us.

All the mystique of the science fictional spaceship is contained in Arthur C. Clarke's novel *Rendezvous With Rama* (1973), which also has a realistic account of the near future possibilities of space travel within the solar system. As in many of Clarke's novels it neatly juxtaposes a careful and restrained anticipation of likely technological developments with a powerful visionary element suggestive of much vaster realms of possibility. "Rama" is the name given by humans to a temporary visitor to our solar system: a hollow cylinder fifty kilometres long and twenty in diameter. The object passes close to the sun in order to boost its velocity, and a human expedition is able to pay a brief visit to it. The humans find their way into the interior of Rama and there they are witness to many wonders: an artificial sun, a Cylindrical Sea, a cyborg "crew". There is no sign of the aliens who built Rama, but their small world continues to function, its ecology becoming briefly active to take advantage of the energy-injection offered by the sun.

Rama keeps its mystique intact by allowing its human visitors only a glimpse of its wonders. Most of its secrets remain concealed, as they should and must be. This is simply a taste of far future possibility, intended to excite the pleasures of anticipation.

A novel set on a human starship like Rama would not be particularly exciting: the timespan of a novel, measured out in the experience of a few human lifetimes, could hardly begin to tell the story of such an artefact. The sheer size of the undertaking which is imagined here reduces human beings to near-negligibility, although even Rama is but the tiniest of motes in an incomprehensibly vast universe. In opening the window on the future by only a tiny crack, Clarke avoids the danger of reducing his ideas to absurdity.

Rendezvous With Rama is one of a number of novels which counteract the naive myth of the "conquest of space" as it was displayed in early pulp SF. Clarke shows that if we are ambitious to travel between the stars we must not simply build ships but small worlds with their own balanced ecologies – and even then might have to absent ourselves from their day-to-day existence while they cross the great empty spaces, perhaps by means of suspended animation.

It is not merely the bigness of Rama and its mission that excites our imagination. There is a sense in which its *smallness* is also attractive. As a vehicle, it is vast, but as a world it is small, and ships are emblems of enclosure as well as means of travel. Rama, like many other starships in SF, is closed, cosy and orderly. In the planned and balanced ecologies that must exist on such starships there is nothing of the chaos and confusion of Earthly life. Rama is a world with a purpose, and has its own inbuilt balance and harmony. This is a prospect we can easily find attractive, and if we insist on seeing this in terms of symbolism then we must conclude that spaceships of this kind are symbolic of the womb rather than the phallus. Clarke's novel reminds us of this in his account of the troubled human affairs which surround the human expedition to the artefact. It is suggested here, as in many other contemporary works, that space travel may be the means by which we can transcend the troubles which afflict the relations between men and between nations. While this assumption remains commonplace, space travel can hardly be expected to lose its mythical significance in SF.

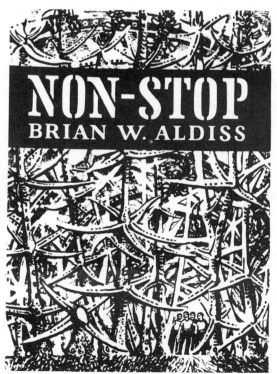

Space Machines are a staple of the science fiction diet and adorn a high percentage of its covers, usually in the form of sleek, highly-technological craft, represented here by Fred Gambino's cover to Leiber's *Ship Of Shadows*. Subtler representations are rarer, as with Christopher Priest's homage to H. G. Wells, *The Space Machine*, and Brian Aldiss's *Non-Stop*, the action of which takes place inside a generation starship.

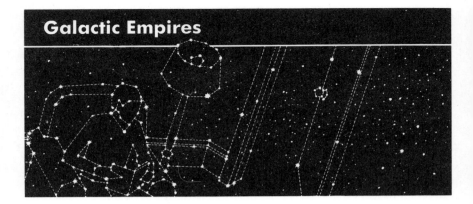

Galactic Empires

THE IDEA OF A GALACTIC EMPIRE has little to recommend it in terms of plausibility. Such a notion collapses the distances between the stars to the scale of the stops on the London Underground or the ports of call on a Mediterranean cruise. This is patently absurd. To some extent, the popularity of Galactic Empires in SF reflects our simple inability to comprehend the real scale of galactic affairs, but the notion has its own aesthetic attractions and it is exceedingly convenient as a literary device in certain kinds of speculative ventures.

The Galactic Empire ("empire" is here used in a metaphorical sense rather than in a narrow political meaning, although a few Galactic Empires really do have emperors and other feudal trappings) provides the perfect imaginative framework for the unfettered science-fictional imagination. Into such a framework can be inserted a multitude of worlds where any and all biological and social systems can be imagined to exist. It is a blank screen onto which any combination of bizarre circumstances and environments can be projected.

The Galactic Empire was established as a convention in modern SF by Isaac Asimov, through his *Foundation* series which ran in "Astounding Science Fiction" between 1942 and 1950. Here, the human race has occupied every habitable world in the galaxy and the Earthly origins of man are merely mythical. In the series the Empire is already disintegrating, after the fashion of the Roman Empire, and it descends into a Dark Age which involves the relative isolation of the member worlds. A secret organization, however, is armed with the techniques of "psychohistory" which will enable them to rebuild galactic civilization into a new and better commonwealth of worlds. None of this makes any sense, but the sheer imaginative audacity of it all is awe-inspiring.

Many other writers followed where Asimov led, often borrowing (as he did) from actual history, or even from historical fiction, in order to shape their inspiration. By the 1950s the image was sufficiently well-established in the mythology of SF to be taken for granted by writers who wanted to use it, and several easily recognizable variants appeared, including the "lost colony" plot, involving the recontacting of a human colony which has been cut off from other worlds long enough to develop interesting cultural eccentricities.

Writers who have made prolific use of the scenario include Jack Vance, most of whose works draw upon the framework, and Cordwainer Smith, virtually all of whose stories fit into a common background: a galactic culture which has its own myths as well as its political institutions and strange subcultures. Some of the most colourful and exotic of modern SF stories use the Galactic Empire background, including *Empire Star* (1966) and *Nova* (1968) by Samuel R. Delany and *The Ring Of Ritornel* (1968) by Charles Harness. The Galactic Empire has even generated its own eccentric species of Ruritanian romance – a tradition begun by Edmond Hamilton with a thinly disguised reprise of *The Prisoner Of Zenda*, *The Star Kings* (1947), and continued in contemporary times by E. C. Tubb, who began in 1967 a series of stories (still incomplete in 1983) in which the hero, Dumarest, searches for lost Earth.

There are two outstanding examples of attempts to use the framework in a more serious way, in order to make comments on the actual patterns seen within history and on the art of politics. One is a loosely aggregated series by Poul Anderson which includes both his "Polesotechnic League" stories about Galactic merchant princes, and the "Terran Empire" series featuring the flamboyant Dominic Flandry, who tries to protect the decadent Imperial system against the day of its inevitable collapse. Here there is an attractive combination of high adventure and observations about the sociological principles embodied in history. The other series, which is more compact and possessed of a much more definite shape, is to be found in the four volumes of James Blish's *Cities In Flight* series (1950-58), collected into a single omnibus in 1970.

In *Cities In Flight* Blish makes use of Oswald Spengler's theory of cyclic history as set out in *The Decline Of The West* (1918-22). Spengler argued that cultures pass through a kind of "life cycle" which can be seen in full in the history of Classical Culture and Arabic Culture. He contended that Western Culture has concluded its creative phase and was doomed to decline; Blish undertook to complete the story of this decline and to chronicle the entire history of the Earthmanist Culture, the next cycle in human affairs, which would have the galaxy as its stage. As if this were not ambitious enough, he made this phase the final one, its end coincident with the death of the universe.

In this series men expand into the galaxy by means of the spindizzy – an antigravity device which will not only power starships but will lift whole cities. The major protagonist of the four novels is the city of New York, which travels the galaxy in search of work, allows the exploration of new worlds, and fights in a galactic war. The scope of the project is magnificent, and its use of Spenglerian theory gives it a coherence that is unique. The apocalyptic conclusion is a satisfactory final flourish.

Of course, Spengler's theory of history is itself an elaborate fiction, but its adoption into this particular kind of SF is entirely appropriate. The Galactic Empire cannot command our belief, but the interpolation of this kind of plausible pseudoscientific theory helps us to suspend our disbelief, strengthening the structure which supports all kinds of particular speculative endeavours. The kind of blank screen which the scenario provides is a great boon to contemporary fiction, because it is a ticket to the furthest reaches of the imagination, where we venture as tourists for pleasure *and* profit.

THE TERM ESP WAS FIRST POPULARIZED by J. B. Rhine in his book *Extra-Sensory Perception* (1934), one of several texts in which he argued that there is experimental evidence for the existence of certain unusual mental abilities: telepathy, clairvoyance, precognition and psychokinesis. SF writers sometimes refer to such phenomena as "psionic powers" or "psi powers". All of these supposed abilities can be traced back to ancient mythology, once being part of the standard repertoire of magicians and witches; there are many modern stories which "rationalize" these ancient stories by supposing that some individuals have always had psionic powers which they did not understand and could only partly control. Since Rhine pioneered the use of experimental tests and statistical analysis in hunting for such powers there has been more or less constant activity in the field of "parapsychology," but most scientists remain sceptical, and perennially suspicious of cheating.

Although mind-reading and clairvoyance have always featured to some extent in popular fiction, it was the popularization of Rhine's work in the 1930s that led SF writers to believe that such things could legitimately take their place among the conventions of SF. A. E. van Vogt's *Slan* (1940) was a very popular story in which telepathic mutants are persecuted by the ordinary men they are destined to replace in the evolutionary scheme. This set the pattern for many other works, including Henry Kuttner's *Mutant* (1953), George O. Smith's *Highways In Hiding* (1956), and Zenna Henderson's long series about "the People." It is significant that in all these stories the sympathies of the reader are enlisted on the side of the mutant supermen; SF readers are not expected to be the kind of people who would stand in the way of progress. Even in stories where the psi-powered superman is malevolent and menacing, as in *The Dreaming Jewels* (1950) by Theodore Sturgeon or *The Power* (1956) by Frank M. Robinson, the hero can always be relied on to turn into a superman himself in order to set things to rights.

The idea that anyone might have these latent powers lurking within him, waiting to emerge and be trained, is a very attractive one. Every Clark Kent wishes that he had a secret identity. SF writers seized upon the hypothesis that anyone walking the streets right now might be superman and yet not know it. Numerous stories have paid serious attention to the psychological problems of adjusting to the realization that one is a superman, to the methodological problems of disciplining one's talents, and to the social problems one will inevitably face in getting along with people (super and non-super). Works of this kind include *Jack Of Eagles* (1952) by James Blish, *The Silent Speakers* (1962) by Arthur Sellings, and *Pstalemate* (1971) by Lester del Rey. The cliché is ingeniously inverted in *Dying Inside* (1972) by Robert Silverberg, which is about the problems of a telepath adjusting to the gradual loss of his power.

Such are the immediate attractions of this theme that relatively few writers have bothered to attempt the difficult task of providing any pseudoscientific account of how ESP might actually work. Blish, in *Jack Of Eagles*, provides one of the notable exceptions. Though relatively few writers have been prepared to imagine whole societies based on the possession of psi-powers – "The Touch Of Your Hand" (1953) by Theodore Sturgeon is one notable example – the best novel in this vein is *The Demolished Man* (1953) by Alfred Bester, in which a future society is policed by a caste of ESPers, thus making the perfect murder even more difficult to commit.

The most striking development in the use of ESP by SF writers has been the use of an evolutionary transformation of men into psi-powered supermen as a necessary solution to our historical and existential plight. This notion of ESP as a panacea for all social problems is seen particularly clearly in Theodore Sturgeon's many psi stories, particularly his novel *More Than Human* (1953). In

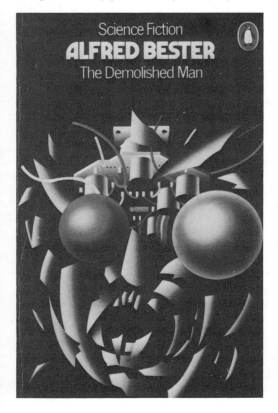

Science Fiction
ALFRED BESTER
The Demolished Man

The ESPer society In Alfred Bester's novel *The Demolished Man* social class is determined not by intellectual ability or (necessarily) wealth, but by the ability to read minds – an ability which has vast social uses and repercussions.

Psi Powers James H. Schmitz was one of the many writers who, in the fifties and sixties, created a whole series of stories featuring telepaths. His featured Telzey Amberdon, an agent of the Overgovernment, but were typical of the lighter, wish-fulfilment aspect of this sub-genre. The use of Rhine cards in the picture gives the whole a pseudo-scientific respectability.

this story a group of social misfits come together to pool their particular wild talents and become a human *gestalt*. At first this group has great difficulty in functioning despite its powers, and requires quasi-maternal protection; later these difficulties are compounded when one of its members dies and has to be replaced. Eventually, though, the *gestalt* learns to get by in the world, and thrives as it acquires a kind of maturity. It then must face the more complicated problem of cultivating an appropriate moral sense before – in a climactic moment of virtual apotheosis – it is permitted to know and be part of the greater community of *gestalts* which will inherit the Earth.

As with all ESP stories *More Than Human* is basically an extravaganza of wishful thinking. It proposes that a collection of social and psychological cripples might be magically transformed into a superhuman unit. Like Jesus, ESP will redeem the most wretched of men – the diseased and the delinquent. No one is beyond the power of its healing grace. Religious imagery is often very obvious in such stories despite the veneer of science-fictional jargon; *More Than Human* is no exception. Many similar psi stories, some more thinly disguised than others, are fantasies about the spiritual redemption of man, Millennarian visions of the world reborn by the intrusion of unashamed miracles into everyday human affairs. The use of pseudoscientific jargon is basically a hard shell to contain a sugary pill.

More Than Human is typical of many stories of the 1950s "psi boom" in SF in setting aside all the sceptical questions about ESP which ought to have occurred to SF writers. The paradoxical implications of precognition are rarely tackled in psi stories of this period; few writers ask how psychokinesis can be made to square with the law of conservation of energy. It is not entirely surprising that SF generated an actual cult at this point in time, which first represented itself as a new psychoanalysis (Dianetics) and later became a religion (Scientology); the attractiveness of the ideas being bandied about was far too great for them to be left to languish in speculative fiction. The ideas remain attractive today, but the fervour of the early 1950s has ebbed away to a considerable extent, testifying to the fact that the existential anxiety into which we were thrown by the revelation of the atom bomb and the hydrogen bomb (mentioned as agents of the apocalypse in the climax of *More Than Human*) is now less hysterical in character.

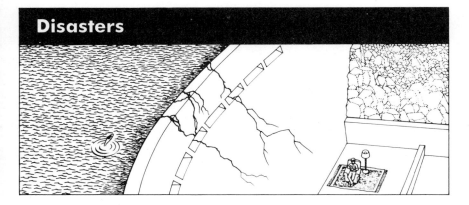

Disasters

ALL HUMAN SOCIETIES ARE HAUNTED by the fear of natural catastrophes, and all ancient mythologies contain images of the world overwhelmed by fire or flood. Such disasters used to be seen as punishments visited upon mankind by angry gods, but in time they came to be reckoned mere accidents of fortune.

Disaster stories were briefly in vogue in the literature of the early 19th century. Thomas Campbell wrote a poem parodied by Thomas Hood, and Mary Shelley wrote a novel, all under the evocative title *The Last Man*. Such stories revived in popularity at the end of the 19th century, when cosmic disasters were all the rage and Earth was continually hit by comets or meteors. Other worlds passed through the solar system, as in "The Star" (1897) by H. G. Wells; earthquakes released poisonous vapours, as in *The Purple Cloud* (1901) by M. P. Shiel; and great plagues were not entirely passé, as witness "The Scarlet Plague" (1912) by Jack London. The sheer variety of catastrophes on offer was exciting. The knowledge that God was not the instigator of disasters was not at all comforting, because it meant that He would not protect us from disaster no matter how well we behaved. London and New York might be obliterated as easily as Sodom and Gomorrah no matter how many virtuous men could stand up to be counted.

There has grown up within modern SF a tradition of disaster stories which, for some reason, is particularly evident and impressive in British SF. There is a post-war sequence of British disaster stories in which the torch is handed on from John Wyndham (*The Day Of The Triffids*, 1951, and *The Kraken Wakes*, 1953) to John Christopher (*The Death Of Grass*, 1956, and *The World In Winter*, 1962) to J. G. Ballard (*The Drowned World*, 1962, *The Drought*, 1964, and *The Crystal World*, 1966) and Brian Aldiss (*Greybeard*, 1964). This preoccupation of British writers with disaster is remarkable in its own right; it is remarkable also that it is this sequence of stories more than any others which helped British SF win a respectability that American SF was as yet denied.

In the post-war period stories of natural catastrophe have been overtaken by stories of man-made catastrophe. There have been many accounts of worlds devastated by nuclear war, including Walter M. Miller's *A Canticle For Leibowitz* (1959) and Edgar Pangborn's *Davy* (1964), but there has also been a profusion of more ironic stories in which irresponsible uses of science and technology have disastrous results. Stories of new inventions which lead to the destruction of

mankind include *Cat's Cradle* (1963) by Kurt Vonnegut and *The Reproductive System* (1968) by John Sladek. Anxieties in the real world about overpopulation and pollution produced a glut of alarmist fantasies, including *Make Room! Make Room!* (1966) by Harry Harrison and two novels by John Brunner: *Stand on Zanzibar* (1968) and *The Sheep Look Up* (1973). Although there was a brief boom in stories of natural disaster during the 1970s, largely encouraged by the cinema, it is man-made catastrophes which now dominate the science-fictional imagination in its apocalyptic mood. These provide obvious scope for the scoring of moral points and the preaching of messages.

The lessons which we are supposed to learn from disaster stories are rather dull ones, for the most part. We are reminded that we have become dependent on

Social suicide Mankind's seemingly lemming-
like desire to end its days on Earth is here
captured in Lucinda Cowell's illustration,
opposite, for *Panic O'Clock*.

the complex organization of our society and its machines, and would have trouble
surviving if we were forced to become subsistence farmers. Many disaster stories
are social Darwinist parables which take cruel delight in telling us that when it
comes to the crunch it will certainly not be the meek who inherit the Earth.
Curiously, though, there is a kind of Romanticism in many disaster stories. It can
be pleasant to imagine having an empty world all to oneself (and a few congenial
companions), and some disaster stories are straightforward wish-fulfilment
fantasies akin to desert island stories. Many modern disaster stories, in fact,
maintain an uneasy balance between bitter realism and nostalgic romance. The
combination is developed with great artistry in the excellent *Earth Abides* (1949)
by George R. Stewart.

The Hero of *Earth Abides*, Isherwood Williams (Ish) is one of a small number
of survivors of a great plague. He gets together with a group of survivors, all more
or less helpless products of their civilization. He is an educated and cultured
man, but finds that all the things he now needs to know will have to be learned
from scratch, mostly by hard experience. His group – self-styled The Tribe by
analogy with the Indians who lived in America before civilization came – has to
learn a whole new way of being, adapting psychologically as well as in their
manner of labouring.

Ish has to stand by as the heritage of civilization rots away. The machines rust
and the books decay. He tries to pass on his own knowledge to the children of the
Tribe, who respect him as a teacher – almost a magician – but they can take from
him only so much as will fit in with their own pattern of needs and interests. Much
of what *he* considers valuable as nourishment for the intellect and the spirit is lost.

The Tribe, knowing that their actions will be important in creating a heritage
for the new future of man, take a serious interest in their rules of conduct, and are
forced to handle several ethical crises – particularly the problems posed by an
outsider who symbolizes the unacceptable face of the old order. Stewart loads the
dice by making the outsider a carrier of venereal disease, and thus makes it easier
for him to be ritually slain. This guilt-tainted act becomes a new Fall, expelling
the Tribe from their conscienceless temporary Eden. In this way, as in many
similar stories, the characters re-enact a fundamental mythological pattern.

Earth Abides, like most disaster stories, is a study of adaptation, and it takes a
familiar line in arguing that psychological adaptation is more important than the
business of producing the means of subsistence. Where writers of such fantasies
differ (and there is a great difference between Stewart, Christopher, and Ballard)
is in prescribing appropriate patterns of psychological adaptation.

Religion and Mythology

AT ONE TIME, all speculative fiction drew upon the religious imagination for its inspiration, although much of the material used was "second-hand," drawn from ancient mythologies which had ceased to command belief. Science fiction is usually defined so as to set it apart from this other kind of imaginative fiction, but in fact it has inherited a good deal from it, and has been drawn back to many of the same concerns. As SF writers have become more interested in moral and metaphysical issues, religious imagery has been imported back into SF, often in disguised form, on a large scale.

There have always been SF writers who have religious beliefs of their own, and some have fused SF and religious fantasy, a notable example being C. S. Lewis in *Out Of The Silent Planet* (1938) and its sequels. Ironically, though, it is often agnostics and atheists who become fascinated with the ideas and ideals of religion, and who use their own cool detachment to scrutinize those ideas and ideals in speculative fiction. Thus H. G. Wells, who adopted a rigorously secularized world-view in *The Time Machine* (1895), produced in the same year *The Wonderful Visit*, a parable in which an unorthodox angel is given a poor welcome in an English village. Olaf Stapledon, in *Star Maker* (1937), was perhaps the first writer to produce a comprehensive account of a God whose activities were in tune with the world-view of SF, but there were to be others.

In the SF pulps religion was initially a sensitive matter, although stories "rationalizing" Biblical mythology (dubbed "Shaggy god stories" by Brian Aldiss) appeared regularly. The favourite story of this kind tells the tale of a catastrophe survived by only two people, whose spaceship makes its way to a pleasant world where they become Adam and Eve. In the 1950s, however, editorial taboos relaxed and there was a boom in religious SF in America. In "The Fire Balloons" (1951) by Ray Bradbury priests encounter sinless beings on Mars. In "The Quest For St. Aquin" (1951) by Anthony Boucher a robot deduces the existence of God and becomes a saint. In *A Case Of Conscience* (1953, expanded 1958) by James Blish a Jesuit is forced to conclude that an alien world is the creation of the devil. In "The Star" (1955) by Arthur Clarke space-travellers discover the alien worlds destroyed by the nova which lighted the way to Bethlehem. In the 1960s several time-travellers tried to find Jesus, and the hero of Michael Moorcock's *Behold The Man* (1966; expanded 1969) actually became

Him. Several new messiahs appeared, most impressively in Philip K. Dick's *The Divine Invasion* (1981). In Barry Malzberg's *Cross Of Fire* (1982) religious experience is delivered by controlled hallucination and used in psychotherapy.

SF writers in this period have also become interested in alien religions and alien gods, often in ways that go beyond hypothetical anthropology. Alien beings are often given the capacity for "true" religious experience, which humans can share. Philip José Farmer's hero John Carmody becomes a priest after an alien religious experience in *Night Of Light* (1959; expanded 1966) and, later in his career, is offered the chance to replace an alien god in "Father" (1955). The hero of Robert Silverberg's *Downward To The Earth* seeks redemption from his sins in alien religious rituals which involve literal rebirth.

Other ancient mythologies have been treated very earnestly in post-war SF. Much of the work of Roger Zelazny features godlike heroes, who often operate in worlds designed in the image of mythological systems. The world of *This Immortal* (1966) is replete with echoes of Greek mythology, while the characters in *Lord Of Light* (1967) have adopted the identities of the Hindu gods. *Creatures Of Light And Darkness* (1969) makes similar use of Egyptian mythology. Samuel R. Delany has embarked upon enterprises which are not dissimilar. The characters in *The Einstein Intersection* (1967) borrow identities promiscuously from all manner of Earthly mythologies as they try to re-create the lost world of human meanings, while *Nova* (1968) is a Promethean Grail epic. Contemporary with these works is the most elegant of SF's several versions of Homer's *Odyssey*, R. A. Lafferty's *Space Chantey* (1968).

Many SF writers use religious ideas purely as metaphors, trying to understand man through his symbols. Some conduct thought-experiments in theology, trying to describe the god implied by the nature of creation. The ideas are inherently very flexible. The most powerful of SF's many excursions into the psychology, sociology, and existential relevance of religion is *A Canticle For Leibowitz* (1960) by Walter M. Miller, which deals with the role played by the Church in the rebuilding of society after a nuclear holocaust.

In the Dark Age which follows the holocaust the Church of St. Leibowitz preserves relics of the old order with no understanding of their significance, and provides the backbone of a rigid social order. In the time of a new Renaissance it finds its faith decaying in the face of scientific thinking which it has itself helped to cultivate. After the dawn of a new Age of Reason it must again fight to preserve what it can, this time trying to secure some tiny fragment of civilization and moral order against a repetition of the holocaust. This is not simply a bitter fantasy of eternal recurrence, however, for in the background of the novel the Wandering Jew goes on his lonely way, waiting for redemption, and "Rachel," the enigmatic sinless second head of the mutant Mrs. Grales, offers evidence of God's continued interest in human affairs. Through the medium of the novel Miller tries to confront yet again all the questions which religious systems have tried to answer, and reminds us of their continued importance.

Some critics have objected to the presence in *A Canticle For Leibowitz* of straightforwardly supernatural material borrowed directly from the mythology of Christianity. Appropriate or not, the embedding of such elements in a novel which is otherwise scrupulously realistic in its speculations gives them a new significance. In religious fantasy *per se* (for example, the novels of Charles

Williams) certain items of faith are taken for granted; in science fiction even the supernatural ideas must be exposed to interrogation and analysis. Where religious fantasy can never quite struggle free from its doctrinal cages, and may always retreat into the alibi that God's ways are inscrutable to man, science fiction will typically insist that the ways of God are there to be investigated carefully, sceptically and without pre-judgement. In religious SF there is frequently an echo of Medieval scholasticism, but without the boundaries set on scholastic argument.

The insertion of religious imagery and metaphysical discussion into *A Canticle For Leibowitz* does not diminish it as SF. It should rather be seen as enrichment. One of the dangers threatening stories of the future is triviality; there are so *many* possible futures that a conscientious analysis of *one* of them may seem irrelevant. If, however, an author can get to grips with issues that will confront us in *any* imaginable future, there is no danger of triviality. Even if God does not exist in the future, we will probably invent Him, and He is always relevant.

Refurbished religions Wholly new religious orders are actually quite rare in science fiction. More often than not the old forms are re-vamped in new settings. In Garry Kilworth's *The Night Of Kadar* it is the Islamic religion that is taken to the stars. Keith Roberts' *The Chalk Giants* calls upon the ancient corn gods for its religious element, whereas James Blish's *Black Easter* is a tale of God and the Devil.

Parallel Worlds and Alternate Histories

THE IDEA THAT OTHER WORLDS EXIST parallel to ours is an old one. In ancient times the other world, close at hand yet very different, was the Land of Faerie or something similar. In the late 19th century there appeared the notion of "other dimensions" (worlds displaced from ours along a fourth spatial dimension), which gave new life to the supposition. The earliest parallel worlds in SF were featured in "Another World" (1895) by J. H. Rosney the elder and "The Plattner Story" (1896) by H. G. Wells. William Hope Hodgson later made considerable use of the notion in his work, most notably in *The Ghost Pirates* (1909).

The most common use of parallel worlds in modern SF is in connection with the notion of alternate time-tracks; there can be imagined an infinity of Earths, lying alongside one another in the fourth dimension, each featuring a slightly different history. Essays in alternate history have long been a favourite game among historians, but as respectable intellectuals the historians have been timid in their ventures. SF writers, by contrast, are anything but timid – what they often lack is a sense of historical coherency. Wars between competing time-tracks appeared quickly in pulp SF, in Jack Williamson's *The Legion Of Time* (1938) and Fritz Leiber's *Destiny Times Three* (1945), but attempts to imagine other worlds where history developed differently were at that time lacking in detail. One of the few writers with sufficient knowledge and understanding of history to carry out such an exercise conscientiously was L. Sprague de Camp, but even his earliest efforts, most notably "The Wheels Of If" (1940), are a trifle faint-hearted and do not ask to be taken too seriously.

The serious attempts to describe alternate worlds which have appeared in the last forty years or so are rather narrowly confined to a handful of favourite hypotheses. The largest number by far deal with worlds in which the allies were defeated in World War II. The earliest of these were published while the war was still being fought; the most recent is Frederick Mullaly's *Hitler Has Won* (1975). Classic examples include *The Sound Of His Horn* (1952) by Sarban and *The Man In The High Castle* (1962) by Philip K. Dick. Americans have also shown a constant interest in the possibility of the Confederacy having won the Civil War – a premise developed in Ward Moore's excellent *Bring The Jubilee* (1953).

It could be argued that neither parallel worlds nor alternative histories have been exploited to the full by SF writers. Many parallel worlds feature simply as

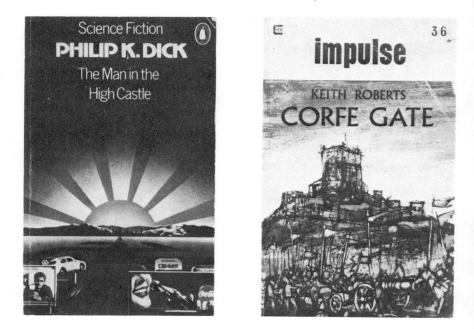

exotic environments in which characters can enjoy fanciful adventures, and it is only in the last fifteen years or so that writers have become ambitious in imagining communication between juxtaposed worlds. Brian Aldiss's *Report On Probability A* (1968) uses the notion for an interesting venture in literary surrealism, while Isaac Asimov, in *The Gods Themselves* (1968), and Bob Shaw, in *A Wreath Of Stars* (1972), have both envisaged parallel worlds where physical laws are different. The limitless potential contained in an infinite plenum of parallel worlds is hardly even glimpsed, although Keith Laumer's *World Of The Imperium* (1962) and Avram Davidson's *Masters Of The Maze* (1965) put the notion to use in exotic adventure stories.

The most interesting group of alternate history stories is perhaps that which deals with alterations to the history of the Christian Church. John Boyd's *The Last Starship From Earth* (1968) is a colourful adventure in this vein, while Kingsley Amis's *The Alteration* (1976) is a satire set in a world where the Holy Roman Empire never disintegrated. The latter hypothesis is more seriously considered in Keith Roberts' *Pavane* (1968), perhaps the most impressive alternate history.

Roberts agrees with the thesis set out in Max Weber's analysis of *The Protestant Ethic And The Spirit Of Capitalism* in describing an alternate England which remains Feudal and technologically primitive, having remained Catholic since the assassination of Elizabeth I, the success of the Spanish Armada and the crushing of the Reformation. The book is a sequence of related stories which look at the lives of half a dozen individuals who are exemplary products of this imaginary world. These include Jesse Strange, a haulier who operates a steam engine and must contend with the depredations of highwaymen; Rafe Bigland, a member of the Guild of Signallers who mans one of a vast series of semaphore

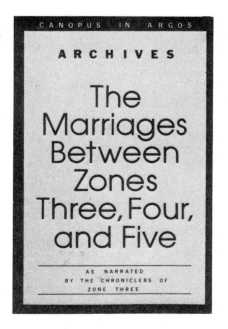

Parallel Worlds and Alternate Universes
"What If?" is a favourite speculative game with science fiction writers; sometimes translated into the past. What if the Germans and the Japanese had won World War II? In Philip K. Dick's *The Man In The High Castle* they had. What if Elizabeth (the Ist) had been assassinated and the Reformation had never occurred in England? She was and it never did in Keith Roberts' *Pavane* (of which "Corfe Gate" was a segment). Alternatively, what if there are layers of this world we cannot see or sense? There are in Doris Lessing's *The Marriages Between Zones Three, Four And Five*.

towers; and Brother John, a monk taken from his artistic labours to act as a recorder for the Inquisition, who eventually rebels against the cruelties of heresy-hunting. The power of the Church is on the wane in this alternate England, and a crucial stand against its tyranny is to be made in the climactic story, "Corfe Gate." The dispute is about taxation, but the implication is that it will spark a wave of dissent that will open the way to a new era – different, of course, from the kind of world which developed out of the Reformation in our world.

Pavane is a bleak book – many of the individual tales are harrowing, and some end tragically – but the plan of the work allows for contrasts of mood; it is also a nostalgic book, reflecting a deep affection for the rural England in which it is set. This rural England, of course, has all but disappeared in *our* twentieth century, but in *Pavane*'s it is preserved – and perhaps always will be, its authentic fairy folk with it. As with many serious excursions into alternate history the real point of this one is to ask whether we might not discover a way to a better world. (We recall, of course, that it is only those who have failed to learn from history who are compelled to repeat it. Alternate histories offer us a way of learning from history.)

Roberts argues quite openly through *Pavane* that contemplation of this imaginary world will help us to see more clearly that which is eternal in human affairs and that which is accidental. Perhaps his estimate of the essential and the peripheral is questionable, but there can be no doubt that this really is the issue at stake. The attempt to imagine how the world might be if a few key events had happened differently must confront us with important questions about the causes of human behaviour. Exercises in imaginary history cannot answer such questions, of course, but it is good that we should be encouraged to face them.

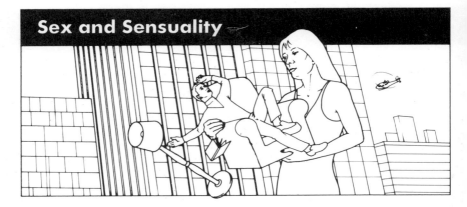

Sex and Sensuality

STANDARDS OF "DECENCY" have always limited the topics for discussion and description in fiction, and it has been argued that this poses special difficulties for SF. Anatole France argued in 1905 that visions of future society would be handicapped by the fact that writers would not dare to assume "the horrible immorality which is to be the morality of the future." Whereas writers of mundane fiction have only had to ask for the freedom to write about the realities of human relationships, SF writers have been required to seek a rather wider licence – to write about all the kinds of relationships, known and unknown, that there might be. This has posed a problem for moralists, who might have difficulty deciding whether description of sex between aliens is more or less disgusting than description of sex between people.

Early SF, for obvious reasons, was mostly coy about sex. American SF suffered more than British SF while it was still mainly confined to the pulp magazines, and only in the post-war period has the situation eased. The main credit for breaking through the barriers of taboo is usually given to Philip José Farmer, whose story *The Lovers* (1952; expanded 1961) dealt with the unfortunate consequences of a love-affair between a man and an alien. Farmer built on this reputation with other stories of strange sexual encounters, including "Open To Me, My Sister" (1960), and a bawdy tale of fertility cults in future America, *Flesh* (1960). More recently, he took advantage of the fact that SF had infiltrated the pornography market, writing explicit novels like *Image Of The Beast* (1968) and *A Feast Unknown* (1969). Others followed where Farmer led, notably Theodore Sturgeon, who was an ardent opponent of moral bigotry in the SF magazines of the 1950s. In "The World Well Lost" (1953) he attacked prejudice against homosexuality, and in *Venus Plus X* (1960) he conducted an interesting Utopian thought-experiment, imagining a society of human hermaphrodites. Fritz Leiber suggested that the future would be a much more liberal time in "Nice Girl With Five Husbands" (1951), and John Wyndham gave serious consideration to the possibility of a male-less society in "Consider Her Ways" (1956).

The permissive era of the 1960s produced a great many stories where sex was imported simply because it could now be done, and a final statement to the effect that all taboos could now be set aside was made with the publication of Harlan Ellison's anthology *Dangerous Visions* in 1967. Explicit sexual description and morbid detail were suddenly all the rage. Relatively few of the stories qualify as speculative fiction *about* sexual matters, but such stories did begin to appear in some quantity. The most sensitive examination of the role of sex in human affairs was provided by Ursula LeGuin in *The Left Hand Of Darkness* (1969), which describes the experiences of an ordinary man in a world where people develop sexual organs to full functional capacity only occasionally, and may become male *or* female depending on circumstance. Sophisticated analyses of future societies which have abandoned contemporary sexual mores can be found in such novels as *334* (1972) by Thomas M. Disch and *Triton* (1976) by Samuel R. Delany. Propagandists for sexual emancipation include Robert A. Heinlein, in *Stranger In A Strange Land* (1961) and subsequent novels, and Norman Spinrad, whose novels *A World Between* (1979) and *Songs From The Stars* (1980) use aspects of the 1960s counterculture as a model for desirable future societies. Several feminist writers have used SF as a vehicle for designing societies free of male domination – often free of males altogether. Examples include Joanna Russ in "When It Changed" (1972) and Marge Piercy in *Woman On The Edge Of Time* (1976).

Most of the points made by these stories of future sex are already familiar; SF is simply used to make them in a new way. There are relatively few new theses about sexual matters propounded in SF. One of the exceptions is an argument about the sexual – or, more correctly, sensual – implications of living in an increasingly artificial and mechanized environment. Mechanically induced sensual experience of orgasmic quality is featured in several stories, but one which suggests that the crucial changes in attitude might already be within our psychological compass is *Crash* (1973) by J. G. Ballard. This novel builds on the common observation that cars – fast, powerful and armour-clad – become a focus for our fantasies of potency. Ballard extrapolates this to draw a perverse equation between orgasm and car crashes.

The hero of the novel, ironically named Ballard, finds that his first car crash is analogous to the loss of his virginity. He revisits the scene of the crash with fascination, becomes erotically involved with the wife of a man killed in it, and becomes obsessed with motorways. He meets other characters whose similar obsessions are even further advanced, and by the end of the story his world has been transformed: he sees it differently, and organizes his life differently within it. It is as though nothing really exists beyond the concrete motorways and their accoutrements, and that life and death are mere matters of driving and crashing.

Crash deserves attention because it is one of the few novels of this liberated era which is still shocking and disturbing. Visions of a sexually free future do not threaten most of us, but what Ballard imagines is not so much a liberation of sexual feeling as an imprisonment of sexuality within the trap of an insidious fetishism. Most of Ballard's recent work presumes that society is being gradually atomized – that we are being detached from our intimate relationships by the "death of affect" as the wellsprings of our emotions dry up. In this future, our intimate involvements will be with the inanimate products of our culture: photographic images and mechanical objects. This argument runs in the opposite direction to the extrapolations of writers like Delany and Spinrad. Ballard suggests that the annihilation of sexual guilt and the advent of honesty in erotic matters might well lead us to realize that what we previously thought of as fulfilment is not in the least fulfilling.

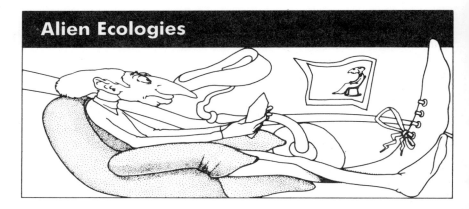

Alien Ecologies

THE IMAGINATIVE TASK of inventing whole ecological systems is a challenging one, whether we are talking about Earthlike environments or worlds very different from our own. Few writers have really taken up the challenge convincingly, but there is a point of respectability at stake for most modern writers. It is generally considered improper not to pay at least some attention to the coherency of imagined worlds; this is especially true now that ecological issues have entered the political arena.

The writer who deserves most credit for importing this kind of conscience into modern SF is Hal Clement. His most famous novel, which presents an ingeniously designed life-system, complete with intelligent beings, adapted to highly unusual physical circumstances, is *Mission Of Gravity* (1953). Another of his works in the same vein is *Cycle Of Fire* (1957). Clement showed that there was much pleasure to be gained from constructing coherent and interesting alien ecologies, and was partly responsible for the invention of the "ecological puzzle story", in which visitors to alien worlds are confronted with enigmas which can be solved via a deeper understanding of the ecological relationships which pertain there. Other exponents of this kind of story are Poul Anderson, whose exercises in alien ecology include *Question And Answer* (1954) and *The Man Who Counts* (1958); Michael Coney, in such novels as *Syzygy* (1973) and *Hello Summer, Goodbye* (1975); and Brian Stableford, in the *"Daedalus"* series (1976-79).

The popularization of ecological terminology has resulted in some popular misunderstanding of the science. There has also been a tendency for ecological notions to be used in a metaphorical fashion: modern uses of the word symbiosis provide an excellent example. In SF, this kind of loosening of meaning has helped to produce an abundance of stories in which the complexity of ecological relationships becomes symbolic of a kind of spiritual harmony. Man, it is presumed, has thrown his own ecosystems out of balance, and has become psychologically alienated from his world. Alien worlds are often put forward as paradigms of perfect harmony, and the one thing that most imaginary alien species in contemporary SF are not is "alienated." Romanticized alien worlds, frequently described with the aid of analogies borrowed from the Biblical myth of the Garden of Eden, are to be found in abundance. Examples include Mark Clifton's *Eight Keys To Eden* (1960), John Boyd's *The Pollinators Of Eden* (1969), and Brian Stableford's *The Gates Of Eden* (1983). Ecological mysticism is also very evident in such novels as *The Green Brain* (1966) by Frank Herbert and *Omnivore* (1968) by Piers Anthony.

SF writers who have taken up the challenge of designing life-systems to fit extreme physical circumstances include Olaf Stapledon, who imagined beings that live in the sun in *The Flames* (1947); Fred Hoyle, who imagined a living cloud of cosmic dust in *The Black Cloud* (1957); and Robert L. Forward, who designed a life-system for the surface of a neutron star in *Dragon's Egg* (1980). One of the favourite exercises in this vein involves designing life-systems which have to face great variations in temperature because their planets have very eccentric orbits. An interesting recent venture along these lines is a trilogy begun with *Helliconia Spring* (1982) by Brian Aldiss. Another favourite is to imagine a life-system which is a single vast organism, like the living ocean in Stanislaw Lem's *Solaris* (1961) or the living forest in Ursula K. LeGuin's "Vaster than Empires and More Slow" (1971).

To be truly comprehensive in their endeavours writers must integrate the ecology of their alien worlds with the sociology and politics of the inhabitants (whether they are indigenous or human colonists). This is rarely accomplished with any degree of plausibility, and one of the few imaginary worlds in modern SF which readers have found convincing is Arrakis in Frank Herbert's *Dune* series (1965-84). The series deals with the "ecological salvation" of a desert world and its people, achieved by the efforts of a messianic hero and his followers.

In *Dune* itself the hero becomes the leader of the desert-dwelling Fremen, and engages in a Holy War whose ultimate object is to irrigate the deserts of Arrakis and regenerate its life-system. The rituals and beliefs of the Fremen all grow out of their desperate need to preserve water. The principal native life-form of the deserts is a gargantuan sand-worm, whose ecological needs preserve the arid environment. The hero uses the sand-worm to help in his war – an ironic use in more than one way, since the sperm of the immensely long-lived worms is a "spice" fabulously valuable to humans because of its life-preserving qualities. The regeneration of Arrakis will involve the extinction of the sand-worms and the end of the spice-supply.

The "spice" produced by the ecology of Arrakis is clearly a magical substance, and the worm is a mythical beast. Quite apart from the charismatic status enjoyed by the hero because of his political role he really is supernaturally blessed. A special kind of wizardry features importantly in the stories, rationalized as psionic power. All of this supernaturalism is so close to the surface of the novels that they can be reckoned as an exercise in futuristic mythology rather than an exercise in scientific speculation. The way in which ecological relationships are made to stand for supernatural ones makes *Dune* one of the archetypal examples of fashionable ecological mysticism, and this may help to explain its great popularity.

Like other novels of its kind *Dune* testifies to the peculiar fascination of ecological awareness. The notion that human beings are part of a vast and complex web of interrelationships, dependent for their existence on the integrity of the web, is one which reminds us to be humble and to be careful of the way in which we use and abuse other species. The quasi-religious note often struck by stories developing this theme is understandable enough.

Magic

MAGIC IS, BY DEFINITION, NOT SCIENCE. It is, therefore, that which cannot be entertained within science fiction. Its banishment, however, has been less than total.

There is a trivial sense in which magic survives in SF by virtue of apologetic jargon. The simple substitution of one specialized vocabulary for another can easily carry a story across the boundary which separates fantasy from SF. Witchcraft can be converted into psionic power, and miracles can be worked by imagining machines to do the trick. Most epics of super-science are magical fantasies dressed up in a new vocabulary, and SF writers are fond of quoting Arthur C. Clarke's dictum that "Any sufficiently advanced technology is indistinguishable from magic". (The dictum is, of course, silly – it all depends who is doing the distinguishing.)

Even if we leave aside this kind of cheating, still magic has its fascinations for SF writers. It is an interesting game to apply the rigorous extrapolative logic of good SF to the premise that certain magical practices do work. This combination of careful extrapolation and absurd premises generated the particular kind of fantasy typical of "Unknown Worlds", the short-lived companion magazine to "Astounding Science Fiction". Within SF itself several writers have played the game of constructing pseudoscientific versions of well-known supernatural phenomena such as shape-shifting (e.g. "There Shall Be No Darkness", 1950, by James Blish) and vampirism (e.g. *I Am Legend*, 1954, by Richard Matheson).

There are some writers who have tried to imagine magic disciplined into an applied science, mostly inspired by the early chapters of James Frazer's *The Golden Bough*, where magic is represented as a kind of proto-science based on presumed natural laws: the law of similarity and the law of contagion. (The first states that one can influence a process by imitating it, or influence an object by operating upon a likeness of it; the second states that objects once in contact remain associated, so that one can influence something by acting upon something else that was once part of it, or once intimately associated with it.) Although the anthropological worth of Frazer's work is very dubious, SF writers have naturally been drawn to ask what the world might be like if these laws had, in fact, proved to be true natural laws and not false ones. Examples of stories which use such "quasi-scientific magic" include some of the classic "Unknown Worlds" stories, including "The Devil Makes The Law" (1940, better known as "Magic, Inc.") by Robert Heinlein and *Conjure Wife* (1943) by Fritz Leiber. A more recent example of a world where magic works and has been disciplined for application is *Operation Chaos* (1971) by Poul Anderson. The most deadly earnest of all SF stories built on the premise that the world really is as the mythology of magic represents it is *Black Easter* (1968) by James Blish.

One of the most interesting series of stories in which magic rather than science provides the basis of "technological advancement" is the Lord Darcy series by Randall Garrett, set in an alternate England. Darcy is a detective whose Sherlockian powers of observation and ratiocination are backed up by the valuable assistance of the master magician Sean O Lochlainn, an expert in "forensic sorcery". The fact that divination works in this world does not make the job of a detective much easier, because all the magic works according to hard and fast rules and murderers can be just as ingenious at confusing conventional methods of finding them out.

The one full-length novel in this series, *Too Many Magicians* (1966), is an elegant locked-room mystery in which a puzzling murder is committed at a convention of sorcerers. How the murderer managed to commit the crime and make his escape is just as puzzling as in any orthodox locked-room mystery, although the reader has to consider a very different array of possibilities and impossibilities. The way in which magic is used by the detectives, and the way in which Lord Darcy reasons his way through the evidence to the only solution permitted by the laws of nature which pertain in his world, is brilliantly ingenious.

It is, of course, entirely appropriate that Garrett's stories in this vein should be detective stories as well as SF stories, because the detective story is the most highly stylized and artificial of all literary genres. Classical detective stories are pure intellectual puzzles, literary game-playing at its most honest and most skilful. This kind of SF can only be taken seriously as an intellectual exercise; it not only benefits from the importation of the rigorous standards of the other genre, but virtually requires it.

There is a certain frivolity in the kind of game which Garrett plays in these stories, and it is commendable that he has the *panache* to borrow also from the conventions of historical fiction. Although these stories are set in the twentieth century of their alternate world, the fact that progress has been based on magic rather than mechanical technology has allowed the survival of the feudal system, and Garrett offers the same romanticized picture of the English aristocracy that can be found in many historical romances. The whole enterprise is a clever joke, carried off with admirable style. The other stories in the series are collected in two volumes as *Murder And Magic* (1982) and *Lord Darcy Investigates* (1982); all three books provide excellent examples of the way in which American SF has cultivated its own rhetorical mode, which is quite distinctive and which has been created out of the dispositions of a handful of influential writers rather than being a logical corollary of any definition of what SF's concerns ought to be.

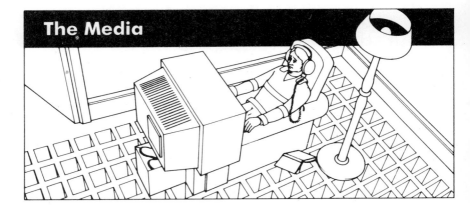

The Media

THE DEVELOPMENT OF MODERN SCIENCE FICTION has run parallel to the evolution of the mass media of communication. Hugo Gernsback, the founder of "Amazing Stories", sold radio sets and ran radio stations in the earliest days of the medium. More recently, Arthur C. Clarke became the prophet of the communications satellite when he drew up specifications in great detail long before *Sputnik* went into orbit.

SF writers in the pre-war years were not much interested in the social effects of the media. Television was usually seen as an adjunct of the telephone rather than as an entertainment medium – a failure of prophecy that was due to lack of interest rather than to lack of foresight. One or two early stories, however, raised alarmist issues that were later to become commonplace. In "The Phantom Dictator" (1935) by Wallace West cinema cartoons are used as a vehicle for political propaganda with the aid of covert "mass hypnosis". In "City Of The Living Dead" (1930) Laurence Manning and Fletcher Pratt imagined a future when people would surrender their sense organs in order to have synthetic experience pumped directly into their brains, living perpetually in pleasant dreams.

Political control of the media for the purpose of manipulating public ideas is common in dystopian novels; even in Aldous Huxley's *Brave New World* (1932) children are indoctrinated by hypnopaedia and the entertainment media are carefully purged of any food for thought. By the time George Orwell wrote *Nineteen Eighty-Four* (1949) there was a much better appreciation of what might be done; the television screens used for surveillance as well as propagandizing remain enduring symbols of subtle and insidious social control. In Ray Bradbury's *Fahrenheit 451* (1953) ordinary people are deliberately denied literacy in order that they may not be able to think for themselves.

Early experiments with subliminal advertising fired the imagination of SF writers, and the application of the discoveries of behaviourist psychology in the same field helped to generate a number of alarmist fantasies, including *The Big Ball Of Wax* (1954) by Shepherd Mead, "The Tunnel Under The World" (1954) by Frederik Pohl and "The Subliminal Man" (1963) by J. G. Ballard. The competition between American TV networks to satisfy their advertisers by grabbing the largest share of the potential audience suggested to SF writers that all moral standards might soon be thrown overboard: ultra-sadistic TV shows are featured in many stories, including "The Pain Peddlers" (1963) by Robert Silverberg. *The Continuous Katherine Mortenhoe* (1975) by D. G. Compton is perhaps the ultimate nightmare of invaded privacy, where a man whose eyes are cameras spies on a dying woman for the delectation of an invisible audience.

The notion that the perfection of artificial media of communication will allow people to retreat into private worlds of synthetic experience is featured in a number of novels, including *The Joy Makers* (1961) by James E. Gunn and *After Utopia* (1977) by Mack Reynolds. The idea has a paradoxical fascination; all the writers who develop it maintain that men must be saved from such a terrible end, while assuming that the temptation to substitute dreams for reality would be well-nigh irresistible. These stories reflect the curious love/hate relationship which exists between the public and the media. We would all feel a tremendous sense of loss if the mass media were to vanish, but we still get anxious about what they might be doing to us, fearing that it might be a kind of moral failure to accept their gifts so gratefully.

The SF novel which displays these anxieties about the media in the most exaggerated and comprehensive fashion is *The Space Merchants* (1953) by Frederik Pohl and Cyril M. Kornbluth. In this novel the political establishment has been taken over by giant corporations whose handmaidens are the advertising agencies. These agencies use every means of persuasion possible to sustain the level of demand, and the people have become slave-consumers whose appetites are manipulated by floods of information, behaviourist trickery, and psychological addiction. The hero of the novel, who works for one of the advertising agencies, is given the job of "selling" a project to colonize and exploit the planet Venus, whose resources are needed to keep the economic wheels turning on Earth. He quickly becomes a casualty of the economic war and has to live a proletarian existence for a while, realizing as he does so the rottenness of the system he is working under. The only sane course, he subsequently discovers, is to get out before its collapse, joining the would-be colonists on Venus in order to make a fresh start.

The Space Merchants is not a subtle novel, and its plot moves in such a fast and furious fashion that it never does become clear exactly who killed who and why, but its sheer boldness gives it a special effectiveness. It presents a picture of a world which has, in essence, gone mad – the whole society is in the grip of an irrational obsession, and paranoia is universal. Ideas like freedom, dignity, and self-fulfilment have simply become impotent. In the thirty years that have passed since the book was first published many people have wondered whether the real world might be heading in that direction. The invocation of the spaceship at the end – a *deus ex machina* to carry the hero away to a new frontier – is a cliché of the day; a spurious upbeat ending which really only serves to confirm the pessimism of the authors. The supposition of the story is that the world, once mad, cannot return to sanity; this, too, is a supposition that many readers find easy to share.

In the real world, research suggests that subliminal advertising may not be much more effective than Huxley's hypnopaedia, and that we rapidly become immunized against the effects of propaganda. It seems highly likely that the media have not done anything dreadful to us yet. Nevertheless, as stories like this testify, we remain apprehensive.

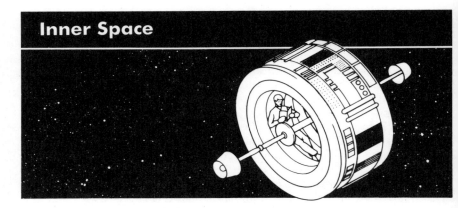

Inner Space

IN A GUEST EDITORIAL called "Which Way To Inner Space?", written for "New Worlds" in 1962, J. G. Ballard suggested that SF writers should abandon their traditional repertoire of ideas, especially those connected with space travel, and should turn their attention instead to the psychological landscapes of private experience, speculating about the possibilities inherent in the world of the mind. This recommendation was in tune with the concerns of the day, and a newly introspective SF grew up in the 1960s. Its exponents were often deemed to constitute a "New Wave", though most denied that they were part of any kind of movement.

Literary "investigations" of psychological possibility existed before SF – and, for that matter, before psychology. Several Romantic and Gothic fantasies from the early 19th century invite consideration as descriptions of psychosis, including E. T. A. Hoffmann's "The Sandman" (1814), which was analysed in a classic essay by Freud, and James Hogg's *Private Memoirs And Confessions Of A Justified Sinner* (1824). Writers as diverse as Virginia Woolf and Franz Kafka can also be nominated as explorers of inner space. Pulp SF likewise produced several ventures into the world of the mind, including L. Ron Hubbard's *Fear* (1940) and several stories in which people are somehow enabled to intrude upon other people's hallucinations.

The new interest in inner space which SF writers of the 1960s found was encouraged by the role played by hallucinogenic drugs in the so-called counter-culture. The notion of "altered states of consciousness" became topical and fascinating when LSD spread from the experimental laboratory to the world at large. Many writers wrote stories about drugs which literally altered reality, including John Brunner in *The Dreaming Earth* (1961) and *The Gaudy Shadows* (1960; expanded 1971). One writer who became preoccupied with worlds of illusion which subvert or absorb reality was Philip K. Dick; such a notion is central to a majority of his works from the early *Eye In The Sky* (1957) through *The Three Stigmata Of Palmer Eldritch* (1964), *Ubik* (1969), and *Flow My Tears, The Policeman Said* (1974) to his last overtly SF novel *The Divine Invasion* (1982). The ultimate SF drug story is *Barefoot In The Head* (1969) by Brian Aldiss, which describes the consequences of psychedelic chemical warfare.

Virtually all of Ballard's own work, of course, follows his prospectus for contemporary SF. He rarely deals with illusions, tending instead to develop elaborate patterns of correspondence between the psychological states of his characters and their physical environments. This is most obvious in short stories like the classic "The Terminal Beach" (1964), but is more elaborately developed in his novels, from early disaster stories like *The Drowned World* (1962) to his recent fantasy of redemption *The Unlimited Dream Company* (1979). Another English writer who has made much of the interweaving of subjective and objective reality is Christopher Priest, in such novels as *Inverted World* (1974) and *A Dream Of Wessex* (1977).

American writers who have a strong interest in private experience and its possibilities (though all have denied belonging to any New Wave) include Harlan Ellison, Thomas M. Disch, and Samuel R. Delany. Ellison's "The Deathbird" (1973) is one of many lurid short stories in which the world undergoes night-marish transformations brought about from within. Disch's *Camp Concentration* (1968) and "The Asian Shore" (1970) both deal with transformations of identity. Delany's *Dhalgren* (1975) is the most detailed and comprehensive study of psychological adaptation to an enclosed world that SF has produced. Other American writers who produced notable inner space stories in this period include Roger Zelazny, whose *The Dream Master* (1966) is a psychoanalytic fantasy of dream manipulation. Barry Malzberg's *Herovit's World* (1973) is a non-SF story about the private inner world of an SF writer.

If there is a single thread connecting all these stories it is that the characters have difficulty in reconciling what goes on inside their heads with what is happening around them. This might be because they are insane or hallucinating, but often it is simply that things no longer make sense – that the certainties of knowledge which once served as psychological anchorages have crumbled. Ballard's protagonists are always remarkably calm and collected in the face of this, but they are exceptional. More typical are Philip K. Dick's protagonists, who are often terrified when they find themselves adrift in uncertainty. This desperate *angst* is perhaps seen to its best advantage in *A Scanner Darkly* (1977), a novel in which Dick reacts fiercely against his earlier fascination with psychotropic drugs.

The hero of this novel, Bob Arctor, is an informer feeding information to the police about the narcotics underworld of the late 1980s. Because he keeps his identity secret from his employers he finds himself in the bizarre situation of

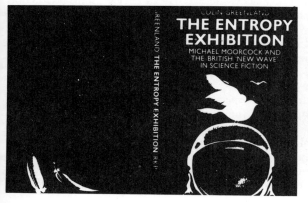

Inner Space J. G. Ballard and *New Worlds* magazine were pioneers of the movement away from Outer Space and into the heads of their hapless protagonists, the realm Ballard termed "Inner Space". Colin Greenland's 1983 study of this phenomenon, *The Entropy Exhibition* traces its various manifestations.

The Inner Realm In much of Nobel Prize-winning author Hermann Hesse's work, the inner-space world of the imagination is dominant, as in *Strange News From Another Star* (1919).

being commissioned to spy upon himself. Unfortunately, his personality is so distorted by the drugs he uses that he takes this commission altogether too seriously; his identity undergoes fragmentation and he becomes lost in a convoluted maze of actions and events. In the end, he becomes a victim of the forces of law and order, but instead of being rescued from his nightmare state he is sentenced to hard labour producing the plants which are the source of the mysterious Substance D: the ultimate destroyer of minds and bodies. He realizes then that there can be no way out of the nightmare. The trap is closed and he is swallowed up. (Some Dick protagonists do manage to find ways back to firm reality, but this is the more common fate.)

Relatively few inner space stories are as nightmarish as this. In other Dick novels where the heroes are permanently detached from certainty, their uncertain worlds at least seem to be places where a man can get by. This one is not. Even those stories which look forward to a time when we can escape the clutches of a dull and oppressive reality, however, recognize the shock of Sartrean *nausea* which is appropriate to the moment when one realizes that one is no longer at home in the world. There may be opportunities in uncertainty, but there is also the threat of disintegration, the possibility of an enclosure in catatonic retreat, and the ultimate certainty of death.

Fantasies of this kind are perhaps specially appropriate to a time of rapid social change, when moral standards are fluid and scepticism has made inroads even into the edifice of scientific theory. When all old beliefs are stricken by a plague of doubt, the fear that we might find nothing to take their place is bound to surface. Such stories have a perennial fascination, particularly for imaginative people who prefer to live in their private fantasies and who find the real world cold and unwelcoming. They serve to remind us of what a hazardous preference that is.

THE SCIENCE FICTION WRITER AT WORK

Introduction
Frederik Pohl

THE WAY SCIENCE-FICTION WRITERS WORK is much the same as any other writers work. That's to say, it's infinitely various. What it is not is a spectator sport. Watching any writer write is about as exciting as watching moss grow; the main diference is that, if you happen to sneeze, moss is not likely to snap your head off for interrupting its train of thought.

The physical parameters of science-fiction writing have widened in the half century and more since it first achieved the status of a separate genre. Around the 1930s the vast majority of the writers in the field were pulpsters. Almost to a man (and to a very occasional woman) their technique was to perch a portable typewriter on a card table in the corner of the living room; the writer put white paper, carbon sheet, and yellow second sheet into the machine, started typing and kept on doing it until he reached "The End". That was it. The stories went out and were published as first drafts (and, of course, were never expected to be seen again after their first appearance in one of the pulps). So it was with Henry Kuttner, George O. Smith, C. M. Kornbluth, and most of the other greats, until perhaps around the mid-1950s. Sometimes the typewriter was not a portable. Doc Smith, creator of the "Skylark" and "Lensman" novels, used an upright Woodstock, vintage of 1915 or thereabouts, for all his work. (As I happen to know because his daughter, Verna, still owns the machine, and not long ago allowed me to write a short story on it.) Doc didn't use a card table, either, at least not after his retirement, because there wasn't room for it in the trailer he and his wife journeyed around the country in. A few more conscientious (or more old-fashioned) writers, Richard Wilson and James Blish among them, generally wrote their first drafts in pencil in small pocket notebooks before typing up the finished product on the old portable. In Wilson's case, the reason was that the jobs that paid his rent and food bills required a lot of travelling; he could balance a notebook on his knee in a train, but not a typewriter.

By and large, they kept those portables smoking. If you wanted to make a living out of writing science fiction in those days you had no choice, since the rates were pitiful. A writer at the top of the field might get two cents a word, possibly even three if he were a superstar; the general horde were lucky to get a penny (often even less), and sometimes had to sue to collect it. There is a mystery novel, *By Rocket to the Morgue*, written by Anthony Boucher under his crime pen-name of H. H. Holmes; it is not science fiction, but it is about science-fiction writers. The characters are all carefully modelled after the real writers of the time, ca. 1940; and there is a funny scene in which everybody's literary agent (the real model was Julius Schwartz, now a senior editor for *Superman*) is visiting his client, representing the real Robert A. Heinlein. Schwartz lies on a sofa with his eyes closed, listening to Heinlein type. He knows that Heinlein averages ten words to the line at two and a half cents a word; every time the bell on the typewriter rings Heinlein has earned 25c and Schwartz ten per cent of that; he hears it tinkle a hundred times before Heinlein quits for the day, and realized that just lying there he has earned $2.50 – not bad pay, he reflects, for taking a fifteen-minute nap. (But not every writer was Heinlein!)

Now the average science-fiction writer has had his horizons widened – or narrowed; he's likely to be spending more of his time travelling (to conventions, booksellers' signing sessions, lecture dates and so on) and is obliged to spend more – *much* more – of his time with editors and agents, hornswoggling out tricky clauses in book contracts. So less of his time is spent in actually writing, more on the ancillary tasks of the writer.

But there are a few who maintain the old tradition. Isaac Asimov, for instance, has a physical addiction to the feel of typewriter keys under his fingertips. I've known this as long as I've known Isaac (which is as long as either of us has been a writer), but it was made vivid for me a few years ago. The Holland-America line invited a bunch of writers aboard its cruise ship *Rotterdam* to view the Apollo 17 Moon launch. Mostly the writers wrote science fiction (Theodore Sturgeon, Robert A. Heinlein, Ben Bova, and so on), but there was a leavening of such mainstreamers as Norman Mailer, Katherine Anne Porter, Hugh Downs, and Carl Sagan. We were a jolly crew, and we jollified a good deal. But Isaac seldom joined us, in ship's bar or on the fantail. He showed up for meals, and most of the rest of the time anyone in the passageway outside his cabin knew where he was by the steady tappety-tap of Book No. 126 (or No. 193, or No. 217) being created. Since then Isaac has switched to a word processor, when one of the manufacturers loaned him a complete outfit for publicity purposes. But the compulsive output will not have changed, for Isaac has never seen a piece of paper he didn't want to write on.

And yet, Isaac is not that different from the rest of us. He's only a little more conspicuous at it. When do writers write? All the time, though not necessarily in any way that is visible from the outside.

It is true that the physical act of putting words on paper is the *sine qua non* of writing. That is how you tell the difference between writers and non-writers; writers write and non-writers just talk about it. But the physical act is only part of the process. When a writer reads he is writing: he reshapes sentences in his mind as he goes along, he identifies this image and that bit of source material, he admires (or deplores) this turn of phrase. When he sees an unusual sight or eavesdrops on a piquant line of conversation, he looks for a place to use it. Perhaps he keeps a notebook to jot these things down – many do. (Though a few, like Robert Sheckley and the late Cordwainer Smith, didn't get as much mileage from their notes as they might have hoped, since Smith's notebook dropped out of his pocket into the Aegean Sea and Sheckley's was stolen, with the rest of his luggage, in the Miami airport.) He may not even be aware of what he is doing. No matter. All those insights and phrases and bits of business work their way down into that pot of soupstock that's always cooking at the bottom of the writer's brain, into which he dips for characters and plots and bits of business.

Of course, a science-fiction writer needs more ingredients in the soup than most writers – he does if he cares about the "science" part, anyway, and most of the better ones do. He needs to find a reliable source for interesting bits of technology and research and scientific conjecture that he can weave into stories. Fortunately there is a familial relationship between one large section of science-fiction writers and one even larger segment of the scientific community. A lot of scientists are present or past science-fiction fans – often they acquired their first impetus to scientific careers through reading science fiction – and retain a sentimental attachment to the field. So it is common for science-fiction writers to be invited to visit campuses, research institutes, observatories, space bases, and all sorts of other places where science and technology are happening. It has become a tradition, for instance, for a group of writers (Heinlein, Bradbury, Poul Anderson, Larry Niven, Jerry Pournelle, and myself among them) to journey to the Jet Propulsion Laboratories in Pasadena to watch the pictures come through as a new space probe nears Jupiter or Saturn. With Jack Williamson I've toured energy installations in New Mexico and Colorado; with James Gunn an advanced transportation facility in Colorado; with Arthur Clarke and Brian Aldiss a series of rocket and vehicular research centres in Japan. Usually there is some staff scientist to give a guided tour. Sometimes it goes beyond the mere tour – as the physicist Robert L. Forward has shown; he provided science-fiction ideas for many writers in the Los Angeles area until finally he decided to write the ideas himself and produced his splendid novel, *Dragon's Egg*.

Perhaps it is because science fiction makes such good use of ideas, scientific and other, that its writers have shown such a marked tendency to collaborate. The brothers Earl and Otto (writing as "Eando") Binder filled the magazines of the 1930s; Fletcher Pratt and his fiancee, Inga Stevens, wrote for *Amazing* even earlier; in the 1950s Poul Anderson with Gordon Dickson, Robert Silverberg with Randall Garrett, and Cyril Kornbluth and I were frequent contributors; now the pace is made by Larry Niven and Jerry Pournelle. The mechanics of collaboration (like the mechanics of marriage!) vary from pair to pair. Perhaps how the words are actually set down is not the important part, though, for all the teams seem to share the trait of positive feedback. A tosses an idea to B; B thinks of some expansions and ornaments and throws it back; A discovers new potentials, and so the story grows. (In the books I've written with Jack Williamson the letters we exchange before actual writing begins often make a stack thicker than the manuscript itself!) My collaboration with Williamson goes on by mail, since we live two thousand miles apart. More commonly the collaborators lock themselves in a room together; but technology may be changing that, as much else – Niven and Pournelle own linked computers. Though they live miles apart, each can read the other's contribution just as it goes onto paper, in his own study.

Even without the special advantages it gives to collaboration, the computer or word processor is beginning to replace the IBM; Williamson, Frank Herbert, Robert Silverberg, and many others have made the switch. They still do have disadvantages. Herbert can't entrust delicate electronics to the muggy climate of his winter home on Maui, so his word processor stays in Washington state; Jack Williamson lost most of a chapter of a novel one Christmas when his wife, Blanche, passed through his study with an armful of metal-foil tree ornaments and capacitance effects wiped his machine's memory. And peripatetic writers like myself have trouble finding a really satisfactory portable. (I do have an electronic portable and love it for its light weight, but for serious work I stay with IBM.)

There is no doubt that the word processor makes writing easier – enough so that Robert Silverberg, who had given up writing for years, now finds the work so painless that he promises to give up giving up writing forever. What is less clear is whether the word processor makes the writing *better*. Those who have made the switch profess to have no doubt that it does; less sure are the stuck-in-the-muds like myself and, for instance, Harlan Ellison (who has not even made the switch to electrics, but still beats on a mechanical upright).

In all the world there are probably no more than a thousand science-fiction writers – five hundred or so in the English-speaking countries, a few score in the Soviet Union, a couple of dozen each in Japan, Germany, France, Italy, and a few other places, down to a bare handful in places like Bulgaria, Korea, and the South American countries. Most write in a room or a corner of a room where they live. Some (like Ray Bradbury) rent an office so they can distance work from leisure; some have full-scale offices in their homes – Harlan Ellison's office wing of the "Ellison Wonderland" in Sherman Oaks, California, is as large as some editorial suites, and has a concert-size stereo and a pool table besides. Many write wherever they are, with whatever facilities are available – Sheckley, world traveller, carries with him a fold-down desk that he sets up in a tent in the Everglades or a trailer parked anywhere he happens to light. None of that seems to matter very much. Whether the tool is pencil, pen, battered portable or $30,000 electronic marvel – whether the work is done on the pulled-down table of an airliner or within a cork-lined room – it isn't the tools or the circumstances that matter, it is the quality of the ideas, the characters, the drama, the poetry, the word-play. Not all science fiction is outstanding in all of these respects. Quite a lot is pretty bad in every one of them. But when it is good – ah, when it is good! Then it feeds the heart and the mind in ways that most writing simply cannot do . . . regardless of where it is written, or in what language, or how, or by whom.

Writers Symposiums When writers get together the second best thing they like to talk about (after rates of payment!) is how they go about the curious business of writing. In the early days there was a much greater sense of the marketplace and the collection of essays in *Of Worlds Beyond* (1948) reflects this. By the time of *Hell's Cartographers* (1975) there was more emphasis upon shaping-experiences and upon the literary aspects of creative writing.

One Man's Work
Poul Anderson

Although the life of a professional writer is, on the whole, a good one, it does inevitably have its special burdens. Among them, after about the five hundredth time, is the question, "Where do you get your ideas?" My reply, truthful but long since stereotyped, is: "Anywhere. If you have that kind of mind, anything at all will suggest a story. It may be something you have personally experienced, or heard about or read about or seen performed. It may be somebody's chance remark, and often that 'somebody' is yourself, free-associating. It may be a dream. It may be a work by another writer, which you realize could be handled quite differently. There's never a dearth of ideas. What counts is what you do with them."

War Of The Wing Men (1958)

This last is, in fact, far more interesting. Given the same theme, or even what looks like the same plot, writers will produce stories entirely unlike each other. (Thus, consider how the life and death of Julius Caesar have been handled literarily over the centuries.) Moreover, the writers will go about their jobs in their own unique ways. I've met a lot of my colleagues and made a small hobby of collecting their working methods. No two are the same.

Hence I can only speak for myself and describe how I proceed. This approach is not necessarily to be recommended to anyone else.

Indeed, in the early stages of a project, mine is a bad example. Inefficiently and unsystematically, I begin thinking about a possible story. During most of this time, I find all sorts of other things to do – puttering in my garden or my workshop, taking long walks, reading, travelling, almost anything that seems unrelated to the task. Yet somehow, in some weird fashion, much of this evasive activity helps make that story take form.

Once I know roughly what I want to do, it's needful to buckle down to specifics. Usually a great deal of background information is called for. It may be found in books, or in discussions with experts, or by visiting actual sites and the like. Even if it comes entirely out of my head – for instance, an imaginary planet – there is a heap of study to do. A setting will not seem real to the reader unless it is first real, in detail, to the author. Many parts of the narrative will be suggested by this or that in its setting.

Meanwhile, and afterward, come the characters, the people whose story this is to be. The relationship between them and the plot is reciprocal. That is, to start with, they must be the kind of individuals to whom the events I have in mind could plausibly happen. A shy scholar won't get involved in wild adventures, except by chance and against his will; nor is a hairy-chested soldier of fortune likely to make discoveries in a laboratory or library. Of course, these extremes are crude. Real human beings are much more subtle and complicated than that, and I make an effort to get well acquainted with my fictional ones. For a novel, I write a biography of each major character, several pages long. It won't appear in the final text, but it will be there in my mind.

Finally comes the making of that text. For me, this is the tail end of the whole process, and generally takes less time than everything that went before. After all, the task now is "merely" to find suitable words with which to describe what happens . . . But that isn't quite true, since I am always surprised along the way. No matter how carefully I thought I had planned, a new aspect of the situation will suddenly show up, or a character will go his own independent way, or . . .

But eventually, somehow, the text will get written; and rewritten; and rewritten: until at last it appears fit to send to market. Thereafter I can only hope that readers will enjoy.

A page of Poul Anderson's manuscript

```
                                1


                    IVORY, AND APES, AND PEACOCKS


        While Solomon was in all his glory, and the Temple was
    a-building                                      measure,
    Manse Everard came to Tyre of the purple. Almost at once, he was
    in peril of his life.

        That mattered little in itself. An agent of the Time Patrol
                            was expendable, the more so if he or she enjoyed
                                               whoever
    the godlike status of Unattached. Those
    Everard could destroy an entire reality. He had come to help rescue it.
                        One
    On a summer's day 950 B.C., the ship that bore him approached
                                        warm
    his destination. The weather was clear, nearly windless, though
                                            landward view
    shimmer a little. Sail furled, the vessel/          creek/ manpower,
                                                        sailors
    and splash, of sweeps, chant of a coxswain posted near the who
                                                seventy
    had the twin steering oars. Around the broad hundred-foot hull,
    wavelets glittered blue, chuckled, swirled. Farther out, dazzlement
    off the water blurred sight of other craft upon it. They were
                                warships
    numerous, ranging from lean/         to tublike rowboats.
    Most                                hailed
                were Phoenician, though many/    from different
    city-states or from the far-flung colonies of these. Some were
                                        or stranger
                quite foreign, Philistine, Assyrian, Achaean, trade
    through the known world flowed in and out of Tyre.

        "Well, Eborix," said Captain Mago genially, "there you have
    her, queen of the sea like I told you she is, eh? What d'you think
    of my town?"
```

The Secret Mind
Ray Bradbury

I had never wanted to go to Ireland in my life.

Yet here was John Huston on the telephone asking me to his hotel for a drink. Later that afternoon, drinks in hand, Huston eyed me carefully and said, "How would you like to live in Ireland and write *Moby Dick* for the screen?"

And suddenly we were off after the White Whale; myself, the wife, and two daughters. From October to April I lived in a country where I did not want to be.

I thought that I saw nothing, heard nothing, felt nothing of Ireland. The Church was deplorable. The weather was dreadful. The poverty was inadmissible. I would have none of it. Besides, there was this Big Fish . . .

I did not count on my subconscious tripping me up. In the middle of all the threadbare dampness, while trying to beach Leviathan with my typewriter, my antennae were noticing the people. Not that my wide-awake self, conscious and afoot, did not notice them, like and admire and have some for friends, and see them often, no. But the overall thing, pervasive, was the poorness and the rain and feeling sorry for myself in a sorry land.

With the Beast rendered down into oil and delivered to the cameras, I fled Ireland, positive I had learned naught save how to dread storms, fogs and the penny-beggar streets of Dublin and Kilcock.

But the subliminal eye is shrewd. While I lamented my hard work and my inability, every other day, to feel as much like Herman Melville as I wished, my interior self kept alert, snuffed deep, listened long, watched close, and filed Ireland and its people for other times when I might relax and let them teem forth to my own surprise.

I came home, assuring one and all, "I'll write nothing ever about the Connemara Lightfoots and the Donnybrook Gazelles". Eire was dead, I insisted, the wake over, her people would never haunt me.

Several years passed.

Then one rainy afternoon Mike (whose real name is Nick), the taxi-driver, came to sit just out of sight in my mind. He nudged me gently and dared to remind me of our journeys together across the bogs, along the Liffey, and him talking and wheeling his old iron car slow through the mist night after night, driving me home to the Royal Hibernian Hotel, the one man I knew best in all the wild green country, from dozens of scores of Dark Journeys.

"Tell the truth about me," Mike said. "Just put it down the way it was."

And suddenly I had a short story and a play. and the story is true and the play is true. It happened like that. It could have happened no other way.

Having dared once, exuberant, I dared again. When Mike vaulted from my machine, others unbidden followed.

And the more that swarmed, the more jostled to fill the spaces.

I suddenly saw that I knew more of the minglings and commotions of the Irish than I could disentangle in a month or a year of writing and unravelling them forth. Inadvertently, I found myself blessing the secret mind, and winnowing a vast interior post-office, calling nights, towns, weathers, beasts, bicycles, churches, cinemas, and ritual marches and flights by name.

Mike had started me at an amble; I broke into a trot which was before long a full sprint. The stories, the plays, were born in a yelping litter. I had but to get out of their way.

Now done, and busy with other plays about science-fiction machineries, do I have an after-the-fact theory to fit playwriting and story-writing?

Yes.

For only after, can one nail down, examine, explain.

To try to know beforehand is to freeze and kill.

Self-consciousness is the enemy of all art, be it acting, writing, painting, or living itself, which is the greatest art of all.

Here's how my theory goes. We writers are up to the following:

We build tensions towards laughter, then give permission, and laughter comes.

We build tensions towards sorrow, and at last say cry, and hope to see our audience in tears.

We build tensions towards violence, light the fuse, and run.

We build the strange tensions of love, where so many of the other tensions mix to be modified and transcended, and allow that fruition in the mind of the audience.

We build tensions, especially today, toward sickness and then, if we are good enough, talented enough, observant enough, allow our audiences to be sick.

Each tension seeks its own proper end, release, and relaxation.

No tension, it follows, aesthetically as well as practically, must be built which remains unreleased. Without this, any art ends incomplete, halfway to its goal. And in real life, as we know, the failure to relax a particular tension can lead to madness.

There are seeming exceptions to this, in which novels or plays end at the height of tension, but the release is implied. The audience is asked to go forth into the world and explode an idea. The final action is passed on from creator to reader-viewer whose job it is to finish off the laughter, the tears, the violence, the sexuality, or the sickness.

Not to know this is not to know the essence of creativity, which at heart, is the essence of man's being.

The art aesthetic is all encompassing, there is room in it for every horror, every delight, if the tensions representing these are carried to their furthest perimeters and released in action. I ask for no happy endings. I ask only for proper endings based on proper assessments of energy contained and given detonation.

The drummer in Dublin tread me lightly through the pubs. The plays and stories wanted to be happy plays and stories. I let them write themselves that way, out of their own hungers and needs, their unusual joys, and fine delights.

Is it the blood of an Irishman that moves his tongue to beauty, or the whiskey that he pours in to move his blood to move his tongue and tell poems and declaim with harps? I do not know. I ask my secret self which tells me back. Wise man, I listen.

So, thinking myself bankrupt, ignorant, unnoticing, I wind up with one-act plays, a three-act play, essays, poems, and stories and a novel about Ireland. I was rich and didn't know it. We are all rich and ignore the buried fact of accumulated wisdom.

So again and again my stories and my plays teach me, remind me, that I must never doubt myself, my gut, my ganglion, or my Ouija subconscious again.

From now on I hope always to stay alert, to educate myself as best I can. But, lacking this, in future I will relaxedly turn back to my secret mind to see what it has observed when I thought I was sitting this one out.

We never sit anything out.

We are cups, constantly and quietly being filled.

The trick is, knowing how to tip ourselves over and let the beautiful stuff out.

Is There A Story In It Somewhere?
Richard Cowper

Seven years ago, describing myself at the age of seventeen I said: "What I did not realize – or was only just beginning to realize – was that you did not *choose* to become a writer, you were chosen. Some genetic accident marked you out from birth and, twist or turn as you might, short of death intervening this was your fate." I wouldn't argue with that today. At least it's true of the kind of writer *I* am, though others might not recognize themselves.

At that point in my life I had reached a sort of 'T' junction. Down one road lay art – specifically painting – down the other, fiction. My innate talents – such as they were – seemed about equally divided between those two modes of self-expression. That I chose to become a writer rather than a painter was, I suppose, due to the dominant strain in my heredity. But unquestionably there is a lot of the artist *manqué* in me still and it tends to surface in my writing. I paint in words and am happiest when the image conceived in my imagination is transferred bright and clear on to the page. Nor should it be forgotten that a writer does have some very real advantages over a painter. He has direct access to his reader's imagination. By choosing his words and images skilfully he can gain his reader's allegiance, lend him his imagination, and (to purloin a phrase) refresh those parts which other arts cannot reach. He can traffic in illusion, feed the hunger of the imagination, and still, with luck, retain his own integrity.

I write science fiction because I am fascinated by the future of mankind. I live in constant awareness that today is yesterday's tomorrow. I am also fascinated by people and without them there would be neither science nor fiction. But between people and science critical stresses develop. They grind against each other like ponderous tectonic plates. On the one hand fallible, emotional, irrational human beings, and on the other this extraordinary creation of theirs, this "Science" which they have apotheosized into a sort of Old Testament Jehovah, an Omnipotence to revere and to fear and to make their sacrifices to. The future is pregnant with conflict. Today the scientists and technologists have become our Egyptian priests, they practise an arcane mystery, and we, the writers of science fiction, must be perpetually alert to expose their human fallibility as we probe into the future which they are preparing for us.

As to the practicalities of my trade, I write all my novels and stories in longhand – usually two drafts and innumerable revisions. I *can* type (just about) but I dislike the racket it makes, whereas the faint whispering of my pen nib as it traces its way across a sheet of paper is soothing to my troubled soul. As for the "ideas" which fuel my stories I often wonder where they come from. Out of my subconscious I suppose, because quite a few of my tales I owe to dreams. But almost anything can trigger off a story – a face seen in a crowd, a line of poetry, even a paragraph in a scientific journal. These are the fragments of grit, the irritants that may one day be transformed into pearls.

As I get older I find myself becoming ever more interested in the subject of "Time"; I sense it leaning down upon me with an inexorable, glacial pressure. At such moments I envy the oak trees I can see on the hillside beyond my study window. What would it be like to be one of them? Would you see the whole world in accelerated motion – clouds rushing across the skies – human lives as brief as mayflies? Would a year seem like a day? I wonder if there's a story in it somewhere . . .

The opening page of "Piper At The Gates Of Dawn"

Wrestling With Words
Christopher Evans

In practical terms I write on a small portable typewriter bought over ten years ago. If I get bogged down – and I frequently do – I may scribble on a notepad until some sense of what I want to say begins to emerge; then I type up these handwritten passages because I need to see how the words look in cold type.

Broadly speaking I do two drafts of everything, plus substantial revisions of the second draft which effectively add up to a further rewrite. The first draft is always the most difficult and heart-breaking. I begin with only a limited idea of my story; frequently I have little more than a beginning, a few crucial scenes, and some vague notion of how it might end. But the very act of writing, of fleshing out the story, changes its texture and emphasis so that what I eventually produce bears only a limited relationship to my original conception. Once I used to despair of this, but I've come to see it as inevitable: I need to write to discover what I am going to say.

My first drafts are sketchy, superficial, frequently ungrammatical and filled with trite phraseology. I know that all I am doing is producing the raw material from which I hope to refine something which possesses a real imaginative dimension. The main effort at this stage is to plod on doggedly to the end and resist the temptation to abandon it all in despair.

The second draft is only marginally easier. But now I usually know where the story has gone wrong and have a clearer sense of what I am actually writing about. I've made lots of notes along the way to remind myself of what needs to be done. The first draft now provides the framework which enables me to re-enter the scenes I've written and attempt to give them more vividness and pertinence. Many passages are cut and new ones substituted; I try to flesh out the characters and give the story a better balance and shape. Often this is a complicated and arduous task, but sometimes a simple thing such as changing a character's name can make all the difference. But because I've been striving to bring everything I've written to life as fully as possible I usually discover that I've over-elaborated, been too descriptive or explanatory. The third draft is therefore mainly a process of refinement and pruning; I try to correct infelicities of expression and aim to pare the text down to its essentials. Often I don't cut enough.

This final stage could, in theory, go on indefinitely since I can always find passages in my work which could be

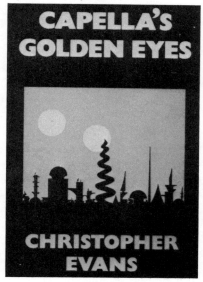

Capella's Golden Eyes (1980)

improved. I never actually finish anything in an absolute sense: I merely abandon it when I decide that I've done all I can reasonably hope to do and that my time would be better spent on a new project. In general I consider a piece of writing to be finished when I can read it through without cringing.

No doubt all this sounds desperately daunting and joyless, not to mention entirely divorced from any external considerations. Yet I always write with an audience in mind, and above all I strive for readability since I want to communicate. I write to please myself but I also hope to please others. And at the heart of it all is the challenge and fascination of wrestling words into some sort of form in which they take on a life of their own.

Mapping Imaginary Countries
Ursula LeGuin

People come up to you if you're a writer, and they say, I want to be a writer. How do I become a writer?

I have a two-stage answer to that. Very often the first stage doesn't get off the ground, and we end up standing around the ruins on the launching pad, arguing.

The first-stage answer to the question, how do I become a writer, is this: You learn to type.

The only alternative to learning to type is to have an inherited income and hire a full-time stenographer.

Well, the person who asked, How do I become a writer, is a bit cross now, and he mumbles, but that isn't what I meant. I want to write short stories, what are the rules for writing short stories? I want to write a novel, what are the rules for writing novels?

Now I say Ah! and get really enthusiastic. You can find all the rules of writing in Fowler's *Handbook of English Usage* and Strunk and White's *Elements of Style*, and a good dictionary (and – as a corrective to Fowler – Miller and Swift's *Words and Women*). There are only a few "rules of writing" not covered in these volumes, and they are to do with the proper preparation of manuscripts for submission to editors. All right, that is stage one of my answer. If the person listens to all that without hitting me, and still says All right, but how *do* you become a writer, then we've got off the ground, and I can deliver stage two. How do you become a writer? Answer: You write.

It's amazing how much resentment and disgust and evasion this answer can arouse. Even among writers. It is one of those Horrible Truths one would rather not face.

The most frequent evasive tactic is for the would-be writer to say, But before I have anything to say, I must get *experience*.

Well, yes: if you want to be a journalist. But I'm talking about fiction. And of course fiction is made out of the writer's experience, his whole life from infancy on, everything he's thought and done and seen and read and dreamed. But experience isn't something you go and *get* – it's a gift, and the only prerequisite for receiving it is that you be open to it. A closed soul can have the most immense adventures and have nothing to show for all that "experience", whereas the open soul can do wonders with nothing. You must write with the imagination, which is the tool of the farmer, the plough you plough your own soul with. You must write from inside, from as deep inside as you can get by using all your strength and courage and intelligence. And that is where books come from. The novelist writes from inside. What happens to him outside, during most of his life, doesn't really matter.

I'm rather sensitive on this point, because I write science fiction, or fantasy, or about imaginary countries, mostly – stuff that, by definition, involves times, places, events that I could not possibly experience in my own life. So when I was young and would submit one of these things about space voyages to Orion or dragons or something, I was told, at extremely regular intervals, "You should try to write about things you know about." And I would say, But I do; I know about Orion, and dragons, and imaginary countries. Who do you think knows about my imaginary countries, if I don't?

But they didn't listen, because they don't understand, they have it all backward. They think an artist is like a roll of photographic film, you expose it and develop it and there is a reproduction of Reality in two dimensions. But that's all wrong, and if any artist tells you "I am a camera", or "I am a mirror" distrust him instantly, he's fooling you, pulling a fast one. Artists are people who are not at all interested in the facts – only in the truth. You get the facts from outside. The truth you get from inside.

OK. How do you get about getting at that truth? What do you do?

You write. You sit down and you do it, and you do it, and you do it, until you have learned to do it. And you do it alone.

It is the experience or premonition of that loneliness, perhaps, that drives a lot of young writers into this search for rules. I envy musicians very much, myself. They get to play together, their art is largely communal; and there are rules to it, an accepted body of axioms and techniques, which can be put into words or at least demonstrated, and so taught. Writing cannot be shared, nor can it be taught as a technique, except on the most superficial level. All a writer's real learning is done alone, thinking, reading other people's books, or writing – practising.

As a writer you are about the freest person that ever was. Your freedom is what you have bought with your solitude, your loneliness. You are in the country where *you* make up the rules, the laws. You are both dictator and obedient populace. It is a country nobody has ever explored before. It is up to you to make all the maps, to build the cities. Nobody else in the world can do it, or ever could do it, or ever will be able to do it again.

Absolute freedom is absolute responsibility. The writer's job, as I see it, is to tell the truth. The writer's truth – nobody else's. It is not an easy job. One of the biggest implied lies going around at present is the one that hides in phrases like "self-expression" or "telling it like it is" – as if that were easy, anybody could do it if they just let the words pour out and didn't get fancy. The "I am a camera" business again. Well, it just doesn't work that way. You know how hard it is to say to somebody, just somebody you know, how you *really* feel, what you *really* think – with complete honesty? You have to trust them; and you have to *know yourself*: before you can say anything anywhere near the truth. And it's hard. It takes a lot out of you.

You multiply that by thousands; you remove the listener, the live flesh-and-blood friend you trust, and replace him with a faceless unknown audience of people who may possibly not even exist; and you try to write the truth to them, you try to draw them a map of your inmost mind and feelings, hiding nothing and trying to keep all the distances straight and the altitudes right and the emotions honest . . . And you never succeed. The map is never complete, or even accurate. You read it over and it may be beautiful but you realize that you have fudged here, and smeared there, and left this out, and put in some stuff that isn't really there at all, and so on – and there is nothing to do then but say OK; that's done; now I come back and start a new map, and try to do it better, more truthfully. And all of this, every time, you do alone – absolutely alone. The only questions that really matter are the ones you ask yourself.

Author's Note:
The above is an amalgamated condensation of some talks I gave in the 1970s to audiences made up of young people who wanted to, or thought they might like to, become professional writers. I could no longer make some of the assertions I made then, for the deeper I go in my writing the harder it is to generalize, and the more I distrust any theory as an element in the practice of any art. However, I don't disagree with anything I said here, and would only add the proviso: All fiction writers are liars, I am a fiction writer, I am telling the truth.

Equipment, Method and the Rest
Larry Niven

Equipment: I used an erasing typewriter until Jerry Pournelle turned me on to a computer. I still don't know much about computers. I buy what Jerry tells me to. At the moment it's a Godbout, and a Diablo printer five or six years old. The Diablo gives me no trouble, so I'm disinclined to upgrade; but my wife tells me I'll want to steal her spinwriter. The new double-sided double-density disks hold a whole novel. My Minolta copier is small, fast, and runs cool and trouble-free. If I can't write it sure isn't the equipment's fault.

Two of the walls in my office are all shelves down to a wider shelf that is all desktop, with tubular lights, and pigeonholes underneath that. It should not be possible to fill up all that space, but the limits are in sight.

Method: The computer has changed my life. I never read anything without rewriting as I go along; it's so bloody easy! By the time I reach the end of a story, it's all final draft. Even so, I never send it in without letting it sit for awhile, then going through it again . . . sometimes several times. That final pass always pays off.

I do a lot of daydreaming. When some of the ideas floating around in my head link together into a story, I begin outlining.

There are a good many half-finished outlines on my disks, and stacks of paper from the pre-computer era. I outline a story all the way through; at least it always feels that way. Later, while I'm writing the story, I always find that I've neglected something.

So I outline in detail, and I build up dossiers on characters, and when I'm sure there's a story I start writing it. Sometimes this involves elaborating the outline, inserting blocks of text into it wherever I feel inspired. Sometimes it's the other way: a block of text riddled with notes to myself in capital letters: DETAIL; DATE?; MINYA POV; DESCRIBE TREEMOUTH; MAYOR'S SON DESCRIPTION, LOOKS LIKE MAYOR BUT TALLER.

If I get bored with a novel, I work on a short story, or another novel, until inspiration returns. (If it's a short-short, I'll just sit down and write it.)

The Fourth Profession (25,000 words) was an exception. When I started it I had no idea where I was going, or even how many skill-pills the bartender-protagonist had swallowed. I was pleasantly surprised all the way. The thing to remember is this: *you can always go back and futz with the beginning.* I put the evidence into the text once I knew what had happened.

Collaborations: are nothing to go into lightly. We must trust each other absolutely. Beyond that, a collaboration is so much more work than a single effort, that the only excuse for writing together is a story that neither author could produce alone.

A complete outline is vital. Or the story will die when we realize that we've gone haring off in different directions.

We always feel free to back up. The nuclear plant in *Lucifer's Hammer* was inserted when Jerry and I were three-quarters finished and having trouble with the ending.

Attitude: It turns out that I don't need to keep regular hours, or to demand a minimum output of myself. I used to. Now I write when I feel like it. Fortunately I feel like it a lot.

Thirty Years of Writing
Robert Silverberg

In the morning: always in the morning. I rise early – usually by six, without benefit of alarm clock – and full of energy, which I want to harness for the benefit of my work before the erosions of the day set in. And I prefer to get my work done in what is normally the cool and foggy time of the day in coastal California, so that the afternoons are free for outdoor life. So the normal story is newspaper, breakfast, trip to post office to pick up the day's mail, and then to work by 8.15 or so. Normally I write until about noon. If the work is going so well that I'm reluctant to break off, I sometimes continue an extra hour. If the day's stint has been disastrously skimpy, I'm apt to continue an extra *two* hours. But I never work past two in the afternoon, and I never work on Saturdays or Sundays except in times of the most dire emergency. (I had a time of the most dire emergency just this winter; but I can't remember how long ago the last one was.)

For the first thirty years of my career I used a standard manual typewriter. I type quickly and well, and the manual seemed to serve my needs satisfactorily. Electric typewriters never pleased me: whenever I tried one, I found myself resting my fingers on the keys while thinking and inadvertently typing a stanza or two of asdf;lkj asdfjlk;. But in the summer of 1982, after typing and retyping a 900-page manuscript, I listened for the first time to the siren song of the word-processor people, and these days I use a Compucorp 685-E. Like all other writers newly converted to word processors, I am boringly evangelical about them, and I discourse to dreary length now on such arcana as megabytes, dedicated keys, and Winchester disks; and, like all the rest, I wonder how I ever managed to do any work on a typewriter. In the typewriter days I found severe headaches setting in after about three hours of work, which I credited to the effects of intense cerebration but which I now see resulted entirely from the clatter of the damned machine; on the word processor I cerebrate just as hard, work an hour or two longer every day, and don't seem to get headaches at all.

The genesis of every story is a quickly jotted idea, image, or sometimes merely a title, set down on the handiest available piece of paper. I develop this into a coherent outline written on the backs of old envelopes; one envelope suffices for a short story, five or six for a novel. I feel ready to begin when a beginning and an ending and a title are clearly in sight. (The middle can take care of itself along the way.) I won't begin an untitled project: my theory is that if I don't have a title for it, I don't really know what it's about. I do sometimes change a story's title after it's written, but I must have a plausible one, at least, at the outset.

A segment of Robert Silverberg's manuscript

```
"Is this what you sought?" the Dutchman asks.

"Yes.  Absolutely."

"I wish you farewell and Godspeed, then!" Noort cries.

"And you -- what will become of you?"

Noort laughs.  "Have no fears for me!  I see my destiny un-
folding!"

Bhengarn, nestled now deep in the ground, enwombed by the earth,
immobile, established already in his new life, looooxxoo watches as
Noort strides boldly forward to the water's edge.  Only slowly, for
an Awaiter's mind is less agile than a Traveler's, does Bhengarn
comprehend what is to happen.

Noort says, xxx "I've found my vocation again.  But if I'm to
travel, I must be equipped for traveling!"

He enters the pond, swimming in broad awkward splashing strokes,
and once again the pure tolling sound is evoked, a delicate carillon
of crystalline transparent tone, and k there is sudden brilliance in
the pond as Noort sprouts the shining scales of a Traveler, and the
jointed limbs, and the strong thick tail.  He scuttles out on the
far side wholly transformed.
```

In the typewriter days I did rough revisions as I went along, then made hand corrections to the first draft and retyped the whole thing. Since the final polish went on during the retyping, I could never entrust the job to anyone else. Now that I use a word processor, I revise to more or less final state as I write, then print out a typed copy and make minor corrections on that, and let the machine take care of producing the final draft. Last year's novel, the last one done on the typewriter, demanded two ghastly months of retyping and polishing; this one, though it was no more swiftly composed in first draft, went to final draft in just two days, thanks to that blessed machine.

It takes me anywhere from five days to a month to finish a short story, five or six months for a novel. Astute students of my bibliography can probably calculate that at those speeds it could not have been possible for me to rack up such an immense total of published works in a mere thirty years, and they would be right: I used to do it a lot faster, a short story in a single sitting, a novel in two or three weeks. I don't know how I managed that, and there are days when I don't believe that I did. But I must have, because platoons of books bearing my name are staring at me from across the room.

And where do I get my ideas? Everywhere. I don't inquire into the process. Whenever I need the next one, it's there. It always has been; I assume it always will. I realize that that's of little use to aspiring writers. But oh! what comfort it is to me!

How I Became A Science Fiction Master in only 15 Minutes a Day John Sladek

Firstly I believe in dressing the part. You can't write science fiction wearing your ordinary everyday writer's uniform. Throw away the tweed jacket with leather elbow patches, the pipe and horn-rim glasses. Shave off that beard. An SF writer can only wear a beard if it looks weird enough.

The usual SF uniform includes a baseball cap with a NASA emblem on it, a T-shirt depicting some comic book superhero, and plenty of buttons with obscure slogans on them ("QUARKS!"). If I can't get all this, I try to make do with a silver jump suit, red cape and fishbowl helmet – jet-propelled roller skates with silver wings on the side being an optional accessory.

The next choice is, how fast to write. SF is famous for authors who churned out novels in five days, short stories in five minutes, and so on. Though no one in SF has so far surpassed Georges Simenon (who probably wore a rubber *pipi* bottle to save leaving the typewriter even for a moment) there have been many speedwriting legends. One prominent scientologist, I understand, back in the 1940s wrote on a special typewriter with extra keys for commonly used words like "intergalactic" and "*spunng*". He also saved time by typing directly onto a roll of toilet paper. Even now there are said to be SF writers whose word processors can't keep up with them – after all, electrons can only move at the speed of light.

Since I write relatively slowly on a manual typewriter, I naturally envy those who can whip out half a novel while I'm trying to make up my mind whether "*spung*" has one *n* or two. Mostly I envy their money. I also envy the money of rich people who do not write, and I envy terrific athletes and those who understand modern physics completely. It always seemed to me that if I really tried, I might achieve partial success at least in any of these fields. I could maybe write a novel in fifty days, or make say half a million. Or at least understand one quark. But I spend all my time writing slowly. One n or two?

Next, how much science to put into my SF. Some writers argue that there must be plenty. I maintain that all is science, anyway. If someone drives a car in a story, that implies the principles of thermodynamics; if he rides a horse, that implies the evolution of horses; if he turns on a water tap, there's fluid dynamics for you. The hard science school might prefer it if we wrote: "He turned the tap and filled a $500ml$ beaker with hydrogen hydroxide . . ." That seems unnecessary to me. Get the science out of our stories, I say, and get the people back in.

Only we can't overdo that, either. One mistake I try to avoid is letting my characters have lives of their own. Authors are always complaining that they create characters who "come to life" and "take over" the story. I say it's just a question of who's the boss. If any of my characters dared try any such rebellion, they'd very soon find themselves back on the street looking for another author, Pirandello maybe. Only once did one of my employees pull anything on me. In *The Müller-Fokker Effect* I invented a minor figure called President Reagan. This cagey guy waited until *after* the novel was published in 1970 and *then* he came to life. I'll make sure that it never happens again.

How I Write
Lisa Tuttle

Sitting at a desk in a room by myself, near a window with no view, on an electric typewriter. Occasionally I'll test out a sentence in longhand on a lined pad, but I've composed on a typewriter since I was twelve.

I imagined myself as someone who writes every day, from nine to one, from two to six, regular, productive, disciplined. That's my fantasy. For reality, take this week: Sunday I spent two hours at my desk and wrote four pages. Monday I walked around the West End with a visitor from America. Tuesday I was at the typewriter from ten until noon, from two until five, and despite many breaks for coffee or Diet Pepsi, reworked one page from Sunday and wrote seven new ones. Most of Wednesday was spent reading someone else's novel. So far today I have written four drafts – eight pages – of this tiny article.

When really driven, working at top speed, I may manage twenty pages in a day, but between three and ten is more usual.

A lot of those pages get thrown away. Ten years ago my first and final drafts were nearly identical, except for neatness. Today I can't read my first drafts without feeling I should give up the hopeless attempt to write. Partly this is because my critical standards are higher now than they were when I was twenty, but objectively I think they are worse because I've changed my habits. I no longer have to squeeze my writing in between classes or a job. Writing is all that I do, and the only proof I have of work is a pile of typed pages. So I work things out on paper which I would once have done in my head. My first drafts are full of blind alleys, failed attempts, unnecessary scenes. By the second draft I have a better idea of what I want to say.

Ideas don't usually come at the typewriter, but away from it. It may look like loafing, but where would the writer be without the epiphany in the bathtub, the connection made while daydreaming or watching TV? I make lists and notes, storing them up for the day when I'll know how to use them.

Bits and pieces come together, sometimes after years. I am startled, looking through old notebooks, to discover just how long a particular idea has been in my head. The seeds of the novel I am writing now go back to a story I wrote while I was still at school. It was a science fiction story. The novel isn't. I'm attracted to the ideas of science fiction, but I'm not primarily a science fiction writer.

Beginning to write, the plot is uncertain, but I have the end in mind, often in precise detail. Those final sentences are, in Dorothea Brande's words, "a raft to swim toward". Later, when the story takes an unexpected direction, I worry about forcing the ending, and decide to change it. But usually I don't have to. I find, when I get there, that the words are right, the details just as I imagined before I understood their full significance. It no longer seems as if I made it up, but as if I managed to find my way to a place that was waiting to be discovered.

Where I Get My Ideas
Gene Wolfe

I wake in the middle of the night to see red eyes staring. They belong to the memory register, and I go back to sleep listening to Duffy swear.

A rat – and it is a rat – is dragging his glasses across the dirt of the hoochie. He swings at it with a bottle of Japanese Scotch, trying to hit the rat, trying to miss his glasses, nearsighted, still a little drunk and half asleep. Of course he misses everything. The soft whoosh of the empty is like the whoosh of my air purifier, a sound half choked with dust.

I hear him rummaging for a flashlight and know he has his .45 in his hand. All of us sleep with guns. Not for the soldiers of the People's Republic, but the pidgin-English slicky-boy thieves of the ROK. If the Chinese come to wake us, standing over the sleeping bags with burp guns—

"Comrade! Comrade!" God, how do you say it in Chinese?

I snuggle down, pulling the blankets, the comforter around my ears. If Duffy fires, I will wake up. It seems terrifying.

No, not Duffy, not the rat; Flip the ugly clown, wearing Duffy's wire-framed glasses. I am myself and Nemo too, fearing to be driven again from the Palace of Slumberland.

Flip flourishes Duffy's gun and fires a flash of light.

And I sit up in bed shaking. The red eyes stare from across the room. (Something horrible is about to happen.) I forgot to turn it off last night.

Or I turned it on last night, turned it on, sitting naked in my fatigues, my mother-bought carpenter's jeans, to write something I have now forgotten. The room seems so cold.

I get up, naked because I always sleep naked, go into the bathroom, run the water and rinse my mouth again and again. I know what the horrible thing is now, and I keep my eyes closed as I brush my teeth.

The windows are gray with summer dawn. The flash of Duffy's automatic has become a globe of light held aloft by a china seal. The seal's name is Thurber: I have written it across his chest in gold stick-on letters. My older daughter gave him to me.

The horrible thing has happened. Father and Mother are dead. (I have an awkward picture, somewhere, of Mother, stooped and old, crouching to lay flowers on Father's grave.)

I have daughters old enough to work, sons in college and high school. Boots is dead too and Lance is gone. Sissy, bought to replace Lance, has gone white at the muzzle.

Where is the little house where Boots stretched before the gas fire, where Mother sat crocheting? The brass bookends like old racing cars? Where is lost Atlantis? Lost in the dust. And only I am left to tell you.

Two hours before Breakfast, three before I must be at work again. Oh, God, let me begin a new one today, begin new in the midst of the old. Help me now. Perhaps I'll think of something.

The Process of Composing
Roger Zelazny

With my novels, I tend to think of the characters first. The story begins to develop as I try these characters in different situations. With shorter fiction I generally get the idea first, and then develop a character to fit whatever it is that I want to do.

As to the original addresses of the characters and ideas, I do not know. I simply encounter them mentally and proceed from there to extend our acquaintanceships. I believe that preparation has something, though not everything, to do with it. I attempt to cultivate a state of preparedness by reading widely – sciences, history, biography, general literature, poetry. I am also very fond of the theatre and of travel.

For a long while I tended to agree with a statement of Malcolm Muggeridge's to the effect that a writer's mind best remembers those things which the writer is best able to write about. In recent years, though, I have come to embrace the corollary – that the more things I can experience, even vicariously, the more things I am better able to remember and to write about. At least, I like to think that this is the case.

Generally, I do not like knowing beforehand how I will end a novel. My ideal method of composition is to begin writing once I know my major character and a few of the situations in which he or she will be functioning – *i.e.*, about thirty percent of the story – if the feeling be present that the story does indeed exist somewhere in the basement of my mind. I enjoy relying upon a subconscious plotting mechanism and discovering its operation as I work. As I said, this is my ideal way of proceeding. It is also a luxury. And this is because it usually takes me half again as long to compose a novel in this fashion than it would if I had outlined the story first.

When speed is essential – which it often is – I will outline. This tightens and tidies, but I sometimes lose something as a result. There is a certain physical and aesthetic exhilaration which comes over me when I write in the first manner and suddenly reach what John Brunner once referred to as the "Aha!" point – the place where everything falls together in my mind and I see the entire story spread out before me like a map or a tapestry, where I realize why I had been inserting some of the material which had been rushing to mind, where the world of the book takes on a life of its own and I need but observe and transcribe rather than continue composing.

Outlines, though, often turn themselves into points of departure for me, revising themselves as I go along, so that the other subconscious process often does come into play of its own accord. I have no fundamental objection to this, as it generally results in a better story than that which I had initially recorded.

Lord Of Light (1967)

I visualize everything in my stories in considerable detail. If I cannot see a person or place clearly I cannot write about them too well. I tend to hear the dialogue, also, when rehearsing it in my mind. I sometimes think that this has something to do with a childhood spent listening to radio dramas.

I try to read for two hours every day and write for two hours every day, on no set schedule. Mornings have been best of late, however.

SCIENCE FICTION WRITERS:
A CONSUMERS' GUIDE

Contributions by: *Brian W. Aldiss, Rob Allen, Colin Greenland, Brian Griffin, Maxim Jakubowski, Roz Kaveney, Tony Richards, Andrew Sawyer, Cyril Simsa, Ritchie Smith, Brian Stableford, David Wingrove*

In making my selection of the 880 writers who are listed here I have adopted some very simple criteria: Are their works available in English?; Have their books been in print in the last twenty-five years, or, if not, can they be considered important influences upon the genre? In almost all cases the writers described are novelists, but as science fiction is a genre which developed from and is still biased towards the short story form, several writers who have not written at novel length have been included.

I have adopted a wide-ranging definition of science fiction, hoping, by that means, to include most of what has, at one time or another and by one party or another, been described as science fiction – from the metafiction of Pynchon to the overt sword-and-sorcery of John Jakes and Robert E. Howard. If, by doing so, I have inferred the width of sf's influences and dispelled, to some degree, the myth of science fiction as "all that rockets and robots stuff", this book has achieved one of its aims: though fans of rockets and robots will find avenues enough to explore within.

The books and short stories listed after each author are recommended as an introduction to the author in question, and to provide a quick appraisal of each book they have been awarded stars, nil to five, for Readability (*R*), Characterization (*C*), Idea Content (*I*), and Literary Merit (*L*). Idea Content is a concept that assesses not merely the originality of the ideas within an sf book, but their influence and impact upon the field in general.

D.J.W.

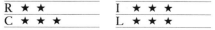

ABBOTT, Edwin A. (1838-1926) English author of *Flatland: A Romance Of Many Dimensions*, which deals with a world which has only two dimensions. It is a hugely enjoyable mathematical romp, deserving of its constant reprinting.

Flatland (1884)

R ★ ★ ★	I ★ ★ ★ ★ ★
C ★	L ★ ★

ABE, Kobo (1924) Japanese novelist known mainly for his work outside the science fiction genre. His three translated works exhibit a strong philosophical bent, possibly from the influence of the French existentialists. *The Woman In The Dunes* (1964) and *The Box Man* (1974) are only peripherally science-fictional, but *Inter Ice Age 4* is recognizably a future-disaster scenario with a central moral dilemma.

Inter Ice Age 4 (1970)

R ★ ★	I ★ ★ ★
C ★ ★ ★	L ★ ★ ★

ABERNATHY, Robert (1924) American writer whose short work appeared in sf magazines in the 1940s and 1950s. His work ranges over space opera, comedy and delightful alien-perspective tales, where Man is contrasted against other creatures. "Junior" (1956) and "Axolotl" (1955) are good introductions to his work.

ABLEMAN, Paul (1927) English novelist whose sf novel, *The Twilight Of The Vilp*, is an entertaining and intelligent psycho-drama, utilizing several genre techniques but ultimately about the craft of authorship.

The Twilight Of The Vilp (1969)

R ★ ★ ★	I ★ ★ ★
C ★	L ★ ★

ABRAMOV, Sergei and **Alexander** Russian sf writers. Only a small amount of their work has been translated. *Horsemen From Nowhere* and *Journey Across Three Worlds* (1973) are standard sf fare, and do not match the work of those other Russian brothers, the Strugatskys (q.v.).

Horsemen From Nowhere (1969)

R ★ ★ ★	I ★ ★
C ★ ★	L ★ ★

ADAMS, Douglas (1952) Unintentional novelist via radio comedy series *The Hitch-Hiker's Guide To The Galaxy* (1978-80), spoofing space opera and other sources of sf cliché. Undergraduate absurdism with a wry sense of paradox, his only work, a trilogy, concerns *Life, The Universe and Everything* (the title of Volume 3). Arthur Dent, the only human survivor when Earth is destroyed, makes a bewildered pilgrim's progress around various corners of space to both ends of time, in the company of assorted blasé humanoid aliens and a depressive robot called Marvin. Adams uses sf as comic extravaganza, purely for fun.

The Hitch-Hiker's Guide To The Galaxy (1979)

R ★ ★ ★ ★ ★	I ★
C ★ ★ ★ ★	L ★

The Restaurant At The End Of The Universe (1980)

R ★ ★ ★ ★ ★	I ★
C ★ ★ ★ ★	L ★

Life, The Universe And Everything (1982)

R ★ ★ ★ ★	I
C ★ ★ ★ ★	L

Douglas Adams

ADAMS, Richard (1920) English ex civil servant whose *Watership Down* – a quest-epic about rabbits – became the Children's Book Of The Year after a round of publisher's rejections. A love of the English countryside, a deep Christianity, and a convincing dramatization of animals' experience mark Adams's fiction, along with remarkably leaden "literary" writing. *Shardik* (1974) (a fantasy in which a bear is seen to be the incarnation of the Power of God) and *The Plague Dogs* (an impassioned attack on vivisection) have to some extent trapped him as a writer about animals. *The Girl In A Swing* – an occult love story – has done little to shift this image.

Watership Down (1972)

R ★ ★ ★ ★	I ★ ★ ★ ★
C ★ ★	L ★ ★ ★

The Plague Dogs (1977)

R ★ ★ ★	I ★ ★ ★
C ★ ★	L ★ ★

The Girl In A Swing (1980)

R ★ ★	I ★ ★
C ★	L ★

ADAMS, Robert (?) American writer of the Horseclans series, begun with *The Coming Of The Horseclans* (1975). His *The Witch Goddess*, the ninth in the series, adds very little to what is essentially a cousin of sword-and-sorcery.

The Witch Goddess (1982)

R ★ ★ ★	I ★
C ★ ★	L ★

ADLARD, Mark (1932) English author of general fiction including sf trilogy set in Tcity, a future Newcastle of automated and regimented leisure based on a new all-purpose material, stahlex. Extraordinarily erudite in his range of references, Adlard convincingly portrays the selfish but cultured executive élite, but his sympathies and the dynamic of his plot tend towards the oppressed no-longer-working classes. His satire is the voice of suppressed rage, verging on the sarcastic. His own professional experience of labour relations, as an executive in the steel industry, informs his story of the frustrations, injustices and inevitable disruption of the city and its managerial hierarchy.

Interface (1971)

R	★ ★ ★	I	★ ★ ★
C	★ ★ ★ ★	L	★ ★ ★

Volteface (1972)

R	★ ★ ★	I	★ ★ ★
C	★ ★ ★ ★	L	★ ★ ★

Multiface (1973)

R	★ ★ ★	I	★ ★ ★
C	★ ★ ★ ★	L	★ ★ ★

ALDISS, Brian W(ilson) (1925) English novelist, editor, poet and critic, whose work covers the very broadest range of modern writing, both within the science fiction field and outside. From the start there has always been far more to Aldiss's work than the immediately-obvious adventure level. *Non-Stop* (1958), his first novel, is not merely an sf mystery set in a generation starship, but also an elaborate questioning of the purpose of modern society, its rituals and its technological over-emphasis. *Hothouse*, a novel composed of connected tales, displays Aldiss's richly exotic and imaginative side, depicting a far-future non-civilized Earth. It won him the Hugo Award in 1962. His fascination with the plasticity of forms – both human and alien – is seen also in the marvellous short story, "Legends Of Smith's Burst" (1959), and has surfaced time and again in his work, most recently in *Enemies Of The System* (1978) and *Moreau's Other Island* (1980), and the long, illustrated poem, *Pile* (1979). The mid-1960s saw a movement in Aldiss's work away from the traditional science-fictional concerns of *The Dark-Light Years* (1964) and *Greybeard* (his most lyrical work, describing a post-"Accident" world where Man is sterile and rapidly dying out) to the extreme speculative statements of his anti-novel, *Report On Probability A* (1968) and *Barefoot In The Head* (1969), which is probably the most complex and sustained stylistic experiment in the science fiction field. The 1970s had Aldiss writing *Billion Year Spree:*

A History Of Science Fiction (1973) and re-evaluating his own writing. *Frankenstein Unbound* (1974) and *The Eighty-Minute Hour* (1974) can be seen more as homages (to Shelley (q.v.) and Dick (q.v.) respectively), than as a new direction. *The Malacia Tapestry*, however, is Aldiss at his very finest, describing an opulent yet degenerative City State in an alternate universe. In this, and in the first two of the *Helliconia* trilogy, *Helliconia Spring* (1982) and *Helliconia Summer* (1983), his rich imaginative powers are in full evidence, inventing and peopling new worlds. Underlying his work, however, is a deep-rooted moral concern for a balance of all the varying aspects of human nature. He is also one of the genre's most prolific short story writers, winning a Nebula for the novella, "The Saliva Tree" (1965).

Hothouse (1962)

R	★ ★ ★ ★ ★	I	★ ★ ★ ★
C	★ ★ ★	L	★ ★ ★

Greybeard (1964)

R	★ ★ ★ ★	I	★ ★
C	★ ★ ★ ★	L	★ ★ ★ ★

The Malacia Tapestry (1976)

R	★ ★ ★ ★ ★	I	★ ★ ★ ★
C	★ ★ ★	L	★ ★ ★ ★

"An Appearance Of Life" (1976)

R	★ ★ ★ ★	I	★ ★ ★ ★
C	★	L	★ ★ ★ ★

ALLEN, Charles Grant (1848-99) English writer, born in Canada. A revolutionary writer in other fields, his work of social criticism, *The British Barbarians*, utilizes the old device of a man from the future presenting his perspective on sexual and social taboos. (See also his time travel story, "The Child Of The Phalanstery.")

The British Barbarians (1895)

R	★ ★	I	★
C	★ ★	L	★ ★

AMIS, Kingsley (William) (1922) English novelist, poet and critic, whose *New Maps Of Hell* (1960) was one of the earliest intelligent commentaries on the sf genre. His own work has occasionally touched upon sf, though only to enrich and accentuate his social satire, which is often bitter but rarely inaccurate. "Something Strange," his first and only venture into magazine fiction (it appeared in *The Magazine of Fantasy and Science Fiction*), is a highly polished psychodrama concerning four people isolated in space. His *The Anti-Death League* (1966) is more exaggerated satire than sf, and *The Green Man* (1969) is a satirical romp through the genres. *The Alteration* must, however, be considered his first full-length sf work, an alternate worlds story, positing what things would be like if the Reformation had not happened (see also Roberts's *Pavane*). His most recent sf offering was *Russian Hide & Seek*, where Amis uses all of his strengths as a contemporary novelist to depict a Russian-controlled Britain 50-plus years after the invasion. Its bleak dénouement is convincing.

"Something Strange" (1961)

R ★ ★ ★ ★	I ★ ★ ★ ★
C ★ ★	L ★ ★ ★

The Alteration (1976)

R ★ ★ ★ ★	I ★ ★ ★
C ★ ★ ★	L ★ ★ ★

Russian Hide & Seek (1980)

R ★ ★ ★ ★	I ★ ★
C ★ ★ ★	L ★ ★ ★ ★

Poul Anderson

AMOSOFF, Nikolai Mikhailovich (1913) Russian novelist whose only translated work is *Notes From The Future*. A scientist suffering from leukaemia is frozen, awoken in 1991 and cured. He rediscovers "purpose" in life, but with a great deal of philosophical reflection.

Notes From The Future (1967; trans. 1970)

R ★ ★ ★	I ★ ★ ★
C ★ ★	L ★ ★ ★

ANDERSON, Chester   American writer of the already-dated *The Butterfly Kid*, a well-written but rather "hip" wish-fulfilment fantasy about Greenwich Village. He also collaborates with Michael Kurland (q.v.).

The Butterfly Kid (1967)

R ★ ★	I ★
C ★	L ★ ★

ANDERSON, Colin   English author of one science fiction novel, *Magellan*, which depicts a post-holocaust City and its intricate and decadent society in an incisive and intelligent manner.

Magellan (197))

R ★ ★ ★ ★	I ★ ★ ★
C ★ ★	L ★ ★ ★

ANDERSON, Poul (1926) One of the writers who are the backbone of the genre, as well as the man who said that writers are competing for the reader's "beer money." A physics graduate of Scandinavian ancestry, Anderson uses both backgrounds in his writing; the science underpins the colourful mythology, sometimes crudely. A genuine if unambitious writer, Anderson has made an attempt to reflect much of human nature in his wide-ranging fiction, from the roguish young Dominic Flandry to the Falstaffian, roguish (but somewhat old) Nicholas van Rijn; however, the trite, traditional adventures that are the apparent substance of his novels are sometimes abrasively trivial when considered with the serious, end-of-empire feeling evoked by some of his later work – Anderson being a citizen of the U.S.A. with considerable knowledge of the obvious historical parallels. Later books have taken a strong stand against ideology (which he usually calls fanaticism), although many readers will be dubious that the foreign capitalism of the Polesotechnic League (effective motto, "All The Traffic Will Bear") is quite the force for civilization and anti-authoritarian liberalism he would have us believe. Books such as *Tau Zero* do, however, show the ability to animate ideas – in this case, quite a profound one, as a group of humans live through the death of the entire universe – and his writing sometimes has a rewarding, sensuous density, and an excellent feeling for local colour.

Piers Anthony

The Star Fox (1965)

R	★	★	★	★		I	★	★	
C	★	★	★	★		L	★	★	★

Ensign Flandry (1966)

R	★	★	★	★		I	★	★	
C	★	★	★			L	★	★	

Tau Zero (1970)

R	★	★	★	★		I	★	★	★
C	★	★	★			L	★	★	

ANSTEY, F. (1856-1934) Pseudonym of Thomas A. Guthrie, notable as a writer of humorous fantasies. *Tourmalin's Time Cheques* is of some interest to historians of sf because it is the first novel to deal with the paradoxical aspects of time travel. His most famous fantasies were *Vice Versa* (1882) and *The Brass Bottle* (1900).

Tourmalin's Time Cheques (1891)

R	★	★	★	★		I	★	★	★
C	★	★				L	★	★	

ANTHONY, Piers (1934) English-born writer, now an American citizen. His full name is Piers Anthony Dillingham Jacob. His first science fiction novel, *Chthon*, was written in lieu of a thesis for his B.A. in Creative Writing. In 1968 he won a novel competition run by *The Magazine of Fantasy and Science Fiction* and Pyramid Books with *Sos The Rope*. He eventually wrote sequels to both books; most of his books are series works and even those planned as trilogies

are apt to be extended by further volumes. His early works were science fiction novels combining intricate, if rather contrived, plots with an exuberant delight in striking ideas. His fondness for crude symbolism makes most of his more earnest novels artificial and a little ponderous, but he writes fluently and his enthusiasm is appealing. It is not surprising, though, that his more popular works have been more playful space operas and outright fantasies. In recent years he has achieved great success with his series of novels set in the magical world of Xanth, and his novels of this kind now regularly reach the paperback bestseller list in the U.S.A. These books tend to be a little patchy but make very easy reading, combining wit and exotic adventure in an attractive fashion. A similar series began with *Split Infinity* (1981) and continued with *Blue Adept* (1981) and *Juxtaposition* (1983). There are six Xanth novels at the time of writing: *A Spell For Chameleon* (1977), *The Source Of Magic* (1979), *Castle Roogna* (1979), *Centaur Aisle* (1982), *Ogre, Ogre* (1982), and *Night Mare* (1983). Of his four science fiction trilogies the one begun with *Sos The Rope*, available in omnibus as *Battle Circle*, is perhaps the best, but he has always given the impression that he might produce much finer work were it not for the fact that the spur of commercial necessity encourages him to overproduce and write too many sequels.

Chthon (1967)

R	★	★	★	★		I	★	★	★	★
C	★	★				L	★	★	★	★

Sos The Rope (1968)

R ★ ★ ★ ★	I ★ ★ ★
C ★ ★	L ★ ★

Cluster (1977)

R ★ ★ ★ ★	I ★ ★
C ★	L ★

ANTILL, Keith   Australian author of the ambitious but overly theatrical novel *Moon In The Ground*, which describes a number of responses to a mysterious alien object, "Pandora," which appears near Alice Springs.

Moon In the Ground (1979)

R ★ ★ ★	I ★ ★
C ★ ★	L ★ ★

ANVIL, Christopher   American writer, pseudonym for Harry C. Crosby Jr. An unspectacular but reliable and prolific author who principally contributed to *Astounding Science Fiction* (and, later, to a lesser extent, to *Analog*) and can now be seen as the epitome of the John W. Campbell (q.v.) Jr. directed and inspired ideas and technology hack, albeit with a sometimes impish sense of humour. He provided *ASF* with over 70 stories, novellas and novelettes but never truly graduated to novel form with only four minor book length titles to his credit. Surprisingly, no collection of his stories has ever been made available.

The Day The Machines Stopped (1964)

R ★ ★ ★	I ★
C ★	L ★

Pandora's Planet (1972)

R ★ ★ ★ ★	I ★ ★
C ★ ★	L ★

Warlord's World (1975)

R ★ ★ ★	I ★ ★
C ★ ★	L ★

APPEL, Benjamin (1907) American writer of one science fiction novel, *The Funhouse*, a satire concerning a nuclear threat to a future America.

The Funhouse (1959)

R ★ ★ ★	I ★
C ★ ★	L ★

ARNOLD, Edwin L(ester Linden) (1857-1935) English writer of science fantasies, popular in his time, but badly dated. His *The Wonderful Adventures Of Phra The Phoenician* (1890) is a metempsychosis tale which is still (just) readable, and the reincarnation theme is again present in a short story, "Rutherford The Twice Born." *Lieut. Gullivar Jones: His Vacation* (a.k.a., *Gullivar Of Mars*) is closest to sf, despite its magic carpet ride to Mars.

Lieut. Gullivar Jones: His Vacation (1905)

R ★ ★ ★	I ★
C ★	L ★

ASH, Fenton   Pseudonym of English writer Frank Aubrey whose lost worlds adventures are rather in the mould of Sir Arthur Conan Doyle (q.v.) and Clarke Ashton Smith (q.v.). *A Queen Of Atlantis; A Romance Of The Caribbean* (1899; as Frank Aubrey) is one such. *A Trip To Mars* is schoolboy fiction of the adventure kind still being regurgitated in the 1930s.

A Trip To Mars (1909)

R ★ ★	I ★
C ★	L ★

ASIMOV, Isaac (1920) American scientist and science fiction writer, born in Russia and naturalized in 1928. His recent return to sf novel writing with *Foundation's Edge* (winner of the Hugo Award for 1983) ended an 11-year spell wherein Asimov produced only a small number of science fiction short stories. Currently a prolific writer of non-fiction (with a scientific, popularizing emphasis), Asimov remains one of the great influences on the genre owing to his work of the 1940s and 1950s. Whilst our engagement in his work is generally at a pure adventure level, Asimov is a master of ideative games. He is equally at home as a thriller writer, and the form of the thriller – usually involving the solution of scientific enigmas and riddles – underpins much of his science fiction. There is a constant and pure sense of astronomical wonder, an almost abstract sense of the poetry of the stars, in his work. However, much of his characterization is crude, and the psychological and emotional range of his work rarely extends beyond the juvenile, as can be seen in the early novels like *The Stars Like Dust* (1951; a.k.a. *The Rebellious Stars*) and *The Currents Of Space* (1952). There is also a series of six overtly juvenile novels, featuring David "Lucky" Starr, a Space Ranger. The one exception is *The End Of Eternity*, which is a far more complex and emotionally more subtle novel than the others; a time travel story which, long ahead of its time, introduced sexual desire as an element in the plot. The Robot stories and the two Robot novels, *The Caves Of Steel* (1954) and *The Naked Sun* (1957), present Asimov's belief in a benevolent Science, opposed to the anti-Technology "Frankenstein" strain in the sf field. However, Asimov is probably best known for his *Foundation* "trilogy" (as of 1983 a "quartet"), a wide-screen space opera written between 1942 and 1950, and based loosely on the rise and fall of the Roman Empire. Its "Psychohistory" element is further evidence of a strong sociological

Isaac Asimov

bias in Asimov's work; for whilst his work is clearly anthropocentric, it rarely deals with the plight of individual man. *The Gods Themselves*, which won both the Hugo and Nebula awards, is again in this vein. Its central idea of connected universes is utilized for an ingenious but essentially adventure-oriented scientific conundrum, the solution of which benefits Mankind in general. With *Foundation's Edge* (1983), Asimov has simply returned to where he left off in the 1940s, and with the success of this sequel on the bestseller lists, further novels in the Foundation series are rumoured to be planned. It remains to see whether the immense changes in the genre can affect Asimov's essentially innocent puzzles.

Foundation And Empire (1952)

R	★	★	★	★	★	I	★	★	★	★	★
C	★	★	★			L	★	★			

The End Of Eternity (1955)

R	★	★	★	★	★	I	★	★	★	★	
C	★	★	★			L	★	★			

The Gods Themselves (1972)

R	★	★	★	★	★	I	★	★	★	★	
C	★	★				L	★				

ASPRIN, Robert (Lynn) (1946) American writer of all-action, high-technology, militaristic adventure stories and novels, such as *The Bug Wars* (1979) and *Tambu* (1979). His fantasy works, such as *Another Fine Myth* (1978), are in a rather heavy-handed and sadistic humorous vein. Asprin utilizes commonplace science fiction and fantasy themes in a haphazard but enthusiastic manner, although with little depth.

The Cold Cash War (1977)

R	★	★	★	I	★	★
C	★			L	★	

Myth Directions (1982)

R	★	★	I	★	★
C	★	★	L	★	

ASTOR, John Jacob (1864-1912) American writer of one early science fiction

novel, *A Journey In Other Worlds: A Romance Of The Future*, notable for featuring an anti-gravity device. It is, however, a view of a future Utopian Earth and a description of a journey to Jupiter.

A Journey In Other Worlds (1894)

R ★ ★ ★	I ★ ★ ★
C ★	L ★ ★

ATKINS, John Alfred (1916) English writer of *Tomorrow Revealed*, an imaginary history told from the year 5000 A.D., and utilizing speculations culled from Wells (q.v.), Huxley (q.v.), Orwell (q.v.), Heinlein (q.v.), Van Vogt (q.v.) and others. The result is a plausible and entertaining future history. He also collaborated with J. B. Pick on a fantasy novel, *A Land Fit For Eros* (1957).

Tomorrow Revealed (1955)

R ★ ★ ★ ★	I ★ ★ ★
C ★ ★	L ★ ★

ATTANASIO, A. A.   American writer whose first novel, *Radix*, has been acclaimed in several respected quarters. However, its laborious and at times quite crude style handicaps it severely. Its ideative content is certainly distinctive, but Attanasio lacks the creative imagination to present his material either forcefully or vividly. The attempted juxtaposition of deep philosophical concerns and fast-action adventure (which Delany (q.v.) succeeds in) fails miserably here.

Radix (1982)

R ★ ★	I ★ ★ ★
C ★	L

AUEL, Jean   Best-selling American author of *The Clan Of The Cave Bear* and its sequel, *The Valley Of The Horses* (1982), both set in the far distant past of Mankind. They are surprisingly well written and very much more than simple adventure stories.

The Clan Of The Cave Bear (1981)

R ★ ★ ★ ★	I ★ ★
C ★ ★ ★	L ★ ★

BAHNSON, Agnew H. Jr (1915-64) American author known for *The Stars Are Too High*, a smoothly written near-future thriller where men pretending to be aliens use a real gravity-driven spacecraft in the attempt to bring Earth's Cold War powers to cooperate.

The Stars Are Too High (1959)

R ★ ★ ★	I ★ ★
C ★ ★	L ★ ★

BAILEY, Hilary (1936) English writer. Once married to Michael Moorcock (q.v.), she also edited the quarterly paperback incarnation of *New Worlds*. An intelligent and delicate stylist, she co-authored (uncredited) M.M.'s *The Black Corridor* and used his character Una Persson in some stories. Her short story output is sparse but includes many much-anthologized stories like "The Fall Of Frenchy Steiner," "Dr Gelabius," (1968) and "Dog Man Of Islington." Her two published novels are not sf, although *Polly Put The Kettle On* is a humorous but affectionate portrayal of many characters familiar from the heyday of the British New Wave.

Polly Put The Kettle On (1975)

R ★ ★ ★	I ★ ★
C ★ ★ ★ ★	L ★ ★ ★ ★

"The Fall Of Frenchy Steiner" (1964)

R ★ ★ ★	I ★ ★ ★
C ★ ★ ★	L ★ ★ ★

"Dog Man Of Islington" (1971)

R ★ ★ ★	I ★ ★
C ★ ★ ★	L ★ ★ ★

BAKER, Scott   American writer who, from writing mildly transcendent novels has recently invested his creative energies in a series of vampire books. *Symbiote's Crown* (1978) is a limited work but of some interest. *Night Child* and *Dhampire* (1982) are cleverly plotted and highly readable horror stories, but add little to an already overworked sub-genre.

Night Child (1979)

R ★ ★ ★	I ★
C ★ ★	L ★

BALL, Brian N. (1932) English writer. Minor practitioner of the genre with a strong vocational scientific bent and a tendency to easy metaphysics. Has published near to ten unspectacular space adventure novels to little acclaim as well as TV series novelizations.

Sundog (1965)

R ★ ★ ★	I ★ ★
C ★ ★	L ★

The Regiments of Night (1972)

R ★ ★ ★	I ★ ★
C ★	L ★

Singularity Station (1973)

R ★ ★	I ★ ★ ★
C ★	L ★

BALLARD, J. G. (1930) The most original and influential British sf writer of the 1960s. An early dissident from the dual orthodoxies of extrovert space adventure and rationalized scientific extrapolation, Ballard determined to use the conventions of sf for a new kind of fiction. His purpose has always been to take account of the imaginative undercurrents of the dominant world-view of the contemporary West. His stories usually describe the observations and ordeals of a central character – typically male, white, middle-aged, educated, solitary, disaffected but comfortably off until the disruption of his environment by some catastrophic force. After a first group of novels in which the force was ecological upheaval, Ballard turned his attention to the depredations of modern technology and especially the media and products of the "communications explosion" – television, advertisement hoardings, cars. Later works have offered something of a synthesis of the elements of both periods, with urban detritus absorbed as totemistic objects in rituals by which the natural order is gloriously transfigured. Commodity

J. G. Ballard

fetishism takes on a new meaning in the light of Ballard's apocalyptic vision. From the first, Ballard's great strength was his style – measured, urbane, vivid, and above all visual. His work was immediately acclaimed by critics, particularly Kingsley Amis (q.v.), as sf written to the highest literary standards, not least because he seemed to be working in line with the respectable British disaster tradition exemplified by John Wyndham (q.v.). When Ballard's radical "fragmented novels" began appearing in 1966, culminating in *The Atrocity Exhibition* (1970), it became apparent he was engaged on something altogether more subversive: William Burroughs (q.v.) and Surrealist painters were principal influences. Ballard's focal character inhabits devastated landscapes which are outward expressions of his state of mind. Other people exist only as figments of his desires and fears. Ballard made popular the term "inner space" to denote the psychological terrain of his fiction. The fact that his introverted hero invariably seeks to embrace the sinister new order he sees inaugurated by the disaster has baffled readers unprepared for Ballard's uncompromising imagination, and the critical establishment has entirely failed to recognize the magnitude of his achievement, however favourable his reviews and enthusiastic his readers.

The Drowned World (1962)

R ★ ★ ★ ★ ★	I ★ ★ ★ ★
C ★ ★	L ★ ★ ★

The Unlimited Dream Company (1979)

R ★ ★ ★ ★ ★	I ★ ★ ★
C ★ ★	L ★ ★ ★

"The Voices Of Time" (1960)

R ★ ★ ★ ★ ★	I ★ ★ ★ ★ ★
C ★ ★	L ★ ★ ★ ★ ★

BANNISTER, Jo   Irish writer of competent but traditional science fiction novels. *The Winter Plain* (1982) and *A Cactus Garden* are available, the latter set on a forest world of Mithras and providing an interesting sf allegory.

A Cactus Garden (1983)

R ★ ★ ★	I ★ ★
C ★ ★	L ★ ★

BARBET, Pierre (1925) French writer, pseudonym for Dr Claude Avice. Also writes as David Maine, Olivier Sprigel and under other pen-names. A prolific but pedestrian author of fast-moving but highly derivative adventure novels and space operas whose reputation outside his home country is flattering to his highly minor status within. A clever improvisator on well-worn themes whose work is very much in the American golden age mould but lacks the clarity and ambition of the U.S. writers of the late 1940s.

Baphomet's Meteor (1972)

R ★ ★ ★	I ★ ★
C ★ ★	L ★

Games Psyborgs Play (1975)

R ★ ★	I ★
C ★	L

The Napoleons Of Eridanus (1976)

R ★ ★ ★	I ★ ★
C ★	L

BARJAVEL, René (1911) French writer. A witty, imaginative author once seen in the post World War II period as a pioneer of the modern genre in France. Deeply pessi-mist after the Hiroshima experience, his later books principally deal with the end of the world theme, until the 1950s when his work took on a reactionary stance and more recent titles have proved naïve and disappointing. *Le Voyageur Imprudent* is one of the earliest and most inventive novels about time paradoxes, while the influential *Ravage* is a harsh dystopia about the disappearance of electricity.

Ravage (1943; trans. as *Ashes, Ashes*)

R ★ ★ ★	I ★ ★ ★ ★
C ★ ★ ★	L ★ ★ ★

Le Voyageur Imprudent (1944; trans. as *Future, Times Three*)

R ★ ★ ★ ★	I ★ ★ ★ ★
C ★ ★	L ★ ★ ★

La Nuit Des Temps (1968; trans. as *The Ice People*)

R ★ ★ ★	I ★ ★
C ★ ★	L ★ ★

BARR, Donald (1921) American writer of one science fiction novel, *Space Relations: A Slightly Gothic Interplanetary Tale*, which title is revealing of the rather tongue-in-cheek space opera within its pages.

Space Relations (1973)

R ★ ★ ★ ★	I ★ ★
C ★ ★	L ★ ★

BARRETT, Geoffrey John   English writer of standard space adventure novels, which plunder rather than utilize the genre's themes. *Slaver From The Stars* (1975) and *The Night Of The Deathship* (1976) are two garish examples of this.

The Lost Fleet Of Astranides (1974)

R ★ ★ ★	I ★
C ★	L

BARRETT, Neal, Jr   American writer who published a number of short stories in the sf magazines of the 1960s and 1970s and graduated to novel length with *Kelwin* (1970). His novels, whilst strictly speaking space operas, have a certain attractively alien atmosphere to them. The Aldair novels, which are essentially quests, are perhaps his most successful.

The Leaves Of Time (1971)

R ★ ★ ★	I ★ ★
C ★ ★	L ★

Aldair, Master Of Ships (1977)

R ★ ★ ★ ★	I ★ ★
C ★ ★	L ★ ★

BARTH, John (1930) American novelist and Professor of English. Words like "metafiction" are often used to describe his books; intensely literary artifices incorporating symbol, myth, fantasy and pastiche of traditional forms. Sometimes unwieldy, his fictions are erudite fables. The best-selling *Giles Goat-Boy* is a quasi-religious, quasi-political comment on the world presented as a university campus in which the goat-raised hero seeks his identity as human and saviour. Greek and Persian myth is the basis for *Chimera*, while *Lost In The Funhouse*, in which Barth explores fictional and narrative conventions, contains one tale, "Night-sea Journey," which in a way is classic sf.

Giles Goat-Boy (1966)

R ★ ★ ★	I ★ ★ ★ ★ ★
C ★ ★	L ★ ★ ★ ★

Chimera (1972)

R ★ ★ ★	I ★ ★ ★ ★
C ★	L ★ ★ ★

Lost In The Fun-house (1968; coll.)

R ★ ★ ★	I ★ ★ ★ ★
C ★	L ★ ★ ★ ★

BARTHELME, Donald (1973) American author who, whilst not in any real sense a genre writer, utilizes elements of the mythological and fantastic to fertilize his dark and opulent surrealism. Some of his short stories border on sf, and the highly modernistic *Snow White* is a fragmentary satire, a kind of Ballard with humour.

Snow White (1967)

R ★ ★ ★	I ★ ★ ★
C ★ ★	L ★ ★ ★

BARTON, William (1950) American author of two highly standard sf novels, *Hunting On Kunderer* and *A Plague Of All Cowards* (1976).

Hunting On Kunderer (1973)

R ★ ★ ★	I
C ★	L

BASS, T. J. (1932) American writer Thomas J. Bassler, whose two science fiction works depict a crowded and regimented future world where a degenerate human race attempts to find meaning. A strong biological knowledge is displayed in both works, matched by an equally potent religious feeling, reminiscent of C. S. Lewis (q.v.).

Half Past Human (1971)

R ★ ★ ★ ★	I ★ ★ ★
C ★ ★ ★	L ★ ★ ★

The Godwhale (1974)

R ★ ★ ★ ★ ★	I ★ ★ ★
C ★ ★ ★ ★	L ★ ★ ★

BATCHELOR, John Calvin American author of *The Birth Of The People's Republic Of Antarctica* who mixes sf and fantasy in his work to present us with a vivid, yet bleak, view of the end of the century. There is an earlier, less successful novel, *The Further Adventures Of Halley's Comet*.

The Birth Of The People's Republic Of Antarctica (1983)

R ★ ★ ★	I ★ ★
C ★ ★	L ★

BATEMAN, Robert (Moyes Corruthers) (1922) English author of pointed novel, *When The Whites Went*, a disaster story where only blacks survive a plague-like disease.

When The Whites Went (1963)

R ★ ★ ★	I ★ ★
C ★ ★	L ★

BATES, Harry (1900) American writer and editor of *Astounding Stories* (1930-33), and *Strange Tales* (1931-33). He wrote short stories as A. R. Holmes and H. G.

Winter, and had one novel published under the pseudonym Anthony Gilmore, *Space Hawk: The Greatest Of Interplanetary Adventures*, an adventure involving his hero Hawk Carse, which links together several of the stories. His story "Farewell To The Master" (1940) was later filmed as *The Day The Earth Stood Still* (1951).

Space Hawk (1952)

R ★ ★ ★	I ★
C ★ ★	L

BAUM, L(yman) Frank (1856-1919) American writer, famous for his Oz novels (and the accompanying series of plays). These essentially juvenile tales appeal to adults also because of the underlying allegory of Technology versus Nature. Baum also wrote a boy's science fiction adventure, *The Master Key: An Electrical Fairy Tale* (1902) – rather whimsical, but nonetheless entertaining.

The Emerald City Of Oz (1910)

R ★ ★ ★ ★ ★	I ★ ★ ★
C ★ ★	L ★

BAX, Martin (1933) English literary editor whose only novel, a symbolic post-holocaust fable, is strongly influenced by J. G. Ballard (q.v.), echoing his stylistic experiments and oblique optimism.

The Hospital Ship (1976)

R ★ ★ ★	I ★ ★ ★
C ★ ★	L ★ ★ ★

BAXTER, John (1939) Australian writer and anthologist who, in his shorter fiction, attempted to combine sound scientific extrapolation with literary qualities. *The Off-Worlders* (1968; a.k.a. *The God Killers*) tells of a colony planet who turn to Satan, while *The Hermes Fall* is a conventional sf disaster novel, describing the collision of a massive meteorite with Earth. Neither novel matches the quality of his shorter work.

The Hermes Fall (1978)

R ★ ★ ★	I ★ ★
C ★	L ★ ★

Barrington J. Bayley

BAYLEY, Barrington J. (1937) English writer. Many of his early short stories were published under the name P. F. Woods, but all his novels are signed with his own name. He is a writer of exotic adventure stories whose fast-moving plots are enlivened by his fascination with odd and esoteric ideas. He is not a particularly fluent writer, but there is perhaps no one else who takes such an obvious delight in exploring the logical consequences of strange ideas. His best novel is *The Fall Of Chronopolis*, about the defeat of an empire established by time travellers across the millennia. Also worthy of note is *The Soul Of The Robot*, one of the better exercises in mechanical existentialism. His short story collection *The Knights Of The Limits* (1978) provides a brilliant array of lively stories packed with ideas. He deserves to have a far greater reputation.

The Fall Of Chronopolis (1974)

R ★ ★ ★ ★	I ★ ★ ★ ★
C ★ ★	L ★ ★ ★

Soul Of The Robot (1974)

R ★ ★ ★ ★	I ★ ★ ★ ★
C ★ ★	L ★ ★ ★

Star Winds (1978)

R ★ ★ ★ ★	I ★ ★ ★
C ★ ★	L ★ ★

BEAGLE, Peter S. (1939) American fantasist, concerned with the elusive – or illusory – phantoms of desire, and the wayward and frequently comic routes by which we pursue them. His weakness for wistful sentimentality is ably offset by his felicity of invention, eloquence of narration, vividness of description and shrewdness of wit. Appropriately, Beagle has also published a study of Hieronymus Bosch.

A Fine And Private Place (1960)

R ★ ★ ★ ★	I ★ ★
C ★ ★ ★ ★ ★	L ★ ★ ★ ★

The Last Unicorn (1968)

R ★ ★ ★ ★	I ★ ★ ★
C ★ ★ ★ ★	L ★ ★ ★

"Lila The Werewolf" (1974)

R · ★ ★ ★	I ★ ★
C ★ ★ ★	L ★ ★

BEAR, Greg(ory Dale) (1951) American poet, novelist and short story writer, whose sf novels, whilst not wholly innovative, possess an intensity of vision and a high degree of intelligence. His first two novels, *Hegira* (1979) and *Psychlone* (1979), have severe flaws which his following books escape. However, it is probably as a short story writer that his greatest strengths currently lie.

Beyond Heaven's River (1980)

R ★ ★ ★	I ★ ★ ★
C ★ ★	L ★ ★ ★

Strength Of Stones (1982)

R ★ ★ ★	I ★ ★
C ★ ★	L ★ ★ ★

"The Wind From A Burning Woman" (1978)

R ★ ★ ★ ★	I ★ ★ ★ ★
C ★ ★ ★	L ★ ★ ★

BEAUMONT, Charles (1929-67) Pseudonym of American writer Charles Nutt, whose short stories appeared throughout the 1950s and 1960s. They are competent, market-tailored productions, the best of which, perhaps, is "The Vanishing American," a contemporary Invisible Man tale.

"The Vanishing American" (1955)

R ★ ★ ★ ★	I ★
C ★ ★	L ★ ★

BEDFORD-JONES, H(enry James O'Brien) (1887-1947) Prolific Canadian writer whose work first appeared in the pulp magazines in 1915 and is in the Rider Haggard (q.v.), Edgar Burroughs (q.v.) mould. He was best known for his work in *The Blue Magazine* in the 1940s (some under the pseudonym Gordon Keyne). Little of his work, however, has any lasting value.

BELLAMY, Edward (1850-98) American author whose work, *Looking Backward, 2000-1887* angered William Morris (q.v.) enough to make him write *News From Nowhere*. It is a glimpse of a machine-ordered future, and has a sequel, *Equality* (1897).

Looking Backward (1888)

R ★ ★	I ★ ★
C ★	L ★

BELYAEV, Alexander (1884-1942) Russian sf writer influenced by Wells (q.v.) and Verne (q.v.), who exerted great influence on the Russian genre between the wars. Several of his works have been translated, such as *The Amphibian* (1928), *The Struggle In Space* (1928), and *Professor Dowell's Head*. The last is a scientific horror story, where a scientist literally steals another's head to obtain his ideas.

Professor Dowell's Head (trans. 1979)

R ★ ★ ★	I ★
C ★ ★	L ★ ★

BENFORD, Gregory (1941) American physicist who emerged into sf writing from fandom and whose fiction has mostly been in collaboration. Although he won a 1975 Nebula for his short story "If The Stars Are Gods" – later expanded into a novel of the same title – in collaboration with Gordon Eklund (q.v.), it wasn't until his fourth novel, *Timescape*, that he showed his

Gregory Benford

potential as a writer. The novel, one of the most innovative time stories of modern sf, demonstrates Benford's ability to explain scientific fact in readable prose. Unfortunately, he was not so successful in his other novels, *The Stars in Shroud* (1978; a.k.a. *Deeper Than The Darkness*), *Shiva Descending* (1980) with William Rotsler (q.v.) and *Find The Changeling* (1980) with Gordon Eklund, which show Benford to be no more than a good writer of hardcore sf.

"If The Stars Are Gods" (1977; with Gordon Eklund)

R	★	★	★	★		I	★	★	★		
C	★	★	★	★		L	★	★	★		

Timescape (1980)

R	★	★	★	★			I	★	★	★	★	★	★
C	★	★	★	★			L	★	★	★	★		

BENNETT, Margot (1912) English writer known for her sole sf novel, *The Long Way Back*, where future Africans visit a degenerate and Stone Age Britain.

The Long Way Back (1954)

R	★	★	★		I	★	★	
C	★	★			L	★	★	

BERESFORD, J. D. (1873-1947) English writer. Author of the early sf classic *The Hampdenshire Wonder*, about a super-

human child born in rural England. He wrote a good deal of innovative short fiction collected in *Nineteen Impressions* (1918) and *Signs and Wonders* (1921), but gave up on science fiction to concentrate on more commercial work after the Great War. He returned briefly to imaginative fiction during World War II, when he produced three sf novels of which the best is *The Riddle Of The Tower*, a nightmarish vision of the future evolution of Mankind, written in collaboration with Esme Wynne-Tyson.

The Hampdenshire Wonder (1911)

R	★	★	★			I	★	★	★	★	
C	★	★	★			L	★	★	★	★	★

Goslings (1913)

R	★	★	★		I	★	★	★	
C	★	★	★		L	★	★	★	★

The Riddle Of The Tower (1944)

R	★	★			I	★	★	★	★
C	★	★			L	★	★	★	★

BERK, Howard (1926) American writer whose one sf novel, *The Sun Grows Cold*, describes the search for identity of a man whose brain has been mind-wiped in a post-holocaust world.

The Sun Grows Cold (1971)

R	★	★	★	★		I	★	
C	★	★				L	★	★

BERRY, Bryan (1930-55) English writer of pulp sf for British magazines. Several very routine novels exist under his pseudonym of Rolf Garner, including *From What Far Star?* (1953) and *The Immortals* (1953).

The Indestructible (1954)

R	★	★	★		I	★	
C	★				L		

BEST, (Oswald) Herbert (1894) American writer of post-holocaust Utopian novel, *The Twenty-Fifth Hour*.

The Twenty-Fifth Hour (1940)

R	★	★	★		I	★	★	★	
C	★	★			L	★			

Alfred Bester

BESTER, Alfred (1913) American sf writer. The plots of Bester's two important novels of the early 1950s are only distinguishable from other space operas of the time by their over-literary debts – *The Demolished Man* to *Crime And Punishment*, *Tiger! Tiger!* (a.k.a. *The Stars My Destination*) to *The Count Of Monte Cristo* – and the extent to which they embody, albeit fairly crudely, psychoanalytic concepts: in the first, Reich (NB the name) is driven to murder by an Oedipus complex while the three major male and three major female characters of the latter can be usefully grouped in patterns of ego, superego and id. What made these books important influences on the New Wave of a decade later was partly a vein of street-credible café-society antinomianism more likely to appeal to the New Wave's exponents and audience than fantasies of steel-eyed technocracy, but more important was the lively expressionism of their telling. Bester was not alone in 1950s magazine sf in his awareness of how modernism had extended the toolbox of narrative and stylistic modes, but he was perhaps the author most flashily prepared to make use of that awareness. *The Demolished Man* has its cinematic dream sequences and its representation of telepathic communication by sentences which intertwine in all directions across the page, whereas *Tiger! Tiger!* has its extensive use of synaesthesia and typographic rebuses. These were tricks largely

new to the genre, and, having been shown to work in entertainments, were now available and acceptable in more serious work. These and his shorter fictions of the same period were less effective in their softer, pontificating sentimental scenes, but one remembers the vigour and the proliferation of throwaway perceptions of the human oddness of the future. Bester's other professional commitments reached a point where he left the field for many years. More recent work has been disappointing.

The Demolished Man (1953)

R ★ ★ ★ ★	I ★ ★ ★ ★
C ★ ★ ★ ★	L ★ ★ ★ ★ ★

Tiger! Tiger! (1956)

R ★ ★ ★ ★	I ★ ★ ★
C ★ ★ ★ ★	L ★ ★ ★ ★ ★

Golem ^{100} *(1980)*

R ★ ★	I ★ ★
C ★ ★	L ★ ★

BIERCE, Ambrose (1842-1914) American writer, some of whose short stories prefigure science-fictional themes. "An Occurrence at Owl Creek Bridge" (in *The Midst Of Life*; coll., 1898) describes a post-death experience, and "Moxon's Master" is an early robot story (in *Can Such Things Be?* coll.). He is unashamedly and often brilliantly gothic, in the manner of (and yet without imitating) Poe (q.v.).

Can Such Things Be? (1893; coll.)

R ★ ★ ★ ★	I ★ ★ ★
C ★	L ★ ★ ★ ★

BIGGLE, Lloyd Jr (1923) American writer, deeply interested in music and the arts. His books display a strong optimism, but, like Asimov's (q.v.), his work is primarily concerned with scientific puzzle-solving, and, for the most part, is undemanding adventure with little concern for characterization. Several of his novels are connected, some in the Cultural Survey series, and five in the Jan Darzek series: *All The Colors Of Darkness, This Darkening Universe* (1975), *Watchers Of The Dark* (1966), *Silence Is Deadly* (1977) and *The*

Whirligig Of Time (1979). Darzek is Earth's representative/councillor to the super-computer "Supreme," which advises the Galactic Synthesis. Whilst entertaining enough, these are lightweight space operas, and Biggle is far more at home when creating alien societies and alien environments. There are three collections of his shorter fiction, including *A Galaxy of Strangers* (1976).

All The Colors Of Darkness (1963)

R ★ ★ ★ ★	I ★ ★ ★
C ★	L ★ ★

Monument (1974)

R ★ ★ ★ ★	I ★ ★ ★
C ★ ★	L ★ ★

The Still Small Voice Of Trumpets (1968)

R ★ ★ ★ ★	I ★ ★ ★
C ★ ★	L ★ ★

BINDER, Eando Pseudonymn used jointly by American brothers Earl Andrew Binder (1904) and Otto Oscar Binder (1911-75), who wrote for *Amazing Stories* in the 1930s and 1940s. *Adam Link: Robot* (1965; serialized 1939-42) and *Puzzle Of The Space Pyramids* (1971; serialized 1937-42) are ingenious, if also superficial, treatments of artificial intelligence and space adventure stories in the regular (i.e. flawed) pulp style.

Anton York, Immortal (1965; serialized 1937-40)

R ★ ★ ★	I ★ ★
C ★ ★	L ★

BISCHOFF, David F(rederick) (1951) American writer of several interesting sf novels (two in collaboration). *Nightworld*, with its galaxy-spanning range and fascination with "mandroids," is a good introduction to Bischoff's lively, charming work.

Nightworld (1979)

R ★ ★ ★ ★	I ★ ★ ★
C ★ ★	L ★ ★

Star Fall (1980)

R ★ ★ ★	I ★ ★
C ★ ★	L ★ ★

BISHOP, Michael (1945) American sf and fantasy writer, Bishop has risen to popularity rather more slowly than many of his contemporaries, perhaps because of the overt and quirky intellectualism of his style and concerns, perhaps because his portrayal of personal evolution and transcendence contains many "depressing" elements – notably in *Stolen Faces* (1977). Much early work – *Catacomb Years* (1979), *A Little Knowledge* (1977) – deals with social pressures in a domed Atlanta, Georgia, eventually released by the arrival and conversion to Christianity of aliens. *Transfigurations* examines the myths implicit in anthropology and in lost race stories; *No Enemy But Time* considers innocence through the love affair between a time traveller stranded in the Pliocene and an Australopithecine woman.

"Allegiances" (1974)

R ★ ★ ★	I ★ ★ ★
C ★ ★ ★ ★	L ★ ★ ★ ★

Transfigurations (1979)

R ★ ★ ★ ★	I ★ ★ ★ ★ ★
C ★ ★ ★ ★	L ★ ★ ★ ★ ★

No Enemy But Time (1982)

R ★ ★ ★ ★ ★	I ★ ★ ★
C ★ ★ ★ ★ ★	L ★ ★ ★ ★ ★

Michael Bishop

BIXBY, (Drexel) Jerome (Lewis) (1923) American editor, screenwriter and short story writer, whose "It's A *Good* Life" is a science fiction classic. Apart from two collections of his shorter work, *The Devil's Scrapbook* (1964) and *Space By The Tale* (1964), most of his sf appeared as screenplays and TV plays.

"It's A *Good* Life" (1953)

R ★ ★ ★ ★ ★	I ★ ★ ★ ★
C ★ ★ ★	L ★ ★ ★

BLACKBURN, John (1923) Lacklustre English writer often using espionage and thriller frameworks with his sf, with a recurrent use of sinister, caricatural Nazis to intensify the would-be gothic mood. His first novel, *A Scent Of New-Mown Hay*, is a clever variation on the mad scientist/bacteriological warfare mode but following works, frequent until the mid-1970s, have made little impact.

A Scent Of New-Mown Hay (1958)

R ★ ★ ★	I ★ ★
C ★	L ★

A Sour Apple Tree (1958)

R ★ ★	I ★
C ★	L ★

Children Of The Night (1966)

R ★ ★ ★	I ★ ★
C ★ ★	L ★

James Blish

BLACKWOOD, Algernon (1869-1951) English writer of strange tales and ghostly stories. The occult and the theme of reincarnation dominate his often beautifully crafted stories.

Julius Le Vallon: An Episode (1916)

R ★ ★ ★	I ★ ★
C ★ ★	L ★ ★

Tales Of The Uncanny And Supernatural (1949; coll.)

R ★ ★ ★ ★	I ★ ★ ★
C ★	L ★ ★ ★

BLISH, James (1921-75) An American writer, Blish was one of the few sf writers of the 1950s educated in biology, and made good use of this specialty in some of the earliest sf novels dealing with genetic engineering: *Titan's Daughter* (1961) and *The Seedling Stars* (the latter is a fix-up of several shorter pieces). He produced one of the most impressive science-fictional future histories in his series of four novels collected as *Cities In Flight* (Revised; 1970), where he borrowed ideas from Oswald Spengler's *Decline Of The West* to give shape and coherence to his account of the rise and fall of the "Earthmanist Culture." He wrote one of the classic sf stories in "A Case Of Conscience," in which a Jesuit priest confronted with an apparently sinless alien world is forced to conclude that it has been created by the Devil in order to delude Mankind into an abandonment of faith. This was expanded into a novel and became the centrepiece of a loose trilogy whose other elements are a fictional biography of Roger Bacon, *Doctor Mirabilis*, and a pair of short novels describing what happens on Earth when a black magician succeeds in liberating the demons imprisoned in Hell. Blish was a careful and economical writer, highly conscientious in extrapolating the premises which he adopted for his stories. Few other writers have tried to be as rigorous in using sf as a medium for experiments in thought, but he always remained mindful of his responsibility to entertain readers and his plots are full of action.

The Seedling Stars (1957)

R	★ ★ ★	I	★ ★ ★ ★
C	★ ★	L	★ ★ ★

"A Case Of Conscience" (1958)

R	★ ★ ★	I	★ ★ ★ ★
C	★ ★	L	★ ★ ★ ★

Doctor Mirabilis (1964)

R	★ ★ ★	I	★ ★ ★
C	★ ★ ★	L	★ ★ ★ ★

BLOCH, Robert (1917) American writer best known for his horror stories, many of which have been adapted for films and TV. He provided the story for the famous Hitchcock film *Psycho*. His one sf novel, *Sneak Preview*, is unimpressive, but he has written some good work in shorter lengths, including a satire about a female-dominated society of the future, "Ladies' Day." The eccentric "One Way To Mars" and "The Strange Flight Of Richard Clayton" are his best sf stories (see *The Best Of Robert Bloch*, 1977), though neither is in his sf collection *Atoms and Evil* (1962). He is a very polished writer, with a ghoulish sense of humour that provides neat surprise endings for his mordant horror stories.

"Ladies' Day" (1968)

R	★ ★ ★ ★	I	★ ★
C	★ ★	L	★ ★

Sneak Preview (1971)

R	★ ★ ★	I	★
C	★ ★	L	★ ★

Strange Eons (1979)

R	★ ★ ★	I	★ ★
C	★	L	★ ★

BLUM, Ralph (1932) American writer, whose *The Simultaneous Man* is, in essence, a spy thriller involving drug-erased memories and a reconstructed, "twin" personality. With his wife, Judy, he also wrote *Beyond Earth: Man's Contact With UFO's* (1974)

The Simultaneous Man (1970)

R	★ ★ ★ ★	I	★ ★
C	★ ★	L	★

BODELSEN, Anders (1937) Danish suspense writer whose novel *Freezing Point* (a.k.a. *Freezing Down*) is a dark and highly stylized version of the Rip Van Winkle theme, involving cryogenics.

Freezing Point (1969)

R	★ ★ ★	I	★ ★
C	★ ★	L	★ ★

BOK, Hannes (1914-64) American author, best known for his illustrative work within the genre (perhaps the most distinctive and gothic style in sf), he did produce one long piece of fiction, *Beyond The Golden Stair* (*Unknown Worlds*, 1942; book form, 1973), and one novel, *Starstone World* (1942).

Beyond The Golden Stair (1942; a.k.a. *The Blue Flamingo*)

R	★ ★ ★	I	★
C	★	L	★

BOLAND, (Bertram) John (1913-76) English writer of three borderline sf-thrillers in the late 1950s. His *Operation Red Carpet* (1959) is interesting in that it depicts a Russian attempt to conquer Britain (see Amis's *Russian Hide & Seek*).

White August (1955)

R	★ ★	I	★
C	★	L	★

BOND, Nelson S. (1908) American writer of 1930s to 1950s, best known for his fantasy stories in *The Blue Book Magazine*, and for his Lancelot Biggs series.

Exiles Of Time (1949)

R	★ ★ ★ ★	I	★ ★
C	★	L	★ ★

Lancelot Biggs: Spaceman (1950)

R	★ ★ ★ ★	I	★ ★
C	★ ★	L	★

BONE, J(esse) F(ranklin) (1916) American writer of several minor sf novels and many short stories. *The Lani People* is generally recognized as being his best work, though even that is flawed. The relationhip of Man to alien races is a favourite theme.

The Lani People (1962)

R ★ ★ ★ ★	I ★ ★
C ★ ★	L ★ ★

Confederation Matador (1978)

R ★ ★ ★	I ★
C ★	L ★

BORGES, Jorge Luis (1899) Argentine writer, highly acclaimed for his essays and spectacularly idiosyncratic short stories. Most of his more famous short pieces are in *Labyrinths* (1962) and *The Aleph and Other Stories* (1949); they very often play with philosophical notions in a speculative way and display an obsession with life as an "amber" of memories. "Tlön, Uqbar, Orbis Tertius" is a brief masterpiece about a strange alternate world which impinges strangely on our own. "Funes The Memorious" describes the existential predicament of a man with a perfect memory. "The Aleph" produces the notion of a point in space where all possible experiences are somehow focused and simultaneously available. These and others are works of awesome imaginative power, and Borges is justly famous as one of the most important and original twentieth-century writers.

"Tlon, Uqbar, Orbis Tertius" (1957)

R ★ ★ ★	I ★ ★ ★ ★ ★ ★
C	L ★ ★ ★ ★ ★

"Funes The Memorious" (1956)

R ★ ★ ★	I ★ ★ ★ ★
C ★	L ★ ★ ★ ★

"The Aleph" (1949)

R ★ ★ ★	I ★ ★ ★ ★ ★
C ★	L ★ ★ ★ ★ ★

BOUCHER, Anthony (1911-68) Pseudonym of William Anthony Parker White, American writer of sf and crime fiction, and also a respected editor. His *Rocket To The Morgue* (1942) is a murder mystery using real science fiction writers of the time as its characters. He is best known,

however, for his delightful "religious" story, "The Quest For St. Aquin," which has inspired most of the great works (like Miller's *Canticle For Leibowitz*) which followed it. He was also editor of *The Magazine Of Fantasy And Science Fiction*.

"The Quest For St. Aquin" (1951)

R ★ ★ ★ ★ ★	I ★ ★ ★ ★
C ★ ★	L ★ ★ ★

BOULLE, Pierre (1912) French writer, better known for his work outside the genre, which inspired various movies including *The Bridge On The River Kwai*. Boulle's reputation within is assured by *Planet Of The Apes*, although it should be stressed that the Charlton Heston film bears little resemblance to the picaresque, almost philosophical tale of the novel. A humanist and a humorist, Boulle's idiosyncratic appreciation of things future comes over best in his short stories.

Contes De L'Absurde & E=MC² (1953, 1957, coll.; trans. *Time Out Of Mind*)

R ★ ★ ★ ★	I ★ ★ ★
C ★ ★	L ★ ★ ★

La Planète Des Singes (1963; trans. *Planet Of The Apes*)

R ★ ★ ★	I ★ ★ ★
C ★ ★	L ★ ★ ★

Le Jardin De Kanashima (1964; trans. *Garden On The Moon*)

R ★ ★ ★	I ★ ★ ★
C ★ ★ ★	L ★ ★ ★ ★

BOUNDS, Sydney J(ames) (1920) English writer who contributed an enormous number of short stories to the British sf magazines during the 1950s and 1960s, together with four highly stereotyped and pedestrian novels.

Dimension Of Horror (1953)

R ★ ★ ★	I
C ★	L

The Robot Brains (1957)

R ★ ★	I ★
C ★	L

BOVA, Ben (1932) American writer who has edited both *Analog* and *Omni* for brief periods of time. He has worked extensively in science journalism and his fiction is mostly set in the near future, dealing with imminent developments in technology. He has written a good deal of juvenile science fiction. His novels for adults are sometimes disappointing because his style is a little stilted and his plotting routine, but he does manage to communicate something of his fervent belief in technological advancement as a way of solving social problems. In spite of this faith, a surprising amount of his work is apocalyptic in tone.

Millennium (1976)

R ★ ★ ★	I ★ ★ ★
C ★ ★	L ★ ★

Colony (1978)

R ★ ★ ★	I ★ ★
C ★ ★	L ★ ★

BOWEN, John (Griffith) (1924) English writer of the fantasy *The Truth Will Not Help Us* (1956) and the mad scientist/disaster novel, *After The Rain*, which is much better than the standard sf fare of its time.

After The Rain (1958)

R ★ ★ ★	I ★ ★ ★
C ★ ★	L ★

BOYCE, Chris (1943) Scottish writer, whose *Catchworld* is a much above average space opera. A second work, *Extraterrestrial Encounter*, is a factual speculation.

Catchworld (1975)

R ★ ★ ★	I ★ ★
C ★ ★	L ★ ★

BOYD, John (1919) Pseudonymn of Boyd Bradfield Upchurch, American sf novelist whose interest in myth, sexual mores and the moral basis of science fiction's well-tried themes, is intelligently and articulately conveyed in his work. He ranges from lyricism to comedy, as in the highly entertaining *Andromeda Gun* (1974). Eight novels appeared between 1968 and 1972, but only a handful since.

The Pollinators Of Eden (1969)

R ★ ★ ★ ★	I ★ ★ ★
C ★ ★	L ★ ★ ★

The Girl With Jade Green Eyes (1978)

R ★ ★ ★	I ★ ★
C ★ ★	L ★ ★ ★

BOYE, Karin Swedish author whose *Kallocain*, depicting a world of socialist totalitarianism, is a potent and memorable piece of writing in the dystopian vein of Zamyatin (q.v.) and Orwell (q.v.).

Kallocain (1940; trans. 1966)

R ★ ★ ★ ★	I ★ ★ ★
C ★ ★ ★	L ★ ★ ★

BRACKETT, Leigh (1915-78) American writer, wife of sf writer Edmond Hamilton (q.v.). In the later part of her career she wrote mainly screenplays, the most famous of which was of Chandler's *The Big Sleep*, though she returned to sf in the last years of her life with the screenplay for *Star Wars II: The Empire Strikes Back*. During the 1940s she made a name for herself writing lush and gaudy adventure stories set mostly on a version of the planet Mars like the one popularized by Edgar Rice Burroughs (q.v.), but more decadent. These exotic romances represent the wilder and more extravagant side of the science-fictional imagination, but are curiously nostalgic in tone, as though regretting their own implausibility in the face of modern astronomical knowledge. She could write in a more realistic vein, as in the post-holocaust novel *The Long Tomorrow*, but is fondly remembered for providing magnificent escapist fantasies spiced with a hint of sad cynicism. Some readers find it difficult to connect with her highly coloured stories, but such novellas as "The Moon That Vanished" (1948) and "Enchantress Of Venus" (1949) remain the best examples of their kind. Her best work was done for the space-adventure magazine *Planet Stories*, including "Queen Of The Martian Catacombs" (1949) and "Black Amazon Of Mars" (1951) – which were, alas, given more sober titles when revised for book publication.

Marion Zimmer Bradley

Shadow Over Mars (1951)

R ★ ★ ★ ★	I ★ ★ ★
C ★	L ★ ★ ★

The Sword Of Rhiannon (1953)

R ★ ★ ★ ★	I ★ ★ ★
C ★	L ★ ★ ★

BRADBURY, Ray (1920) Bradbury has always been concerned with what is called "original participation" between the human spirit and the Spirit of Nature. In *The Martian Chronicles* (1950), Mars is actually a series of conflicting "collective representations" of Nature; and the poetic drama of the successive Earth missions to Mars has lost none of its imaginative impact. The book culminates in what might be a higher synthesis: a recognition by Earth's survivors of the Mars within themselves. In 1957, Bradbury followed this up with the Nature-worship of *Dandelion Wine*, a poeticized childhood autobiography. It begins with young Douglas Spaulding being invaded (Martian-fashion) by the Nature Spirit; it ends with the understanding that Nature exists *within* Douglas, despite Death and Time. Bradbury's preoccupation with conflicting weathers of the soul is spread throughout his many collections: he has made Summer and Autumn, "the Cold Wind and the

Ray Bradbury

Warm," his very own, by demonstrating how we are part of them and vice-versa. In *Something Wicked This Way Comes* (1963), a fantasy novel, a "Summer" boy and his friend, a child of Autumn, deal characteristically with a dark carnival of cyclic Evil run by the Illustrated Man – the eponymous "hero" of a classic collection, who is evil because totally subsumed by the patterns of Nature. In *The Halloween Tree* (1972), Pip, a child of Summer, is sought amid Egyptian death-chambers, death-dealing Gods of Harvest, and the wintry gargoyles of Notre Dame. In the end, Pip is "internalized": his name, in the form of a candy skull, is sacramentally eaten by his friends. These basic themes and motifs recur throughout Bradbury's voluminous short stories. Generally, he favours the interdependence of the Dark Night and Summer of the Soul, and actively defends the former in his play, *Pillar Of Fire* (1975), and in the classic book-burning dystopia, *Fahrenheit 451*.

The Martian Chronicles (1951)

R ★ ★ ★ ★ ★	I ★ ★ ★ ★ ★
C ★ ★ ★ ★ ★	L ★ ★ ★ ★ ★

Fahrenheit 451 (1954)

R ★ ★ ★ ★ ★	I ★ ★ ★ ★ ★
C ★ ★ ★ ★ ★	L ★ ★ ★ ★ ★

"The Emissary" (in *The October Country*, 1956)

R ★ ★ ★ ★ ★	I ★ ★ ★
C ★ ★ ★ ★ ★	L ★ ★ ★ ★ ★

BRADLEY, Marion Zimmer (1930) American writer. Her best-known work is the long Darkover series, which features the conflicts between representatives of a galactic civilization and the inhabitants of the planet Darkover, whose culture is dominated by telepathic groups. The earlier stories in the series are straightforward adventure stories, more fantasy than science fiction, but as the books gathered a loyal following Bradley began to devote more serious effort to developing an elaborate history and geography for Darkover, and used her plots for earnest analyses of the psychology of human relationships. She was one of the first writers to capitalize on the feminist interest in science fiction which grew in the 1970s. Her work has diversified in recent years, and she has ventured into serious mainstream fiction with her novel *The Catch Trap* (1979), about circus life, and into Arthurian fantasy with her recent best-seller, *The Mists Of Avalon* (1983). Bradley is not a particularly original writer – her earliest novels were virtually exercises in pastiche, heavily influenced by Leigh Brackett (q.v.) and Henry Kuttner (q.v.) – but she has the virtue of many sf fans-turned-writers, that she loves her work and can immerse herself in her imaginary worlds to the extent that she knows them in intimate detail and can write about them with great conviction. Darkover recommends itself to its fans not simply as an imaginary place where stories are set but as an alternate reality, a legitimate object for careful study and the cultivation of expertise.

The Bloody Sun (1964)

R ★ ★ ★	I ★ ★
C ★ ★	L ★ ★

The Heritage Of Hastur (1975)

R ★ ★ ★	I ★ ★
C ★ ★	L ★ ★ ★

The Ruins Of Isis (1978)

R ★ ★ ★	I ★ ★
C ★ ★	L ★ ★

BRAUTIGAN, Richard (1935) American off-beat novelist whose works occasionally touch upon the concerns of sf and fantasy. *In Watermelon Sugar* is vaguely an Utopian fantasy, whilst *The Hawkline Monster, A Gothic Western* (1974) toys with the Frankenstein theme. Hard sf fans might find him far too trivial.

In Watermelon Sugar (1968)

R ★ ★ ★	I ★ ★
C ★	L ★ ★

BRETNOR, Reginald (1911) American writer who, like Asimov, was born in Russia. Bretnor's fast-paced and witty Papa Schimmelhorn stories and three critical symposia edited by him are his main achievements in the field. He uses the pseudonym Grendel Briarton to write the Ferdinand Feghoots stories, again in a humorous vein.

The Complete Feghoot (1975; coll.)

R ★ ★ ★	I ★ ★ ★
C ★ ★	L ★

The Schimmelhorn File (1979; coll.)

R ★ ★ ★ ★	I ★ ★
C ★ ★	L ★

BRIN, David   American author, whose *Startide Rising* is a wide-screen space opera written with acute intelligence, which manages to convey a real sense of a varied civilization that spans five galaxies and countless alien races.

Startide Rising (1983)

R ★ ★ ★ ★	I ★ ★ ★
C ★ ★ ★	L ★ ★ ★

BRODERICK, Damien (1944) Australian writer and anthologist who, after being published in the late 1960s and early 1970s, has only recently come to notice again with *The Judas Mandala* (1982). Broderick's acute and highly literary sensibility – his extreme care for style and craft – does not prevent his work from being both accessible and entertaining.

Sorceror's World (1970)

R ★ ★ ★ ★	I ★ ★ ★
C ★ ★	L ★ ★ ★

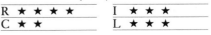

BROOKS, Terry   English writer of science fantasy. His *Sword Of Shannara* is much in the vein of stereotyped sword-and-sorcery.

Sword Of Shannara (1977)

R ★ ★ ★	I ★
C ★	L

BROWN, Fredric (1906-72) American writer. One of the first genuine humorists in the history of sf, Brown paved the way for other authors like Sheckley (q.v.) and Vonnegut (q.v.). His other claims to fame lie in his mastery of the short-short story, which he perfected to an art, and his consummate thrillers, some of which, like *Night Of The Jabberwock* (1950), contain fantasy elements. An underrated craftsman, Brown excelled even in the realm of ideas with classic stories like "Arena," about an interstellar war settled by individual arm-to-arm combat or the lunatic "Placet Is A Crazy Place" (1946). *The Mind Thing* (1961) and *Project Jupiter* (1953) are unspectacular novels, overshadowed by the unforgettable *What Mad Universe*, a zany parallel universe and a splendid satire of sf and the hilarious Earth invasion yarn *Martians, Go Home*. Many of his splendid

John Brunner

collection are still in print.

"Arena" (1944)

R ★ ★ ★	I ★ ★ ★
C ★ ★	L ★ ★

What Mad Universe (1949)

R ★ ★ ★ ★	I ★ ★ ★ ★
C ★ ★ ★	L ★ ★

Martians, Go Home (1955)

R ★ ★ ★ ★ ★	I ★ ★ ★
C ★ ★	L ★ ★

BROWN, James Cooke (1921) American writer of *The Troika Incident*, in which three astronauts are sent into the year 2070 and return to describe a socialist Utopia. Heavily ideative, but sophisticated in its manner.

The Troika Incident (1970)

R ★ ★ ★	I ★ ★ ★ ★
C ★ ★	L ★ ★

BROWN, Rosel George (1926-67) American writer whose premature death ended a promising career in the sf field. Her tough female protagonists were ahead of their time. She wrote a space opera *Earthblood* (1966) with Keith Laumer (q.v.), and her solo posthumous novel, *The Waters Of Centaurus*, is an interesting variation on the galactic policeman tale, with a female cop.

The Waters Of Centaurus (1970)

R ★ ★ ★	I ★
C ★ ★	L ★

BRUNNER, John (Kilian Houston) (1934) English writer. He was one of the most prolific writers of sf during the 1960s, but slowed down considerably in the 1970s, partly because of a serious illness. Although his reputation was compromised by his productivity, Brunner was one of the most respected British writers in the genre for many years, the climax of the early phase in his career being attained with a series of long alarmist novels about the dangers threatening near-future civilization. *Stand On Zanzibar* is perhaps the best novel about the dangers of overpopulation, and *The Sheep Look Up* (1972) an outstanding polemic against pollution. *The Jagged Orbit* (1969) and *The Shockwave Rider* deal with other worrying trends in human affairs. In the last few years he has begun publishing again, releasing a massive non-fantasy novel about Mississippi riverboats and two relatively minor sf novels, the better of which is *Players At The Game Of People* (1980). Brunner has always been a careful and highly professional writer; even among his minor works there are some well-crafted novels of ideas, including the fix-up novel of alternate histories *Times Without Number* (1962) and the sombre sf mystery *Total Eclipse* (1974). His major works use techniques borrowed from John Dos Passos, building up a cultural background by means of fragmentary vignettes, newspaper items, advertising slogans, quotations from books, etc. Use of these methods helps flesh out his visions of the near future so that they become unusually complex while remaining believable. He is at his best when there is a didactic element in his writing – his style benefits from rhetorical fervour. Even at his coolest and most scrupulous, though, as in the early novel *The Whole Man* (also known as *Telepathist*), he is effective in recruiting the sympathy of the reader for his characters. He is an underrated writer whose best works have been out of print too long.

The Whole Man (1964)

R	★ ★ ★ ★	I	★ ★ ★ ★
C	★ ★ ★	L	★ ★ ★

Stand On Zanzibar (1968)

R	★ ★ ★	I	★ ★ ★
C	★ ★ ★	L	★ ★ ★ ★

The Shockwave Rider (1975)

R	★ ★ ★	I	★ ★ ★
C	★ ★ ★	L	★ ★ ★ ★

BRUST, Steven   American writer of *Jhereg*, which starts promisingly and degenerates into a fairly standard sf/sword-and-sorcery novel. Nonetheless he has the potential to develop into a reasonable writer.

Jhereg (1983)

R	★ ★ ★	I	★ ★
C	★	L	★

BRYANT, Ed (1945) American writer. He has long been considered one of the most promising young American sf authors but the high hopes held out for him have never truly come to fruition in novel form, a genre he has never successfully tackled. His short stories are poetic, memorable and accomplished, witness to a strong regionalist sensitivity and full of vivid imagery ("Particle Theory," (1980) "Shark"). His Cinnabar stories, linked in a collection, re-create a lazy far-future California where man has been replaced by strange artifacts, and are his most accomplished effort to date. A slow, meticulous writer, Ed Bryant's forthcoming first genuine novel (he has committed a TV novelization with Harland Ellison (q.v.)) should see him at the forefront of adventurous sf.

Among The Dead; And Other Events Leading Up To the Apocalypse (1973; coll.)

R	★ ★ ★	I	★ ★
C	★ ★ ★	L	★ ★ ★

"Shark" (1973)

R	★ ★ ★ ★	I	★ ★ ★ ★
C	★ ★	L	★ ★ ★

Cinnabar (1976; coll.)

R	★ ★ ★	I	★ ★ ★
C	★ ★ ★	L	★ ★ ★

BRYNING, Frank (Bertram) (1907) Australian short story writer, who also wrote as F. Cornish. His works are heavily biased towards the hard sciences and are generally sound pieces of engineering, both stylistically and in terms of content. Some of his later pieces utilize aborigines in an antagonistic manner.

"Nemaluk And The Star-Stone" (1977)

R	★ ★ ★	I	★
C	★	L	★

BUDRYS, Algis (1931) Shortened form of Algirdas Jonas Budrys, Lithuanian writing sf in English and resident in the U.S.A. since adolescence. As a critic Budrys is usually perceptive and often subtle; excess of charity towards fellow-writers prevents him from being more than occasionally at his best. Among the themes which (if one is prepared to simplify this particularly sophisticated writer) can be distinguished in his work is the role of the hero or, to be more precise, the nature of a man capable of intervening significantly in political or other events. It is because Michaelmas is presented as both benevolent and hard-working that we accept him, in the movie named for him, as the secret and competent ruler of Earth. Significantly, Michaelmas and his computer rule the world by selecting and occasionally falsifying facts; their eventual opponent is an alien intelligence capable of altering the objective structure of reality; these powers are shown as pragmatically equivalent. The alien can be seen as both an alternate author. Many of Budrys's characters, particularly in his work of the late 1970s, can be seen as judged morally – according to whether their manipulation of reality produces good or bad art. Intertwined with all this, particularly in early work, are the perhaps personally relevant themes of identity and exile; Martino, in *Who?*, is deprived of any hope of agenthood because no one can be sure who he is; it is by accepting, in the literal reality of multiple duplications of himself, the implications of the self-alienation of his death wish that Barker in *Rogue Moon* can solve a deadly lunar labyrinth. Budrys is one of the few writers of sf whose characters are not only credible but also adults; his reputation can only grow.

Who? (1958)

R	★	★	★	★	★	I	★	★	★	★	
C	★	★	★	★	★	L	★	★	★	★	★

Rogue Moon (1960)

R	★	★	★	★	★	I	★	★	★	★	
C	★	★	★	★	★	L	★	★	★	★	★

Michaelmas (1977)

R	★	★	★	★	★	I	★	★	★	★	
C	★	★	★	★	★	L	★	★	★	★	

BULGAKOV, Mikhail (1891-1940) Russian science fiction author who combines the tradition of Wells (q.v.) and Verne (q.v.) with a strong surrealist streak. His *The Master And Margarita* is a *sui generis* classic, wherein Satan visits Moscow. He has written several sf plays, too, *Bliss* (a utopian story) included. One of his earliest works, *The Heart Of A Dog*, is also sf.

The Heart Of A Dog (1927)

R	★	★	★	I	★	★	
C	★	★		L	★	★	★

The Master And Margarita (1966)

R	★	★	★	★	I	★	★	★	
C	★	★	★		L	★	★	★	★

BULMER, (Henry) Kenneth (1921) Prolific English author whose pseudonyms are many but whose sf work has mainly appeared as Alan Burt Akers, Philip Kent, Tully Zetford, Manning Norvil and under his own name. Whilst there is little to recommend him in literary terms, Bulmer is an exceedingly honest and morally concerned writer and there is usually more to his novels than just a good read. He has a great weakness at plotting, however, which continually detracts from the overt adventure element. The Alan Burt Akers novels are all in the Dray Prescot series, which began with *Transit To Scorpio* (1972) and is on its way to 30 volumes already. There are

Anthony Burgess

about 50 sf novels under his own name, the bulk of which is pure space opera, and the best of which is probably *The Wizard Of Starship Poseidon* (1963). The bulk of his shorter fiction was published in British sf magazines in the 1950s and early 1960s. He is also known as an anthologist, with the *New Writings In Sf* series.

The Doomsday Men (1968)

R ★ ★ ★	I ★
C ★	L ★

A Fortune For Kregen (1979; as Alan Burt Akers)

R ★ ★ ★	I ★
C ★ ★	L

Star City (1974; as Tully Zetford)

R ★ ★ ★	I ★ ★
C ★	L

BUNCH, David R.   American writer whose fascinating series of vignettes and short stories about Moderan, a super-technological society of the post-wars future, appeared between 1959 and 1970. Bunch has written more than 30 other sf stories, but no novels. Despite this limited output he is one of the field's true originals.

Moderan (1971)

R ★ ★ ★ ★	I ★ ★ ★ ★ ★
C ★ ★	L ★ ★ ★ ★

BURGESS, Anthony (1917) English writer, known primarily for his mainstream fiction. Although he hates genre sf he remains paradoxically fascinated by its themes, and cannot resist dabbling in futuristic fantasy. His novel *A Clockwork Orange* achieved belated notoriety thanks to Stanley Kubrick's film. More recently he has inserted futuristic material into works where it is counterpointed by other material: an essay on Orwell in *1985*; a biography of Freud and the score of a musical comedy about Trotsky in *The End Of The World News*. His obvious unease makes the science-fictional parts of these later works weak and sickly, but *A Clockwork Orange* still remains an effective moral fable.

A Clockwork Orange (1962)

R ★ ★ ★	I ★ ★ ★ ★
C ★ ★ ★ ★	L ★ ★ ★ ★

The Wanting Seed (1962)

R ★ ★ ★	I ★ ★
C ★ ★ ★	L ★ ★ ★

The End Of The World News (1982)

R ★ ★	I ★ ★
C ★ ★	L ★ ★ ★

BURKS, Arthur J. (1898-1974) Prolific American writer, mainly of short fiction for the science fiction and fantasy pulps of the 1930s and 1940s. Works like the novel *The Great Amen* (1938) are overtly fantasy, but even his science fiction is garish and rather fantastic in nature. *The Great Mirror* (serialized 1942) has been reprinted.

The Great Mirror (1942/1952 in book form)

R ★ ★	I ★
C ★ ★	L

BURROUGHS, Edgar Rice (1875-1950) American writer who began writing in his mid-thirties, having failed at almost everything else. He became quickly successful marketing unashamed daydreams of an exotic and uninhibited character. *A Princess Of Mars* was the first of 11 volumes

Edgar Rice Burroughs

set on a romantic Mars which has become part of modern folklore, and which influenced many later writers, including Leigh Brackett (q.v.) and Ray Bradbury (q.v.). *Tarzan Of The Apes* began an even longer series, introducing one of the twentieth century's three great hero-myths. Although Tarzan's adventures supposedly happen in Africa, his jungle is just as much a dream-world as Mars, *Pellucidar* (1923) (a world in the centre of the Earth) and *The Land That Time Forgot* (a lost island inhabited by prehistoric survivals). Burroughs is clearly an unsophisticated writer, and although he is the most widely imitated writer of the century, none of the copies of his work retain the flavour of his originals. Unfortunately, the same harsh judgement must be passed on all his own later works, which are feeble self-plagiarisms. All his good work was done before 1930; after that he lost his magic touch. This is not altogether surprising, in that one of his virtues is a frank naivety – the kind of commodity which is bound to perish with time. His style is easy to mock and his stories are utter nonsense, but Burroughs appeals directly, without embarrassment or undue artifice, to the secret desires, dreams and illusions whose repression creates the need for escape into fantasy worlds. In his own field he was a writer of great talent.

A Princess Of Mars (1912)

R	★ ★ ★ ★ ★	I	★ ★
C	★	L	★ ★ ★

Tarzan Of The Apes (1912)

R	★ ★ ★ ★ ★	I	★ ★
C	★ ★ ★ ★	L	★ ★ ★

The Land That Time Forgot (1924)

R	★ ★ ★ ★	I	★
C	★	L	★ ★

BURROUGHS, William S. (1914) American writer. Although not specifically a sf author, William Burroughs has borrowed wholesale from sf imagery and genre concepts while, on the other hand, extending a major influence on many sf writers of New Wave persuasion. A master of dark irony, literary montage and drug-induced surrealism, his books have the relentless logical lunacy of nightmares. Although he has used sf for its metaphorical power, Burroughs also harbours a good knowledge and affection for the genre and his use of sf tropes is very knowing.

The Naked Lunch (1959)

R	★	I	★ ★ ★ ★
C	★ ★ ★ ★	L	★ ★ ★

Nova Express (1964)

R	★	I	★ ★ ★
C	★ ★ ★	L	★ ★ ★

Cities Of The Red Night (1981)

R	★ ★ ★	I	★ ★
C	★ ★ ★	L	★ ★ ★

BUSBY, F. M. (1921) American writer whose first story was published in 1957, but whose novels have only begun to appear in the late 1970s. His best work has probably been achieved at short story length, in bizarre visions like "Tell Me All About Yourself" (1973), a depiction of a brothel for necrophiliacs. His longer work is overtly space opera and has so far fallen into two series. *Cage A Man* (1973) is the first work in the Barton series which, in *The Proud Enemy* and *All These Earths* (1978), never quite delivers the excitements it promises. His *Rissa Kerguelen* trilogy, describing the adventures of his female protagonist, is much better but follows a highly similar format. *The Long View* (1976) and *Zelde M'Tana* (1980) continue that series.

The Proud Enemy (1975)

R	★ ★ ★	I	★ ★
C	★ ★	L	★ ★

Rissa Kerguelen (1976)

R	★ ★ ★ ★	I	★ ★
C	★ ★	L	★ ★

"The Learning Of Eeshta" (1973)

R	★ ★ ★	I	★ ★
C	★ ★ ★	L	★ ★ ★

BUTLER, Octavia (1947) American novelist, most of whose work has fallen into the Patternist series, which began with

Patternmaster (1978) and continued recently with *Wild Seed* (1980). These novels deal with the social grouping of people possessed of paranormal abilities, and range over a vast period of time (although most of their action is near-contemporary). Technology and fantasy are blended to create a colourful, if sometimes patchy, background for the works, and the central ideas are only properly examined – in all their logical and moral aspects – in *Mind Of My Mind*, where Butler's eloquence and storytelling abilities are best displayed. She has not yet achieved her early promise, but could prove to be one of the genre's most influential writers in the 1990s.

Mind Of My Mind (1977)

R ★ ★ ★ ★	I ★ ★ ★ ★
C ★ ★ ★	L ★ ★ ★

Survivor (1978)

R ★ ★ ★ ★	I ★ ★ ★
C ★ ★	L ★ ★

BUTLER, Samuel (1835-1902) English writer, relevant for his Utopia *Erewhon* and its sequel, *Erewhon Revisited*. The former is an intelligently written anti-Darwinian tale set in a New Zealand which has banned all machines. Whilst it lacks the coherence and consistency expected from modern science-fictional Utopias, its satire is still sharp. The sequel detracts somewhat from its charms, but is nonetheless readable.

Erewhon (1872)

R ★ ★ ★ ★	I ★ ★ ★
C ★	L ★ ★ ★

Erewhon Revisited (1901)

R ★ ★ ★	I ★ ★
C ★ ★	L ★ ★

BUTTERWORTH, Michael (1947) English writer and editor who wrote several experimental short stories for *New Worlds* in the 1960s, six *Space 1999* novelizations and a trilogy of science fiction/fantasy novels based on the rock group Hawkwind, and co-authored (partially) with Michael Moorcock (q.v.). There is a vast disparity of achievement in his work.

The Time Of The Hawklords (1976)

R ★ ★ ★	I ★ ★
C ★ ★	L ★ ★

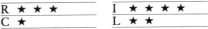

CABELL, James Branch (1879-1958) American writer. Most of his works, including some eccentric texts which are not stories, are assimilated into the *Biography Of The Life Of Manuel*, 21 volumes linking the affairs of an imaginary town in Virginia and an imaginary mythology relating to happenings in the magical medieval French province of Poictesme. This unique combination of the modern novel and the *chanson de geste* has a substantial cult following, and many readers rate Cabell the major American fantasist of the century. The best fantasy novels from the series are witty, elegant, clever and luxurious. *Jurgen* was fortunate enough to become notorious when there was a move to ban it because of some delicately bawdy scenes full of playful innuendo.

Jurgen (1919)

R ★ ★ ★	I ★ ★ ★ ★
C ★ ★	L ★ ★ ★ ★

The High Place (1923)

R ★ ★ ★	I ★ ★ ★ ★
C ★ ★	L ★ ★ ★ ★

Something About Eve (1927)

R ★ ★ ★	I ★ ★ ★ ★
C ★ ★	L ★ ★ ★ ★

CAIDIN, Martin (1927) Prolific American writer of non-fiction books (many with a technical bias) who has produced a dozen novels within the sf field. His *Cyborg* (1972) and its sequels were adapted to become TV's *The Six Million Dollar Man*. He is essentially an adventure writer who uses his technical knowledge to very good effect in his novels. *Marooned* was filmed.

Marooned (1964)

R ★ ★ ★	I ★ ★ ★ ★
C ★	L ★ ★

CALDWELL, (Janet Miriam) Taylor (Holland) (1900) Best-selling American author whose two works in the genre are the politically right-wing and nightmarish *The Devil's Advocate*, attacking by portraying the excesses of an American socialist Utopia in 1970, and the rather lightweight fantasy *Your Sins And Mine* (1956).

The Devil's Advocate (1952)

R ★ ★ ★	I ★ ★
C ★ ★	L ★ ★

CALISHER, Hortense (1911) American author of one science fiction novel, *Journal From Ellipsia*, an alternate world story with a strong metaphysical concern which yet manages to remain entertaining and at times comic.

Journal From Ellipsia (1965)

R ★ ★ ★	I ★ ★ ★
C ★ ★	L ★ ★

CALVINO, Italo (1923) One of the best known modern Italian writers, Calvino first came to prominence with the trilogy *Our Ancestors* (1951-59); drawing on folklore and the Romance, it went against the tone of socially committed realism prevalent in Italy at the time. His later works explore other systems of imagery, and (under the influence of structuralism) become increasingly abstract; of these, *Cosmicomics* (1965), which explores the imagery of science, is probably closest to sf. His most unusual book is *Invisible Cities* (1972), a series of brilliant fragments, each of which encodes an insight into the nature of perception into the description of a city which exemplifies it.

Our Ancestors (1951-59)

R ★ ★ ★ ★ ★	I ★ ★ ★ ★ ★
C ★ ★ ★ ★	L ★ ★ ★ ★ ★

Cosmicomics (1965)

R ★ ★ ★ ★ ★	I ★ ★ ★ ★ ★
C ★ ★ ★	L ★ ★ ★ ★

Invisible Cities (1972)

R ★ ★ ★ ★	I ★ ★ ★ ★ ★
C ★ ★ ★	L ★ ★ ★ ★ ★

CAMERON, John   American author of *The Astrologer*, a quasi science fiction novel about a second Virgin Mary and her progeny.

The Astrologer (1972)

R ★ ★ ★	I ★ ★ ★
C ★ ★	L ★

CAMPBELL, J(ohn) Ramsey (1946) English writer of horror stories and novels, and winner of the British Fantasy Award for *In The Bag*. His works embrace sf devices, but are more normally straight horror stories. Interesting are *Demons By Daylight* (1975) and *To Wake The Dead* (1981). There is a bizarre and disturbing streak in his work which marks him out as an original. His best work to date is, perhaps, *The Nameless*.

In The Bag (1978)

R ★ ★ ★ ★	I ★ ★
C ★ ★	L ★ ★

The Nameless (1981)

R ★ ★ ★ ★ ★	I ★ ★ ★
C ★ ★ ★	L ★ ★ ★

Italo Calvino

CAMPBELL, John W. Jr (1910-71)

American writer and long-time editor of *Astounding Science Fiction*, later *Analog*. He was the main influence shaping the development of magazine sf in the 1940s, promoting the genre as a realistic medium for entertaining experiments in extrapolation. The fiction he wrote under his own name before becoming an editor is extravagant and almost-unreadable space opera, but he wrote some first-rate material for *Astounding* under the name Don A. Stuart before he virtually gave up writing at the end of the 1930s.

"Who Goes There?" (1938)

R ★ ★ ★ ★	I ★ ★ ★ ★
C ★	L ★ ★ ★

The Moon Is Hell (1950)

R ★ ★	I ★ ★
C ★	L ★

CAPEK, Karel (1890-1938)

Czech novelist, playwright and essayist. He is best known as the author of the play *R.U.R.*, which introduced the word "robot" into several languages. His play *The Makropoulos Secret* (1925) deals with immortality, while his novel *Krakatit* (1925) is an early story about the issues of conscience involved in the invention of extremely powerful explosive devices. *The Absolute At Large* and *War With The Newts* are both classic satires in the same mould as *R.U.R.*, proposing that scientific discovery will unleash such forces that the human world will be devastated. Capek believed, and argued most persuasively, that no good would come from contemporary trends in human affairs. Had he not died when he did he would have suffered the same fate as his brother Josef, who died in a concentration camp. He is without parallel as a writer of anti-scientific fables.

R.U.R. (1921)

R ★ ★	I ★ ★ ★
C ★ ★	L ★ ★ ★ ★

The Absolute At Large (1922)

R ★ ★ ★ ★	I ★ ★ ★ ★
C ★ ★ ★	L ★ ★ ★ ★ ★

War With The Newts (1936)

R ★ ★ ★	I ★ ★ ★
C ★ ★ ★	L ★ ★ ★ ★

CAPON (Harry) Paul (1912-69)

English writer, mainly of juveniles and barely known in the U.S.A. where his writing never penetrated. Interesting is a trilogy beginning with *The Other Side Of The Sun* and continuing with *The Other Half Of The Planet* (1952) and *Down To Earth* (1954). Another five novels in the science fiction vein exist, but none are strong enough to deserve reprinting.

The Other Side Of The Sun (1950)

R ★ ★ ★	I ★ ★ ★
C ★ ★	L ★

CARD, Orson Scott (1951)

American writer who is only just emerging as a major talent in the genre, his work thus far almost equally divided between science fiction and fantasy. His first collection, *Unaccompanied Sonata and Other Stories* (1981), showed that he was an accomplished technician with words, but it is only with the publication of four novels that his true strengths and weaknesses can be gauged. Like many contemporary writers who utilize a hybrid form of sf and fantasy, Card loves detailed maps. *A Planet Called Treason* is a failed hybrid, illogical and derivative, but *Hart's Hope*, more overtly fantasy (but again with a map!), is far more successful. *Songmaster* (1982) is again in the fantasy vein, while *The Worthing Chronicle* (1983) is "galaxy-spanning adventure." His work has thus far best been summarized by critic John Clute: "At the heart of all his work to date [lies] a compulsive cold technical polish," and there is an undeniable harshness to his work which may or may not prove his trademark.

A Planet Called Treason (1980)

R ★ ★ ★	I ★ ★
C ★ ★	L ★ ★

Hart's Hope (1983)

R ★ ★ ★ ★	I ★ ★ ★
C ★ ★	L ★ ★ ★

CARR, Jayge   American author of several fine works which are evidence of a new and considerable talent within the field. *Leviathan's Deep*, whilst utilizing familiar space opera devices (a galaxy-wide system of human-colonized planets), is a novel of character, and its central sf idea is complementary to a story of love and betrayal. *Navigator's Syndrome*, Carr's latest work, whilst less artistically successful, is nonetheless quite brilliant in its depiction of the backwater world of Rabelais and its complex social relationships.

Leviathan's Deep (1979)

R ★ ★ ★	I ★ ★
C ★ ★ ★	L ★ ★ ★

Navigator's Syndrome (1983)

R ★ ★ ★	I ★ ★
C ★ ★ ★	L ★ ★

CARR, John Dickson (1906-77) American writer of detective novels, some of which incorporate the sf element of time travel: *The Devil In Velvet* (1951), *Fear Is The Same* (1956; under his pseudonym, Carter Dickson), and *Fire, Burn!* The last is an excellent hybrid of the two genres.

Fire, Burn! (1956)

R ★ ★ ★ ★ ★	I ★ ★ ★
C ★ ★	L ★ ★

CARR, Terry (1937) American writer and editor. He has been far more prolific as an anthologist than as a writer, and his reputation still hangs on the fact that he was editor of the influential series of "Ace Specials" – original paperback novels of high quality and ambitious nature, issued in the late 1960s and early 1970s. Apart from some potboilers his only sf novel is *Cirque*, an effective story of a far-future city under a peculiar metaphysical threat. Along with his best short stories (like "The Dance Of The Changer And Three" (1968)) it shows him to be a writer of considerable skill and imaginative power, but no great energy.

Cirque (1977)

R ★ ★ ★	I ★ ★ ★
C ★ ★ ★	L ★ ★ ★

CARROLL, Lewis (1832-98) Pseudonym of British mathematician Charles L. Dodgson, author of the classic children's stories *Alice's Adventures In Wonderland* and *Through The Looking Glass*. The archetypal victim of a peculiarly innocent Victorian species of paedophilia, Carroll composed for the nine-year-old Alice Liddell a long, fantastic tale to while away a picnic afternoon, and later reconstructed it for publication. Dodgson was a pioneer of symbolic logic, and these two "nonsense" novels, especially the second, are masterpieces of twisted and subverted rationality which hold a powerful fascination for all devotees of intellectual perversity. They are pleasant, dreamy, sentimental and ruthlessly anarchic, and their influence is very widespread in modern fantasy and sf.

Alice's Adventures In Wonderland (1865)

R ★ ★ ★ ★ ★	I ★ ★ ★ ★ ★
C ★ ★ ★ ★	L ★ ★ ★ ★ ★

Through The Looking Glass (1871)

R ★ ★ ★ ★ ★	I ★ ★ ★ ★ ★
C ★ ★ ★ ★	L ★ ★ ★ ★ ★

CARTER, Angela (1940) English novelist, radio playwright and journalist whose rich gothic and symbolist inheritance is from France rather than England; she also spent crucial years in Japan. Her writing is powerful, often baroque but always fiercely

Lewis Carroll

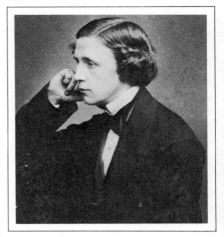

controlled. Her central concern is with sex, with the vigorous contours and bizarre inversions of human desire, and especially with the autonomy of the individual imagination. Carter draws upon sf as upon melodrama, horror, folktale and dream for a vocabulary of potent images and distortions. The worlds of her fiction, often presented as decadent, may be ostensibly present, future or timeless, but her vision always pierces the contemporary heart.

Heroes And Villains (1969)

R ★ ★ ★ ★ ★	I ★ ★
C ★ ★ ★ ★	L ★ ★ ★ ★

The Infernal Desire Machines Of Dr Hoffman (1972)

R ★ ★ ★ ★ ★	I ★ ★ ★
C ★ ★	L ★ ★ ★ ★ ★

"The Courtship Of Mr Lyon" (1979)

R ★ ★ ★ ★ ★	I ★ ★
C ★ ★ ★ ★	L ★ ★ ★ ★ ★

CARTER, Bruce (1922) Pseudonymn of prolific English writer Richard Alexander Hough. In science fiction he has produced two enjoyable, if undemanding juveniles, *The Perilous Descent* (1976) and *Buzzbugs*.

Buzzbugs (1977)

R ★ ★ ★ ★	I ★
C ★	L ★

CARTER, Lin(wood Vrooman) (1930) American writer/editor. Most of Carter's prolific output is based on motifs developed by earlier generations of pulp writers. His main influences have been Robert E. Howard (q.v.) (to whose "Conan" epic Carter has himself contributed) and Edgar Rice Burroughs (q.v.). The Thongor sword-and-sorcery series rises no higher than pale pastiche; the "Callisto" books are a more effective tribute to E.R.B.'s Martian heroic fantasies. Carter's success is perhaps firmest in his non-fiction. Although marked by the same facetious humour and uncritical enthusiasms as his fiction, his introductions to Tolkien (q.v.) (*Tolkien: a look behind "The Lord Of The Rings,"* 1969) and Lovecraft (q.v.) (*Lovecraft: a look behind*

the *Cthulhu Mythos*, 1972) are useful to the fantasy enthusiast and his *Imaginary Worlds* (1973), a survey of fantasy literature, essential. As anthologist and editor for the Ballantyne adult fantasy list from 1969 to 1972 Carter was responsible for the publication of many classic fantasy novels; it is probably true to say that this, rather than his fiction, marks his solid and undoubted contribution to the genre.

Thongor At The End Of Time (1968)

R ★ ★	I ★ ★
C ★	L ★

Jandar Of Callisto (1972)

R ★ ★ ★	I ★
C ★	L ★

Sky Pirates of Callisto (1973)

R ★ ★	I ★ ★
C ★	L ★

CARTER, Robert (1954) English author of one sf novel, the intelligent thriller, *The Dream Killers*, which deals with a post civil war England and mind-manipulation.

The Dream Killers (1981)

R ★ ★ ★	I ★ ★ ★
C ★ ★	L ★ ★

CARVER, Jeffrey A.   English writer of juvenile space quest series, beginning with *Star Rigger's Way* (1978) and continuing with *Panglor*.

Panglor (1982)

R ★ ★ ★	I ★ ★
C ★	L ★

CHALKER, Jack Laurence (1944) American author and editor who founded Mirage Press, to publish non-fiction sf books, and then became a prolific writer producing an average of two novels a year since 1976. He came to prominence with his Well World series, featuring the immortal space adventurer Nathan Brazil, which began with *Midnight At The Well Of Souls* and continued with the short story "Forty Days and Nights in the Wilderness" (1978) and the novels *Exiles At The Well Of*

Souls (1978), *Quest For The Well Of Souls* (1978), *The Return Of Nathan Brazil* and *Twilight At The Well Of Souls* (1980). An extra protagonist, Mavra Chang, replaces Brazil as the central character in *The Wars Of The Well*, told in Volumes 2 and 3. As with *Web Of The Chozen*, the Well World series introduces Chalker as an entertaining storyteller of alien beings and worlds. His other work, which includes *A Jungle Of Stars* (1976), *Dancers In The Afterglow* (1978) and another series, *The Four Lords Of The Diamond*, continues these themes.

Midnight At The Well Of Souls (1977)

R	★	★	★	★	★	I	★	★	★	★
C	★	★	★	★	★	L	★	★	★	

The Wars Of The Well (1980)

R	★	★	★	★		I	★	★	★
C	★	★	★	★	★	L	★	★	★

CHANDLER, A. Bertram (1912) English-born writer, now an Australian citizen. He spent most of his life in various Merchant Navies, and this influences his sf to a very considerable extent. Most of his stories feature small trading starships working among the Rim Worlds on the edge of a galactic civilization. These are basically sea stories transplanted into outer space, but that transplanting opens up all kinds of plots and strange situations which can have no parallel in real sea stories. Chandler is a pedestrian writer, but his works have a unique flavour that is valued by many readers. His plotting is usually poor, but there is a certain intimacy and charm about his descriptions of spaceship life that makes them readable. His more recent works have taken advantage of a relaxation of editorial taboos to unveil a preoccupation with sex that is not to the advantage of the stories.

The Rim Of Space (1961)

R	★	★	★	I	★
C	★	★		L	★

The Deep Reaches Of Space (1964)

R	★	★	★	I	★
C	★	★		L	★

CHANT, Joy (1945) American author of three science fantasy novels set on the world Rahike. Whilst she is a strongly feminist writer, her work has a lightness of touch which is appealing. In her world the female is dominant, and, unfortunately, her male characters can be as cardboard as the most chauvinistic male writer's female creations.

The Grey Mane Of Morning (1977)

R	★	★	★	I	★	
C	★	★		L	★	★

When Voiha Wakes (1983)

R	★	★	★	★	I	★	★
C	★	★			L	★	★

CHAPDELAINE, Perry A. (1925) American author of very routine sf novel, *Swampworld West*, which concerns trouble with the alien natives and Earth's colonists on a distant planet. Another novel, *The Laughing Terran* (1977), is about as bad as its title.

Swampworld West (1974)

R	★	★	I	★
C	★		L	

CHARBONNEAU, Louis (Henry) (1924) American writer of tightly plotted science fiction adventures, using the full range of science fiction's themes. He is rather formularistic at times, but can present some interesting twists to old standards, as in *The Sentinel Stars* (1964) and *Barrier World* (1970).

No Place On Earth (1958)

R	★	★	★	★	I	★
C	★				L	★

The Sensitives (1968)

R	★	★	★	I	★
C	★			L	★

CHARNAS, Suzy McKee (1939) American sf writer. McKee's overtly feminist post-atomic novels *Walk To The End Of The World* (1974) and *Motherlines* portray a brutal male-dominated dystopia and a far from totally idealized nomadic society of independent women. They are notable for some rather cavalier treatment of scientific plausibility and for a strongly characterized heroine who comes slowly to a maturity unusually convincing for sf. Charnas has yet to produce the planned third volume. Linked to these thematically is *The Vampire Tapestry*, in which a male predator is shown as trapped and doomed by his needs.

Motherlines (1979)

R ★ ★ ★	I ★ ★ ★
C ★ ★ ★ ★	L ★ ★ ★

"Scorched Supper On New Niger" (1980)

R ★ ★ ★	I ★ ★ ★
C ★ ★ ★	L ★ ★ ★

The Vampire Tapestry (1980)

R ★ ★ ★ ★	I ★ ★
C ★ ★ ★ ★	L ★ ★ ★ ★

CHAYEFSKY, Paddy (1923) American stage and screen writer, responsible for the novel and screenplay of *Altered States*, a work which describes the search for the origins of consciousness in Man. It is a subtle work and in places is perhaps over-technical, yet its scope and intelligence are impressive.

Altered States (1978)

R ★ ★ ★ ★	I ★ ★ ★ ★ ★
C ★ ★	L ★ ★ ★

CHERRYH, C. J. (1942) American writer Carolyn Jane Cherryh, who, in a manner reminiscent of the genre's earliest days, uses the name C. J. Cherryh (the additional "h", an exotic touch) for both her fantasy and science fiction. Surprisingly she did not come to prominence in the sf field until 1976. Since then she has proved one of the most prolific and yet consistently good writers of science fiction and science fantasy in the field and has won the major awards for her work. Her obvious delight in creating and peopling a relatively near-future galaxy with alien races and human colonies is in the very mainstream of sf concerns, but only in works like *Downbelow Station* does it become traditional space opera, with battling spacecraft and inter-galactic intrigues. *Hestia* (1979) displays Cherryh's belief in strong narrative matched by strong characterization (and its muddy planet might well be a study for Downbelow). The three novels in *The Book Of Morgaine* (1979) tell of a galaxy permeated by "gates" in space and time which have malfunctioned and must be guarded. Her *Faded Sun* series, *Kesrith*, *Shon'Jir* (1978) and *Kutath* (1979), is again a portrait of an alien culture; a rich and fascinating imaginative feat. If there is a fault in her work it is that, in depicting her alien worlds, she over-utilizes the trick of an unfamiliar vocabulary, necessitating – as in *Hunter Of Worlds* (1977) – an extensive glossary. She has been charged, also, with being derivative, and there is no doubt that in novels such as *Serpent's Reach* (1980) and *The Well Of Shiuan* (1978; part of *The Book Of Morgaine*) she does fail to provide a distinctive voice. Perhaps the sheer range of her work and its adventure-orientation has retarded her stylistic development, even though her fascination with words is clear (she has a B.A. in Latin and an M.A. in Classics). Despite this, her novels are evidence of a maturation of the space opera, and *Downbelow Station* justly deserved the Hugo Award for its depiction of not merely the huge screen effects but a number of individual portraits. *Port Eternity* (1982) is a somewhat less successful attempt to blend myth and science fiction, a flawed attempt

C. J. Cherryh

at re-telling the Arthurian legend, using clones for the characters. *The Pride Of Chanur* (1982) is a more stirring and successful work, perhaps indicative that Cherryh is happiest when dealing with alien races in adventure situations. A fantasy element is always implied if never overt, but in *The Dreamstone* (1983) it is central. The Celtic atmosphere is vividly captured as she describes the coming of Man to the faery Ealdwood. Unlike most contemporary fantasy novels, it displays a deep understanding of the allegorical and mythical elements it uses. Its sequel, *The Tree Of Swords And Jewels*, is, if anything, much better. To emphasize this apparent split in Cherryh's concerns between space opera and fantasy, her latest work returns to the human/alien-on-colony-world format which, for the first time, shows some signs of strain and weak characterization. *Forty Thousand In Gehenna* (1983) has faint undertones of *The Tempest* (especially in the naming of the alien ariels and calibans) but is otherwise the story of how a colony planet develops in 200 years of social mutation. Cherryh is and will doubtlessly continue to be one of the contemporary genre's most influential writers and the best of her work is probably to come.

The Faded Sun; Kesrith (1978)

R ★ ★ ★ ★	I ★ ★
C ★ ★ ★	L ★ ★

Downbelow Station (1981)

R ★ ★ ★ ★	I ★ ★ ★
C ★ ★ ★	L ★ ★

The Tree Of Swords And Jewels (1983)

R ★ ★ ★ ★ ★	I ★ ★
C ★ ★ ★	L ★ ★ ★

CHESNEY, Sir George (Tomkyns) (1830-95) English author of the definitive future-war novel of its time, *The Battle Of Dorking: Reminiscences Of A Volunteer*, which depicted the future invasion of England by Germany.

The Battle Of Dorking (1871)

R ★ ★ ★	I ★ ★
C ★	L ★

CHESTERTON, G(ilbert) K(eith) (1874-1936) English writer famous for his Father Brown detective stories, whose science fiction novels are pastorals, with a certain Utopian quality to them. *The Napoleon Of Notting Hill* is perhaps the most typical of these, although *The Flying Inn* is perhaps his finest defence of purely English traditional values. *The Man Who Was Thursday: A Nightmare* (1908) is a delightful fantasy-cum-satire with a group of anarchists led by God.

The Napoleon Of Notting Hill (1904)

R ★ ★ ★	I ★ ★ ★
C ★ ★	L ★ ★

The Flying Inn (1914)

R ★ ★ ★ ★	I ★ ★
C ★ ★ ★	L ★ ★

CHILSON, Robert (1945) American writer whose output has been limited both in quality and quantity. His technophilic novels and short stories are typical *Analog* fare. *The Star-Crowned Kings*, a space opera, and *The Shores Of Kansas* (1976), about time travel, add little to either sub-genre.

The Star-Crowned Kings (1975)

R ★ ★ ★	I ★
C ★ ★	L ★

CHRISTOPHER, John (1922) Pseudonym used by English writer Sam Youd for his science fiction. During the 1950s he established a reputation as a writer of disaster stories with such novels as *The Death Of Grass* and *The World In Winter*, but from the late 1960s until the present virtually all his sf has been aimed at a juvenile audience, including several trilogies. His best work is in the vein of John Wyndham's (q.v.) more successful books, facing ordinary people with extraordinary situations in which they must fight to survive. The uncompromising social Darwinism of his early books makes them rather bleak. His juvenile novels are mostly rather formularistic but have proved very successful despite a constant didactic undercurrent which champions individualism against various forms of collectivism.

The Death Of Grass (1956)

R ★ ★ ★	I ★ ★
C ★ ★ ★	L ★ ★ ★

The World In Winter (1962)

R ★ ★ ★	I ★ ★
C ★ ★ ★	L ★ ★ ★

CLARKE, Arthur C(harles) (1917)
English-born resident of Sri Lanka, whose
championing of the science in science fiction has won him a massive worldwide following, as has the Kubrick film of his "The
Sentinel" (1951), *2001: A Space Odyssey*
(novelized 1968). He has written some of
the most perfect extrapolative tales in the
genre, and balances strict technological
accuracy with a vivid, almost religious belief in *otherness*. "A Meeting With
Medusa," his award-winning novella about
the investigation of Jupiter's red spot, is
deservedly rated as one of the major works
in sf. Clarke's early work could be summarized as space-engineering tales. In his
shorter fiction there is more diversity and
humour, but in his novels – such as *The
Deep Range* (1957) and *A Fall Of Moondust*
(1961) – there is an unconvincing wooden-
ness, especially in his characterization. His
best work, therefore, is marked by an
absence of human foci, where the marvellous and mystical nature of *things* is evoked.
In this sense Clarke is a hieroglyphicist,
seeking meanings from forms. *The City And
The Stars* (1956; a revised version of *Against
The Fall Of Night*, 1948) evokes our
sense of wonder at the City, Diaspar, rather
than at the trite anarchy/stability theme.
Childhood's End, however, is justifiably
rated as one of the seminal sf novels of the
1950s, where devil-like superior aliens
come to Earth to assist Mankind in achiev-
ing his cosmic destiny. There is a hiatus in
Clarke's major work between 1961 and
1973, when *Rendezvous With Rama* appeared. *Rama* is one of the genre's major works,
describing the close transit and exploration
of a giant alien spacecraft. As in the best of
Clarke's work, it conveys perfectly a
scientific sense of enigma – of undiscovered depths to existence. *Imperial Earth*

(1975), with its greater human emphasis,
shows Clarke's limitations as a novelist, but
is nonetheless an impressive work. *The
Fountains Of Paradise* (1979) again displays
Clarke at his best, describing the construction of a 22,000-mile high elevator to a
spaceport orbiting the Earth. Again, the
sheer wonder of massive artifacts is vividly
created, and, for once, the human relation-

Arthur C. Clarke

ships, whilst dwarfed by the elevator and its
implications, are reasonably depicted. His
latest work, *2010: Odyssey Two* (1982), a
sequel to the film novelization, is far more
human and less technologically oriented
than its predecessor, showing off aspects of
Clarke's unashamedly mystical side. Also
of importance is a book of Clarke's scientific essays, *The View From Serendip* (1977),
partly autobiographical and partly about his
fascination with Sri Lanka.

Childhood's End (1953)

R ★ ★ ★ ★	I ★ ★ ★
C ★ ★	L ★ ★ ★

The City And The Stars (1956)

R ★ ★ ★ ★	I ★ ★ ★
C ★	L ★ ★

Rendezvous With Rama (1973)

R ★ ★ ★ ★ ★	I ★ ★ ★ ★ ★
C ★	L ★ ★ ★

"A Meeting With Medusa" (1971)

R ★ ★ ★ ★ ★	I ★ ★ ★ ★ ★
C ★ ★	L ★ ★ ★ ★

CLEMENT, Hal (1922) Pseudonym used by American writer Harry C. Stubbs for his sf. He is often held up as the prime example of the "hard" sf writer because of the scrupulous attention he pays to matters of scientific detail in designing his alien worlds. He delights in fitting exotic life-forms to peculiar physical circumstances. *Mission Of Gravity* is set on a world that rotates so quickly on its axis that its surface gravity varies from three times Earth-normal to several hundred. *Cycle Of Fire* is set on a world with a very eccentric orbit, so that it experiences extremes of heat and cold. His writing is not particularly elegant and his plotting tends to be far from intricate, but he can build up considerable suspense in his tales of people trying to use their intelligence and knowledge to get them out of awkward predicaments.

Mission Of Gravity (1954)

R	★ ★ ★		I	★ ★ ★ ★
C	★		L	★ ★

Cycle Of Fire (1957)

R	★ ★ ★		I	★ ★ ★
C	★		L	★ ★

Star Light (1971)

R	★ ★ ★		I	★ ★ ★
C	★		L	★ ★

CLIFTON, Mark (1906-63) American writer who, whilst he produced only a small corpus of work in his ten years of writing sf, was highly influential on the field in the U.S.A. His E.S.P. stories, his bleak view of humanity and yet his perceptive psychological understanding of individuals, make him an author worth close study. *They'd Rather Be Right* (1957; with Frank Riley; a.k.a. *The Forever Machine*) is the archetypal Clifton story about the new race of ESPers emerging. *Eight Keys To Eden* is perhaps the exception to these stories, a clever ecological puzzle story which is also a satire of our contemporary civilization.

Eight Keys To Eden (1960)

R	★ ★ ★ ★		I	★ ★ ★
C	★ ★ ★		L	★ ★ ★

When They Come From Space (1962)

R	★ ★ ★		I	★ ★ ★
C	★ ★		L	★ ★

"Remembrance and Reflection" (1958)

R	★ ★ ★ ★		I	★ ★ ★
C	★ ★		L	★ ★

CLINGERMAN, Mildred (McElroy) (1918) American short story writer, whose charming fantasies are best termed "soft science fiction" (in the Spielberg-ET vein!) but retain their appeal.

A Cupful Of Space (1961; coll.)

R	★ ★ ★ ★		I	★
C	★ ★		L	★ ★

CLUTE, John (1940) Canadian author and critic, resident in England. His novel, *The Disinheriting Party*, is a complex and fascinating search for reality and identity with one of the most bizarre endings in literature. Its experimental and enigmatic nature makes it slightly inaccessible to the casual reader, but its lyrical obsessiveness has great appeal.

The Disinheriting Party (1977)

R	★ ★		I	★ ★ ★ ★
C	★ ★ ★		L	★ ★ ★ ★

COBLENTZ, Stanton A(rthur) (1896-1982) Prolific American novelist, poet and short story writer, who first appeared in the sf magazines with *The Sunken World* (serialized 1928; published in book form, 1949). His strength was descriptive rather than imaginative, and his works, such as *The Blue Barbarians* (1931/1958) and *After 12000 Years* (1929/1950) now seem badly dated. However, the non-technological bias and the satiric purpose underlying his work was unusual for its time and formed the pattern for many writers, like Sheckley (q.v.) and Pohl (q.v.), who followed him.

Hidden World (1957)

R	★ ★ ★		I	★ ★
C	★		L	★

COGSWELL, Theodore R(ose) (1918) American short story writer whose *Spock*

Messiah (novelization, 1976) is rather an aberration within his opus. His work has a great range, but at its best blends a technological wonder with a poetic lyricism. "The Wall Around The World" (1953) and "Early Bird" (1973) are good examples of this. Two collections of his short fiction are available. *The Wall Around The World* and *The Third Eye* (1968)

The Wall Around The World (1962; coll.)

R ★ ★ ★ ★	I ★ ★ ★
C ★ ★	L ★ ★

COLE, Everett B. (1910) American writer of the Philosophical Corps series (three of which were published as *The Philosophical Corps*). This galactic-ranging thought-police have a humane ideological "war" against dissenters and cultural disturbers. Five other Philosophical Corps stories are not included in the collection.

The Philosophical Corps (1961; coll.)

R ★ ★ ★	I ★ ★
C ★ ★	L ★

COMPTON, D. G. (1930) English writer. He is a rather downbeat writer of alarmist stories of the near future; a realist who presents convincing accounts of unheroic characters trying to get by in desperate – sometimes apocalyptic – circumstances. His relentless pessimism has prevented him becoming widely popular but his

artistry commands admiration and he has a small but enthusiastic following. His plots usually deal with new moral dilemmas that arise as a result of the march of progress; for this reason even his earliest works retain their topicality. He is underrated and deserves to be read much more widely. He has never been a prolific writer, but, with the exception of the eccentric and interesting *Ascendancies* (1980) he has published very little in the last seven or eight years.

Farewell Earth's Bliss (1966)

R ★ ★ ★	I ★ ★ ★
C ★ ★ ★	L ★ ★ ★

Synthajoy (1968)

R ★ ★	I ★ ★ ★
C ★ ★ ★ ★	L ★ ★ ★ ★

The Steel Crocodile (1970)

R ★ ★ ★	I ★ ★ ★
C ★ ★ ★ ★	L ★ ★ ★ ★

CONDON, Richard (Thomas) (1915) American author of the best-selling sf/spy-thriller *The Manchurian Candidate*, later filmed, which is one of the better Cold War novels that appeared on the genre's borderline at the time.

The Manchurian Candidate (1959)

R ★ ★ ★ ★ ★	I ★ ★
C ★ ★ ★	L ★ ★

CONEY, Michael G(reatrex) (1932) English writer now resident in Canada. A spate of novels appeared from him in the early 1970s, most of them transposing an English "West Country" setting to other planets. *Mirror Image* (1972), his first novel, is typical of Coney's lyrical use of fairly standard sf ideas. His books are strongly atmospheric, but when he departs from the coastal settings he knows so well (as in *Friends Come In Boxes* (1973) and *Winter's Children* (1974)) the weakness of plotting is starkly evident. *Syzygy* and *Mirror Image*, two seemingly quite separate novels, were cleverly combined in the delightful *Brontomek!* (1976), which is essentially a colony-planet tale in the oldest traditions of the genre. His best novel, however, is prob-

Michael G. Coney

ably *Hello Summer, Goodbye,* where the science-fictional idea complements one of the most charming and poignant love stories in the genre. *The Ultimate Jungle* (1979) and *The Human Menagerie* (1981) are slight departures from his normal themes and not so successful, but with *Cat Karina* (1982) he seems back on form.

Syzygy (1973)

R ★ ★ ★	I ★ ★
C ★ ★ ★	L ★ ★

Hello Summer, Goodbye (1975)

R ★ ★ ★ ★ ★	I ★ ★ ★
C ★ ★ ★ ★	L ★ ★ ★

Charisma (1975)

R ★ ★ ★ ★	I ★ ★ ★
C ★ ★ ★	L ★ ★ ★

CONQUEST, (George) Robert (Ackworth) (1917) English writer and editor in the sf field (with Kingsley Amis (q.v.)). He is largely responsible for the growing academic acceptance of sf in England.

CONRAD, Paul (1924) Pseudonym of English writer Albert King, prolific in many genres (and also as Albert King and Mark Bannon, Scott Howell and Christopher King). His work, however, is a minor contribution to the field, and works like *Ex Minus* and *The Last Man On Kluth V* (1975) will probably not last.

Ex Minus (1974)

R ★ ★ ★ ★	I ★ ★
C ★	L ★

The World Of Jonah Klee (1975; as Christopher King)

R ★ ★ ★ ★	I ★ ★
C ★ ★	L ★

CONWAY, Gerard F.   Minor American sf writer who also writes as Wallace Moore. His novels are standard space operas.

Mindship (1971; a.k.a. *Universe,* 1974)

R ★ ★ ★	I ★
C ★	L ★

COOPER, Edmund (1926-82) English writer whose fiction is mostly derivative, replaying standardized sf scenarios. Like many other British writers, he dabbled extensively in stories of the breakdown of civilization following a natural catastrophe or atomic holocaust. At his best, in the sober story of a human castaway on an alien world, *A Far Sunset,* or in the lively satire, *Son Of Kronk,* he has much to offer, but most of his novels are careless and lacklustre. Those written during the last decade of his life – during which time he became an alcoholic – are very poor, and are notable primarily for his extreme anti-feminist views.

A Far Sunset (1967)

R ★ ★ ★	I ★ ★
C ★ ★ ★	L ★ ★

Son Of Kronk (1970)

R ★ ★ ★	I ★ ★
C ★ ★	L ★ ★

Who Needs Men? (1972)

R ★ ★	I
C	L ★

COOPER, Louise   English writer of *Lord Of No Time,* a sword-and-sorcery novel in which Time is stopped. An above average writer, she has yet to make any real mark on the genre.

Lord Of No Time (1977)

R ★ ★ ★ ★	I ★ ★
C ★ ★ ★	L ★ ★

COOPER, Susan (1935) English-born former journalist now resident in the U.S.A., Cooper has written one adult sf novel (*Mandrake,* 1964), but is justly celebrated for her fantasies for children, the five-volume *The Dark Is Rising* sequence. *Over Sea, Under Stone* (1968) hovers uneasily between powerful myth and jovial family-adventure story, but its sequels introduce Will Stanton, the 11-year old who is also the last of the Old Ones and, later, the mysterious albino Bran. The resonant imagery of Celtic ritual and Arthurian legend takes fuller control to propel the plot to a satisfying victory of Light over Dark and emancipation from both.

The Dark Is Rising (1973)

R ★ ★ ★ ★	I ★ ★ ★ ★
C ★ ★ ★	L ★ ★ ★ ★

The Grey King (1975)

R ★ ★ ★	I ★ ★ ★
C ★ ★ ★	L ★ ★ ★

Silver On The Tree (1977)

R ★ ★ ★	I ★ ★ ★
C ★ ★ ★	L ★ ★ ★

COOVER, Robert (Lowell) (1932) American novelist and short story writer whose work involves certain absurd elements more normally associated with the sf field's black satirists (Sheckley (q.v.), Sladek (q.v.)). See his collection *Pricksongs And Descants* (1969).

COPPELL, Alfred (1921) Name used by American writer Alfredo José de Marini y Coppell Jr. He has produced a series of space operas for juveniles, but is best known for *Dark December*, a post-holocaust trek across a devastated U.S.A., and essentially a survival tale.

Dark December (1960)

R ★ ★ ★	I ★ ★
C ★ ★	L ★

COPPER, Basil English writer of sf-horror stories. *The Great White Space* is more purely generic than *House Of The Wolf* (1983), a neo-Victorian thriller involving werewolves.

The Great White Space (1974)

R ★ ★ ★	I ★
C ★ ★	L ★

CORLEY, James (1947) English writer whose work has never quite lived up to his potential. *Benedict's Planet* (1976) is a pot-boiler, whereas *Orsini Godbase* has much in common with Sheckley's work, intelligent, humorous and sharply incisive, if a touch inaccessible in places. There is also a third

sf novel, *Sundrinker* (1981).

Orsini Godbase (1978)

R ★ ★ ★	I ★ ★ ★ ★
C ★ ★	L ★ ★

CORREY, Lee (1928) Pseudonym of American writer George Harry Stine. *Starship Through Space* (1955) is a juvenile. *Contraband Rocket*, an unexceptional work, is his only serious contribution to the genre.

Contraband Rocket (1956)

R ★ ★ ★	I ★
C ★	L ★

COULSON, Juanita (1933) American writer who, like her husband Robert (q.v.), graduated from being a fan. She co-authors with Robert Coulson on an sf family saga, of which *Outward Bound*, an adventure-oriented novel, is a part.

Outward Bound (1982)

R ★ ★ ★	I ★
C ★	L ★

COULSON, Robert (Stratton) (1928) American writer who has collaborated on a handful of books with Gene De Weese (q.v.) and one with Piers Anthony (q.v.) (*But What Of Earth?* (1976)). His solo novel, *To Renew The Ages*, is a post-holocaust novel involving telepathy, told in a direct commercial way with few stylistic frills.

To Renew The Ages (1976)

R ★ ★ ★ ★	I ★ ★
C ★	L ★

COVER, Arthur Byron (1950) American writer who has yet to make a real impact on the genre. His first novel, *Autumn Angels*, is a parody of power fantasy set in the far future. The second, *The Sound Of Winter* (1976), is a post-holocaust love story and far more successful stylistically.

Autumn Angels (1975)

R ★ ★ ★	I ★ ★ ★
C ★ ★	L ★ ★ ★

COWPER, Richard (1926) Pseudonym of English writer, John Middleton Murry, whose mainstream novels are published as Colin Murry. His science fiction output is oriented towards fantasy. His early novels, *Breakthrough, Phoenix* (1968) and *Domino* (1971) rely heavily upon paranormal experiences – a mistrust of pure rationality which is a hallmark of Cowper's work – and concentrate upon the workings of this fantastic element within a contemporary framework. In *Clone* (1972), *Worlds Apart* (1974) and *Profundis* (1979) Cowper uses science fiction as a vehicle for social satire (in *Worlds Apart* satirizing the sf field itself). Probably his best work, however, has been produced since 1974. The publication of *The Twilight Of Briareus* marked the fusion of an accomplished literary style with Cowper's favourite theme, that of depicting a world where some disaster (flood, social/economic collapse, mass sterility) has decimated the population and returned Mankind to a medieval state. However, Cowper's popularity as an sf author has resulted from the publication of several novellas in *The Magazine of Fantasy And Science Fiction*, and from his novel *The Road To Corlay*, a sequel to the novella "Piper At The Gates Of Dawn" (1976). A third part of this series – called by Cowper "The White Bird Of Kinship," and concerned with the development of a quasi-religious brotherhood 1,000 years from now – *A Dream Of Kinship* (1981) is once more concerned with simple, human values, asserting them strongly against religious dogmatism and materialism. The series was completed with *A Tapestry Of Time* (1982), where the moral questions raised in the previous segments were finally faced and, in one sense, answered. Cowper is undoubtedly producing some of the finest and most memorable writing in the genre. Two of his earlier novels, written under the name of Colin Murry, are also worthy of note for their peripheral sf interest; *Recollections Of A Ghost* (1960) and *A Path To The Sea* (1961).

Breakthrough (1967)

R	★	★	★	★	★	I	★	★		
C	★	★	★	★		L	★	★	★	★

The Twilight Of Briareus (1974)

R	★	★	★	★	★	I	★	★		
C	★	★	★			L	★	★	★	★

The Road To Corlay (1978)

R	★	★	★	★	★	I	★	★	★	
C	★	★	★			L	★	★	★	★

"The Custodians" (1975)

R	★	★	★	★	★	I	★	★	★	
C	★	★				L	★	★	★	★

CRAWFORD, Ned   English writer whose first novel, *Naming The Animals*, is a competent but hackneyed closed environment story with an Edenic twist.

Naming The Animals (1980)

R	★	★	★	I	★		
C	★			L	★	★	

CRICHTON, Michael (1942) American author, screenwriter and film director. His works are often science fiction thrillers, although *Westworld* (1974) deals with a future robot-manned fun park, and *Eaters Of The Dead* (1976) is, in effect, a re-telling of the Beowulf myth. *The Andromeda Strain* and *The Terminal Man* (1974) were both made into films, and are highly sculpted, intelligent and fast-paced entertainments.

The Andromeda Strain (1969)

R	★	★	★	★	★	I	★	★	★	
C	★					L	★	★	★	

John Crowley

CROWLEY, John (1942) American writer whose *Little, Big* won the 1982 World Fantasy Award. He has only been working within the genre for eight years but is already recognized as one of the major talents produced by the field, if not the first science fiction writer of true literary standing. All of his work displays a masterful command of the written medium, matched with a visual sense that ranks with the genre's best. *The Deep*, his first novel, is a haunting mythopoeia, a science fictional *Macbeth*. Crowley's fascination with kings continued in *Beasts* (1976), which depicts a near-future world where Leos (genetically produced but self-breeding Man-Lions) are fighting for their survival. *Engine Summer* had Crowley changing tack with a lyrical science fantasy told by its protagonist Rush-Who-Speaks to one of the mysterious Angels. It is, perhaps, the finest example of a closed environment riddle story, fascinating and ultimately powerful. *Little, Big,* however, is his most impressive work to date, not simply a marvellous, sprawling (and yet tightly plotted) work, but a great novel (which compares with LeGuin's *The Dispossessed*). To call it simply a fantastic family saga is to undervalue its richness and its eloquence. Crowley is one of the few rare writers who can combine intellectual acuteness with lyrical power. He will undoubtedly continue to create the next generation of sf's classics.

The Deep (1975)

R	★ ★ ★ ★ ★	I	★ ★ ★ ★ ★
C	★ ★ ★ ★ ★	L	★ ★ ★ ★

Engine Summer (1979)

R	★ ★ ★ ★	I	★ ★ ★ ★ ★
C	★ ★ ★ ★	L	★ ★ ★ ★

Little, Big (1981)

R	★ ★ ★ ★ ★	I	★ ★ ★ ★ ★
C	★ ★ ★ ★ ★	L	★ ★ ★ ★ ★

CUMMINGS, Ray (1887-1957) American writer who was writing sf for the pulp magazines before the emergence of specialized sf pulps. He wrote numerous space operas and time travel stories but is best remembered for his microcosmic romances in which characters shrink in order to visit worlds on the surface of Rutherfordian atoms. His style is childish and he proved unable to adapt it as the genre became more sophisticated, but there is a naïve excitement in his best work which allows it to retain a certain period charm.

"The Girl In The Golden Atom" (1919)

R	★ ★ ★	I	★ ★ ★
C		L	★

The Man Who Mastered Time (1924)

R	★ ★ ★	I	★ ★
C		L	★

The Princess Of The Atom (1929)

R	★ ★ ★	I	★ ★
C		L	★

CURVAL, Philippe (1929) French writer, pseudonym for Philippe Tronche. An elegant stylist, particularly successful in creating alien as well as erotic atmospheres, Curval is one of France's foremost contemporary sf authors with almost 20 novels to his credit, including many well-received mainstream volumes.

L'Homme À Rebours (1974)

R	★ ★ ★	I	★ ★ ★
C	★ ★	L	★ ★ ★ ★

Cette Chère Humanité (1976; trans. as *Brave New World*)

R	★ ★ ★	I	★ ★ ★ ★
C	★ ★ ★	L	★ ★ ★ ★

Y'A Quelqu'un? (1979)

R	★ ★ ★ ★	I	★ ★ ★ ★
C	★ ★	L	★ ★ ★

DAHL, Roald (1961) Welsh writer of children's books and horror/fantasy stories, and one (subsequently rewritten) sf novel, *Some Time Never: A Fable For Supermen* (1948; previously *The Gremlins*, 1943).

His work is often bitter and quite frequently unoriginal, but he is extremely popular for all that.

Some Time Never (1948)

R ★ ★ ★	I ★
C ★	L ★

DALEY, Brian   American author of *Tron*, the novelization of the Disney film about an expert games-player trapped inside a super games-machine.

Tron (1982)

R ★ ★ ★	I ★ ★
C ★	L ★

DALLAS, Ian   Scottish author of *The Book Of Strangers*, which, like Kilworth's (q.v.) *The Night Of Kadar*, if more overtly, deals with the Islamic faith in an unspecified future setting. It is only peripherally science-fictional, however.

The Book Of Strangers (1973)

R ★ ★	I ★
C ★ ★	L ★ ★

DANIEL, Yuli (1925) Russian writer, imprisoned for his work by the Soviet authorities. His highly satirical short stories, collected and translated in *This Is Moscow Speaking and other Stories*, are outspoken but exceptional only in their social context.

This Is Moscow Speaking (1968; coll.)

R ★ ★ ★	I ★ ★
C ★	L ★ ★

DANN, Jack (1949) American writer whose work emerged in the 1970s, some of it in collaboration with George Zebrowski (q.v.). He has since collaborated with Gardner Dozois (q.v.), and Jack C. Haldeman III (q.v.). His first novel, *Starhiker*, was an ambitious work, depicting Earth as a backwater, a relay-station for the big cross-galaxy starships of the alien Hrau. The adventures of Bo, its hero, are dream-like, yet ultimately unadventurous and Dann fails to integrate all the elements of his plot. *Junction* is a far more effective work, equally metaphorical yet with the

tension *Starhiker* lacked. In these two works, and in his 40-plus shorter works (some of which, like "Amnesia" in *Timetripping* (coll.), are amongst the best written sf stories ever), the influence of literary figures like Kafka (q.v.) and Borges (q.v.) have, without doubt, left their mark on his work.

Starhiker (1977)

R ★ ★ ★	I ★ ★ ★
C ★ ★	L ★ ★ ★

Junction (1981)

R ★ ★ ★ ★	I ★ ★ ★
C ★ ★ ★	L ★ ★ ★ ★

Timetripping (1980; coll.)

R ★ ★ ★ ★ ★	I ★ ★ ★
C ★ ★	L ★ ★ ★ ★

DARNAY, Arsen   American writer of *A Hostage For Hinterland*, a study of post-holocaust America and its last cities and tribes.

A Hostage For Hinterland (1976)

R ★ ★ ★	I ★
C ★	L ★

DAVENTRY, Leonard (1915) English writer of *A Man Of Double Deed*, a competently written post-holocaust telepathy story. Another five sf novels, published in the early 1970s, are far less effective, and the recent *You Must Remember Us* (1981) is a rather jaded offering.

A Man Of Double Deed (1965)

R ★ ★ ★ ★	I ★ ★
C ★ ★	L ★ ★

Twenty-One Billionth Paradox (1971)

R ★ ★ ★	I ★ ★
C ★	L ★

DAVIDSON, Avram (1923) American writer of sf and fantasy. Davidson's witty and original novels and short stories have not had the popularity they deserve, partly because of a joy in erudition that sometimes skirts wilful obscurity, partly because of a certain structural looseness in most of his longer fictions, partly because of a wit that risks degenerating into the facetious and the cute, and partly because many of his most interesting cycles of stories and novels have turned out thus far to be abortive projects. Not untypical of his shorter fiction is the early Hugo-winning "Or All The Seas With Oysters" (1958), a study of two contrasted character types in the course of which we learn a lot about bicycles and the origins of wire coat-hangers. He started to write longer sf adventure novels in the 1960s; perhaps the most successful of these is *Masters of the Maze*, in which a True Adventure writer combats alien insects across time and space; Davidson's talents are not least well exemplified by the fact that the hero's pulp writing, the psychology of the Chulpex and the various exotic locations are all credible. Many of his fantasies take place in alternate worlds; typical is *Peregrine: Primus*, in which the bastard son of the last pagan king in Europe wanders a Dark Age full of comic arguments about obscure points of Christian and other doctrine.

Or All The Seas With Oysters (1962; coll.)

R	★ ★ ★ ★	I	★ ★ ★
C	★ ★ ★ ★	L	★ ★ ★ ★

Masters Of The Maze (1965)

R	★ ★ ★ ★	I	★ ★ ★
C	★ ★ ★ ★	L	★ ★ ★ ★

Peregrine: Primus (1971)

R	★ ★ ★ ★	I	★ ★ ★ ★
C	★ ★ ★ ★	L	★ ★ ★ ★ ★

DAVIDSON, Lionel (1922) English writer of crime novels, whose marginally sf novels reflect more of an interest in Israel (where he resides) than in the genre. *The Sun Chemist* is a science-puzzle story, but is more thriller than sf.

The Sun Chemist (1976)

R	★ ★ ★ ★	I	★ ★
C	★ ★ ★	L	★ ★

DAVIES, Leslie Purnell (1914) English writer and painter who writes as L.P. Davies. He was most active in the late 1960s and early 1970s, when he produced ten genre novels. He is essentially a thriller writer and uses the sf field in the same manner, in novels like *The Alien* (1968), *The Paper Dolls* (1964) and *Genesis Two*. All are densely plotted, suspense-oriented works, more slick than serious.

The Artificial Man (1965)

R	★ ★ ★ ★	I	★ ★ ★
C	★	L	★ ★

Genesis Two (1971)

R	★ ★ ★ ★ ★	I	★ ★
C	★ ★	L	★

DAVIS, Gerry English writer and co-author, with Kit Pedler (q.v.), of the Doomwatch novel, *Mutant 59: The Plastic Eaters* (1972), *Brainrack, The Dynostar Menace* (1976), and several Dr Who novelizations for children.

Brainrack (1974; with Kit Pedler)

R	★ ★ ★	I	★ ★
C	★	L	★ ★

DE BERGERAC, (Savinien) Cyrano (1619-55) French author of *The States And Empires Of The Moon* (1657) and *The States And Empires Of The Sun* (1657) (collected and translated as *Other Worlds*), two speculative, slightly whimsical and highly amusing stories which anticipate sf's later obsession with space travel and alien environments.

Other Worlds (1965)

R	★ ★ ★ ★	I	★ ★ ★ ★ ★
C	★ ★	L	★ ★ ★ ★

DE CAMP, L. Sprague (1907) American writer. He was the most prolific contributor to the excellent fantasy magazine *Unknown* durings its short life in 1939-43. The Harold Shea series, begun with *The Incomplete Enchanter* (1941), which he wrote with Fletcher Pratt (q.v.), best encapsulates the *esprit* of the magazine. His classic alternate history story, *Lest Darkness Fall*, also appeared there. Most of his sf is witty and lightweight, the greater part of it falling into the Viagens Interplanetarias series. His

L. Sprague de Camp

plotting is weak, most of his stories featuring journeys through exotic territory, but the entertainment value of his work is always high. His fine historical novels set in the classical world are much better than his sf or his fantasy deserving both attention and respect, and he is also well-known for his non-fiction books on ancient tech nology and archaeology. He has done a great deal of work in collaboration, most recently with Lin Carter (q.v.), with whom he has written many stories featuring Robert E. Howard's (q.v.) sword-and-sorcery hero, Conan.

Lest Darkness Fall (1941)

R	★ ★ ★ ★	I	★ ★ ★
C	★ ★ ★	L	★ ★ ★

Rogue Queen (1951)

R	★ ★ ★	I	★ ★
C	★ ★	L	★ ★

The Hostage of Zir (1977)

R	★ ★ ★	I	★ ★
C	★ ★	L	★ ★

DEFONTENAY, C(harlemagne) I(schir)   French writer of the early, anthropological novel, *Star; ou Psi de Cassiopée* (1854), translated as *Star* (1975), more valuable for its early attempts at scientific speculation than for its entertainment.

Star (1854/1975)

R	★ ★ ★	I	★ ★
C	★	L	★ ★

DE FORD, Miriam Allen (1888-1975) American writer and editor, who wrote over 30 science fiction short stories. Two collections of her work show her to be happiest when toying with time travel themes.

Xenogenesis (1969; coll.)

R	★ ★ ★ ★	I	★ ★
C	★ ★	L	★

Elsewhere, Elsewhen, Elsehow (1971; coll.)

R	★ ★ ★	I	★
C	★ ★	L	★

DEIGHTON, Len (1929) English best-selling author of spy thrillers, whose *Billion-Dollar Brain* (1966) and *SS-GB* are marginally science-fictional, the latter being a kind of alternative history, where the Germans won World War II.

SS-GB (1978)

R	★ ★ ★ ★	I	★ ★ ★
C	★ ★	L	★ ★

DELANY, Samuel Ray (1942) Black American sf and fantasy writer and critic, Delany published his first novel at 20, but even in his earliest books (*The Jewels Of Aptor* (1962) and *The Fall Of The Towers* (1970)) we find the concerns and traits that have characterized all of his work – the recapitulation (often by characters aware of what they are doing) of mythic patterns, notably the Grail quest; the productive interfaces between a sleazily glamorous semi-criminal street world, an artistic bohemia and a slumming ruling class; emotionally intense sexual relationships movingly portrayed and often homosexual – Delany is declaredly bisexual; an optimistic viewpoint that has little to do with the success or survival of his protagonists; a strong visual sense which sometimes moves on from setting a scene to cluttering it up. These all reached their most generally accepted peak in *The Einstein Intersection* (1967), *Nova* and a small body of short

Samuel Ray Delany

stories such as the Hugo-winning novella "Time Considered as a Helix of Semi-precious Stones." Of Delany's later work, *Dhalgren* (1975) achieved major popularity, probably for its depiction of the polymorphous violent and/or sexual encounters between the inhabitants of a ruined city, and a fair measure of critical disapproval for what was described as wantonly perverse and self-indulgent experimentalism. *Triton* (1976) is a moving attempt at a Stendhalian novel of character growth, whose protagonist, Bron, changes sex in an attempt to make reparation for earlier machismo; some readers have found the length of the novel exceeds their sympathy for the hero/heroine. The episodic heroic fantasies *Tales of Neveryon* and *Neveryona* (1983) retreat somewhat from stylistic experiment but carry a considerable freight of ideological commitment and intellectual concern, attempting to extend the sensibilities of that usually dunder-headed genre by applying to it the insights of feminism, linguistics, structural anthropology and the holistic perception of economic and political organizations found in the French historian Fernand Braudel. The same concerns make Delany a difficult but often perceptive critic.

Nova (1968)

R	★	★	★	★	★	★		I	★	★	★		
C	★	★	★	★	★	★		L	★	★	★	★	★

"Time Considered as a Helix of Semi-precious Stones" (1969)

R	★	★	★	★		I	★	★	★	★
C	★	★	★			L	★	★	★	

Tales of Neveryon (1979; coll.)

R	★	★	★			I	★	★	★	★	★
C	★	★	★	★		L	★	★	★	★	

DELILLO, Don   American novelist whose fourth novel is a science fiction story, *Ratner's Star*, a fairly standard tale of communication from the stars (which turn out to be from our own far distant human past). Delillo is highly literary, but he simply cannot use genre materials and is far too flippant.

Ratner's Star (1976)

R	★	★		I	★	
C				L	★	★

DEL REY, Lester (1915) American writer, who now edits heroic fantasy novels for Ballantine books under the imprint of his own name. He wrote some good short fiction for *Astounding* during its greatest years, 1939-42, and his one important novel, *Nerves*, is expanded from a novella published then. Although he wrote a good deal in the 1950s, including several juvenile sf novels, his work of this period was mostly mediocre; he never seems to have fulfilled his early potential. *Nerves*, about an accident at a nuclear power plant, remains topical even after 40 years, although the science in the story is now way out of date.

Nerves (1956)

R	★	★	★		I	★	★	★
C	★	★	★		L	★	★	★

Police Your Planet (1956)

R	★	★		I	★	★
C	★			L	★	★

Pstalemate (1971)

R	★	★		I	★	★
C	★			L	★	★

DENT, Lester (1905-59) American author and inventor of Doc Savage (a hero utilized by Philip José Farmer (q.v.) in several books). He was a crude pulp writer who nonetheless created a powerful, adventurous figure.

The Man Of Bronze (1933)

R ★ ★ ★ ★	I ★
C ★ ★	L ★

DE QUINCEY, Thomas (1785-1859) English writer, friend of Wordsworth, author of *Confessions Of An English Opium Eater* (1856) and also of *Klosterheim* (his only novel), a tale of gothic horror which prefigures much of the more garish side of the sf field.

Klosterheim (1832)

R ★ ★ ★	I ★
C ★ ★	L ★ ★ ★

DERLETH, August (1909-71) American writer, primarily noted for his non-fantasy stories set in his home state of Wisconsin. He was a great admirer of H. P. Lovecraft (q.v.) and founded Arkham House in 1939 in order to publish Lovecraft's work. Arkham House became one of the leading publishers of weird fiction. Most of his own work was done for *Weird Tales*, but it does include a number of sf stories. Derleth was also important as an early sf anthologist. His sf is collected in *Harrigan's File* (1975)

Philip K. Dick

The Trail Of Cthulhu (1962)

R ★ ★	I ★ ★
C ★	L ★ ★

"McIlvaine's Star" (1952)

R ★ ★ ★	I ★ ★ ★
C ★	L ★

DeWEESE, (Thomas Eu)Gene (1934) American technical writer on space navigation and sf fan, who has written (solo and with Robert Coulson (q.v.)) a number of clever adventure novels, nine of them in sf. He began by writing *Man From U.N.C.L.E.* novelizations and has never quite stopped being an sf fan (two of his collaborated novels are set at sf conventions). His writing is fun but instantly forgettable.

The Wanting Factor (1980)

R ★ ★ ★	I ★
C ★	L

DIAMOND, Graham   American writer of a sado-masochistic soft-porn series which is notable mainly for its utter failure to take itself seriously; a garish potpourri of myth, power-fantasy and sword-and-sorcery. Four books exist so far in the series, which describes adventures in The Empire of the Haven.

Samarkand Dawn (1980)

R ★ ★	I
C	L

DICK, Kay (1915) English author of *They; A Sequence Of Unease*, which describes a near-future authoritarian England. Her experimental style is an interesting departure from normal sf tale-telling.

They; A Sequence Of Unease (1977)

R ★ ★ ★	I ★ ★
C ★ ★	L ★ ★ ★

DICK, Philip K(endred) (1928-82) American writer, whose death robbed the field of perhaps its first great talent. His work must be seen as a continuous whole, for themes developed in some novels are subsidiary to others, and vice versa, such that it forms a coherent world-view. His best-known novel is the Hugo Award-winning *The Man In The High Castle* (1962), where Germany and America won the War. The emphasis on things Germanic is strong throughout his highly philosophical and yet ever-amusing and entertaining work. His very first novel, *Solar Lottery*, is one of the cleverest débuts in sf, and typifies much of his work where VanVogtian adventure meets Kantian philosophy and Eastern metaphysics. Though much of his writing is clearly unrevised and was produced as a means of earning money, nonetheless even his poorest works (i.e. *Dr Futurity* (1960), *The Crack In Space* (1966)) are marked by his natural compassion and unique vision. Mars is a constant frontier setting in his work, and massive multinational corporations have usurped the power of nations. Robots of every kind suffer existential dilemmas whilst the humans wonder what is real and what false. His plotting takes much from the thriller format, though few of his books depend on gimmick endings; they can all be read again for their ideative content. Essentially, however, he will be remembered and re-read because of the deep compassionate concern of his work – his emphasis on Caritas and Empathy – particularly in classic works like *Flow My Tears, The Policeman Said* (1974), *Do Androids Dream Of Electric Sheep?* (filmed as *Blade Runner*), a concern which never neglected the darkest side of life. His later work is marked by a fascination with street-wise young girls and with the drug-oriented nature of late-1960s, early-1970s California, which he captures perfectly in his semi-mainstream novel, *A Scanner Darkly*. All of his sub-themes, however, are subsumed in a general concern with Perception; with how we might see things as they really are, and, occasionally, with why it is advisable that we should not. Absurd aliens and believable humans are juxtaposed to produce a kind of comic-book-real feel to his best work, as in *The Game-Players Of Titan* (1963), *Clans Of The Alphane Moon* (1964) and *The Three Stigmata Of Palmer Eldritch* (1964). The latter (and *Clans*) deals with forms of mental illness, and in particular with paranoid schizophrenia, a theme underlying all his

later work, and often compared to the robot-state. Dick was undoubtedly, in his range of metaphysical concerns and ideas, the foremost investigator of the philosophical, practical and human consequences of changes in reality. His too-often sloppy style hides what is the most perceptive and acute intelligence to be found in science fiction, an intelligence too overtly and un-artistically displayed in two late works, *Valis* (1980) and *The Divine Invasion* (1981). His final work, *The Transmigration Of Timothy Archer* (1982) is evidence that Dick was undergoing a further change of direction, shedding some of his latter-day didacticism.

Solar Lottery (1955; a.k.a. *World Of Chance*)

R	★	★	★	★	I	★	★	★	★
C	★	★			L	★	★	★	

Do Androids Dream Of Electric Sheep? (1968)

R	★	★	★	★	★	I	★	★	★	★	★
C	★	★	★	★		L	★	★	★	★	

Martian Time-Slip (1963; a.k.a. *All We Marsmen*)

R	★	★	★	★	★	I	★	★	★	★	★
C	★	★	★	★		L	★	★	★		

A Scanner Darkly (1977)

R	★	★	★	★	★	I	★	★	★	★
C	★	★	★	★		L	★	★	★	★

DICKINSON, Peter (1927) An eclectic English writer, Dickinson has published a mock-scholarly study of dragons (*The Flight Of Dragons*, 1979), a series of prize-winning thrillers which sometimes flirt marginally with sf (*King and Joker*, 1976) is set in an alternative present with a different Royal Family), a heavy-handed science-fictional satire on racism (*The Green Gene*, 1974) and a wide-ranging series of children's books, many of which use such sf themes as a rejection of technology, telepathy, an alien being in an abandoned mine, and the survival of prehistoric monsters. Often, as in the *Changes* trilogy, his plots are as much fantasy as sf (and *The Blue Hawk* is pure fantasy) but his use of these themes as springboards for effective story-telling rather than ends in themselves

Gordon R. Dickson

make him worth reading by any age group.

Changes (1975; coll.)

R ★ ★ ★ ★	I ★ ★
C ★ ★ ★	L ★ ★ ★

"The Gift" (1973)

R ★ ★ ★	I ★ ★
C ★ ★ ★	L ★ ★ ★

The Blue Hawk (1976)

R ★ ★ ★ ★	I ★ ★ ★
C ★ ★	L ★ ★ ★

DICKSON, Gordon R(upert) (1923) Canadian-born American sf and fantasy writer. Many of his novels are fairly routine adventure stories, principally notable for the extent to which the usual anthropocentricity of such novels and their adherence to traditionalist views of fortitude and persistence, are both deeply felt and intellectually examined. This essential seriousness often makes Dickson's work more effective than one might expect from someone with such overt limitations as a writer. He is an unadventurous writer and lacks facility, yet often surpasses his limits to write with a real power and fervour. A novel like *Time Storm*, for example, does an impressive job of conveying just how unhappy and alienated the omnicompetent cosmos-saving traditional hero is likely to be; the somewhat metaphysical universal catastrophe is displayed with clarity and visual precision. Much of Dickson's most serious effort for the last two decades has gone into the Childe cycle, 12 novels (3 contemporary, 3 historical, 6 science fiction) and linked shorter material, designed to demonstrate a postulated revolution in human sensibility between the Fifteenth Century and a future in which Earth's colonies have developed into Splinter Cultures, each embodying an aspect of human nature. The science-fictional part of this series is sometimes known as the "Dorsai" cycle, and includes the Hugo Award-winning short story, "Soldier, Ask Not" (1965), depicting the Dorsai, a Spartan-like race specially bred to be warriors. Those aspects most important to the cycle as a whole appear to be the Warrior, the Believer and the Mystic, and the shift in sensibility towards a mature individual autonomy which includes an empathic regard for the significance of others. The culmination of the cycle, *The Final Encyclopaedia*, makes all of this surprisingly coherent and non-cranky. The slightly simplistic characterizations to which Dickson is prone are effective here as human embodiments of ideas; he has made eloquent use of genre conventions to create an imposing book out of material which might have proved intransigent to a writer more sophisticatedly literary.

"*Call Him Lord*" (1966)

R ★ ★ ★ ★	I ★ ★
C ★ ★ ★	L ★ ★ ★

Time Storm (1977)

R ★ ★ ★ ★	I ★ ★ ★
C ★ ★ ★ ★	L ★ ★ ★ ★

The Final Encyclopaedia (1983)

R ★ ★ ★ ★	I ★ ★ ★ ★ ★
C ★ ★ ★ ★	L ★ ★ ★ ★

DISCH, Thomas M. (1940) American writer who has travelled extensively in Europe. He was one of the Americans who became involved with Michael Moorcock's (q.v.) *New Worlds* in the 1960s, taking advantage of its liberal policies to publish some excellent *avant garde* sf, including his bold novel *Camp Concentration*, which offers an intimate account of the experiences of a man whose intelligence is artificially boosted. Only a small fraction of his work from the 1970s was sf, and there was a long gap between his brilliant fix-up novel of the near future, *334*, and the equally fine *On Wings Of Song*. He is an exceptionally witty writer and can write with a subtle but scalding irony. In a more earnest mood, though, he is a powerful writer expert in building up tension, with a magnificent eye for environmental detail. He is one of the most accomplished stylists presently working in the sf field, and one of the best contemporary American short story writers. His images of the future are generally pessimistic, and he sometimes seems to be taking a morbid delight in watching the suffering of his characters, but he is so deft and seductive that the reader ends up sharing his *schadenfreude*.

Camp Concentration (1968)

R ★ ★ ★	I ★ ★ ★
C ★ ★ ★ ★	L ★ ★ ★

334 (1972)

R ★ ★ ★	I ★ ★ ★
C ★ ★ ★ ★	L ★ ★ ★ ★

On Wings Of Song (1980)

R ★ ★ ★ ★	I ★ ★ ★ ★
C ★ ★ ★ ★	L ★ ★ ★ ★

Thomas M. Disch

DOLINSKI, Mike (1923) American author of *Mind One* – an interesting novel which portrays what happens when a new drug produces telepathy as a side-effect.

Mind One (1972)

R ★ ★ ★	I ★ ★
C ★ ★	L ★

Stephen Donaldson

DONALDSON, Stephen (1947) American writer and creator of Thomas Covenant, the Unbeliever, a leper whose adventures are chronicled in a series of thickish fantasy novels, currently run to six volumes and with the promise of more. *Lord Foul's Bane* introduces Covenant as he is spirited into the Land – a magical world not totally unlike Tolkien's Middle Earth – where he begins a reluctant quest against the evil Lord Foul, who seeks to destroy the Land. Covenant, who is hailed as a saviour because he wears a white gold band (his wedding ring) – a symbol of power – does not believe that the Land exists and convinces himself that he cannot defeat the evil force. Finally, as Covenant witnesses the magical healing properties of the earth and air and the magic woven out of wood and stone by his followers, he utilizes his unwanted power to coerce and banish Lord Foul. Covenant's adventures continue with *The Illearth War* (1979) and *The Power That*

Preserves (1977) and with the Second Chronicles, *The Wounded Land, The One Tree* and *White Gold Weilder* (1983). In the second trilogy, Donaldson introduces Linden Avery, a disillusioned female doctor and gives Lord Foul the Sunbane, a meteorological weapon, to thwart Covenant, no longer an unbeliever.

Lord Foul's Bane (1977)

R	★	★	★	★		I	★	★	★	
C	★	★	★	★	★	L	★	★	★	★

The Wounded Land (1980)

R	★	★	★	★		I	★	★	★	★	
C	★	★	★	★	★	L	★	★	★	★	★

The One Tree (1981)

R	★	★	★	★	I	★	★	★
C	★	★	★	★	L	★	★	★

DORMAN, Sonya (1924) While she has produced only one novel, and that a juvenile, this American writer is noted for her tightly written and often metaphysical stories. One of the most sensitive writers in the field, she has a distinctive style and an unique vision of what is human. Her sf stories are all to this end – making us see just what *is* human.

Planet Patrol (1978)

R	★	★	★	I	★
C	★	★		L	★	★	★

"Cool Affection" (1974)

R	★	★	★	★	I	★	★
C	★	★		L	★	★	★

"Peek-A-Boom" (1980)

R	★	★	★	★	I	★	★
C	★	★		L	★	★	★

DOUAY, Dominique (1944) French writer. Although his work displayed a strong influence of Dick and his compatriot Jeury, Douay's first decade of publications showed him to be a strong, forceful and sensitive writer at ease in the murky areas of "inner space" and, sometimes, political fiction. Since becoming a Cabinet aide in the new French socialist government, however, his fiction has come to a sad halt.

Strates (1978)

R	★	★		I	★	★	★
C	★	★	★	L	★	★	★

La Vie Comme Une Course De CharA Voiles (1978)

R	★	★	★	I	★	★	
C	★	★	★	L	★	★	★	★

L'Impasse-Temps (1980)

R	★	★	★	★	I	★	★	★
C	★	★	★		L	★	★	★

DOYLE, Sir Arthur Conan (1859-1930) British writer, most famous for his Sherlock Holmes stories and his historical novels, but also one of the pioneers of British scientific romance. His first sf novel, *The Doings Of Raffles Haw* (1892), is very weak, and some of his other imaginative works are almost overpowered by the fascination with spiritualism which overtook him in later life, but the first two books featuring Professor Challenger – *The Lost World* and *The Poison Belt* – are classics. He was at his best when writing in a relaxed manner, exploiting his remarkable instinct for dramatic description and incident.

The Lost World (1912)

R	★	★	★	★	I	★	★	★	★
C	★	★	★	★	L	★	★	★	★

The Poison Belt (1913)

R	★	★	★	★	I	★	★	★	
C	★	★	★		L	★	★	★	★

The Maracot Deep (1929)

R	★	★	★	I	★	★
C	★	★		L	★	★

DOZOIS, Gardner (1947) American writer, who has produced some of the best crafted stories in the sf field since the mid-1970s. He is far from prolific, yet has a reputation for thoughtful and very stylish writing, which utilizes and transforms standard sf themes. His collaboration with Geo. Alec Effinger (q.v.) *Nightmare Blue* (1977), is a potboiler, but his own novel, *Strangers*, is a superbly written and highly poignant tale of the love of an Earth man for an alien woman. His fiction is partly collected in *The Visible Man* (1978).

Strangers (1978)

R ★ ★ ★ ★	I ★ ★
C ★ ★ ★	L ★ ★ ★ ★

"A Special Kind Of Morning" (1971)

R ★ ★ ★ ★ ★	I ★ ★
C ★ ★ ★	L ★ ★ ★ ★

DRAKE, David A. (1945) American writer whose work lacks imagination and has, thus far, been rather derivative. Since 1979 he has produced a stream of garish novels and short stories, many of which utilize a power-fantasy or future-war scenario. *Hammer's Slammers* (1979) displays the War theme, *The Dragon Lord* (1981), the power-fantasy.

Sky Ripper (1983)

R ★ ★ ★	I ★
C ★	L

DRENNAN, Paul   English author of a rather poor first (and only?) novel, *Wooden Centauri*, depicting a future utopia. The book has very little to recommend it.

Wooden Centauri (1975)

R ★ ★	I
C	L

DRURY, Allen (Sturat) (1918) American writer, usually of politically oriented novels. His *Come Nineveh, Come Tyre* extrapolates into the near future, to show America collapsing after Communist subversion. *The Throne Of Saturn* (1971) again has the Russians as the villains, this time attempting to foil America's first manned mission to Mars.

Come Nineveh, Come Tyre (1973)

R ★ ★ ★ ★	I ★ ★
C ★	L ★ ★

DUDINTSEV, Vladimir (1918) Russian writer of *A New Year's Tale*, a semi-mystical story of the discovery of cheap energy through relaxation. Slightly moralistic and condemned by Soviet authorities after its appearance.

A New Year's Tale (1956; trans. 1960)

R ★ ★ ★	I ★
C ★ ★	L ★ ★

DUNCAN, David (1913) Popular American author who wrote the script for a version of *The Time Machine*, and several for *Outer Limits*. Five novels appeared in the sf vein between 1949 and 1957, including *Occam's Razor*, which tells how an experiment taps another space-time continuum. Essentially a standard sf adventure, despite its ideative content.

Occam's Razor (1957)

R ★ ★ ★	I ★ ★
C ★	L ★

DUNN, Saul (1946) Pseudonym of English publisher Philip M. Dunn, whose three novels in the Steeleye saga were reputedly cobbled together by his secretaries during odd lunch hours. They certainly read as if the rumour were true, being the worst examples of space opera to be found between covers.

The Coming Of Steeleye (1976)

R	I
C	L

DUNSANY, Edward Plunkett (1878-1957) Prolific Irish writer, essayist and dramatist, whose highly wrought prose continues to exert an enormous influence over the development of style in "otherworld" fantasy. Principally consolatory, escapist fiction, his own heroic romances describe a world in which magic, defined as broadly as can be, is always about to vanish with the departing hero or the setting sun: the Spanish "Golden Age" or an oriental fabulous past, seen nostalgically but often with a wry and subtle humour. Later stories, the Jorkens series, take the insular but popular form of adventures recounted in the smoking room of a gentlemen's club.

The King Of Elfland's Daughter (1924)

R ★ ★ ★ ★ ★	I ★
C ★	L ★

DURRELL, Lawrence (1912) English novelist and poet probably best known for his *Alexandria Quartet* (completed in 1960) and for his immaculate and richly elaborate prose style. His two sf works, *Tunc* and *Nunquam* (1970), known together as *The Revolt Of Aphrodite*, describe the antics of Felix Charlock and his supercomputer Abel, which can predict the future. The science-fictional element here is used as extended metaphor in these highly sculpted and first-rate novels.

Tunc (1968)

R ★ ★ ★ ★	I ★ ★ ★ ★ ★
C ★ ★ ★	L ★ ★ ★ ★ ★

ECKERT, Alan W.   English author of *The Hab Theory*, a technical science-thriller, well written, but ultimately unsatisfying. He lacks the visionary streak necessary to become more than a fiction-making scientist.

The Hab Theory (1977)

R ★ ★ ★	I ★ ★ ★
C ★	L ★

EDDISON, (Eric Rucker) (1882-1945) An English civil servant who wrote heroic fantasy in the Grand Style, owing more to the gods and heroes of Greece and the sophisticated villains of the Renaissance than broad-thewed barbarians. Love and war, underscored by a fascinating if obscure philosophy, are his themes. His rich prose owes something to the archaism of William Morris's romances, but more, directly, to the early seventeenth century; one source perhaps for the romantic and political intrigue featured in the world of *The Worm Ouroboros* and more strongly in the related (unfinished) Zimiamvian trilogy, set in its Valhalla and twentieth-century England.

The Worm Ouroboros (1922)

R ★ ★ ★	I ★ ★ ★ ★ ★
C ★ ★ ★	L ★ ★ ★

EDMONDSON, G. C. (1922) Mexican writer José Mario Garry Ordoñez Edmondson y Cotton used this name for his sf writing. His major theme is the contact and clash of alien civilizations and races, and even in his time travel novel, *The Ship That Sailed The Time Stream*, a parody of that sub-genre, he manages to encounter any number of races in the past. His later novels are more serious and less impressive.

The Ship That Sailed The Time Stream (1965)

R ★ ★ ★ ★	I ★ ★
C ★ ★	L ★ ★

The Aluminium Man (1975)

R ★ ★ ★	I ★ ★
C ★	L ★

EDWARDS, Peter (1946) English author of *Terminus*, a post-holocaust tale of Eurafrican society with strong characterization but a slightly dubious *raison d'être*. Its adventure elements are intelligently handled.

Terminus (1976)

R ★ ★ ★ ★	I ★ ★
C ★ ★ ★	L ★ ★

EFFINGER, Geo(rge) Alec (1947) American writer, who produced four *Planet Of The Apes* books in the 1970s, but is a much better stylist than those novels allow for. He has collaborated with Gardner Dozois (q.v.) and Jack Dann (q.v.), but is best encountered through his solo novels, *What Entropy Means To Me*, a pastiche of quest stories with a high technical polish, and the muted but interesting space romance, *Those Gentle Voices* (1976). He is young enough and talented enough to be worth watching in the 1980s.

What Entropy Means To Me (1972)

R ★ ★ ★	I ★ ★
C ★ ★	L ★ ★ ★

Irrational Numbers (1976; coll.)

R ★ ★ ★ ★	I ★ ★ ★
C ★	L ★ ★ ★

EHRLICH, Max (Simon) (1909) American writer of numerous borderline sf novels in the last three decades. Some are overtly science-fictional, like *The Big Eye* (1951), a planetary collision tale. *The Edict* is an interesting overpopulation story, presented in a rather awkward manner.

The Edict (1971)

R	★	★		I	★	★
C	★			L	★	

EISENSTEIN, Phyllis (1946) American writer of both fantasy and science fiction. She seems easiest as a fantasist, as in *Sorceror's Son* (1979), a pleasant but undemanding read. Her science fiction is more awkward but perhaps more interesting and more promising. *Shadow Of Earth* is an alternative world story which allows Eisenstein to examine women's roles (the alternate world is a feudal twentieth-century American after the success of the Spanish Armada). *In The Hands Of Glory* is straightforward space opera with a strong female protagonist.

Shadow Of Earth (1979)

R	★	★	★	I	★	★
C	★	★		L	★	★

In The Hands Of Glory (1982)

R	★	★	★	I	★	★
C	★	★		L	★	

EKLUND, Gordon (1945) American writer whose work appeared in the 1970s. Despite winning a Nebula Award for his novella "If The Stars Are Gods" (subsequently rewritten at novel length with Gregory Benford (q.v.), his work is rarely that original and is occasionally badly flawed artistically. The broad range of his themes and interests makes up for this somewhat, and his best work seems to be politically oriented, such as *All Times Possible*, which depicts a left-wing American revolution. A recent series, developed from E. E. Smith's (q.v.) idea, began with *Lord Tedric* (1978), and is again rather patchy. At best his writing is both imaginative and highly intelligent, but, alas, at worst it is simply irritating, as in "Red Skins."

All Times Possible (1974)

R	★	★	★	★	I	★	★
C	★	★			L	★	★

Dance Of The Apocalypse (1976)

R	★	★	★	I	★
C	★	★		L	★

"Red Skins" (1981)

R	★	★	I
C	★		L

ELDER, Michael (1931) English writer and actor, who has written a number of standard sf novels in the 1970s, varying in range but not in achievement.

Mindslip (1976)

R	★	★	I	★
C	★		L	★

ELDERSHAW, M. Barnard (1897) Pseudonym of Australian writer Marjorie Faith Barnard. A historian, her only sf novel, *Tomorrow And Tomorrow And Tomorrow*, is a retrospective upon the Australia of the 1920s and 1930s through the eyes of a man from the future.

Tomorrow And Tomorrow And Tomorrow (1947)

R	★	★	★	I	★		
C	★	★		L	★	★	★

ELGIN, (Patricia Anne) Suzette Haden (1936) American poet and novelist, also a professor of linguistics. Her "feminist" novels in the Coyote Jones series, which began with the novella "For The Sake Of Grace" (1969), suffer from occasional structural weaknesses, but are nonetheless intelligent adventures with more than a superficial purpose. *The Communipaths* was the first of these novels, and two others, *At The Seventh Level* (1972) and *Furthest* (1971) complete this sequence. A new series, the Ozark fantasy trilogy, has been recently begun by Elgin, with *Twelve Fair Kingdoms*, a blend of fantasy and sf, again with a slight feminist purpose but with a counterbalancing readability. Her professional training and a fascination with communication informs her work.

The Communipaths (1970)

R ★ ★ ★	I ★ ★
C ★ ★	L ★ ★

Twelve Fair Kingdoms (1982)

R ★ ★ ★ ★	I ★ ★
C ★ ★ ★	L ★ ★ ★

ELLIOT, John (1918) English writer best known for his collaborations with Fred Hoyle (q.v.), *A For Andromeda* and *Andromeda Breakthrough* (1964), TV serials which were later novelized. One solo novel, *Dragon's Feast* (1970), is marginally sf, but essentially a political thriller.

A For Andromeda (1962; with Fred Hoyle)

R ★ ★ ★ ★	I ★ ★ ★
C ★	L ★

ELLIOT, Sumner Locke (1917) American writer born in Australia. Better known for his work in the mainstream, Locke produced one sf novel, *Going*, which echoes the preoccupations of his other work – escape from a mundane and ultra-suburbanized society.

Going (1975)

R ★ ★ ★	I ★
C ★ ★	L ★ ★

Harlan Ellison

ELLISON, Harlan (1934) American author, journalist, and scenarist; some sf. Ellison began making his impact in the mid-1960s with a succession of, then, highly controversial short stories. His themes – sexuality, violence, hypocrisy, alienation – reflected the social turmoil of America at that time. His aggressive, flamboyant style seemed perfectly to match that subject matter and if he has usually seemed too prolific for his own good, he has hit the target often enough to win him more Hugos (7½) and Nebulas (3) than any other writer in the field. The importance of his role in extending the traditional boundaries of sf, his influence on the work of younger luminaries, cannot be overestimated. He was the catalyst and leader of the American New Wave with his editorship of the two massive anthologies *Dangerous Visions* (1967) and *Again, Dangerous Visions* (1972), both of which won special citations from the World Science Fiction Convention. He also holds the distinction of being the only scenarist ever to win the Writers Guild of America Award three times, all for sf scripts. With the demise of the American "youth movement," and perhaps with the coming of greater age and maturity, Ellison has managed to prune the more bombastic elements from his prose style, and, though his themes and subject matter retain their shock factor, he has increasingly concentrated on more personal, often semi-autobiographical stories. He remains as much today as 18 years ago an important writer, constantly worth watching. His collections *Deathbird Stories* (1975) and *Strange Wine* (1978) are of especial note.

"I Have No Mouth And I Must Scream" (1967)

R ★ ★ ★ ★ ★	I ★ ★ ★ ★ ★
C ★ ★ ★ ★	L ★ ★ ★ ★

"Croatoan" (1975)

R ★ ★ ★ ★ ★	I ★ ★ ★ ★ ★
C ★ ★ ★ ★	L ★ ★ ★ ★ ★

"Jeffty Is Five" (1977)

R ★ ★ ★ ★ ★	I ★ ★ ★ ★ ★
C ★ ★ ★ ★	L ★ ★ ★ ★

EMSHWILLER, Carol (1921) American short story writer, whose work has been collected in *Joy In Our Cause*. She is a great experimental fantasist, ignoring the pulp stereotypes and focusing upon a poetically intense form of literature.

Joy In Our Cause (1974)

R ★ ★ ★	I ★ ★
C ★ ★	L ★ ★ ★

ENGDAHL, Sylvia (Louise) (1933) American writer of intelligent juveniles which compare with the very best in the field (LeGuin's *Earthsea*, for instance). Her *Heritage Of The Star* is an exceptional and serious work about a boy's search (and thirst) for knowledge. *The Far Side Of Evil* (1974) is far less successful but no less serious in intent. Her work compares with the best in the adult field.

Heritage Of The Star (1973; a.k.a., *This Star Shall Abide*)

R ★ ★ ★ ★	I ★ ★ ★
C ★ ★ ★	L ★ ★ ★

Enchantress From The Stars (1974)

R ★ ★ ★ ★	I ★ ★
C ★ ★	L ★ ★ ★

ENGLAND, George Allan (1877-1936) American writer and rival of Edgar Rice Burroughs (q.v.), whose work mainly pre-dates the establishment of the pulp magazines in 1926. He is best known for the five volumes of *Darkness And Dawn*, a post-holocaust, last-man-and-last-woman story.

Darkness And Dawn (1914)

R ★ ★	I ★ ★
C ★ ★	L ★

ENGLAND, James   English writer whose one sf novel, *The Measured Caverns*, is a rather tired re-hash of the "enclosed environment" story, with Sanctuary and Outside.

The Measured Caverns (1978)

R ★ ★	I ★
C ★	L ★

ENSTROM, Robert   American writer whose work within the genre is uninspired and in the tradition of E.E. "Doc" Smith, pure and hackneyed space opera.

Encounter Program (1977)

R ★	I
C	L

ERDMAN, Paul E. (1932) American novelist and specialist on economics and politics. His best-selling *The Crash of '79* uses basic science-fictional techniques (a historical retrospective from 1984) as a means of expressing a what-if situation.

The Crash of '79 (1976)

R ★ ★ ★ ★	I ★ ★ ★
C ★ ★	L ★ ★

ESHBACH, Lloyd Arthur (1910) American writer and publisher, whose Fantasy Press was influential in establishing science fiction as a book-length genre. His own work, which is entirely composed of short fiction, adds little to the pulp material of the 1930s, 1940s and early 1950s.

The Tyrant Of Time (1955; coll.)

R ★ ★	I ★
C ★	L

EVANS, Christopher (1951) Welsh writer whose two sf novels show a rapid movement away from genre concerns. *Capella's Golden Eyes* (1980) deals with a cut-off colony world and its enigmatic aliens. *The Insider* is a novel of internalization and alienation, set firmly on earth and in a contemporary framework – more like Camus than Clarke.

The Insider (1981)

R ★ ★ ★	I ★ ★ ★
C ★ ★ ★	L ★ ★ ★

EVANS, E(dward) Everett (1893-1958) American writer of macabre fantasy and supernatural tales, but most of whose work is not particularly memorable. He published mainly in the 1950s and has not often been reprinted.

Man Of Many Minds (1953)

R ★ ★	I ★ ★
C ★	L ★

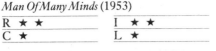

FAIRMAN, Paul W. (1916-77) American writer whose competent but uninspired novels (some of them novelizations) appeared mainly in the 1960s. Whatever theme he tackles – be it over-mechanization, alien invasion or time travel – he adds little that is new. Some of his work was written in collaboration with and under the name of Lester Del Rey (q.v.). Some are overtly juveniles.

I, The Machine (1968)

R ★ ★	I
C ★	L ★

The Forgetful Robot (1970)

R ★	I
C	L ★

FANTHORPE, R. Lionel (1935) Phenomenal English writer who produced more than 100 novels and many hundreds of short stories under his own name and many pseudonyms for Badger Books between 1957 and 1965. At his height he was writing (or rather dictating) two per week. Many of them are astonishingly awful, but his sheer tirelessness attracts admiration. His intelligence is not often evident in the stories but his enthusiasm is, and connoisseurs hunt through them for private jokes and displays of eccentric virtuosity. In recent years he founded his own publishing company to issue *The Black Lion*, a Burroughsian (q.v.) fantasy written in collaboration with his wife Patricia.

Android (1962; as Karl Zeigfried)

R ★	I
C	L

The Black Lion (1979)

R ★ ★	I ★
C ★	L ★

FARJEON, J(oseph) Jefferson (1883-1955) English author of one sf novel, a rather tired last-man story, told through his diaries to aliens who land on a dead earth.

Death Of A World (1948)

R ★ ★	I ★
C ★	L ★

FARLEY, Ralph Milne (1887-1963) American writer, mainly active in the pre-war magazines. His most famous series is *The Radio Man* (1924; book form, 1948), and not much of his Burroughsian (q.v.) science fantasy is readable today. His Venus is as garishly unfeasible and impossible as Burroughs's Mars, but less powerful in its conception.

The Radio Beasts (1925/1964)

R ★	I ★
C ★	L ★

FARMER, Philip José (1918) Prolific American writer of 60 books and countless short stories, written mostly since the 1950s after being awarded a Hugo in 1953

Philip José Farmer

for "Most Promising New Author." The accolade came as a response to his 1952 novella "The Lovers," which depicted a relationship between a human male and an alien female in a strong sexually explicit narrative. Farmer returned to the theme of sex in sf with the novels *Flesh* (1960), *Image Of The Beast* and *Blown* (1968), his writing bordering almost on the pornographic. In *A Feast Unknown* (1969), the pornographic element is heightened further as the two protagonists, Lord Grandrith (supposedly Tarzan) and Doc Caliban (supposedly Doc Savage), engage in sado-masochistic duels. Farmer would later write fictional biographies of Tarzan and Doc Savage. Throughout his fiction the adventure story is prevalent but he has been prone to verbosity, especially with his Riverworld and Tier World series. *To Your Scattered Bodies Go* and *The Fabulous Riverboat* (1971) began the award-winning Riverworld concept, but as Farmer eventually completed the series with *The Dark Design* (1977) and *The Magic Labyrinth* (1978), it was evident that the idea of the entire human race being resurrected along the banks of a river, endlessly circling a world, and the exploits of numerous famous historical characters seeking to discover the secret of the planet clearly bored him. The same fault occurs in the otherwise excellent Tier World novels – *Maker Of Universes* (1965), *The Gates Of Creation* (1966), *A Private Cosmos* (1968), *Behind The Walls Of Terra* (1970) and *The Lavalite World* (1977), the last novel a disappointing conclusion to the adventures of Kickaha-Wolff in the artificially created pocket universes, constructed by immortal humans, and populated with exotic aliens. Farmer uses classical folk legend and history to blend the novels into entertaining fantasy novels. Where he has concentrated on fundamental sf themes Farmer has emerged as one of the best writers in the field, with many excellent novels, although his best work seems to be from his early years. In particular *A Woman A Day* 1960; a.k.a. *Timestop*), *The Gate Of Time* (1966), *Night Of Light* (1966), *Traitor To The Living* (1973) and the collection *Strange Relations* (1960) stand out where he has attempted conventional sf ideas.

"The Lovers" (1952)

R ★ ★ ★	I ★ ★ ★ ★
C ★ ★ ★ ★	L ★ ★ ★ ★ ★

Image Of The Beast (1968)

R ★ ★ ★ ★	I ★ ★ ★ ★
C ★ ★ ★	L ★ ★ ★ ★

To Your Scattered Bodies Go (1971)

R ★ ★ ★ ★ ★	I ★ ★ ★ ★ ★
C ★ ★ ★ ★ ★	L ★ ★ ★ ★ ★

FARREN, Mick (1943) English writer and one time member of the rock group, The Deviants. His surreal, rock-oriented novels, and in particular his trilogy, *The Quest Of The DNA Cowboys* (1976), *Synaptic Manhunt* (1976) and *The Neural Atrocity* (1977), are best described, perhaps, as hippy-gothic. He is also known as a commentator on the genre.

The Texts Of The Festival (1973)

R ★ ★ ★ ★	I ★ ★ ★
C ★ ★	L ★ ★

Mick Farren

FAST, Howard (Melvin) (1914) Prolific American writer, whose contribution to the sf field has been limited both in quality and quantity. He has written sf since 1932, but only sporadically. His stories are workmanlike but unimpressive, and, at their worst, trite.

The Hunter And The Trap (1967)

R ★ ★	I ★
C ★	L ★

A Touch Of Infinity (1973; coll.)

R ★	I
C	L

FAST, Jonathan (David) (1948) American writer whose work is fast-paced and humorous but with an underlying serious intent. His two novels in the sf field are evidence of a playful attitude towards the genre which suggest he will never write an important work.

The Secrets Of Synchronicity (1977)

R ★ ★ ★	I ★
C ★ ★	L ★

FAWCETT, Edgar (1847-1904) American writer, mostly noted for his realistic novels, who produced a number of what he called "realistic romances" between 1888 and 1895. These are close in spirit to Wells's scientific romances, and include *Solarion*, a story of a dog with artificially enhanced intelligence, and *The Ghost Of Guy Thyrle*, an impressive cosmic voyage story. The style of the novels is artificial and somewhat florid, but they provide interesting accounts of the war of ideas between science and religion. Fawcett was heavily influenced by Herbert Spencer and the Positivists, but wondered whether moral decadence might follow the decline of religious faith. His works should be reprinted, if only out of academic interest.

Solarion (1889)

R ★ ★ ★	I ★ ★ ★ ★
C ★ ★ ★	L ★ ★ ★

The Romance Of Two Brothers (1891)

R ★ ★ ★	I ★ ★ ★
C ★	L ★ ★

The Ghost Of Guy Thyrle (1895)

R ★ ★ ★	I ★ ★ ★ ★
C ★ ★	L ★ ★ ★

FEARN, John Russell (1908-60) English writer who used many pseudonyms, especially for the paperback novels which he produced very prolifically in the early 1950s. He did a good deal of work for the American sf pulps in the 1930s, but his greatest success was the long series of stories he wrote for the *Toronto Star Weekly*, featuring a superwoman called the Golden Amazon. His style is frankly abysmal, but there is a fervid excitement in his work which can be quite effective. In the guise of his most familiar pseudonym he edited the short-lived juvenile sf magazine *Vargo Statten's Science Fiction Magazine.*

The Intelligence Gigantic (1943)

R ★ ★	I ★
C	L

The Golden Amazon (1944)

R ★ ★	I ★
C	L

The Grand Illusion (1953)

R ★ ★	I ★
C ★	L ★

FELICE, Cynthia American writer, whose *Eclipses* is stronger for its characterization than for its sf elements, telling of Serensunar, a colony planet which has suddenly to accommodate refugees from a troubled Earth. There is an earlier novel, *Godsfire* (1978).

Eclipses (1983)

R ★ ★ ★ ★	I ★
C ★ ★ ★	L ★ ★

FINGAL, Marc English writer whose first novel, *Memory Of Tomorrow*, a delightful if not unique work, was self-published. Its mixture of contemporary English setting and alien intrusion is almost traditional.

Memory Of Tomorrow (1982)

R ★ ★ ★	I ★
C ★ ★	L ★ ★

FINNEY, Charles G(randison) (1905) American writer, famous for his Dr Lao works, which, in their strange mixture of fantasy and metaphysics have exerted great influence on the genre, and in particular upon Ray Bradbury (q.v.).

The Circus Of Dr Lao (1935)

R	★ ★ ★	I	★ ★ ★
C	★ ★	L	★ ★ ★

FINNEY, Jack (1911) American author whose work is stamped with a strong escapist quality. His disaffection with contemporary society and his wistful longing for another time, or a *different* now, is deeply poetic, and even his most garish work, *The Body Snatchers* (filmed as *Invasion Of The Body Snatchers*) is not so much an alien invasion story as a statement of Finney's sense of the growing inhumanity in us. The associated theme is time travel into a more perfect past.

The Body Snatchers (1955)

R	★ ★ ★ ★	I	★ ★ ★
C	★ ★	L	★ ★

Time And Again (1970)

R	★ ★ ★ ★	I	★ ★
C	★ ★	L	★ ★ ★

FISCHMAN, Bernard American writer of the flabby and over-sentimentalized borderline sf novel, *The Man Who Rode His 10-Speed Bicycle To The Moon*, a wish-fulfilment fantasy for ageing executives.

The Man Who Rode His 10-Speed Bicycle To The Moon (1979)

R	★ ★	I	
C	★	L	★

FISK, Nicholas (1923) English children's writer of predominantly, but not exclusively, sf. His books are firmly geared to the modern world although they frequently display a jaundiced view of what it might become. He writes for the bright pre-teen or young teenager; of mysterious invasions (*Trillions*, 1971 and *Grinny*), or drab futures in which sparks of individuality splutter fitfully, contrasted against a more "authentic" past (*Time Trap, A Rag, A Bone And A Hank Of Hair*, 1980). In the delight-ful *Wheelie In The Stars*, teenagers fight boredom on a distant planet by rebuilding a motorbike. Fisk's novels are higher-than-normal quality sf for an age group traditionally ill-served by the genre.

Grinny (1973)

R	★ ★ ★ ★	I	★ ★
C	★ ★	L	★ ★ ★

Time Trap (1976)

R	★ ★ ★	I	★
C	★ ★	L	★ ★

Wheelie In The Stars (1976)

R	★ ★ ★ ★	I	★ ★ ★
C	★ ★	L	★ ★ ★

FITZGIBBON, (Robert Louis) Constantine (1919) Irish writer (born in America) whose sf novels have a strong political flavour to them. *The Iron Hoop* describes a fortified city in World War III, while *The Golden Age*, a much more recent work, is almost mythical in its construction, with a divided world and the four Horsemen loose.

The Iron Hoop (1949)

R	★ ★ ★	I	★ ★
C	★	L	★ ★

The Golden Age (1975)

R	★ ★ ★	I	★ ★ ★
C	★ ★	L	★ ★

FLAMMARION, Camille (1842-1925) French astronomer and writer who utilized fiction to imaginatively convey his speculative ideas. His major works, published in France throughout the late nineteenth century, were translated in the 1890s and found a wide audience. His imagination covered most of the themes which are now recognized as science-fictional, and *Urania* (1890; three stories) and *Omega: The Last Days Of The World* were great works of scientific popularization (more so, perhaps, than those of Wells (q.v.) and Verne (q.v.)).

Omega: The Last Days Of The World (1894)

R	★ ★ ★	I	★ ★
C	★	L	★ ★

FLEMING, Ian (Lancaster) (1908-64) English writer whose James Bond series utilizes a wide range of sf techniques and gimmickry. Whilst many of these now seem extremely dated, Fleming's mixture of thriller and tehnological gadgetry has created a best-selling borderline between the two genres. His only overtly science-fictional novel is *Moonraker*.

Moonraker (1955)

R ★ ★ ★	I ★ ★ ★
C ★ ★	L ★ ★

FONTENAY, Charles L(ouis) (1917) Brazilian-born American writer and journalist, who wrote many stories for *If* magazine in the late 1950s. His intelligent variations on standard sf themes are still eminently readable. *Twice Upon A Time*, *Rebels Of The Red Planet* (1961) and *The Day The Oceans Overflowed* (1964) are routine sf adventures.

Twice Upon A Time (1958)

R ★ ★ ★ ★	I ★ ★
C ★ ★	L ★

"The Heart's Long Wait" (1957)

R ★ ★ ★ ★	I ★ ★
C ★ ★ ★	L ★ ★

FORD, John M. American writer, whose *The Princes Of The Air* is a fairly standard space adventure, pirates, empires, space-battles and all – one of a spate of high-action adventures coming out in the wake of *Star Wars*.

The Princes Of The Air (1982)

R ★ ★ ★	I
C ★	L ★

FORSTCHEN, William R. American writer, whose *Ice Prophet* is a rather tiresome story about a future Earth which is frozen over. Like Coney's *Winter's Children*, it shows a more savage world where survival is all but it is never vivid.

Ice Prophet (1983)

R ★ ★	I ★
C ★	L ★

FORSTER, E(dwin) M(organ) (1879-1970) English writer whose reputation as a literary figure is unquestioned. Much of his shorter fiction touched upon science-fictional themes, sometimes overtly, as in "The Machine Stops," which remains one of the most forceful condemnations of machine progress and social over-organization. Other of his works are delightful fantasies where the mundane and the fantastic sit side by side.

"The Machine Stops" (1909)

R ★ ★ ★ ★	I ★ ★ ★
C ★	L ★ ★ ★

Collected Short Stories (1947)

R ★ ★ ★	I ★ ★ ★
C ★ ★	L ★ ★ ★

FORWARD, Robert L. American writer whose sf debut, *Dragon's Egg*, about the education and transcendance of an alien race, is an ambitious but flawed work. Its ability to fascinate despite its lack of craft is evidence that, with time, Forward could become an important writer within the genre.

Dragon's Egg (1980)

R ★ ★ ★	I ★ ★ ★
C ★	L ★ ★

FOSTER, Alan Dean (1946) American writer who has written a number of film novelizations, including *Dark Star* (1974), *Alien* (1979), *The Black Hole* (1979) and several Star Trek books. His own works can be sharply divided between those novels that fall into his University of the Commonwealth series, which are action-adventure stories, and his shorter fiction, which presents Foster's more serious and personal statements. Four of the connected "Commonwealth" novels deal with the exploits of Philip Lynx, or Flinx, a telepathic youngster in search of his origins. These works, such as *Tar-Aiym Krang* (1972) and *The End Of The Matter* (1977) are good, intelligent adventures, highly colourful and reminiscent in some ways of Poul Anderson (q.v.). He represents sf's modern mainstream.

Icerigger (1974)

R	★ ★ ★ ★	I	★ ★
C	★ ★ ★	L	★ ★

Splinter Of The Mind's Eye (1978)

R	★ ★ ★ ★	I	★ ★
C	★ ★	L	★ ★

The Man Who Used The Universe (1983)

R	★ ★ ★ ★	I	★ ★ ★
C	★	L	★ ★

FOSTER, M(ichael) A(nthony) (1939) American writer, whose four sf novels so far published are all to do with genetic manipulation. The first two were about the "1er," a race of genetically created super-humans. There is much in common with Frank Herbert's *Dosadi Experiment* (q.v.) in these stories, *The Gameplayers Of Zan* (1977) and *The Warriors Of Dawn* (1975). Something about the structure of these books is unsatisfactory, but in the later pair of genetic novels, about the morphodites (shape-changers) there is a marked improvement in craft. These are essentially space operas with a semi-erudite flavouring.

Transformer (1983)

R	★ ★ ★	I	★ ★
C	★ ★	L	★ ★

FOX, Gardner F(rancis) (1911) American writer whose comic book work has undoubtedly coloured his science fiction. Prolific in several genres, his sf, most of it published in the 1960s, is formularistic and often trite adventure. His effects are Van Vogtian in all but imaginative potency.

The Arsenal Of Miracles (1964)

R	★ ★ ★ ★	I	★
C	★	L	★

FRANCE, Anatole (1844-1950) Nobel prize-winning author of the classic fantasy *The Revolt Of The Angels*, in which a free-thinking fallen angel tries to interest his fellows in a new rebellion. *The White Stone*, which includes a vision of the future, is a brilliant philosophical novel about the difficulties besetting would-be prophets.

The White Stone (1905)

R	★ ★ ★	I	★ ★ ★ ★
C	★ ★	L	★ ★ ★ ★

The Revolt Of The Angels (1914)

R	★ ★ ★ ★	I	★ ★ ★ ★
C	★ ★ ★ ★	L	★ ★ ★ ★ ★

FRANCIS, Richard   English writer, whose one sf novel, *Blackpool Vanishes*, is a curious and humorous mystery which is both social satire and a parody of the sf genre's tropes.

Blackpool Vanishes (1979)

R	★ ★ ★ ★	I	★ ★
C	★ ★	L	★ ★ ★

FRANK, Pat (1907-64) Pseudonym of American writer Harry Hart. Three science fiction novels appeared from him between 1946 and 1959, mostly concerned with the effects of atomic war (he also wrote the non-fiction book, *How To Survive The H-Bomb, And Why* (1962)).

Mr. Adam (1946)

R	★ ★ ★	I	★
C	★	L	★

Alas, Babylon (1959)

R	★ ★	I	★ ★
C	★	L	★

FRANKE, Herbert W. (1927) Austrian author, and the foremost German-language sf writer. Not all of his work has yet been translated, but it seems that his talent is equal to the best of the British and American writers. *The Orchid Cage* (1961; trans. 1973) is a deeply considered work about an alien planet which changes the humans who explore it. *The Mind Net* (1961; trans. 1974) is less dry in tone and suggests a further side to this writer. Franke teaches cybernetics aesthetics at the University of Munich.

Zone Null (1970; trans. 1974)

R	★ ★ ★	I	★ ★ ★
C	★ ★	L	★ ★

FRANSON, Robert Wilfred American writer whose *The Shadow Of The Ship* is an entertaining and rich alternate universe story; much more than a run-of-the-mill space adventure.

The Shadow Of The Ship (1983)

R	★ ★ ★ ★	I	★ ★
C	★ ★	L	★ ★

FRAYNE, Michael (1933) English writer of thoughtful satiric books which are overtly science-fictional more in their devices than in their themes. *A Very Private Life* is perhaps his most interesting sf work, a stimulating, almost philosphical book which is essentially a dystopian tale. *The Tin Men* (1965) and *Sweet Dreams* (1973) are also of interest.

A Very Private Life (1968)

R	★ ★ ★ ★	I	★ ★ ★
C	★ ★	L	★ ★

FREEDMAN, Nancy (1920) American writer whose novel, *Joshua Son Of None* is a life of the clone of John F. Kennedy.

Joshua Son Of None (1973)

R	★ ★ ★	I	★
C	★ ★	L	★ ★

FRIEDBERG, Gertrude (1908) American writer known for her excellent and sometimes mesmerizing sf novel, *The Revolving Boy*, which chronicles the life of a super-normal boy, born in free fall, who has the ability to pick up signals and communications from an alien civilization.

The Revolving Boy (1966)

R	★ ★ ★ ★	I	★ ★ ★
C	★ ★ ★	L	★ ★ ★

FYFE, H(orace) B(rowne) (1918) American short story writer whose one sf novel, *D-99*, is an alien-human clash of racial "personalities," competently told. His shorter work is quite varied in theme but never in its quality. His series of stories about the Bureau of Slick Tricks is amusing and compassionate, and includes the novel.

D-99 (1962)

R	★ ★ ★	I	★
C	★ ★	L	★ ★

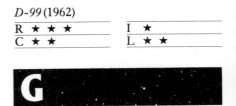

GALLICO, Paul (William) (1897-1976) American writer, two of whose novels are borderline sf. *The Snow Goose* (1941) prefigures other, later animal fantasy novels, while *The Foolish Immortals* is the story of a youth who remains eternally young.

The Foolish Immortals (1953)

R	★ ★ ★	I	★
C	★ ★	L	★ ★ ★

GALLUN, Raymond Z. (1911) American writer who wrote a good deal for the pulp magazines in the 1930s and produced occasional pieces thereafter. When most stories of human contact with aliens were lurid tales of interplanetary war Gallun stood out as an advocate of tolerance and understanding. His fiction is sometimes awkward but always lively and occasionally striking. His only recent novel, *The Eden Cycle*, is an intelligent and sensitive story of immortality which should have attracted more attention.

"Old Faithful" (1934)

R	★ ★ ★	I	★ ★ ★
C	★	L	★

The Eden Cycle (1974)

R	★ ★ ★	I	★ ★ ★
C	★ ★ ★	L	★ ★ ★

GALOUYE, Daniel F(rancis) (1920-76) American writer and journalist, whose work mainly appeared in the sf magazines in the 1950s and early 1960s. He is best known for *Dark Universe* – a post-holocaust tale with a difference; the survivors live like moles in an underground culture. But while all of his novels are ingenious and well-crafted, none of them are an improvement on *Dark Universe*. *Simulacron-3* is perhaps Galouye's most original work, hinging upon the discovery that the world is only a mathematical model and not a true reality: an experiment. Galouye can be compared to Dick (q.v.) in this respect – that his tales construct and question alternative but credible realities. Unlike Dick he creates no memorable characters and his humour and compassion are not immediately evident.

Dark Universe (1961)

| R ★ ★ ★ ★ | I ★ ★ ★ |
| C ★ ★ | L ★ ★ ★ |

Lords Of The Psychon (1963)

| R ★ ★ ★ ★ | I ★ ★ |
| C ★ ★ | L ★ ★ |

Simulacron-3 (1964, a.k.a. *Counterfield World)*

| R ★ ★ ★ ★ | I ★ ★ ★ |
| C ★ | L ★ ★ |

GARDNER, John (Champlin) (1933-82) American author whose work is only marginally science-fictional. He is better known as a poet and mainstream writer, but his *Grendel* is an excellent work of imaginative reconstruction, telling the Beowulf myth from the monster's viewpoint.

Grendel (1971)

| R ★ ★ ★ ★ ★ | I ★ ★ ★ |
| C ★ ★ | L ★ ★ ★ ★ |

GARNER, Alan (1934) English novelist, dramatist and poet who, confining his attention in space, primarily, to his home village in Cheshire, has developed the most formidable assault on time – personal, generational, historical, cosmic – of any contemporary fantasist. For Garner, correspondences and echoes in history are identities; myths struggle out at each age, no matter what material they have to work with. Garner's element is earth, his prose like stone carving, dense, strong, inflexible. It is inexplicable that such an elliptic, concentrated style would have found its main market among juvenile readers, except for Garner's choice of adolescent characters, whose impulses and yearnings have not yet suffered the muting of maturity.

Alan Garner

The Owl Service (1967)

| R ★ ★ ★ | I ★ ★ ★ |
| C ★ ★ ★ ★ ★ | L ★ ★ ★ ★ |

Red Shift (1973)

| R ★ ★ | I ★ ★ ★ |
| C ★ ★ ★ ★ ★ | L ★ ★ ★ ★ ★ |

"The Stone Book" (1976)

| R ★ ★ ★ | I ★ ★ ★ |
| C ★ ★ ★ ★ | L ★ ★ ★ ★ |

GARNETT, David S. (1947) English writer of adventure novels within the sf medium, beginning with *Mirror In The Sky* (1969). Several novels were published in the early 1970s, but since then his output has dropped considerably. Recent shorter work has shown evidence of considerable potential.

The Forgotten Dimension (1975)

| R ★ ★ ★ | I ★ ★ |
| C ★ ★ ★ | L ★ ★ |

GARRETT, Randall (1927) American writer, prolific throughout the 1950s, with more than 100 short stories and a handful of novels (some with Robert Silverberg (q.v.) as Robert Randall, and some with Laurence M. Janifer (q.v.) as Mark

Phillips). It is difficult to isolate Garrett's main concerns because his work is so wide-ranging, being written for so many different markets under different pseudonyms. Despite his output, the standard of his work is generally high and has grown better over the years. His recent Lord Darcy series, set in an alternative twentieth century where Magic works are a blend of mystery thriller and science fantasy. *Too Many Magicians* is the major work in the series, but see also "The Eyes Have It" (1964). His "psi" stories and his space operas have less to recommend them, but are nonetheless good genre fiction.

The Shrouded Planet (1957; with Robert Silverberg as Robert Randall)

R ★ ★ ★	I ★ ★
C ★	L ★ ★

Too Many Magicians (1967)

R ★ ★ ★ ★	I ★ ★ ★
C ★ ★	L ★ ★ ★

GARY, Romain (1914) Pseudonym of French writer Romain Kacewgari, much respected for his mainstream fiction. His fascination with Nazi atrocities is evident in several of his works, where he utilizes a transference device, such that victim becomes torturer, as in *On A Dark Night* (1949). An early novel, *Tulipe* (1946), describes the world taken over by the blacks, while the fairly recent *The Gasp* is almost pure sf.

The Gasp (1973)

R ★ ★ ★ ★	I ★ ★
C ★ ★	L ★ ★ ★ ★

GASKELL, Jane (1941) English writer who, after a precocious fairy tale début at the age of 16 with *Strange Evil*, soon established herself – long before the genre was in vogue – as a master of heroic fantasy with her Atlantean trilogy, full of barbarians, unclad princesses and sorcery (*The Serpent*, *Atlan* and *The City*). Her later work became more erotic but topheavy with unnecessary symbolism and she is now partly forgotten, not having published any new novel in almost a decade.

Strange Evil (1957)

R ★ ★ ★	I ★ ★
C ★ ★	L ★ ★

The Serpent (1963), *Atlan* (1965) and *The City* (1966)

R ★ ★ ★ ★	I ★ ★ ★
C ★ ★ ★	L ★ ★

Some Summer Lands (1977)

R ★ ★ ★	I ★ ★
C ★ ★ ★	L ★ ★ ★

GAWRON, Jean Mark   American writer, whose two stylish and experimental novels have both had science-fictional themes and settings. *An Apology For Rain* is a quest through a surreal landscape, a post-war America. *Algorithm* (1978) is a rich ambiguous work, where algorithm becomes a way of thought.

An Apology For Rain (1974)

R ★ ★	I ★ ★ ★
C ★	L ★ ★ ★

GENTLE, Mary (1956) English author, whose *Golden Witchbreed* is a sensitively written first novel, describing the exploits of an envoy to an ancient alien civilization.

Golden Witchbreed (1983)

R ★ ★ ★	I ★ ★
C ★ ★ ★	L ★ ★

GENTRY, Curt (1931) American writer, whose single sf work is *The Last Days Of The Late, Great State Of California*, a pseudo-historical account of the San Andreas fault disaster.

The Last Days Of The Late, Great State Of California (1968)

R ★ ★	I ★
C ★ ★	L ★

GEORGE, Peter (Bryan) (1924-66) English writer, whose novel, *Two Hours To Doom*, shows the lunacy leading up to nuclear war and was later filmed as *Dr Strangelove: Or, How I Learned To Stop Worrying And Love The Bomb*. Another novel, *Commander-1* (1965) is, aptly enough, a post-holocaust tale.

Two Hours To Doom (1958; a.k.a. *Red Alert*; re-written as *Dr Strangelove*)

R ★ ★ ★	I ★
C ★ ★	L ★ ★

GERNSBACK, Hugo (1884-1967)

American writer best known as the founder of *Amazing Stories* in 1926, the first proper magazine of "Scientifiction." His own writing is instantly forgettable, ultra-melodramatic and actually worse than most of the pulp fiction he published.

Ralph 124C41 + : A Romance Of The Year 1660 (1925)

R	I ★
C	L

GERROLD, David (1944) Pseudonym of

American writer Jerrold David Friedman. His work seems more firmly anchored in the 1950s than in contemporary genre concerns. The influence of Asimov (q.v.), Bradbury (q.v.), Clarke (q.v.) and Heinlein (q.v.) is strong in his work, and whilst he has created little that is unique, he does utilize old themes in an inventive manner. *When Harlie Was One* is about a super-intelligent computer; *The Man Who Folded Himself* is a clever time-paradox tale with an updated homosexuality theme; *Deathbeast* (1978) is a rather poor tale of hunters going back in time 100 million years.

When Harlie Was One (1972)

R ★ ★ ★	I ★ ★
C ★	L ★ ★

The Man Who Folded Himself (1973)

R ★ ★ ★ ★	I ★ ★ ★
C ★ ★	L ★ ★

A Matter For Men (1983; Volume 1 of *The War Against The Chtorr*)

R ★ ★ ★ ★	I ★
C ★ ★	L ★ ★

GESTON, Mark S(ymington) (1946)

American writer who has yet to fulfil the promise of his first novel, *Lords Of The*

Hugo Gernsback

Starship. All of his novels depict far-future Earth involved in galactic warfare. The dream-like texture of his works is attractive and has, thus far, received less critical acclaim than it deserves.

Lords Of The Starship (1967)

R ★ ★ ★ ★	I ★ ★
C ★ ★ ★	L ★ ★ ★

The Day Star (1972)

R ★ ★ ★	I ★ ★
C ★ ★	L ★ ★

GIBSON, Colin   New Zealand writer,

whose *The Pepper Leaf* is a near future survivalist tale.

The Pepper Leaf (1971)

R ★ ★	I ★ ★
C ★	L ★ ★

GIESY, J(ohn) U(lrich) (1877-1947)

American writer, most of whose work appeared between 1910 and 1924 in the pulp magazines (especially *Argosy* and *All-Story Weekly*). Four of his longer serials were published as novels in the 1960s. The garish imaginative streak in his work is definitely Burroughsian (q.v.), but memorable all the same.

Palos Of The Dog Star Pack (1918/1965)

R ★ ★ ★	I ★ ★
C ★	L ★

GILBERT, Stephen (1912) English writer of *Ratman's Notebooks*, later filmed as *Willard*; more a contemporary horror story than sf.

Ratman's Notebooks (1968; a.k.a. *Willard*)

R ★ ★ ★ ★	I ★
C ★ ★ ★	L ★ ★

GLOAG, John (1896) English writer, an expert in the field of architecture and the history of furniture. Between 1932 and 1944 he produced a sequence of excellent scientific romances, all bitterly critical of contemporary trends which seemed likely to lead Europe into a new and catastrophic Great War. He stopped writing sf when his fears came true. *Tomorrow's Yesterday* is a brilliant satire in which a species of sapient cats review the history of the humans they have replaced. *Winter's Youth* is a scathing political satire in which members of an incompetent government experiment with rejuvenation. Gloag was one of the outstanding sf writers of the 1930s and his books ought to be reprinted.

Tomorrow's Yesterday (1932)

R ★ ★ ★ ★	I ★ ★ ★ ★
C ★ ★	L ★ ★ ★ ★

The New Pleasure (1933)

R ★ ★ ★ ★	I ★ ★ ★ ★
C ★ ★ ★	L ★ ★ ★ ★

Winter's Youth (1934)

R ★ ★ ★ ★	I ★ ★ ★ ★
C ★ ★ ★ ★	L ★ ★ ★ ★ ★

GOBLE, Lou   American author of *The Kalevide*, an unusual fantasy, based on the Estonian national epic, the *Kalevipoeg*. It is a stirring folk epic which borrows little from sword-and-sorcery or the modern clichés of fantasy. A pure strain.

The Kalevide (1983)

R ★ ★ ★ ★ ★	I ★ ★
C ★ ★	L ★ ★ ★

GODWIN, Tom (1915) American writer famous for "The Cold Equations," one of the genre's classic short stories, where a stowaway girl has to be jettisoned to save a spacecraft. It is typical of Godwin's *oeuvre*, in which psychodrama and cold scientific fact are interlaced, simply but skilfully.

Beyond Another Sun (1971)

R ★ ★ ★	I ★ ★
C ★ ★	L ★ ★

"The Cold Equations" (1954)

R ★ ★ ★ ★ ★	I ★ ★ ★ ★ ★
C ★ ★	L ★ ★ ★

GOGOL, Nikolay (1809-52) Russian writer whose stories contain elements of the fantastic and the absurd. "The Nose" is a brilliant and hilarious tale of a man who has his nose stolen and goes in search of it. Other works, like *Taras Bulba* (1833) and *Dead Souls* (1842) are semi-historical novels with a strong mystical element. His most memorable tale, however, is "Diary Of A Madman," – the classic hilarious study of the illogic of insanity. Whilst not overtly sf, Gogol's stories prefigure much that has since appeared in the genre.

"The Nose" (1833)

R ★ ★ ★ ★ ★	I ★ ★ ★
C ★ ★	L ★ ★ ★ ★

"Diary Of A Madman" (1834)

R ★ ★ ★ ★ ★	I ★ ★ ★ ★ ★
C ★ ★	L ★ ★ ★ ★

GOLD, H(orace) L(eonard) (1914) American writer, best known for his editorship of *Galaxy Science Fiction*, one of the most innovative of magazines of the 1950s. His own work is collected in *The Old Die Rich*, witty entertainments which are evidence of Gold's sharp and perceptive intelligence.

The Old Die Rich And Other Science Fiction Stories (1955)

R ★ ★ ★	I ★ ★
C ★	L ★ ★

GOLDIN, Stephen (1947) American writer who, since his first novel in 1975, has become one of the most prolific writers in the genre. He has continued "Doc"

Smith's (q.v.) space opera, the Family d'Alembert, very much in Smith's fast-action pulp vein. His own work is mainly intelligent adventure with occasional satiric and humorous pieces. Some of his stories achieve a remarkable poignancy, and "The Last Ghost" (1971) was runner-up for a Nebula award. There is an emphasis upon optimistic, up-beat endings in his novels (not so in his shorter fiction) which seems a response to commercial pressures in part, yet, on examination, proves to be Goldin's philosophy of coming through.

Imperial Stars (1976; part of Family d'Alembert series)

R ★ ★ ★	I ★
C ★	L ★

The Eternity Brigade (1980)

R ★ ★ ★	I ★ ★
C ★ ★	L ★ ★

GOLDING, William (Gerald) (1911)

English mainstream author, acclaimed for his work throughout the world. His first novel, *Lord Of The Flies* (1954) is sf only in that a nuclear war is being fought offstage: the degeneration of the children to savagery, however, may be seen as a theme within sf's repertoire. His second novel, *The Inheritors*, returns us to the clash of Neanderthal with Cro-Magnon, as seen through the eyes of Lok of the tribe. It is, perhaps, the classic anthropological-sf work. Golding's obsession with forms of perception – with different kinds of seeing – emerged in *Pincher Martin* (1956; a.k.a. *The Two Deaths Of Pincher Martin*) where the hero is dead throughout the book, and in the medieval story of *The Spire* (1964). "Envoy Extraordinary" is overtly science-fictional – a delightful, thoughtful and comic story about anachronistic inventions in Ancient Roman Egypt. However, his best work to date is also peripherally science-fictional: *Darkness Visible* on one level is the story of one of the four figures of the Apocalypse come to Earth and made to conform to English society. The award of the Nobel Prize for literature in 1983 accurately reflects his stature.

The Inheritors (1955)

R ★ ★ ★ ★ ★	I ★ ★ ★ ★ ★
C ★ ★ ★ ★ ★	L ★ ★ ★ ★ ★

"Envoy Extraordinary" (1956)

R ★ ★ ★ ★	I ★ ★ ★
C ★ ★	L ★ ★ ★

Darkness Visible (1979)

R ★ ★ ★ ★ ★	I ★ ★ ★ ★ ★
C ★ ★ ★ ★ ★	L ★ ★ ★ ★ ★

GORDON, Rex (1917)

Pseudonym of English writer Stanley Bennett Hough, who published eight sf novels in the 1950s and 1960s. Some are Cold War thrillers, like *Extinction Bomber* (1956) and *Beyond The Eleventh Hour* (1961). His best-known work, however, is probably *No Man Friday*, a Robinson Crusoe story set on Mars.

No Man Friday (1956; a.k.a. *First On Mars*)

R ★ ★ ★	I ★ ★
C ★	L ★ ★

The Yellow Fraction (1969)

R ★ ★	I ★ ★
C ★	L ★

GORDON, Stuart (1947)

Pseudonym of Scottish writer Richard Gordon. His first novel, *Time Story* (1972), was an interesting début, but he is best known for his trilogy *One-Eye* (1973), *Two-Eyes* (1974) and *Three-Eyes* (1975), which depicts the city of Phadraig where normalcy prevails. A mixture of wizardry, exotic settings, telepathy and spiritual quests makes the trilogy slightly garish, but there are greater depths to it than most sf sagas. There is a serious intent behind the colourful surface of Gordon's work, but unfortunately his style often obscures it. *Suaine & The Crow-God* (1975) revealed Celtic influences on his work, but in the recent novel, *Smile On The Void*, the mythic element is more subdued and Gordon's dislike of materialism has grown prominent.

Smile On The Void (1981)

R ★ ★ ★	I ★ ★ ★
C ★ ★	L ★ ★

GOTLIEB, Phyllis (Fay) (1926) Canadian writer and poet whose carefully crafted and intensely visualized sf is quite distinctive. The normal expectations of sf adventure are often denied by her as she focuses more upon moral questions than upon a dynamic of events. *Sunburst* was an impressive first novel about paranormal powers and the potentiality of human transcendence, but it was with *O Master Caliban* that the full richness of her poetic gift was given expression, in a tale about survival, myth and creativity. A third novel, *A Judgement Of Dragons* (1980), is similarly polished, if less impressive.

Sunburst (1964)

R ★ ★ ★	I ★ ★ ★
C ★ ★	L ★ ★ ★

O Master Caliban (1976)

R ★ ★ ★ ★	I ★ ★ ★
C ★ ★ ★	L ★ ★ ★

GOULART, Ron(ald Joseph) (1933) American writer who began writing in the 1950s. He takes traditional science fiction themes and has fun with them by exaggeration or by simply showing how silly they can be. Many of his characters are straight cardboard cut-outs, stumbling through plastic worlds which travesty or satirize the American consumer society. One of the great delights in his work (as in Dick (q.v.) and Sheckley (q.v.)) is the proliferation of independent and quirky robots. His space operas are set in the Barnum System and feature the Chameleon Corps, including novels like *The Sword Swallower, Spacehawk Inc.* (1974) and *A Whiff Of Madness* (1976). He has written a number of Vampirella novels from the comic strip character and is presently publishing novels at a frightening rate of three to six a year. Three Flash Gordon novels appeared in 1974 under his pseudonym Con Steffanson.

The Sword Swallower (1968)

R ★ ★ ★ ★	I ★ ★
C ★	L ★ ★

Shaggy Planet (1973)

R ★ ★ ★	I ★ ★
C ★ ★	L ★

The Wicked Cyborg (1978)

R ★ ★ ★ ★	I ★ ★
C ★ ★	L ★ ★

GRANT, Charles L. (1942) American writer whose short stories appeared in the sf magazines throughout the 1970s. He has won two Nebula awards for his short fiction, with "A Crowd Of Shadows" (1976) and "A Glow Of Candles, A Unicorn's Eye" (1978). He started publishing at novel length in 1976 with the first of his Parric family series, *The Shadow Of Alpha*. Much of his work borders upon the horror genre, and his books are filled with disenchanted loners, but the Parric series seems central, with 20 stories (long and short) planned in it (more than ten written). In it a Plague-wind has devastated and depopulated a North America of the future. Other elements combine to make the brew richer, but not by much, and Grant's best work exists outside of the Parric tales. *Shadows* (1981) and *Fears* (1983) are fairly standard horror collections.

The Ravens Of The Moon (1978)

R ★ ★ ★	I ★ ★
C ★ ★	L ★ ★

Legion (1979; Parric series)

R ★ ★ ★	I ★
C ★	L ★ ★

GRAVES, Robert (Ranke) (1895) English poet and novelist who wrote one Utopian novel, *Seven Days In New Crete*, an encounter by a poet with the Poet-Magicians of the future – all presented as a kind of Keatsean Vision. The poet's role is to fracture the stasis, which has produced mediocrity, and allow creativity to emerge again. His short story "The Shout" (1929) might also be seen as borderline sf.

Seven Days In New Crete (1949; a.k.a. *Watch The North Wind Rise*)

R ★ ★ ★	I ★ ★ ★
C ★	L ★ ★ ★

GRAY, Alasdair   Scottish author of *Lanark*, a rich literary work which describes the arrival of Lanark, an enigmatic figure, in the desolate city of Uthank. At times comic, poignant, bitter and devastatingly honest (about Glasgow, the *real* Uthank), Gray has produced one of the most impressive début novels in any genre.

Lanark (1981)

R ★ ★ ★ ★ ★	I ★ ★ ★ ★ ★
C ★ ★ ★	L ★ ★ ★ ★

GRAY, Curme   American writer of an sf-thriller, *Murder In Millennium VI*, which is as notable for the matriarchal society depicted as for the fascinating murder mystery.

Murder In Millennium VI (1952)

R ★ ★ ★ ★	I ★ ★
C ★	L ★ ★

GREEN, Joseph (Lee) (1931) American writer who established himself in the English sf magazines. His work often takes the form of scientific puzzle-solving (in the mode of Asimov (q.v.), though lacking Asimov's ideative verve). *Conscience Interplanetary* is probably as good an introduction to his work as any other, with its rather unimaginative use of genre materials, centrally concerned with a human-alien interaction on a distant planet.

Conscience Interplanetary (1972)

R ★ ★ ★	I
C ★	L ★

GREENHOUGH, Terry (1944) English writer, who also writes as Andrew Lester (*The Thrice Born*, 1976). His tale of Time and alien beings, *Time And Timothy Grenville*, is an interesting if rather too slowly paced work.

Time And Timothy Grenville (1975)

R ★ ★ ★	I ★ ★
C ★	L ★

GREENLEAF, William   American author of *The Tartarus Incident*, which mixes hard science with exotic and alien adventure. Unoriginal but highly entertaining, Greenleaf will undoubtedly prove popular.

The Tartarus Incident (1983)

R ★ ★ ★ ★	I ★
C ★	L ★

GREENLEE, Sam (1930) American author of *The Spook Who Sat By The Door*, a dark tale of C.I.A. interests and a nationwide uprising of blacks; highly contemporary at its time.

The Spook Who Sat By The Door (1969)

R ★ ★ ★	I ★
C ★ ★	L ★ ★

GRIFFIN, Brian (1941) English novelist and sf critic, whose two sf novels are ambitious but flawed ideative exercises. His first work, *The Nucleation* (1977), depicts a power-struggle 500 years hence, where the outcome will affect not merely society, but morality and the universe itself. *The Omega Project* is a much better work, describing once again small human creatures struggling to find coherence in a vast and incomprehensible cosmos. Both works suffer from over-cerebration.

The Omega Project (1978)

R ★ ★ ★	I ★ ★ ★
C ★	L ★ ★

GRIFFIN, Russell M.   American author whose third novel, *The Blind Man And The Elephant*, is marginally sf. It is a darkly satiric look at contemporary America, in the vein of Sladek (q.v.) and Vonnegut (q.v.), involving Macduff, an "Elephant man" type monster. At times bleak, horrific or simply hilarious, it is an eminently good read.

The Blind Man And The Elephant (1982)

R ★ ★ ★ ★ ★	I ★ ★ ★
C ★ ★ ★	L ★ ★ ★

GRIFFITH, George (1857-1906) English journalist who produced a great many futuristic stories for serialization in newspapers and magazines owned by C. Arthur Pearson. *The Angel Of The Revolution* is one of the works which helped to generate the genre of scientific romance in the 1890s – a future-war story featuring airships and submarines. Griffith delighted in scenes of mass destruction, and his revolutionary socialism provided a nice counterpoint to the reactionary future-war novels of William le Queux (q.v.). His work deteriorated rapidly after 1900, probably because he became an alcoholic – he died of cirrhosis of the liver. His fluent journalistic style makes him very readable, but his inventiveness could not keep pace with his productivity.

The Angel Of The Revolution (1893)

R	★ ★ ★	I	★ ★ ★
C	★	L	★ ★

Olga Romanoff (1894)

R	★ ★ ★	I	★ ★ ★
C	★	L	★ ★

A Honeymoon In Space (1901)

R	★ ★	I	★ ★
C	★	L	★ ★

GROVE, Frederick Philip (1879-1948) Canadian author of *Consider Her Ways*, a satiric novel involving the giant ant, Wawaquee, and her view of humanity.

Consider Her Ways (1947)

R	★	I	★ ★
C	★	L	★

GUIN, Wyman (Woods) (1915) American author, active but not prolific in the 1950s and 1960s. His only sf novel, *The Standing Joy*, is a parallel Earth story of no great originality. His best work is collected in *Living Way Out*, which includes his best story, "Beyond Bedlam" (1951), where a future Earth has obligatory drug-induced schizophrenia, solving by this means Man's outward schizophrenia (wars, etc.).

The Standing Joy (1969)

R	★ ★ ★	I	★ ★
C	★	L	★

Living Way Out (1967; a.k.a. *Beyond Bedlam*)

R	★ ★ ★ ★	I	★ ★ ★
C	★	L	★ ★

James Gunn

GUNN, James E. (1923) American writer and teacher who was influential in importing sf into the curricula of American colleges. His better novels tend to be compounded out of shorter pieces which explore the consequences of particular premises in different time periods. *The Joy Makers* tracks the development of a society run by a cult of hedonists, while *The Immortals* studies the circumstances which develop when it is discovered that the immortality naturally possessed by a small minority can be transferred via blood transfusions. Gunn has a tendency to pomposity which occasionally makes his work dull or sententious, but at his best he is a careful and methodical writer who can provide much food for thought.

The Joy Makers (1961)

R	★ ★ ★	I	★ ★ ★ ★
C	★ ★	L	★ ★ ★

The Immortals (1962)

R	★ ★ ★	I	★ ★ ★ ★
C	★ ★	L	★ ★ ★

The Listeners (1972)

R	★ ★ ★	I	★ ★ ★
C	★ ★ ★	L	★ ★ ★

GUNN, Neil M(iller) (1891-1973) Scottish writer, most of whose lyrically beautiful work is outside of the genre. Several of his novels have a fantastic basis, but *The Green Isle Of The Great Deep* is a deeply imagined dystopian vision, as poignant as a love story, yet picturing a benevolent totalitarian state. It is a rich and deeply spiritual book, unrecognized as yet by the genre of which it is a classic. Another of Gunn's stories, *The Serpent* (1948), deals with time travel.

The Green Isle Of The Great Deep (1944)

R ★ ★ ★ ★ ★	I ★ ★ ★
C ★ ★ ★ ★	L ★ ★ ★ ★ ★

GUTTERIDGE, (Thomas Gordon) Lindsay (1923)

English writer who often fuses the science-fictional with mystery/suspense elements, as in *Cold War In A Country Garden* (1971) and *The Doppleganger Gambit* (1979). They are charming stories and three of them have a micro-man who is a quarter of an inch high (Matthew Dike), as their spy-hero.

Killer Pine (1973)

R ★ ★ ★ ★	I ★
C ★ ★	L ★ ★

HAGGARD, Sir H(enry) Rider (1856-1925)

English writer whose stories contain elements of the fantastic. Although none of his work is pure science fiction, novels like *King Solomon's Mines* and *She* (1887), with their sense of lost worlds, immortal beings and reincarnated ancients, are the model for many science fiction stories, as is Haggard's love of richly detailed and exotic settings (Africa in most of his tales).

King Solomon's Mines (1885)

R ★ ★ ★ ★	I ★ ★
C ★ ★	L ★ ★

Ayesha (1905)

R ★ ★ ★	I ★ ★
C ★ ★	L ★ ★

HAIBLUM, Isidore (1935)

American writer whose work is permeated by his Yiddish humour and is generally excessively complex plot-wise. *The Tsaddik Of The Seven Wonders* (1971), his first novel, is a perfect example. In other novels, however, Haiblum works in the Hammett-Chandler tradition, using hard-boiled heroes in alternative world settings, as in *Transfer To Yesterday*.

The Wilk Are Among Us (1975)

R ★ ★ ★	I ★
C ★	L ★

Transfer To Yesterday (1973)

R ★ ★ ★ ★	I ★
C ★ ★	L ★

HALDANE, J(ohn) B(urdon) S(anderson) (1892-1964)

Although this English writer and scientific speculator published very little which is recognizably science fiction, his essays, like *Daedalus; or, Science And The Future* (1923) and *The Last Judgement: A Scientist's Vision Of The Future Of Man* (1927), are science-fictional in their mode of enquiry. One short story, "The Gold Makers," and an incomplete novel, *The Man With Two Memories*, exist.

The Man With Two Memories (1976)

R ★ ★ ★	I ★
C ★ ★	L ★ ★

"The Gold Makers" (1932)

R ★ ★	I ★ ★
C ★	L ★

HALDEMAN, Jack C(arroll) (1941)

American writer, and brother of Joe Haldeman, with whom he has written *There Is No Darkness* (1983). His own solo work is dominated by two kinds of story, the sports tale of his shorter fiction ("Home Team Advantage" (1977)), and the rather crude space adventure of his novels, one of which is a Star Trek novelization.

Vector Analysis (1978)

R ★ ★	I ★
C ★	L ★

Perry's Planet (1980)

R ★ ★ ★	I
C ★	L ★

Joe Haldeman

Joe Haldeman

HALDEMAN, Joe (William) (1943)
American writer and winner of a Hugo and
Nebula for his future-war novel, *The Forever War*. Haldeman's experience of war
and his training in physics and astronomy
are factors which make his adventures so
convincing. But Haldeman is much more
than a contemporary up-date of Robert
Heinlein (q.v.), whose *Starship Trooper* is
often cited as a major influence; his work
shows a concern for stylistic experimentation, as in *Mindbridge* (1976), and for the
effects of war on individuals rather than as
a wide-screen sociological spectacle. Much
of his work is extrapolated directly out of
his experiences in Vietnam, yet none of it is
simply a soldier's tale. The two Attar
novels, written as Robert Graham, are
more in the spy-thriller vein than pure
hardcore sf, but in *All My Sins Remembered*
and *Worlds* (1981), the first in a trilogy,
Haldeman has markedly progressed from
his impressive début. His short stories are
hard-edged and highly polished and
"Tricentennial" won another Hugo.
Strangely enough, Haldeman admits to
Delany (q.v.) as being amongst his influences.

The Forever War (1975)

R ★ ★ ★ ★ ★	I ★ ★ ★ ★
C ★ ★ ★	L ★ ★ ★

All My Sins Remembered (1977)

R ★ ★ ★ ★	I ★ ★ ★
C ★ ★	L ★ ★ ★ ★

"Tricentennial" (1976)

R ★ ★ ★ ★ ★	I ★ ★ ★
C ★ ★	L ★ ★ ★ ★

HALDEMAN, Linda   American
writer, whose *Enbae: A Winter's Tale* is
more a horror-fantasy than sf, featuring
chiefly the conjuring-up of Asmodeus.

Enbae: A Winter's Tale (1982)

R ★ ★ ★	I ★
C ★	L ★ ★

HALL, Sandi   American writer in the
new radical-feminist mould, whose *The
Godmothers* is an alternate time-track novel,

allowing the author to make comparative
studies of women's conditions in past, present and future. It is a flawed but interesting experiment; evidence of a new and vital
use of the genre.

The Godmothers (1982)

R ★ ★ ★	I ★ ★
C ★ ★	L ★ ★ ★

HAMILTON, Andrew   English writer
of one interesting sf novel, *The Host Man*,
wherein the legal complications regarding
the first brain-transplant are investigated.
Who *is* the surviving personality? the novel
asks, with intelligence and a good sense of
humour in places.

The Host Man (1975)

R ★ ★ ★ ★	I ★ ★ ★
C ★ ★	L ★ ★

HAMILTON, Edmond (1904-77)
American writer, husband of Leigh
Brackett (q.v.). He was one of the pioneers
of pulp space opera, and most of his early
stories are extravagant tales of worlds at
war, with genocidal climaxes. In the 1940s
he wrote the Captain Future series of
juvenile pulp novels, in which the world is
constantly saved from alien threats. His
work matured with the genre, and though
he always remained a purveyor of action-
adventure fiction, he wrote some thoughtful stories in the 1950s which are much

more sober in tone. His plotting was always rather stereotyped, and he had a tendency to return again and again to formulae which once proved successful. *The Star Kings* is a science-fictional version of *The Prisoner Of Zenda*, and his other good space operas also have a hint of the swashbuckling Ruritanian romance about them. His earliest stories are now unreadable but some of his work from the late 1940s and 1950s is enjoyable in an unpretentious fashion. *The Best Of Edmond Hamilton*, edited by Leigh Brackett, is an interesting collection but another at least as good could be culled from his work in shorter lengths.

The Star Kings (1949)

R ★ ★ ★ ★	I ★ ★
C ★	L ★ ★

City At World's End (1951)

R ★ ★ ★	I ★ ★
C ★	L ★ ★

The Haunted Stars (1960)

R ★ ★ ★	I ★ ★ ★
C ★ ★	L ★ ★

HARDING, Lee (John) (1937) Australian writer whose shorter fiction appeared in the 1960s but has turned to novel-writing since the mid-1970s. His work deals with love, reality and identity, and utilizes science-fictional metaphors to explore character. He is not an outstanding stylist but is highly conscious of literary possibilities. His juveniles are not, therefore, of the usual pulp adventure kind (see *Misplaced Persons* 1979; a.k.a. *Displaced Persons*).

A World Of Shadows (1975)

R ★ ★ ★	I ★ ★
C ★ ★	L ★

The Weeping Sky (1977)

R ★ ★ ★	I ★ ★
C ★ ★ ★	L ★ ★

HARNESS, Charles L. (1915) American writer, active for a brief period in the early 1950s and now publishing regularly again following his retirement. His experience as a patent attorney shows up in several of his works, most notably "The Alchemist" and the recent *The Venetian Court*. His *Flight Into Yesterday* (a.k.a. as *The Paradox Men*) is a classic VanVogtian space opera – a futuristic costume drama bristling with throwaway ideas. His short novel "The Rose" is also a classic – a lavishly decorated fable about the enmity of art and science, based on Oscar Wilde's fable "The Nightingale and the Rose." His recent work does not quite recapture the magnificent ideative verve of his early work, but it is lively and eminently readable.

Flight Into Yesterday (1949)

R ★ ★ ★ ★	I ★ ★ ★ ★
C ★ ★ ★	L ★ ★ ★ ★

"The Rose" (1953)

R ★ ★ ★	I ★ ★ ★ ★
C ★ ★ ★	L ★ ★ ★ ★

The Ring Of Ritornel (1968)

R ★ ★ ★ ★	I ★ ★ ★ ★
C ★ ★	L ★ ★ ★

HARRISON, Harry (Max) (1925) American writer who began as an illustrator and first published fiction in 1951. Much of his work in the late 1950s and 1960s was published in *Astounding Science Fiction*, where he developed a reputation

Harry Harrison

for fast-paced adventure which often had a darkly ironic streak to it. Slippery Jim DiGriz, the stainless steel rat of his series of books, began life there, and his *Deathworld* trilogy emerged first in *Astounding*. Most of his novels appeared in book form in the 1960s, when Harrison (with Aldiss (q.v.)) was active also as an editor. His most memorable and certainly funniest creation was *Bill, The Galactic Hero*, which displays Harrison's dark and pessimistic humour at its best. Robots, matter-transmitters, future police states, alternative worlds (a Victorian one in *Tunnel Through The Deeps*), colliding comets and generation starships are all subjects which Harrison has explored in his varied and colourful work. However, he is best (if anonymously) known for *Make Room! Make Room!* (1966) which was an overpopulation story, later filmed as *Soylent Green*. No stylist, he yet possesses a keenly expressive prose in his best work. Most recently he has turned to a form of space opera in his series "To The Stars," borrowing skilfully from the genre and shaping his material in a manner quite distinctive; wide-eyed, wry and sometimes wicked.

The Stainless Steel Rat (1961)

R ★ ★ ★ ★ ★	I ★ ★
C ★ ★ ★	L ★ ★

Bill, The Galactic Hero (1965)

R ★ ★ ★ ★ ★	I ★ ★
C ★ ★ ★	L ★ ★

Tunnel Through The Deeps (1972; a.k.a. *A Transatlantic Tunnel, Hurrah!*)

R ★ ★ ★ ★	I ★ ★ ★
C ★	L ★

HARRISON, M. John (1945) English novelist and story writer. Though at first powerfully influenced by J. G. Ballard (q.v.) (*The Committed Men*, his first novel, is a distinctly post-Ballard story of deviant excursions after catastrophe) and Michael Moorcock (q.v.) (with whom he collaborated on Jerry Cornelius material), Harrison's voice and direction have always been firmly individual. Much of his fiction is set in a polymorphous everlasting city, Viri-

M. John Harrison

conium. Making use of forms from sword-and-sorcery, space opera and horror fiction, Harrison pursues an idiosyncratic vision: often grim, but with a strong vein of sardonic humour and sensual detail. Typically, his characters make ill-assorted alliances to engage in manic and often ritualistic quests for obscure objectives. Out of the struggle, unacknowledged motives emerge, often to bring about a frightful conclusion, which, it is suggested, was secretly desired all along. Harrison's vivid, highly finished prose convinces the reader of everything. His most recent work is beginning to be sunnier.

The Committed Men (1971)

R ★ ★ ★ ★	I ★ ★ ★
C ★ ★ ★ ★	L ★ ★ ★

A Storm Of Wings (1980)

R ★ ★ ★	I ★ ★ ★
C ★ ★ ★ ★ ★	L ★ ★ ★ ★

"The Quarry" (1983)

R ★ ★ ★ ★ ★	I ★ ★ ★
C ★ ★ ★ ★ ★	L ★ ★ ★ ★

HARTLEY, L(eslie) P(oles) (1895-1972) English novelist best known for his Eustace and Hilda trilogy. He wrote one sf novel, a post World War III tale of a totalitarian state where absolute equality is the rule, reminiscent of Orwell (q.v.).

Facial Justice (1960)

R ★ ★ ★ ★	I ★ ★
C ★ ★ ★	L ★ ★ ★ ★

HARTRIDGE, Jon (1934) English writer whose two sf novels, *Binary Divide* (1969) and *Earthjacket* are intelligently but unimaginatively constructed and written. They are essentially satires on contemporary society which utilize sf as metaphor.

Earthjacket (1970)

R ★ ★	I ★
C ★	L ★ ★

HAWKES, Jacquetta (1910) English writer and wife of J. B. Priestley, she is better known as an archaeologist and fabulist, but did produce one sf novel in *Providence Island: An Archeological Tale* – about the discovery of survivors from the Paleolithic discovered in an extinct volcano.

Providence Island (1959)

R ★ ★ ★	I ★ ★ ★
C ★	L ★ ★ ★

HAWTHORNE, Nathaniel (1804-64) American writer whose influence upon American literature is huge. His obsession with the fantastic nature of ordinary things – a reading of the surface of things as a hieroglyphic for some deeper reality – is a heritage of his family's puritan past. In his stories this emerges as a dark symbolism, as in "The Minister's Black Veil" (1836) and "Young Goodman Brown" (1835). They would be classed as "Horror" stories now, but stories like "Wakefield," the sketch for a story in which a man simply leaves his wife for long years and then, having lived in the next street, returns, is pure psychological sf of the most contemporary kind. His novels, again, are in a symbolist/horror vein, and *The House Of The Seven Gables* would be claimed by the genre if it were published today. Half of the material that regularly appears in *The Magazine Of Fan-*

tasy And Science Fiction can be seen to have the direct or indirect influence of Hawthorne stamped upon it.

The House Of The Seven Gables (1851)

R ★ ★ ★ ★ ★	I ★ ★ ★ ★
C ★ ★ ★ ★	L ★ ★ ★ ★ ★

"Wakefield" (1835)

R ★ ★ ★	I ★ ★ ★ ★ ★
C ★	L ★ ★ ★

"Rappaccini's Daughter" (1844)

R ★ ★ ★ ★	I ★ ★ ★
C ★ ★	L ★ ★ ★ ★

HAY, George (1922) English writer and editor. Three of his novels appeared in the 1950s, together with a pseudonymously published sf thriller, *Terra!* (1953). His enthusiasm is undoubted, his talent – as displayed in his early novels – questionable.

This Planet For Sale (1952)

R ★ ★	I ★ ★
C ★	L

HEINLEIN, Robert A. (1907) American author who is, in every sense, a past master of science fiction, though his half-century writing career is now in its twilight. A storyteller above all, this inventor of the "future history" is a quintessential old-school American: and his early pretensions to political and social criticism troubled no one – in the 1940s. In those days, Heinlein wrote of rites of passage in his "adult" novels as well as his "juveniles." Typically, a youth undergoes ordeals – usually on some kind of frontier – and these produce adulthood for the protagonist and a poised moment of quiet in the narrative; both the novel for adults *Starship Troopers* (1959) and the excellent juvenile *Beetween Planets* follow this pattern, and there is great emphasis on *earning* your place in the universe. The notably pre-sexual and pre-adult nature of Heinlein's early work may have been a strength, however, as his art is not well-adapted for emotional complexities. Invention – irising doors, superb talking aliens such as "Sir Isaac Newton" from Venus, the terrifying "puppet masters" –

Robert A. Heinlein

and simple, usually sentimental, emotion are his strengths. In the 1960s the controversial bestseller *Stranger In A Strange land* (1961) may have been liberating for its author, but the novel is a crude power-fantasy said to have inspired the mass-murderer Charles Manson. Most later works, like *Time Enough For Love* (1973) and *The Number Of The Beast* (1980), have incidental interest only, as does *Friday* (1982); this last novel, his latest, is mere picaresque, a loosely satirical collection of colourful anecdotes and essays only. For his invention and sheer narrative aggression, though, and the genuinely heroic and epic scope of *The Moon Is A Harsh Mistress*, Heinlein at his best may deserve the epithet "great."

The Puppet Masters (1940)

R ★ ★ ★ ★	I ★ ★ ★
C ★ ★ ★ ★	L ★ ★ ★

Between Planets (1951)

R ★ ★ ★ ★	I ★ ★ ★
C ★ ★ ★	L ★ ★ ★

The Moon Is A Harsh Mistress (1966)

R ★ ★ ★ ★ ★	I ★ ★ ★ ★
C ★ ★ ★ ★	L ★ ★ ★ ★

HEMINGWAY, Amanda (1955) English writer, whose one sf novel is a highly literate thriller, set on the art-obsessed world of Fingstar. The science-fictional elements remain unassimilated, however, and she appears more comfortable when writing atmospheric horror stories such as "The Alchemist" (1981).

Pzyche (1982)

R ★ ★ ★	I ★ ★ ★
C ★ ★ ★	L ★ ★

HENDERSON, Zenna (1917-83) American writer whose two novels about "The People" are really short story collections, loosely joined together. A wistful fantasy vein inhabits her sf, and most of her stories are about more-than-human aliens living amongst us, humanoids of extraterrestrial origin who have been with us since the 1890s. She has been accused of sentimentalism, but her deep humanistic streak makes her highly readable.

Pilgrimage: The Book Of The People (1961)

R ★ ★ ★ ★	I ★
C ★ ★ ★	L ★ ★

The People: No Different Flesh (1966)

R ★ ★ ★	I ★
C ★ ★	L ★ ★

HENNEBERG, N(athalie) C. (1917-77) Russian-French wife of Charles Henneberg (German-French) who was first his collaborator and then finished many of his manuscripts. Most of her work is fast-action adventure with a fantastic streak.

The Green Gods (*Les Dieux Verts*, 1961; trans. 1980)

R ★ ★ ★	I ★ ★
C ★	L ★ ★

HENSLEY, Joe L. (1926) American writer who publishes infrequently in the sf magazines. His only sf novel to date, *The Black Roads*, is a post-holocaust story about a mobile society, slickly told. His shorter work is often dark and never dull, and his friendship with Harlan Ellison (q.v.) is possibly an influence on many of these stories.

The Black Roads (1976)

R ★ ★ ★	I ★ ★
C	L ★

"Lord Randy, My Son" (1967)

R ★ ★ ★	I ★ ★
C ★ ★	L ★ ★

HERBERT, Brian   American writer, and son of Frank Herbert. His first novel, *Sidney's Comet*, is a highly inventive satire, set in 2605. Earth is threatened by a comet composed of its own consumer garbage and two men are given the task of saving the Earth while everyone else gets on with the elections.

Sydney's Comet (1983)

R ★ ★ ★ ★	I ★ ★ ★
C ★ ★	L ★ ★

HERBERT, Frank (1920) American novelist whose work explores the themes of evolved intelligence, genetic engineering, immortality, and paranormal mind powers. He is, of course, best known for *Dune* and its sequels, wherein he created what is sf's most convincing alien environment, meticulously detailed and practically a character in itself. But the desert planet Arrakis is only a part of Herbert's complex story of political and religious manipulation, and the novel's focus is the "Dune

Frank Herbert

Messiah," Paul Atreides, one of the most powerfully developed characters in science fiction. *Dune Messiah* (1969), *Children Of Dune* (1976) and *God Emperor Of Dune* (1981) continued the epic, and a fifth, *Heretics Of Dune* is, in Herbert's words, "about the evolution and devolution of the Bene Gesserit." Others may yet follow. Herbert's sf career began in 1952, and before the publication of *Dune* about 20 short stories and one novel appeared, although none of them presaged the achievements of his later work. The novel, *The Dragon In The Sea* (1956; a.k.a. *Under Pressure*) is a psychodrama set aboard a submarine of the future. Herbert's manner of juxtaposing internalized soliloquy against enigmatic external action to create a dynamic interplay was first developed in this novel. *Dune* was his second full-length work, and five other novels appeared in quick succession before the Dune sequel. Whilst none of these is exceptional, Herbert's voice is clear in each of them, pursuing his favourite theme of developed and unusual forms of mentation, as in *The Green Brain* (1966), where mutated insects form a single hive-mind. *The Santaroga Barrier* (1968) shows the same thing happening within a contemporary human framework. His most impressive work outside the Dune sequence began to appear in 1970 with the publication of *Whipping Star*, which chronicles the early adventures of Jorj X. McKie, an Agent of the multi-species ConSentiency's Bureau of Sabotage. That novel and *The Godmakers* are subtle intellectual puzzles which demand much of their readers, and in each case a vast and complex universe is inferred through the narrow range of events shown to us. *The Dosadi Experiment*, a sequel to *Whipping Star*, is the most complicated and yet most successful of Herbert's novels barring *Dune*, and, in depicting a savage future where brutal manipulaion of individuals is the norm rather than exceptional, he suggests that the future promises a new technological barbarism rather than the flowers of humanism. Some might say that Herbert's works, filled as they are with psychics, religious fanatics, powerful aliens, élites and masses, are simply intellectual power fantasies, and his obsession with supermen (created or emergent) seems to bear something of this out. But there is nothing of the power fantasy's lust for blood and glory in Herbert's work: there is only dread necessity in the face of evil men and totalitarian regimes, and so his work possesses a realism that power fantasy lacks. Of late he has written two novels with Bill Ransom, *The Jesus Incident* (1979) and *The Lazarus Effect* (1983), as well as several solo novels, one of which, *The White Plague* (1982), was a bestseller.

Dune (1965)

R ★ ★ ★ ★ ★	I ★ ★ ★ ★ ★
C ★ ★ ★ ★	L ★ ★ ★

The Godmakers (1972)

R ★ ★ ★ ★	I ★ ★ ★
C ★ ★ ★	L ★ ★ ★

The Dosadi Experiment (1978)

R ★ ★ ★ ★	I ★ ★ ★ ★ ★
C ★ ★ ★	L ★ ★ ★

HERBERT, James (1943) English writer whose blend of hard science and the paranormal makes him of interest to the sf reader. Nothing he has written is overtly science-fictional, and is more in the horror/disaster vein, but in books like *The Rats* his starting point is pure sf – a nuclear test which produces mutant rats. These fast-paced and slick bestsellers are sensational rather than ideative, but, as in *The Dark* (1980), operate on the imagination in the same way as sf, taking us into an area just beyond probability.

The Rats (1974)

R ★ ★ ★ ★	I ★
C ★ ★	L ★ ★

HERSEY, John (Richard) (1914) American writer more active in other fields than sf. His novel *The Child Buyer* is a story of cold economics in the near future: child prodigies are dealt with as commodities in a dystopian world. *White Lotus* is perhaps his most interesting book; in it China conquers the U.S.A. early in the twentieth century. It is one of the more interesting parallel world stories. *My Petition For More Space* (1974) is, as the title suggests, an overpopulation/future-tyranny story.

The Child Buyer (1960)

R ★ ★ ★	I ★ ★
C ★ ★	L ★ ★

White Lotus (1965)

R ★ ★ ★ ★	I ★ ★ ★
C ★ ★	L ★ ★

HERZOG, Arthur (1928) American writer of *The Swarm* (1974), in which African bees mutate, become a hive-mind and invade North America. Another sf work, *Earthsound* is both less garish and less interesting: premonitions of earthquakes are ignored by East Coast Americans. *Make Us Happy* (1978) describes an American dystopia 1,000 years from now.

Earthsound (1975)

R ★ ★	I ★
C ★	L ★

HESSE, Hermann (1877-1962) German novelist, poet and essayist, who won the Nobel Prize for Literature in 1946. Always a writer who utilized the fantastic as an expression of his essential dissatisfaction and mistrust of mechanical realism, his only overtly "science-fictional" novel is *The Glass Bead Game* (a.k.a. *Magister Ludi*), a chronicle of a future Earth where, after the chaos of the twentieth century and its constant wars, a game is formed amongst the intellectual élite in a Utopian state, Castalia. A complex and fascinating work, it is, in essence, a summation of Hesse's mature thought. For the more fantastic strain in Hesse, the final section of *Steppenwolf* (1927) and early stories such as "Strange News From Another Star" (1919) are recommended.

The Glass Bead Game (1943)

R ★ ★ ★ ★ ★	I ★ ★ ★ ★ ★
C ★ ★ ★ ★	L ★ ★ ★ ★ ★

"Harry The Steppenwolf" (1928)

R ★ ★ ★ ★	I ★ ★ ★
C ★ ★	L ★ ★ ★ ★

HIGH, Philip E(mpson) (1914) Prolific English author, most of whose work appeared in the late 1950s and early 1960s in British sf magazines and, at novel length, in American paperbacks. They are fast-action space adventures for the main part with a great deal of intelligent speculation tucked away in them. His best novel is *The Time Mercenaries*, where a time-displaced submarine fights off aliens on behalf of a passive, conformist humanity, but a number of his finely crafted novels are worth investigation.

The Time Mercenaries (1968)

R ★ ★ ★ ★	I ★ ★
C ★ ★	L ★ ★

Fugitive From Time (1978)

R ★ ★ ★	I ★ ★
C ★	L ★

HILDICK, E(dmund) W(allace) (1925) English writer for the American market. Only a small amount of his work – which is basically juvenile fiction – is science-fictional. One fine example is *Time Explorers Inc.*, interesting despite its structural flaws.

Time Explorers Inc. (1976)

R ★ ★ ★	I ★ ★
C ★	L ★ ★

HILL, Douglas (1935) Canadian writer of space juveniles. Simply told but containing an underlying intelligence they are enjoyable entertainments.

Exiles In Colsee (1983)

R ★ ★ ★	I ★
C ★	L ★ ★

HILTON, James (1900-54) English writer of the lost world story, *Lost Horizon*, which tells of Shangri-La, a lost valley in Tibet. The aspect of the novel which is most overtly science-fictional is the longevity of the dwellers in Shangri-La.

Lost Horizon (1933)

R ★ ★ ★	I ★ ★
C ★ ★	L ★ ★

HINGLEY, Ronald (Francis) (1920) English writer of *Up Jenkins!*, which depicts a post civil war Britain, divided into North and South (Free/Totalitarian).

Up Jenkins! (1956)

R ★ ★	I ★
C ★	L ★

HJORTSBERG, William (1941) American fantasy writer who sometimes sets his work in future Utopias. His first novel, *Alp* (1969), is one such, and *Gray Matters* is another. *Gray Matters* is interesting in that it deals with transcendence via a system of cybernetic wombs and synthetic bodies. It ends with the return of the purely human into the world.

Gray Matters (1971)

R ★ ★ ★ ★	I ★ ★ ★
C ★ ★	L ★ ★

HOBAN, Russell (1925) American writer, formerly for children, turned adult novelist after emigrating to England in 1969. England has since provided crucial geographical and historical material for his work, especially *Riddley Walker*, set in a post-nuclear Kent. Perceptive, with a wry sense of humour, Hoban is also a deeply romantic writer, concerned with extracting meaning from the chaos of experience. He concentrates on the emotions of his characters, weaving them into patterns of manifold symbolism and fluent mystical apprehensions. Resolute but obscurely motivated, they make their various quests for new life in landscapes of loss and dereliction. Hoban has no particular interest in or purpose for sf, but his imagination freely transgresses boundaries between fantasy and reality, natural and supernatural. The world of *The Lion Of Boaz-Jachin And Jachin-Boaz* (1973) is obviously our own, but lions are extinct there; *Riddley Walker* blends medieval Christianity and atomic physics into a new mythological language.

Riddley Walker (1980)

R ★ ★	I ★ ★ ★ ★
C ★ ★ ★	L ★ ★ ★

HOCH, Edward D. (1930) American writer of detective stories. Three of his works blend sf and the detective thriller, using the same characters, Carl Crader and Earl Jazine. They are ingenious tales set in the twenty-first century. Some of his short stories in a similar vein, only featuring Simon Ark, have been collected.

The Frankenstein Factory (1975)

R ★ ★ ★	I ★ ★
C ★	L ★

The Judges Of Hades And Other Simon Ark Stories (1971; coll.)

R ★ ★ ★ ★	I ★ ★
C ★ ★	L ★ ★

HODDER-WILLIAMS, (John) Christopher (Glazebrook) (1926) English novelist, whose first sf novel was *Chain Reaction* (1959), a work which, like *Fistful Of Digits* and *The Main Experiment* (1964), concerns itself with the problem of asserting individuality in a progressively machine-oriented world. Their admirable social concern is, however, spoilt by melodramatic effects, and most are best read as straight thrillers with a scientific *frisson*.

Fistful Of Digits (1968)

R ★ ★ ★ ★	I ★ ★ ★
C ★ ★	L ★ ★

The Silent Voice (1977)

R ★ ★ ★	I ★ ★
C ★	L ★

HODGELL, P.C.   American writer, whose *God Stalk* is the first novel in a fantasy trilogy in the vein of Leiber's (q.v.) *Lankmar* stories. A rich and often bizarre work.

God Stalk (1983)

R ★ ★ ★ ★	I ★ ★
C ★ ★	L ★ ★

HODGSON, William Hope (1877-1918) English writer killed in World War I. He wrote a great many weird stories of the sea, including the classic "The Voice In The Night." He played a major part in developing the mythology of the Sargasso Sea, but his most effective sea stories assume that there are parallel worlds inhabited by monsters into which luckless ships might stray. *The House On The Borderland* is also a story of touching worlds which climaxes with an astonishing vision of the far future. Much more elaborate is *The Night Land*, a long and stylized account of the monstrous life-forms inhabiting a dying Earth.

The House On The Borderland (1908)

R ★ ★ ★	I ★ ★ ★ ★ ★
C ★	L ★ ★ ★ ★

The Ghost Pirates (1909)

R ★ ★ ★	I ★ ★ ★
C ★ ★	L ★ ★ ★

The Night Land (1912)

R ★	I ★ ★ ★ ★ ★
C ★	L ★ ★ ★ ★

HOFFMAN, Lee (1932) American writer who works more in the Western genre than in science fiction. Her sf is thoughtful and deals with human personality under different conditions and at different times. There is no stylistic trickery, yet her writing is lucid and extremely visual. There is always plenty of action, as in *The Caves Of*

Robert Holdstock

Karst (1969) and *Always The Blacknight* (1970), but never is it only simplistic adventure.

Change Song (1972)

R ★ ★ ★	I ★ ★
C ★ ★	L ★ ★

HOGAN, James P(atrick) (1941) English novelist active in the sf field since the late 1970s. Most of his work is speculative and looks to the near future concernedly. His sense of impending crisis is constant, and in novels like *The Genesis Machine* he realistically portrays scientists trying to come to grips with that crisis. His characterization is often weak, but his examination of ideas is always first-rate.

The Genesis Machine (1977)

R ★ ★ ★ ★	I ★ ★ ★
C ★	L ★ ★

HOLDSTOCK, Robert (1948) One of an emergent generation of young English sf writers, his novels are involved and rather ponderous fusions of ideas drawn from science and mythology. He has improved steadily over the years and as his style becomes smoother he promises to produce some fine work in future. His preoccupation with the dark depths of human nature which are encoded in the symbolism of Celtic mythology is a little irritating at present, but he will surely become more versatile as he progresses.

Eye Among The Blind (1976)

R ★ ★	I ★ ★ ★
C ★ ★	L ★ ★

Earthwind (1977)

R ★ ★	I ★ ★ ★
C ★ ★ ★	L ★ ★ ★

"Mythago Wood" (1981)

R ★ ★ ★	I ★ ★ ★
C ★ ★ ★	L ★ ★ ★

HOLLAND, Cecilia (1943) American writer best known for her historical novels, she has published one lengthy sf book, *Floating Worlds*, describing a future Anarchist Earth involved in an Inner-System planetary war. Intelligent space opera, her usual eloquent gifts often depart in this over-complex tale.

Floating Worlds (1976)

R ★ ★	I ★ ★
C ★ ★	L ★ ★

HOLLIS, H. H. (1921) Pseudonym of American writer Ben Rhamey, his delightfully eccentric stories have yet to be collected, despite the fact that he has been twice nominated for Nebula awards. "Sword Game" (1968), which begins as a circus act and ends as a tale of universal reality, is a good introduction to Hollis's distinctive work.

HOLLY, Joan Hunter (1932) American writer Joan Carol Holly, whose first sf novel was *Encounter* (1959). She has been trained in psychology and the confrontation of Man and Alien in that book is typical of her work. Several novels appeared in the early 1960s, and, after a break from illness, she has returned to the field with a number of straightforward adventure novels, of which *Death Dolls Of Lyra* (1977) is a fine example.

The Grey Aliens (1963)

R ★ ★ ★	I ★
C ★ ★	L ★ ★

HOOVER, H. M. English writer of polished sf juveniles which utilize myth, fantasy and generic materials to create rich future worlds. Good characterization and a lucid style make Hoover a writer to watch. *The Delikon* (1978) is about a future Earth dominated by long-lived aliens. *This Time Of Darkness* is a rite-of-passage novel, set in a totalitarian city of the future.

This Time Of Darkness (1982)

R ★ ★ ★ ★	I ★ ★
C ★ ★	L ★ ★

HOSKINS, Robert (1933) American writer and editor who has turned to the novel length in the 1970s after establishing a minor reputation for his shorter sf. His works are space adventures of a fairly un-pretentious kind, wherein sophisticated cultures and barbarian races meet and clash. His Alnians trilogy utilizes the idea of "stargates" left by an ancient alien race.

The Shattered People (1975)

R ★ ★ ★	I ★ ★
C ★	L ★

To Escape The Stars (1978; Alnians series)

R ★ ★ ★ ★	I ★
C ★ ★	L ★

HOWARD, (John) Hayden   American author of *The Eskimo Invasion*, essentially an overpopulation story, but different in its humane treatment of the fast-breeding but benevolent Esks.

The Eskimo Invasion (1967)

R ★ ★ ★	I ★ ★
C ★ ★	L ★ ★

HOWARD, Robert E. (1906-36) Ameri-can writer who published prolifically in the pulps in the last ten years of his life, before committing suicide. He wrote many highly coloured historical fantasies, adding magic to one particular series which he sold to
Robert E. Howard

Weird Tales, thus becoming the founding father of sword-and-sorcery fiction and beginning a fashion in mighty barbarian heroes. A boom in this kind of fiction in the late 1960s brought him posthumous fame and fortune, and a substantial industry has grown up around his name, new adven-tures of his chief characters being chroni-cled by several experts in pastiche. His writing is unsophisticated but his obsessive fascination with violence is unparalleled and his work can be breathtakingly exciting until one tires of it, at which point it be-comes irritatingly tedious. None of his imitators can quite recapture his fervour.

Conan The Conqueror (1935)

R ★ ★ ★ ★	I ★ ★
C ★	L ★ ★ ★

Almuric (1939)

R ★ ★ ★	I ★
C ★	L ★

HOWELLS, William Dean (1837-1920) American author best known in the sf field for his linked novels *A Traveller From Altruria* (1894) and *Through The Eye Of A Needle*. In the first, a traveller from Altruria, a future Utopia where Christian and Democratic values are taken literally, visits contemporary America. In the second the traveller takes a bride back to Altruria.

Through The Eye Of A Needle (1907)

R ★ ★	I ★ ★
C ★	L ★ ★

HOYLE, Fred (1915) English scientist, the *enfant terrible* of astronomy. His sf novel *The Black Cloud* is a classic story of first contact between humans and an intelligent cloud of interstellar gas. Recently, in col-laboration with Chandra Wickramasinghe, he has developed the hypothesis that life actually involved inside such clouds, and that they not only seeded the Earth 2 billion years ago, but still transmit viruses to Earth via comets. In general his sf is less exciting than his non-fictional conjectures; he is a pedestrian writer, though not as pedestrian as his son Geoffrey (q.v.) who has collab-orated with him on most of his more recent stories. His main virtues are his imaginative power and his knowledge of the way scientists work, but he has been understandably reluctant to invest much time in sf.

The Black Cloud (1957)

R ★ ★ ★	I ★ ★ ★ ★
C ★ ★	L ★ ★ ★

October The First Is Too Late (1966)

R ★ ★ ★	I ★ ★ ★
C ★ ★	L ★ ★ ★

The Inferno (1973; with Geoffrey Hoyle)

R ★ ★	I ★ ★ ★
C ★	L ★ ★

HOYLE, Geoffrey (1942) English writer and son of Fred Hoyle, Astronomer Royal and sf author, with whom he has collaborated on a number of sf novels, the best of which is perhaps *Fifth Planet*, a mixture of hard science and science fantasy. *The Inferno* (1973), a disaster scenario, is better written but not as entertaining.

Fifth Planet (1963; with Fred Hoyle)

R ★ ★ ★ ★	I ★ ★
C ★	L ★

HUBBARD, L. Ron (1911) American writer and founder of the cult of Scientology. He was a prolific pulp writer from 1938 to 1950, when he discovered an even easier way to make money. He recently returned to sf with his long space opera *Battlefield Earth* (1985). An attempt by his son to have him declared legally dead is the cause of much controversy; Hubbard claims to be still alive but is coy about appearing to prove the point. His best work is outstanding within the pulp tradition: "Typewriter in the Sky" is a fine fantasy about a man who gets trapped within a story written by a pulp writer, while "Fear" is a brilliant exercise in psychological horror. *Final Blackout* is a grim novel in which Europe is devastated by World War II and an American lieutenant tries to establish a libertarian state in the ruins of London. He had great imaginative power, and it is something of a tragedy that he turned it to such a perverse purpose.

Slaves Of Sleep (1948)

R ★ ★ ★ ★	I ★ ★ ★
C ★ ★	L ★ ★ ★

Return To Tomorrow (1954)

R ★ ★ ★	I ★ ★ ★
C ★ ★	L ★ ★ ★

HUDSON, William Henry (1841-1922) English writer born in the Argentine. His Utopian novel *A Crystal Age* depicts a matriarchal society in the future, balanced with nature. Another such evolutionary vision exists in *Green Mansions* (1904).

A Crystal Age (1887)

R ★ ★ ★	I ★ ★
C ★ ★	L ★ ★

HUGHES, Monica English writer of juvenile science fiction. Her work uses the genre's materials skilfully but unimaginatively, and essentially these are quite ordinary stories where the hero or heroine solves a problem or confronts and surmounts his or her growing pains (as in *The Keeper Of The Isis Light*, 1980). Her psychology is a touch out of step with contemporary children, but the adventure element in her stories and the intelligence displayed in them (without lecturing) make up for that.

The Tomorrow City (1978)

R ★ ★ ★ ★	I ★ ★
C ★ ★	L ★ ★

HUGHES, Zach (1928) Pseudonym of American writer, Hugh Zachary, who has produced more than ten novels in the sf field since 1973. His first book, *The Book Of Rack The Healer*, is considered his best; a post-holocaust tale, depicting the fragmentation of Man into four species. Other of his works share a disaster format (*Tide*, 1974, and *The St. Francis Effect*, 1976). He is very good at re-using well-worn genre clichés and giving them a breath of new life.

The Book Of Rack The Healer (1973)

R ★ ★ ★ ★	I ★ ★
C ★ ★	L ★ ★

HULL, E(dna) M(ayne) (1905-75) American writer, and wife of A. E. Van Vogt (q.v.), with whom she collaborated on two novels, *Planets For Sale* (1954) and *The Winged Man*. She adds little to Van Vogt's (q.v.) normal heady mixture of power-fantasy and fast-paced adventure.

The Winged Man (1966)

R	★ ★ ★	I	★ ★
C	★	L	★

HUNTER, Evan (1926) Pseudonym of American writer S. A. Lombro (who also wrote as Richard Marsten and Hunt Collins). He did the screenplay for Hitchcock's *The Birds*, but most of his sf has been for juveniles. *Find The Feathered Serpent* (1952), *Rocket To Luna* (1952; as Marsten) and *Danger: Dinosaurs!* (1953; as Marsten) share the common factors of being easily readable and unchallenging. His one novel as Hunt Collins, *Tomorrow's World*, is much better, positing two extreme poles of society in the near future; ultra-hedonists and ultra-puritans. Lombro is best known, however, for his writings as Ed McBain.

Tomorrow's World (1956)

R	★ ★ ★	I	★ ★
C	★	L	★

HUNTER, Norman (1899) English author of the Professor Branestawm series of juvenile books. His scientific inventions are vaguely sf.

The Peculiar Triumph Of Professor Branestawm (1970; coll.)

R	★ ★ ★	I	★
C	★	L	★

HUXLEY, Aldous (1894-1963) Huxley's is one of the most extraordinary life trajectories of the twentieth century, from the exclusive enclaves of Eton and Balliol to a death in California adrift on L.S.D. Huxley is now best remembered for his brilliant anti-Utopia, *Brave New World*, in which science supports a new eudemonism. Among his other novels, there are sf notes in the mordant *After Many A Summer* (1939), and the post-nuclear *Ape And*

Essence (1948). Disgust eventually gave way to guru-dom, and Huxley's last novel, *Island*, depicts a Utopia which blandly embraces the drugs and sensualities his more incisive work rails against.

Brave New World (1932)

R	★ ★ ★ ★	I	★ ★ ★ ★ ★
C	★ ★	L	★ ★ ★ ★

Island (1962)

R	★ ★ ★ ★	I	★ ★ ★
C	★ ★	L	★ ★ ★

HYNE, C(harles) J(ohn) Cutliffe (Wright) (1864-1944) English writer of the turn of the century, whose works, such as *The New Eden* (1892) and *The Lost Continent*, are tolerable scientific melodramas which have aged badly. He is interesting nonetheless as a progenitor of many of the field's themes.

The Lost Continent (1900)

R	★ ★ ★	I	★ ★
C	★	L	★

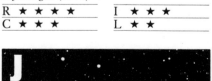

ING, Dean American writer, and author of *Soft Targets*, a good sf thriller about international terrorists, and *Pulling Through* (1983), part-novella, part non-fiction article about the nuclear holocaust to come.

Soft Targets (1979)

R	★ ★ ★ ★	I	★ ★ ★
C	★ ★ ★	L	★ ★

JACKSON, Shirley (1919-65) American writer, best known for her horror stories and dark psychological studies. Some of her work overlaps sf concerns, as in *The Sundial* (1958) and her famous horror novel, *We Have Always Lived In The Castle*, recently and deservedly reissued.

We Have Always Lived In The Castle (1962)

R	★	★	★	★	I	★	★
C	★	★			L	★	★

JAKES, John (1932) American pulp writer who produced a good deal of undistinguished sf before suddenly becoming a runaway bestseller with a series of novels spanning American history since the revolution. His best work tends to be amiable comedy after the fashion of his sword-and-sorcery skit, *Mention My Name In Atlantis*, but some of his short fiction is rather striking and *On Wheels* is a curiously effective novel about a gypsy clan who live on the interstate highways of America and never stop. If he ever finds it worth his while to return to sf writing he might produce some good work.

Mask Of Chaos (1970)

R	★	★	★	I	★	★
C	★	★		L	★	★

Mention My Name In Atlantis (1972)

R	★	★	★	I	★	★
C	★	★		L	★	★

On Wheels (1973)

R	★	★	★		I	★	★	★
C	★	★			L	★	★	

John Jakes

JAKOBER, Marie (1941) Canadian writer of *The Mind Gods*, a complex and thought-provoking novel, depicts the clash of tolerance and intolerance on two separate planets. It is darkly real in its outcome.

The Mind Gods: A Novel Of The Future (1976)

R	★	★	★	I	★	★	★
C	★	★		L	★	★	★

JANIFER, Laurence M. (1933) American writer Larry Mark Harris, who also writes as Mark Phillips. His work is highly routine, with stock situations and characters consistently thrown into unremarkable juxtaposition.

Slave Planet (1963)

R	★	★	I	
C			L	★

JEFFERIES, (John) Richard (1848-87) English novelist whose interest in Nature dominates his work. His two books, *Sir Bevis: A Tale Of The Fields* (1881) and *Bevis: The Story Of A Boy* (1882) tell of a gifted youngster who can communicate with bird, bee and flower. A delightful tale, beautifully told, it is bettered only by his future history, *After London; or, Wild England*, which is a post-holocaust novel of some power and intensity of expression.

After London; or, Wild England (1885)

R	★	★	★	★	I	★	★	★	
C	★	★			L	★	★	★	★

JENSEN, Axel (1932) Norwegian author of the dystopian novel, *Epp*. Epp is a retired citizen of a future Utopia, wherein he is a hopeless and despairing unit. Vividly told psychological novel.

Epp (1965; trans. 1967)

R	★	★	★	I	★	★
C	★	★	★	L	★	★

JEURY, Michel (1934) French writer. Generally considered the most prominent of today's French sf authors, Jeury is a prolific ideas man who, after an early infatuation with Dick (q.v.), time travel and alternative worlds, is maturing into a splendid conceptualist as well as a popular writer. There are two distinct strands in his career: long, ambitious novels about the nature of reality and shorter but more frequent adventure yarns and series for a larger readership.

Le Temps Incertain (1973; trans. as Chronolysis)

R ★ ★ ★	I ★ ★ ★
C ★ ★ ★	L ★ ★ ★

Soleil Chaud Poisson Des Profondeurs (1976)

R ★ ★ ★	I ★ ★ ★ ★
C ★ ★	L ★ ★ ★

Les Yeux Géants (1980)

R ★ ★ ★	I ★ ★ ★ ★
C ★ ★ ★	L ★ ★ ★ ★

JOHANNESSON, Olof (1908) Pseudonym of Swedish scientist and writer, Hannes Alfven, winner of the Nobel Prize for Physics (1970). His *The Tale Of The Big Computer* posits (frighteningly) that Man was only an intermediary means of creating the ultimate life-form on Earth, the computer. Pessimistic or ironic, it is a chilling future vision.

The Tale Of The Big Computer (1966; trans. 1968)

R ★ ★ ★	I ★ ★ ★
C	L ★

JOHNS, W(illiam) E(arl) (1893-1968) English writer, famous for his Biggles adventures (all juveniles), some of his work was sf-oriented, and featured a hero, Rex Clinton, whose adventures in space were rather Flash Gordon-ish. They have charm, but little science. Surprisingly enough, however, they are ecologically and socially conscious works – opposed to warfare and waste.

The Death Rays Of Ardilla (1959)

R ★	I ★
C ★	L ★

JONES, D(ennis) F(eltham)   English writer whose *Colossus* (which has two lesser

sequels) is much praised for its portrayal of the super-computer designed to safeguard the Western world, and which links up with its Russian counterpart to rule the world wisely but firmly. His recent *Earth Has Been Found* (1979; a.k.a. *Xeno*) is a good read with nasty insectile aliens.

Colossus: The Forbin Project (1966)

R ★ ★ ★ ★ ★	I ★ ★
C ★	L ★ ★

JONES, Langdon (1942) English story writer, editor, poet and composer deeply involved in the *New Worlds* experiment. His fiction is anxiously concerned with the search for transcendence of the captivity of time and uncertain identity. Formally experimental and eclectic, inspired by music, all his best writings are in his collection, *The Eye Of The Lens* (1972).

"The Eye Of The Lens" (1968)

R ★ ★	I ★ ★ ★
C	L ★ ★

"Garden Of Delights" (1969)

R ★ ★ ★	I ★
C ★ ★ ★	L ★ ★

JONES, Neil R(onald) (1909) American writer whose popular Professor Jameson series first appeared in the magazines in the 1930s and in paperback form in the 1960s. The whole forms a future history of the twenty-fourth to twenty-sixth centuries, with benevolent robots and a reincarnated man of the twentieth century, Jameson himself. Charming and un-selfconscious, they have influenced a number of writers, including Isaac Asimov (q.v.).

The Sunless World (1967)

R ★ ★	I ★
C ★ ★	L ★

JONES, Raymond F. (1915) American writer whose *This Island Earth* was filmed. Much of his work was either juvenile or straightforward space opera, but his work in the 1970s is more diverse, whilst still retaining pure sf ideas and a direct story line.

This Island Earth (1952)

R	★ ★ ★ ★	I	★
C	★	L	★

Renegades Of Time (1975)

R	★ ★ ★	I	★
C	★	L	★

JOSEPH, M(ichael) K(ennedy) (1914) English-born New Zealand writer, whose work is sadly neglected. It has a surface colour which is pure space opera, but its depths are just as rich; complex, philosophical and at times allegorical, as in *The Hole In The Zero. The Time Of Achamuth* (1976) is more of a thriller in time, but has similar depths.

The Hole In The Zero (1967)

R	★ ★ ★ ★	I	★ ★ ★ ★
C	★	L	★ ★ ★

KAFKA, Franz (1883-1924) Czech author whose influence on the science fiction field is, surprisingly, quite recent, and, some would say, partly questionable. Undoubtedly the more acutely self-conscious sf writers of the late 1960s and 1970s looked to Kafka as a stylistic model, along with Samuel Beckett, William Burroughs (q.v.) and Borges (q.v.), utilizing Kafka's love of enigmatic and absurd situations to create their own landscapes of the mind. As far as his own work is concerned, it is more fabular than science-fictional, although the satiric and fantastic elements in stories such as "Metamorphosis," "The Burrow," "In The Penal Settlement" (1914), "Josephine The Singer, or The Mouse-Folk" (1924) and "A Report To An Academy" (1917) overlap with the concerns of much modern, intelligent sf. None of his three novels can really be said to be sf in any way, although again their distinctive style has influenced – if sometimes at second-hand – a small amount of the more speculative and philosophical work being produced in the field.

"Metamorphosis" (1913)

R	★ ★ ★ ★ ★	I	★ ★ ★ ★ ★
C	★ ★ ★	L	★ ★ ★ ★ ★

"The Burrow" (1923)

R	★ ★ ★	I	★ ★ ★ ★ ★
C	★ ★ ★	L	★ ★ ★ ★ ★

KANTOR, Mackinlay (1904-77) American author of *If The South Had Won The Civil War*, one of the best of many works on this alternative world theme.

If The South Had Won The Civil War (1961)

R	★ ★ ★	I	★
C	★ ★	L	★

KAPP, Colin (1928) English writer who blends a poetic vision of physics with an understanding of the human personality in his work. He is far from being the most original of writers but, in his early work, could create a genuine sense of scientific awe.

The Patterns Of Chaos (1972)

R	★ ★ ★	I	★ ★
C	★ ★	L	★ ★

The Ion War (1978)

R	★ ★ ★	I	★
C	★	L	★

KARINTHY, Frigyes (1887-1938) Hungarian writer who has written two sequels to Swift's *Gulliver's Travels*, his wit perhaps more savage but no less misogynistic, and sharpened by the dark events of this century.

Voyage To Faremido And Capillaria (1916/1922; trans. 1966)

R	★ ★	I	★ ★
C	★	L	★ ★

KARP, Colin (1922) American writer of a single interesting sf novel, *One*, a dystopian work, which depicts a totalitarian and cruel-to-be-kind future U.S.A.

One (1953; a.k.a. *Escape To Nowhere*)

R	★ ★	I	★
C	★	L	★ ★

Anna Kavan

KAVAN, Anna (1901-68) Pseudonym of French writer Helen Woods Edmonds, who committed suicide after years of heroin addiction. Her work is hauntingly atmospheric and paradoxically rich in its echoing bleakness. Her intense and involuted imagery forms a surreal landscape of the psyche in a manner similar to, but perhaps more potent and dream-like, than Ballard's (q.v.). Schizophrenia, paranoia, mirror-selves and an imagistic language of dreams marks her fiction as being close to Kafka's (q.v.) in intent, though her work lacks his humour. *Ice*, a story of pursuit and identity in a world engulfed by a new Ice Age, is the most overtly generic of her novels, though *Sleep Has His House* (1948; a.k.a. *House Of Sleep*) prefigures much of the New Wave. Her short stories in the collections *Asylum Piece* (1946) and *Julia And The Bazooka* (1970) frequently involve elements of the absurd and fantastic more normally found in the sf field.

Ice (1967)

R	★ ★ ★ ★ ★	I	★ ★ ★ ★ ★
C	★ ★ ★	L	★ ★ ★ ★ ★

KEA, Neville   English writer of standard sf adventures such as *The Glass School* (1981), *The Rats Of Megaera* (1981) and *The World Of Artemis*.

The World Of Artemis (1981)

R	★	I	★
C		L	★

KELLER, David H(enry) (1880-1966) American writer and psychologist whose work in the 1930s and 1940s reflected his profession in its thematic concerns. His style is crude but was suitable for the pulps for which he mainly wrote.

The Solitary Hunters, And The Abyss (1948)

R	★ ★	I	★
C	★	L	

KELLEY, Leo P(atrick) (1928) American writer of standard sf adventures which are tainted by a rather pessimistic and callous form of sociological determinism. Most of his work is written for juveniles,

and since 1979, he has proved highly prolific in that genre.

Time Rogue (1970)

R	★ ★	I	★
C		L	★

On The Red World (1979)

R	★	I	★
C		L	★

KELLEY, William Melvin (1937) American writer of one lovely borderline sf novel, *A Different Drummer*, a Faulkner-like picture of an imaginary southern state of the U.S.A. where the blacks up and leave. Two other books, *Dem* and *Dunsford Travels Everywheres* (1970), are delightful mixtures of mainstream techniques and sf themes, with an underlying deep concern for black rights.

A Different Drummer (1962)

R	★ ★ ★ ★	I	★ ★
C	★ ★	L	★ ★ ★

Dem (1967)

R	★ ★ ★	I	★ ★
C	★	L	★ ★ ★

KERSH, Gerald (1911-68) Russian-born English writer, whose work often incorporates sf elements. Some of his shorter fiction is clearly sf, like "Whatever Happened To Corporal Cuckoo?" (1953), where the protagonist has lived 500 years. A few of his novels have been borderline sf of an intelligent and highly emotional kind.

The Great Wash (1953; a.k.a. *The Secret Masters*)

R ★ ★ ★	I ★ ★
C ★ ★	L ★ ★

KEY, Alexander (Hill) (1904-79) American writer for the very young, whose popular and simply crafted stories, *Sprockets: A Little Robot* and *Rivets And Sprockets* (1964), formulated his fiction for the next 15 years. There is a deep moral (but not moralizing) concern behind his adventures which offsets his tendency to over-sentimentalize in his stories.

Sprockets: A Little Robot (1963)

R ★ ★ ★	I ★ ★
C ★	L ★ ★

KEYES, Daniel (1927) American writer who, whilst he has produced very little, did write one of the sf field's classic short stories (later extended into a novel and filmed as *Charlie*), "Flowers For Algernon," which tells of Charlie Gordon, whose I.Q. is artificially boosted and then regresses. It is one of the most touching scientific fables in the genre. The novel, which loses the first-person immediacy of the shorter version, is nonetheless a forceful condemnation of scientific experimentation on human subjects. Six other short fictions and one borderline sf novel, *The Touch* (1968), exist.

"Flowers For Algernon" (1959)

R ★ ★ ★ ★ ★	I ★ ★ ★ ★
C ★ ★ ★ ★ ★	L ★ ★ ★ ★

Flowers For Algernon (1966)

R ★ ★ ★ ★	I ★ ★ ★ ★ ★
C ★ ★ ★	L ★ ★ ★ ★

KILLOUGH (Karen) Lee (1942) American writer whose novels have begun to appear since 1979. It is difficult as yet to assess her worth, but her early work suggests that her mixture of science fiction and

the mystery/thriller format – a fusion which looks at human problems within a vast perspective – may produce something of real value.

The Doppleganger Gambit (1979)

R ★ ★ ★ ★	I ★ ★
C ★ ★	L ★ ★

KILWORTH, Garry (1941) English writer who emerged in the late 1970s with a series of finely crafted science fiction works. *In Solitary* (1977), a taut first novel, depicts a future Earth ruled by bird-like aliens. His second novel, *The Night Of Kadar*, was a richer work, with allusions to the Islamic religion, and memorable for its character Fdar. *Split Second* is a work which combines anthropology and psychology in an excellently structured thriller. *Gemini God* (1981) suffers somewhat from having been cut for publication, but tells of telepathic twins and an expedition to New Carthage, an alien planet, where a new religion is born. His work thus far is most memorable for his humane portrayals of characters.

The Night Of Kadar (1978)

R ★ ★ ★ ★	I ★ ★
C ★ ★ ★	L ★ ★

Split Second (1979)

R ★ ★ ★ ★	I ★ ★
C ★ ★ ★	L ★ ★ ★

"Blind Windows" (1982)

R ★ ★ ★ ★	I ★
C ★ ★	L ★ ★

KING, Stephen (1947) American horror writer. The world's best-selling author, with most of his novels already adapted into major motion pictures, King has demonstrated his skilful grasp of both conventional horror – vampires, haunted houses, possession – and more contemporary, scientific subject matter such as telekinesis and telepathy. His long, loosely plotted novels have centred on two themes in particular: first, the creation of horror out of commonplace, everyday situations; second, the menace inherent in massive, uncontrollable American organizations. *Firestarter*, for example, uses as its villains the members of a C.I.A.-type network, while the fanatical religious movement depicted in *The Dead Zone* (1979) bears an alarming resemblance to America's "Moral Majority." Not generally noted as a great "character" author, King has managed, however, to draw particular comment for his uncanny depictions of young children, most especially the five-year-old "Danny" in *The Shining*. In 1978 he published a collection of often remarkably proficient short stories, *Night Shift*. He has produced one of the few extensive historical and critical assessments of the horror genre, *Danse Macabre* (1981). On the lighter side he has taken time off to script and even act in the spoof horror movie *Creepshow* in collaboration with cult director George Romero. The extreme readability of King's novels, combined with his ability to intertwine the instantly identifiable with the bizarre, satanic, and macabre, guarantees him a massive and devoted following.

Salem's Lot (1975)

R ★ ★ ★ ★ ★	I ★ ★
C ★ ★ ★	L ★ ★ ★ ★

The Shining (1977)

R ★ ★ ★ ★ ★	I ★ ★ ★
C ★ ★ ★ ★	L ★ ★ ★

Firestarter (1980)

R ★ ★ ★ ★ ★	I ★ ★
C ★ ★ ★	L ★ ★

KING, Vincent (1935) Pseudonym of English writer Rex Thomas Vinson. His work has never received the attention it deserves, and has always been treated as straightforward suspense-style sf with dystopian leanings, but in works like *Light A Last Candle* (1969) and *Candy Man* (1971) he weaves a fascinating spell. His use of traditional sf themes has a distinct originality to it.

Time Snake and Superclown (1976)

R ★ ★ ★ ★	I ★ ★
C ★ ★	L ★ ★

KINGSBURY, Donald American author of *Courtship Rite*, an interesting first novel about a libertarian society coping with an alien planet environment; an exhilarating, if not always comfortable, read.

Courtship Rite (1982)

R ★ ★ ★	I ★ ★ ★
C ★ ★	L ★ ★

KIPLING, (Joseph) Rudyard (1865-1936) English author, two of whose short story collections might be considered to include sf stories, although this is more a use of the supernatural than speculative material.

A Diversity Of Creatures (1917)

R ★ ★ ★	I ★
C ★	L ★ ★

KIPPAX, John (1915-74) Pseudonym of English writer John Charles Hynam. His shorter fiction was published regularly in the British sf magazines in the 1950s and a series of sf novels – essentially space operas – in the 1970s, co-authored with Dan Morgan (q.v.) for the main part.

Where No Stars Guide (1975)

R ★ ★ ★	I ★ ★
C ★	L ★

KLEIN, Gerard (1937) French writer, prolific in his own language. A small part of his work has been translated, amongst it *Starmaster's Gambit*, a space opera which seeks the secrets of the universe, and discovers the source of sentience, and *The Day Before Tomorrow* (1972), an adventure in time, with much tampering of reality going on. Klein's work covers a wide range of styles and subjects and much of it (especially his early work) has a poetic richness to it.

Starmaster's Gambit (1958; trans. 1973)

R ★ ★ ★ ★	I ★ ★ ★
C ★	L ★ ★

KLINE, Otis Adelbert (1891-1946) American writer and editor of *Weird Tales*. His own fiction was rather poor standard pulp adventure with crude racist and sexist undertones. Nowadays, it would be categorized as sword-and-scorcery. Few of his nine novels are readable.

Maza Of The Moon (1930)

R	I
C	L

KNEALE, (Thomas) Nigel (1922) English writer of the Quatermass novel, plays, screenplays and television plays. Alien beings try to establish a colony on Earth, and Professor Quatermass prevents them – after several thrilling episodes?

Quatermass (1979)

R ★ ★ ★	I ★ ★
C ★	L ★

KNIGHT, Damon (1922) American writer and editor. He produced a great deal of good sf, much of it satirical, in the 1950s, but for the last 20 years has mostly been active as an editor, responsible for the *Orbit* series of original anthologies which promoted the careers of Gene Wolfe (q.v.) and Knight's wife Kate Wilhelm (q.v.). His novels are mostly undistinguished, though he wrote some good novellas, and the best of his work is to be found in his collections. He is a polished and methodical writer whose recent handbook for writers, *Creating Short Fiction*, dissects several of his own

Arthur Koestler

pieces to show how they work. It may be this preoccupation with mechanics that has dried up the spring of his creativity. "The Country of the Kind," set in a world where there is almost no crime, is about the intolerable loneliness of a man ostracized for anti-social behaviour – it remains a classic of the genre and demonstrates the ingenuity and delicacy which makes his best work so memorable.

A For Anything (1959)

R ★ ★ ★	I ★ ★ ★
C ★ ★ ★	L ★ ★ ★

Mind Switch (1965)

R ★ ★ ★	I ★ ★
C ★ ★	L ★ ★

The World And Thorinn (1980)

R ★ ★	I ★ ★
C ★ ★	L ★ ★

KNIGHT, Norman L(ouis) (1895-1970) American writer who published a number of melodramatic stories for *Astounding* in the 1930s and early 1940s, but is best known for his collaboration with James Blish on *A Torrent Of Faces*.

A Torrent Of Faces (1967)

R ★ ★ ★ ★	I ★ ★ ★ ★
C ★	L ★ ★

KOESTLER, Arthur (1905-83) Hungarian-born writer who became a British subject in 1948. Two of his works can be classified as science fiction, *The Age Of Longing* (1951), which is more a metaphor for the helplessness of France in the Cold War years of the 1950s, and *The Call Girls: A Tragi-Comedy*, which is really a fictionalized symposium of 12 different attitudes to disaster; an overview of contemporary philosophical approaches to reality. Koestler is probably most influential via his philosophical and speculative works like *The Act Of Creation* (1964) and *The Ghost In The Machine* (1967).

The Call Girls: A Tragi-Comedy (1972)

R ★ ★	I ★ ★ ★ ★ ★
C ★	L ★ ★ ★

Jerzy Kosinski

KOMATSU, Sakyo (1931) One of the major Japanese science fiction writers, his most notable work, *Japan Sinks*, has been translated. It is a catastrophe story on an epic scale. The geological speculation in the work is impressive and highly convincing.

Japan Sinks (*Nippon Chinbotsu*, 1973; trans. 1976; a.k.a. *The Year Of The Dragon*)

R	★ ★ ★ ★ ★	I	★ ★ ★ ★
C	★	L	★ ★

KOONTZ, Dean R(ay) (1945) Prolific American author whose work varies greatly in quality. Most of his novels were written in the early 1970s, many of them more in the horror vein than sf. There is a definite gothic streak to his work and a relish for dark situations, as in *Demon Seed*, a Frankenstein-tale of a computer creating itself in the flesh (later filmed). Most impressive, perhaps, is his vision of the far-distant future in *Nightmare Journey* (1975) and his cyberdetective in *A Werewolf Among Us*. His output has diminished recently.

Demon Seed (1973)

R	★ ★ ★ ★ ★	I	★ ★ ★
C	★	L	★ ★

A Werewolf Among Us (1973)

R	★ ★ ★ ★	I	★ ★
C	★ ★	L	★ ★

KORNBLUTH, Cyril M. (1923-58) American sf and fantasy writer. Kornbluth, perhaps best known for his collaborations with Frederik Pohl (q.v.), was, as an adolescent, one of the intellectual leading spirits of the Futurians and, in his mature writing, is perhaps the central exemplar of that group's merits and defects. To the collaborations with Pohl and to his own best work he brought a sceptical attitude to stock assumptions that derives at least partly from being part of the first generation to grow up with pulp sf and is, perhaps, best embodied in *The Syndic*, in which, after the breakdown of international order and credit, New York and environs are an aimiable libertarian muddle where a bene-volent Mafia holds the ring. Kornbluth's scepticism extends both to the conventional pieties and to his own creation – this society is threatened by both the tattered remnants of the old U.S.A. and by a Chicago where the Mob has created a feudal tyranny instead. His other sf novels, *Not This August* (1955) and *Takeoff* (1952), are considerably more conventional treatments of a Soviet-dominated U.S.A. and a first space flight. Kornbluth's most important work is probably in his underrated short stories with their occasional interesting experimentalism "The Last Man Left In The Bar" (1957), and their tough-minded compassion for the humanly guilty ("The Altar At Midnight," with its scientist who drunkenly tries to exculpate himself from the use and side effects of his discoveries). Kornbluth's science fiction, like Pohl's, is politically sophisticated to an extent unusual in the period; some have found his constitutional liberalism marred by his obsession with eugenics and species degeneration.

The Syndic (1953)

R	★ ★ ★ ★	I	★ ★ ★ ★
C	★ ★ ★	L	★ ★ ★ ★

"The Mindworm" (1950)

R ★ ★ ★ ★	I ★ ★ ★
C ★ ★	L ★ ★ ★ ★

"The Altar At Midnight"

R ★ ★ ★ ★	I ★ ★ ★
C ★ ★ ★ ★	L ★ ★ ★ ★ ★

KOSINSKI, Jerzy (1933) American mainstream writer much of whose work is of a fabular nature, as in *Being There*, with its allegory of garden and gardener, and the progress of the innocent Chance to the highest post in government.

Being There (1970)

R ★ ★ ★ ★ ★ ★	I ★ ★ ★ ★ ★
C ★ ★ ★	L ★ ★ ★ ★

KOTZWINKLE, William   American author, some of whose works (fabulations) are directly sf. *Doctor Rat* is an allegory, but told by a laboratory rat: Man's inhumanity to his fellow creatures is perfectly captured, but without being in the least sentimental. *Hermes 3000* (1972) is also of interest.

Doctor Rat (1976)

R ★ ★ ★ ★ ★	I ★ ★ ★ ★
C ★	L ★ ★ ★

Henry Kuttner

KURLAND, Michael (Joseph) (1938) American writer whose earliest work was in collaboration with Chester Anderson. He is also known as a thriller/mystery writer. His solo sf novels are well-written portraits of different societies and alternative worlds (i.e. *The Whenabouts Of Burr*, 1975). A heavy satirical element pervades his books as in *The Unicorn Girl* (1969).

Tomorrow Knight (1976)

R ★ ★ ★	I ★
C ★ ★	L ★ ★

KURTZ, Katherine (1944) American writer known primarily for her science fantasy series about Deryni, an alternative world where a group of paranormal humans are being persecuted by the Church. Its medieval flavour and its well-crafted prose makes the whole series an interesting read.

Deryni Rising (1970)

R ★ ★ ★ ★	I ★ ★
C ★ ★	L ★ ★

Camber Of Culdi (1976)

R ★ ★ ★ ★	I ★ ★
C ★	L ★ ★

KUTTNER, Henry (1914-58) American writer. Most of his work after 1940 was done in collaboration with his wife C. L. Moore (q.v.). The two used several pseudonyms for work of varying tone and content, most notably Lewis Padgett and Laurence O'Donnell. Kuttner's early work was routine space opera, but he and Moore played a considerable role in leading genre sf to maturity with their work for *Astounding*. Kuttner was astonishingly versatile, equally at home writing comic sf, luxuriant fantasies in the vein of A. Merritt (q.v.), and careful extrapolations. "Mimsy Were The Borogoves" is a classic story in which parents helplessly watch their children educated into superhumanity by alien toys. Kuttner's premature death was a great loss to the genre, all the more so because C. L. Moore would not carry on without him. Although much of his work seems dated now, because he was so expert at writing for particular markets and so sensitive to the topicality of his subjects, his artistry remains admirable.

Fury (1947)

R ★ ★ ★	I ★ ★ ★
C ★ ★	L ★ ★ ★

Mutant (1953)

R ★ ★ ★	I ★ ★ ★
C ★ ★ ★	L ★ ★ ★

The Well Of The Worlds (1953)

R ★ ★ ★	I ★ ★
C ★ ★	L ★ ★

L

LAFFERTY, R(aphael) A(loysius) (1914) American writer whose first sf was published in 1960. His freewheeling style and *outré* subject matter have caused many to apply the adjective "surrealist" to his fiction, although the traditions of the American "tall tale" and the late-medieval Morality seem to share equal, billing. A prolific short story writer, Lafferty is arguably at his best in this form; his novels are rambling, but rewarding. He writes of conspiracies, strange secret sub-groups of human and alien, and hard-drinking hell-raisers evoked against a kind of Irish-Catholic mysticism. The down-home folksiness of his characters and style contrasts with the strangeness of his subject matter, as does his bizarre, often black humour, with topics of high metaphysical seriousness – for example, the novel *Fourth Mansions*. His use of sf's conventional images is wide-ranging, fresh, and imaginative, and he is capable, as in the story "Among The Hairy Earthmen," (1966) of giving the hoariest of sf ideas a serious *frisson*.

Fourth Mansions (1969)

R ★ ★	I ★ ★ ★
C ★ ★	L ★ ★ ★ ★

The Devil Is Dead (1971)

R ★ ★ ★	I ★ ★ ★ ★
C ★ ★	L ★ ★ ★ ★

LAKE, David (John) (1929) Australian writer whose imaginative strengths have never quite found the correct vehicle of expression. He can create marvellous alien worlds, like that in *Walkers On The Sky* (1976), but a simplistic adventure story prevents the novel from being more than an average read. Likewise, his two Dextra books are strong in ideas but weak in characterization. This mixture of strengths and weaknesses makes his work irritating and at times disappointing, yet he has the capacity occasionally to write superb science fiction.

The Man Who Loved Morlocks: A Sequel To The Time Machine As Narrated By The Time Traveller (1981)

R ★ ★ ★ ★	I ★ ★ ★
C ★	L ★ ★ ★

LANG, Andrew (1844-1912) Scottish writer whose volumes of fables and tales for children, which began with *The Blue Fairy Book* (1889), have had some influence on the fantasy genre, but it is in his adult short fiction that Lang displays his interest in themes that prefigure science fiction. One example is "The End Of Phaeacia," a lost race story.

In The Wrong Paradise And Other Stories (1886; coll.)

R ★ ★ ★	I ★ ★
C ★	L ★ ★

LANGE, Oliver American author of *Vandenberg*, a novel which describes Russia's easy conquest of America. The protagonist, Vandenberg, fights to the death.

Vandenberg (1971)

R ★ ★ ★	I ★
C ★ ★	L ★ ★

LANGFORD, David (1953) English writer of humorous short sf, one sf novel and a book of science fact/speculation, *War In 2080* (1979), which is comparable to the very best of Asimov's scientific popularizations and deals humanely with the problems of modern warfare. His novel, *The*

Space Eater, is a hard science adventure, entertaining and yet flawed. He is certain to become one of the genre's more popular writers, however.

The Space Eater (1982)

R ★ ★ ★ ★ ★	I ★ ★ ★
C ★ ★	L ★ ★

LANIER, Sterling E. (1927) American sf writer. Lanier is principally known for the tales his Brigadier Ffellowes tells round a clubland fireplace, in each of which he escapes from some monster or supernatural entity; these are more frightening then their adherence to formula might lead one to expect. His post-atomic quest story, *Hiero's Journey*, is notable for even more bigger and better monsters.

"The Syndicated Time" (1978)

R ★ ★ ★	I ★ ★
C ★ ★	L ★ ★

"Ghost Of A Crown" (1976)

R ★ ★ ★	I ★ ★
C ★ ★	L ★ ★

Hiero's Journey (1973)

R ★ ★ ★	I ★ ★
C ★ ★	L ★ ★ ★

LASSWITZ, Kurd (1848-1910) German philosopher, historian and writer whose sf novel, *Two Planets*, depicts a confrontation between Mankind and a superior Martian culture. The Martians conquer Earth, rule benignly, degenerate, are overthrown, and both species are deemed equal, Earth becoming an Utopia.

Two Planets (1897; trans. as *Auf Zwei Planeten*, 1971)

R ★ ★ ★	I ★ ★
C ★	L ★ ★

LATHAM, Philip (1902) Pseudonym of American writer and astronomer Robert Shirley Richardson, active in the sf field in the 1940s and 1950s. He wrote two juvenile sf novels, *Five Against Venus* (1952) and *Missing Men Of Saturn*, both of which are notable for their scientific content, if

David Langford

not particularly for their style.

Missing Men Of Saturn (1953)

R ★ ★ ★	I ★ ★
C ★	L ★

LAUMER, Keith (1925) American sf writer. Laumer was first noticed for the farcical template series in which dashing young diplomat Retief cuts through the absurd obfuscations of his senior colleagues to confound Earth's enemies. More important work applies a similar verve to darker matters; Laumer's heroes go through rites of passage to attain personal and often species transcendence but the losses they suffer in the process are emotionally credible and genuinely tragic. The hero of *A Plague Of Demons* is transformed into a super-powered cyborg by agents of a benevolent international conspiracy then, captured by lupine aliens, his "washed" brain is made to run a vast war machine on the moon; he reasserts his personal identity and leads a revolt. Laumer is not noted for effective female characters or for even the smallest sneaking sympathy with un-American values. His career has in recent years been hindered by major illness.

Dinosaur Beach (1971)

R	★	★	★	★	I	★	★	★
C	★	★	★		L	★	★	★

Retief's Ransom (1975)

R	★	★	★	★	I	★	★	
C	★	★			L	★	★	

A Plague Of Demons (1967)

R	★	★	★	★	I	★	★	★
C	★	★	★		L	★	★	★

LE CLEZIO, J(ean)-M(arie) G(ustave) (1940) French writer, few of whose sf-oriented absurdist fictions have been translated into English. His work might be judged from *The Giants*, where the mind's hallucinatory matter is made manifest in a future city.

The Giants (1973; trans. as *Les Géants*, 1975)

R	★	★	★		I	★	★	★
C	★				L	★	★	

LEE, Tanith (1947) English writer whose work spans the whole range of horror, fantasy and science fiction. She is probably at her best when writing sword-and-sorcery of an epic kind, as in the Birthgrave series of novels. Initiations and quests are at the

Ursula K. Le Guin

heart of her writing, and though her protagonists often possess awesome mental powers she retains a very human emphasis throughout her work. She began as a writer for juveniles with novels like *The Dragon Hoard* (1971) but has become prolific as an adult fantasist. There is often no definite boundary in her work between the different horror, fantasy and sf elements, and they are cleverly co-ordinated in a single plot. The simplicity of her prose is deceptive, for she can create highly lucid and memorable scenes from simple elements, and the trials and tribulations of her heroes and heroines are powerfully conveyed. Her Birthgrave series, set in a far-future world, of which *Quest For The White Witch* (1978) and *Drinking Sapphire Wine* are a part, reveals her as a writer with a great but as yet untapped potential. At present she is a powerful storyteller but could, as suggested by moments in novels like *Electric Forest*, become a memorable fabulist.

The Birthgrave (1977)

R	★	★	★	★	I	★		
C	★	★			L	★	★	

Drinking Sapphire Wine (1977)

R	★	★	★		I	★		
C	★	★			L	★	★	

Electric Forest (1979)

R	★	★	★	★	I	★	★	
C	★	★	★		L	★	★	

LEGUIN, Ursula K(roeber) (1929) American writer who, since the publication of her first novel, *Rocannon's World* (1966), has exerted more influence on the sf field than any other writer. She possesses a rare visual talent which, presented in her immaculate and economic prose gives her work a startling vividness. There is an underlying concern for a "balance" of all things which is essentially Taoist in its conception, and many of her stories enact a marriage of opposites. Her fantasy trilogy – ostensibly a juvenile, but one of the finest adult books also – *Earthsea*, is a search for "balance" presented through the education of a young Wizard, Ged; a search that leads him even into death's kingdom at one stage. *The Left Hand Of Darkness* was the novel with which LeGuin made her mark on the genre. A spellbinding work, it describes the world of Winter and its androgynous inhabitants, as seen through the eyes of the Envoy, Genly Ai. There are always memorable central characters in LeGuin's work, but none more memorable than Shevek in *The Dispossessed*, which is arguably the finest sf novel yet written. The scientific speculation by which an instantaneous transmitter (an *ansible*) is created, is utterly plausible, yet this is only secondary to the story of two worlds, one like ours and one an anarchist state; one richly fertile, the other barren. Shevek is the focus wherein things meet and, after acute disharmony, are ultimately balanced. The novel won both the Hugo and Nebula awards and remains the peak of LeGuin's achievement to date. Her shorter fiction covers a wide range from fantasy to contemporary fable, and is typified by excellent works such as "Vaster Than Empires And More Slow" (1971), "An Die Musik", and the recent "Sur" (1982). All of the early novels, bar *The Lathe Of Heaven* (1969), were set in the same future universe where the Hain organize a peaceful League of All Worlds; a wise, intelligent race older than Man. This setting has been dropped in recent works, and LeGuin has set several short stories and one novel, *Malafrena* (1979), in an imaginary nineteenth-century Eastern European country. This movement from a directly science-fictional landscape to a historical/political one has helped to sharpen her moral edge, but has, unfortunately, meant that some of the visionary magic has departed from her recent work. *Threshold* (1980, a.k.a. *The Beginning Place*) is a juvenile quest novel with a difference (for it asks what you do when the dragon is slain and real life lies ahead of you), and with it LeGuin seems to have written herself out of the sf field. Several short stories have suggested that she may yet return to sf, but her interest in feminism and Taoism and too great an academic scrutiny upon her work appears to have made her look elsewhere (in particular to poetry) for expression. A whole generation of young sf writers, male and female, look to her as their mentor, just as an earlier generation looked to Heinlein (q.v.).

The Left Hand Of Darkness (1969)

R	★ ★ ★ ★ ★	I	★ ★ ★ ★ ★
C	★ ★ ★ ★ ★	L	★ ★ ★ ★ ★

Earthsea (1977; individual novels published 1968, 1971, 1973)

R	★ ★ ★ ★ ★	I	★ ★ ★
C	★ ★ ★ ★	L	★ ★ ★ ★

The Dispossessed (1974)

R	★ ★ ★ ★ ★	I	★ ★ ★ ★ ★
C	★ ★ ★ ★ ★	L	★ ★ ★ ★ ★

"An Die Musik" (1961)

R	★ ★ ★ ★ ★	I	★ ★
C	★ ★	L	★ ★ ★ ★ ★

LEIBER, Fritz (1910) American sf and fantasy writer. Leiber's long and distinguished career has left its mark on most of the sf and fantasy sub-genres. His heroic fantasies featuring the Grey Mouser and Fafhrd brought to the form a redeeming cynicism and wit, notably in the novel *The Swords Of Lankhmar* (1968); his horror fiction largely abandons the traditional imperatives for specifically urban dreads. He contributed to the time travel story the concept of the Change War, in which both

Fritz Leiber

sides alter history in an attempt to remove the other's origins and are seen (particularly in *The Big Time*) as agents of a new sort of evolution. A body of effective short social satires from the 1940s and 1950s (notably "Coming Attraction" (1951) and "The Girl With Hungry Eyes" (1949) – the latter discussed at length by Marshall McLuhan as a paradigm of media-influenced sexuality) culminated in *A Spectre Is Haunting Texas* in which a gangling actor from an orbital colony becomes the figurehead of a revolt against racial tyranny. Leiber's own theatrical background contributed to his fiction both a myth of backstage camaraderie (the time soldiers in *The Big Time*, the revolutionaries in *Spectre*) and a notable sense of pace and timing. *The Wanderer* (1964) is an interesting fusion of multi-viewpoint disaster novel and space opera which explores, adventurously for its time, various sorts of sado-masochistic sexuality. His fiction of the 1970s is chastened, discursive and confessional: the traditional sf topic of alternate worlds is used in "Catch That Zeppelin" (1975; a Hugo and Nebula winner) for an only partly fictional essay on old age and its sense of lost possibilities. The horror novel *Our Lady Of Darkness* is overtly a transformation of some tragic passages in Leiber's own life and a portrayal in art of how it helped him survive them.

The Big Time (1961)

R ★ ★ ★ ★	I ★ ★ ★ ★
C ★ ★ ★	L ★ ★ ★

A Spectre Is Haunting Texas (1969)

R ★ ★ ★ ★	I ★ ★ ★
C ★ ★	L ★ ★ ★

Our Lady Of Darkness (1977)

R ★ ★ ★ ★	I ★ ★ ★ ★
C ★ ★ ★ ★	L ★ ★ ★ ★

LEINSTER, Murray (1896-1975) Pseudonym used by American writer Will F. Jenkins for most of his sf. He began writing sf for the pulps before there were specialist sf magazines, and continued right through to the 1960s, adapting his style and subjects to suit the market as it developed. Some of his early work was innovative –

notably, "Sidewise In Time" (1934), an early story of time disruption – but for the most part he was a thoroughgoing professional who seemed to fit in so well with his environment that he almost faded into the background. He wrote a great many potboilers but was a thoroughly competent entertainer whose better work repays attention.

The Forgotten Planet (1954)

R ★ ★ ★	I ★ ★
C ★	L ★ ★

The Other Side Of Nowhere (1964)

R ★ ★ ★	I ★ ★
C ★ ★	L ★ ★

Time Tunnel (1964)

R ★ ★ ★	I ★ ★
C ★ ★	L ★ ★

LEM, Stanislaw (1921) Polish writer whose erudite, intelligent and witty use of science fiction has established him as Europe's foremost sf writer. His academic champions view him as a creator of modern parables in which Mankind's limitations are defined in encounters with the alien. The less critical and more average sf reader will find him a deeply philosophical satirist of great inventive power, whose work often amuses but more often creates a genuine sense of intellectual wonder. This is not to say that he lacks compassion, simply that the humour is the medium for its expression: a truly Polish outlet in these times. Some works are more memorable as pure sf than others, notably *Solaris* (filmed by Tarkovsky), which depicts a sentient alien planet, and the collections of stories featuring Pirx The Pilot, including *Tales Of Pilot Pirx*, which are perhaps Lem's most overtly didactic tales. *Memoirs Found In A Bathtub* (1971; trans. 1973) is a satire on militarism and its surrounding paranoid madness, whilst *The Cyberiad: Fables For The Cybernetic Age* is a rather charming story-cycle about two robot-constructors. Opinions differ greatly within the field concerning Lem's ultimate worth, and though he seems not to have influenced science fiction as greatly as several far less talented

Stanislaw Lem

American sf writers, those he has affected with his highly crafted and impressively thoughtful work are creating what is, perhaps, that part of the genre which will last the test of time.

Solaris (1968; trans. 1970)

R ★ ★ ★	I ★ ★ ★ ★ ★
C ★ ★	L ★ ★ ★

Tales Of Pilot Pirx (1968; coll.)

R ★ ★ ★ ★	I ★ ★ ★ ★
C ★ ★	L ★ ★ ★

The Cyberiad (1967; trans. 1974; coll.)

R ★ ★ ★ ★	I ★ ★ ★ ★
C ★ ★ ★	L ★ ★ ★

L'ENGLE, Madeleine (1918) American writer prolific in other genres and only active in the sf field since the mid-1970s, although the first volume in her Time trilogy was published in 1962. Her work is almost allegorical in its use of science-fictional metaphor, the outer world reflecting the inner life of her characters. One novel, *A Ring Of Endless Light*, exists out of the Time sequence.

A Wind In The Door (1973)

R ★ ★ ★	I ★ ★
C ★ ★	L ★

LEOURIER, Christian (1948) French author of *The Mountains Of The Sun*, which depicts a future catastrophe on Earth (a great flood) and the return, centuries later, of the Martian colonists. A story of the integration of two highly different cultures.

The Mountains Of The Sun (1971; trans. as *Les Montagnes Du Soleil*, 1974)

R ★ ★ ★	I ★ ★
C ★ ★	L ★ ★

LE QUEUX, William (Tufnell) (1864-1927) English writer of fast-paced and exotic thrillers and romances. His sf is of the future-war/invasion kind, with *The Great War In England In 1897* (1894) and *The Invasion Of 1910*, both of them pieces of speculative journalism with the spice of sensationalism and scare-mongering. Germany is the enemy in both cases.

The Invasion Of 1910; With A Full Account Of The Siege Of London (1906)

R ★	I ★ ★
C ★	L ★

LESSER, Milton (1928) American writer, prolific in the thriller/mystery genre. In sf he wrote mainly juveniles (sometimes as Adam Chase) in the 1950s and early 1960s few of which are more than fast-paced space opera.

Recruit For Andromeda (1959)

R ★ ★	I
C	L ★

LESSING, Doris (1919) Expatriate Rhodesian novelist, resident in England. Lessing has come to the attention of the sf audience most prominently with her continuing series "Canopus In Argos: Archives," though sf tropes traditional and modern have featured in her work since *The Four-Gated City* (1969). This fifth volume of the Children of Violence sequence takes her story of Martha Quest up to the disastrous end of the twentieth century: Britain is classified as "Destroyed Area II," polluted with nerve-gas and radioactive fallout. Lessing's original concern was with the politics of personal conduct in an unjust and self-destructive society. Sf gave her techniques for questioning a culture as a whole, and a standpoint for moral warnings of the "If this goes on . . ." kind. More recently, Lessing's feminism has been displaced by her adoption of the Sufi faith. Political protest still resonates through her fiction, but now in the context of lamenting the Fall and seeking a redemptive orderly life of wise passivity. The sf she has read has been mainly British – Wells (q.v.), Stapleton (q.v.), Lewis (q.v.), Wyndham (q.v.). She follows their tradition of using sf as a vehicle for speculation on civilization and ethics. The Canopus books are written as the archives of a wise and benign interstellar empire of which Earth (Shikasta) is the most benighted and disobedient colony.

Briefing For A Descent Into Hell (1971)

R	★ ★ ★		I	★ ★	
C	★ ★ ★		L	★ ★ ★	

The Memoirs Of A Survivor (1974)

R	★ ★ ★ ★		I	★ ★ ★	
C	★ ★ ★ ★		L	★ ★ ★	

Shikasta (1979)

R	★ ★ ★		I	★ ★	
C	★ ★ ★ ★		L	★ ★ ★	

C. S. Lewis

LEVIN, Ira (1929) Successful American writer most of whose novels have been filmed. His fantasy *Rosemary's Baby* helped to initiate the cinematic horror boom of the late 1960s and 1970s. His next three novels were all sf, and all are vivid cautionary tales about the misuse of science, ranging from the ironic satire *The Stepford Wives*, in which the men of a small town replace their wives with robots, to the slightly ponderous dystopian novel *This Perfect Day*. *The Boys From Brazil*, about an attempt to clone dozens of replicas of Hitler, is a highly effective thriller. Levin's strength is his plotting, which is delicately ingenious. He seems fascinated by the exploitation of women, extraordinary varieties of which are presented in all his works.

This Perfect Day (1970)

R	★ ★ ★		I	★ ★	
C	★ ★		L	★ ★	

The Stepford Wives (1972)

R	★ ★ ★		I	★ ★	
C	★ ★ ★		L	★ ★ ★	

The Boys From Brazil (1976)

R	★ ★ ★ ★		I	★ ★ ★	
C	★ ★ ★		L	★ ★ ★	

LEWIS, C. S. (1898-1963) Lewis is considered by many to be the H. G. Wells of Christendom; and our introduction to Lewis, as to Wells (q.v.), is likely to be through his sf. Lewis called it "theologized" sf; though only in the case of *Perelandra (Voyage To Venus)* is this likely to feel obtrusive. *Out Of The Silent Planet* (1938) deals with Mars: an unfallen hierarchical society, doomed in the evolutionary scheme of things. Ransom, the donnish hero, grapples with Terran scientists who look towards a very different future hierarchy. *Perelandra* (1943) foreshadows the New Creation, complete with new Adam and Eve. Satan tries to restage *Paradise Lost*, and Ransom tries to stop him. *That Hideous Strength* (1945) has conflicting angelic pasts and futures fighting it out through human agents in a present-day university town devastated by perverted science. Those doubting the complexity of

Lewis's mind are directed to *The Dark Tower* (1977), a related fragment; and *Till We Have Faces*, a psychological retelling of the Cupid and Psyche myth. The seven related novels which comprise *The Chronicles Of Narnia* (1950-56) postulate a parallel universe of talking beasts, in which God is incarnate as a Lion: another doomed hierarchy, which actually dies in the final book (*The Last Battle*). Human and Narnian history have a complex interrelationship, and the entire series is a successful and highly readable combination of Swift, Kenneth Grahame, and Plato.

That Hideous Strength (1945)

R ★ ★ ★ ★ ★	I ★ ★ ★ ★ ★
C ★ ★ ★	L ★ ★ ★ ★

Till We Have Faces (1956)

R ★ ★ ★ ★	I ★ ★ ★ ★ ★
C ★ ★ ★ ★ ★	L ★ ★ ★ ★ ★

The Lion, The Witch And The Wardrobe (1950)

R ★ ★ ★ ★ ★	I ★ ★ ★ ★ ★
C ★ ★ ★	L ★ ★ ★

LEWIS, (Ernest Michael) Roy (1913) English author of *What We Did To Father*, a humorous work which utilizes evolutionary theory anachronistically – by setting itself in the Pleistocene and having the evolutionary debate in the mouths of cavemen. A delightful and irreverent book.

What We Did To Father (1960; a.k.a., *The Evolution Man/ Once Upon An Ice Age*)

R ★ ★ ★ ★ ★	I ★ ★
C ★ ★	L ★ ★

LEWIS, (Harry) Sinclair (1885-1951) American writer, known in the sf field for his work, *It Can't Happen Here*, which portrays the development of a Nazi-style totalitarian régime in the U.S.A. It has dated more than most dystopian novels because of its contemporary frame of reference.

It Can't Happen Here (1925)

R ★ ★	I ★ ★ ★
C ★ ★	L ★ ★

LIGHTNER, Alice (Martha) (1904) American writer of juvenile science fiction novels which, whilst simple in structure and style, express quite complex intellectual and moral questions with a degree of lucidity.

The Day Of The Drones (1969)

R ★ ★ ★ ★	I ★ ★ ★
C ★ ★	L ★ ★

LINDSAY, David (1878-1945) English writer whose fantasy novels have a philosophic and esoteric flavour to them. His *A Voyage To Arcturus* is undoubtedly a classic work of science fantasy which is one of the most perfect blends of adventure and idea, depicting Maskull's metaphysical picaresque to meet the god-like Crystalman behind the layers of illusion. The posthumously published *The Violet Apple* is a fascinating mixture of contemporary sexual mores (1920s) and a visionary glimpse of the past glories of Eden and its tree of knowledge. Lindsay is, quite clearly, one of this century's foremost fantasists.

A Voyage To Arcturus (1920)

R ★ ★ ★ ★	I ★ ★ ★ ★ ★
C ★ ★	L ★ ★ ★ ★ ★

The Violet Apple (1976)

R ★ ★ ★ ★ ★	I ★ ★ ★ ★
C ★ ★ ★	L ★ ★ ★ ★

LINKLATER, Eric (Robert Russell) (1899-1974) Scottish writer of a number of sf novels for juveniles with strong fantasy and speculative elements. An adult novel, *The Impregnable Women*, is expressive of its time of publication in being an up-date of *Lysistrata*.

The Impregnable Women (1938)

R ★ ★	I ★ ★
C ★	L ★ ★

LLEWELLYN, (David William) Alun (1903) English-born Irish writer, known in sf circles for his novel *The Strange Invaders*, which is set in a new Ice Age. In a Russia of the future, Marx, Lenin and Stalin are the tribal gods of a degenerate and barbarian culture; a culture attacked by Mankind's heirs, sentient lizard-like creatures.

The Strange Invaders (1934)

R ★ ★ ★ ★	I ★ ★ ★
C ★ ★	L ★ ★ ★

LOFTING, Hugh   English author of the Dr Dolittle Books. His *Doctor Dolittle In The Moon* is his only marginally sf book, wherein his hero travels by giant moth to the Moon, whereupon there are indescribable colours. It is a highly evocative juvenile.

Doctor Dolittle In The Moon (1929)

R ★ ★ ★	I ★ ★
C ★	L ★ ★

LOGAN, Charles (1930) English writer whose novel, *Shipwreck*, is a modern Crusoe-like story of the last survivor of a disaster, abandoned on an alien world, Tamsis, who sets out to explore his environment, succeeds but, true to the logic of the story, dies. A well-told début.

Shipwreck (1975)

R ★ ★ ★ ★ ★	I ★ ★
C ★ ★	L ★ ★

LONDON, Jack (1876-1916) American writer, mainly noted for his non-fantasy work. He wrote several important sf short stories, including "The Scarlet Plague," a celebrated disaster story. His novels include a prehistoric fantasy, *Before Adam* (1907); an account of an unsuccessful socialist revolution in America, *The Iron Heel*; and the story of a man whose personality is set free from his body during periodic punishments in prison, *The Star Rover*. He was perhaps the most important American writer of Wellsian scientific romance and has particularly influenced American sf authors.

The Iron Heel (1907)

R ★ ★ ★	I ★ ★ ★
C ★ ★ ★	L ★ ★ ★

The Star Rover (1915)

R ★ ★ ★	I ★ ★ ★
C ★ ★ ★	L ★ ★ ★

LONG, Charles R(ussell) (1904) American author of two fairly standard sf novels, utilizing a wide range of science fiction hardware and ideas (telepathy, immortality, aliens, parallel worlds, etc.). His imaginative powers and story-telling abilities do not match his ambition, especially in *The Infinite Brain* (1957).

The Eternal Man (1964)

R ★ ★	I ★ ★
C ★	L ★

LONG, Frank Belknap (1903) American writer, more noted for his weird fiction than his sf. He was a member of the literary circle surrounding H. P. Lovecraft (q.v.) and his best work is in the Lovecraftian vein. He wrote a good deal of sf in the early 1960s, but most of it is derivative and undistinguished. The collection *The Hounds Of Tindalos* (1946) contains his best work, though most of his early pulp sf is in *The Rim Of The Unknown* (1972).

The Horror From The Hills (1931)

R ★ ★	I ★ ★
C ★	L ★

Woman From Another Planet (1960)

R ★	I
C	L

Lest Earth Be Conquered (1966)

R ★	I
C	L

LONGYEAR, Barry B.   American writer who, winning Hugo and Nebula awards for his work, has come to prominence in the last few years. His fiction, however, is far from an award-winning quality, and is often simply poor mainstream fiction given an artificial colouring and flavouring of sf gimmickry. *Circus World* (1983) and the earlier *City Of Baraboo* (1981) are lightweight and, at their worst, trivial works about circus antics in space, whereas *Manifest Destiny* is a sentimental, cardboard melodrama about future warfare, which doubtlessly calls on memories of Vietnam rather than speculative ideas of what war will be like. *Elephant*

World, another circus novel, is simply appalling in every sense, and hints that Longyear has very little to offer the sf genre.

Manifest Destiny (1980)

R ★	I
C	L ★

Elephant World (1983)

R	I
C	L

LOOMIS, Noel M(iller) (1905-79) American writer who also wrote one sf novel as Silas Water (*The Man With Absolute Motion* (1955)). Many of his short stories appeared in the sf magazines between 1945 and 1970, none of which are more than stock scientific adventure. The same can be said of his too-neat novel, *City Of Glass.*

City Of Glass (1955)

R ★ ★	I ★
C ★	L ★

LOVECRAFT, H(oward) P(hillips) (1890-1937) American writer whose work for *Weird Tales* in the 1920s and 1930s can be viewed as a sub-genre in itself, creating an alternate mythology of dark underworld gods, the Cthulhu Mythos, within which a number of his contemporaries set their tales. His longest piece of fiction, *At The Mountains Of Madness*, is part of the Mythos and is typical of the rest, if not, perhaps, the finest story in the sequence. Lovecraft creates dark and sometimes horrific scenarios which, in their tense and gothic style, can seem like the visions of a madman. The formless entity dominates his work, an impalpable threat which lies beneath everything he wrote, and which was possibly an expression of his strange lifestyle. His stories are often garishly overwritten and occasionally fail to fulfil their simple tale-telling function, but at his best there is an atmospheric intensity which transcends the limitations of his cluttered prose, as in "The Dunwich Horror" (1929). To say that he is in the tradition of Poe (q.v.) is not to devalue his originality

and idiosyncracity, particularly in his vision of a world where even the most familiar object or person can be revealed to be part of an alien and wholly inimical universe.

At The Mountains Of Madness And Other Novels (1964)

R ★ ★ ★ ★	I ★ ★
C ★ ★	L ★ ★

The Colour Out Of Space (1964; coll.)

R ★ ★ ★	I ★ ★
C ★	L ★

The Dunwich Horror (1945; coll.)

R ★ ★ ★ ★	I ★ ★ ★
C ★ ★	L ★ ★

H. P. Lovecraft

LOVESEY, Andrew (1941) English author of *The Half-Angels*, an allegorical work where the protagonist is transported to an alien world to undergo a quest. He uses a mixture of fantasy and sf elements quite professionally, if not originally.

The Half-Angels (1975)

R ★ ★ ★	I ★
C ★	L ★ ★

LOWNDES, Robert A(ugustine) W(ard) (1916) American writer and editor. He published four fairly mundane novels in the 1950s and early 1960s which had a basic action-adventure formula, but is much better in his shorter fiction which is of the Lovecraft/Ashton-Smith school. Much of his shorter work was published under pseudonyms, such as Paul Dennis Lavond, Mallory Kent and Wilfred Owen Morley.

The Puzzle Planet (1961)

R ★ ★	I ★
C	L ★

LUCAS, George (1944) American film-director/producer who wrote the noveliza-tion of his own film, *Star Wars*, which, whilst it captures something of the film's fast-paced sense of wonder, cannot, un-fortunately, match the film's visual qualities.

Star Wars: From The Adventures Of Luke Skywalker (1976)

R ★ ★ ★ ★ ★	I ★
C ★ ★	L ★ ★

LUNDWALL, Sam J(errie) (1941) Swedish writer, active in sf fandom since the 1950s. He is a good sf satirist and much of his work has been translated into English. His activities as editor and pub-lisher of sf have made him the father figure of Swedish sf.

King Kong Blues (1974; a.k.a., *AD 2018: or, The King Kong Blues*)

R ★ ★ ★	I ★ ★
C ★	L ★

LUPOFF, Richard A(llen) (1935) American writer, highly active in the sf field since the mid-1970s. He has produced much which is simple fast-action narrative, but his fixed-up novel (rewritten from four shorter pieces), *Space War Blues*, is a quite exceptional piece of science fiction, as readable for its experiments in linguistic expression (colloquial viewpoints) as for its moving story of racial warfare in a future where the dispersal of racial types to separate planets has occurred. His fantasy novel, *Sword Of The Demon*, shows a similar care for materials, its research into

Japanese mythology and literary style car-ried out in depth. Unlike many colder and more intellectual writers Lupoff uses his experiments in prose to illuminate his stories and not obfuscate; to reveal other-ness through a difference in expression. He seems comfortable in whatever style he adopts and, though the bulk of his work is fairly routine, has the ability to write the very best science fiction.

Space War Blues (1978)

R ★ ★ ★ ★ ★	I ★ ★ ★ ★
C ★ ★ ★	L ★ ★ ★ ★ ★

Sword Of The Demon (1977)

R ★ ★ ★ ★	I ★ ★ ★ ★
C ★ ★	L ★ ★ ★

LYMINGTON, John (1911) Pseudonym of English writer John Newton Chance. He was prolific in the 1960s and has begun to publish again in recent years, although without any real consideration of the maturation in the sf field in the interim years. His work is essentially space opera, told slickly but unimaginatively. *The Night Of The Big Heat* (1959), his first novel (later filmed), is typical; an uninspired alien in-vasion story.

A Caller From Overspace (1979)

R ★ ★	I ★
C	L ★

LYNN, Elizabeth (1946) Winner of Best Novel and Best Short Story at the 1980 World Fantasy Awards, with *Watchtower*, the first novel in her *Chronicles Of Tornor* trilogy, and "The Woman Who Loved The Moon," the title story from her only short fiction book. Her first novel, *A Different Light*, is a conventional sf story, not dis-similar in style to her later work, yet is a seriously flawed piece of fiction. Not the case, though, with her stories of the Land of Arun. Sketching the history and culture of the land over 500 years through the eyes of three vastly different characters – swordsman Ryke in *Watchtower*, telepath Kerris in *The Dancers Of Arun* (1979) and the visionary Sorren in "The Northern Girl" (1980) – she blends telepathy with

Anne McCaffrey

martial art to produce an excellent fantasy in the sword-and-sorcery tradition.

A Different Light (1978)

R ★ ★ ★	I ★ ★
C ★ ★ ★	L ★ ★

Watchtower (1979)

R ★ ★ ★ ★	I ★ ★ ★
C ★ ★ ★ ★	L ★ ★ ★

"The Woman Who Loved The Moon" (1979)

R ★ ★ ★ ★	I ★ ★ ★
C ★ ★ ★ ★	L ★ ★ ★

LYTTON, (Edward George Earle) Bulwer (1803-73) English writer who often used the occult in his work, but is known in the sf field for his Utopian work *The Coming Race*, which depicts an underground society, the Vril-ya, who have been in existence for thousands of years. Its delight in technology is evident, and it was a marked influence on Wells (q.v.).

The Coming Race (1871)

R ★ ★ ★	I ★ ★
C ★	L ★ ★

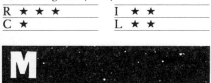

McCAFFREY, Anne (Inez) (1926) American writer permanently living in Ireland. She is famous for her fantasy series depicting the world of Pern, where dragons and dragonriders fight a perpetual battle against the Threads, a life-devouring substance thrown out by Pern's companion planet. The idea, ingenious in itself and dramatically and vividly portrayed in *Dragonflight* and *Dragonquest* (1971), has, perhaps, been overworked in an effort to please her readers' requests for ever-more sequels. The original stories, "Weyr Search" (1967) and "Dragonrider" (1967/8) won, respectively, the Hugo and Nebula awards. A juvenile series, including *Dragonsong* (1976) and *Dragonsinger* (1977), are again set on Pern, but feature a young heroine, Menolly. They are lesser works but entertaining enough. Better are McCaffrey's early non-series novels, like *Restoree* (1967), a melodramatic but nonetheless gripping kidnap-and-mutilation-by-aliens tale (in the American tradition of Mary Rowlandson's "Captivity"), and *Decision At Doona* (1969), a frontier-planet story which again depicts confrontation with sentient aliens. Most interesting, however, is *The Ship Who Sang*, about a defective human, Helva, who is cybernetically linked to a spaceship, so that, in effect, she becomes the ship. McCaffrey is often accused of sentimentality, yet her depiction of cruel necessities acts as a balance to this. There is a love in her work (especially in the Pern works) of a cruder, almost medieval cultural framework, wherein characters can better express their intrinsic selves, and her characterization is memorable because of this. There is some evidence, however, that more recent works, such as *Get Off The Unicorn* (1977) and *The Coelura*, are far less imaginative than her earlier work and tend towards fantasy clichés.

Dragonflight (1968)

R ★ ★ ★ ★ ★	I ★ ★ ★ ★
C ★ ★ ★	L ★ ★ ★

The Ship Who Sang (1969)

R ★ ★ ★ ★ ★	I ★ ★
C ★ ★ ★	L ★ ★ ★

The Coelura (1983)

R ★ ★ ★	I ★
C ★ ★	L ★ ★

MacAPP, C. C. (1917-71) Pseudonym of American writer Carroll M. Capps, whose work appeared in the sister magazines *If* and *Worlds Of Tomorrow* in the 1960s. His second novel, *Worlds Of The Wall*, is an interesting depiction of an other-dimensional world.

Worlds Of The Wall (1969)

R ★ ★ ★	I ★ ★
C ★ ★	L ★

MACAULEY, Robie   American author of *A Secret History Of The Time To Come*, a fast-action post-holocaust story which adds little to a crowded sub-genre.

A Secret History Of The Time To Come (1982)

R ★ ★ ★	I
C ★	L ★ ★

McCLARY, Thomas (Calvert) American writer who produced some work as Calvin Peregoy. His two novels *Rebirth, When Everyone Forgot* (1944) and *Three Thousand Years* are evolutionary tales with a nasty sting in their tails.

Three Thousand Years (1954)

R ★ ★	I ★
C ★	L ★

McCOLLUM, Michael   American author of *Life Probe*, where an alien probe/spacecraft seeks Earth's help in refitting – bargaining its vast, alien knowledge for all of Earth's economic resources. In the bargain the Pan-Africans lose out. A strange, frighteningly racist book in its conclusion of the-stars-or-bust.

Life Probe (1983)

R ★ ★ ★	I ★
C ★	L ★

McCUTCHAN, Philip (1920) English writer whose sf novels are slick thrillers content to use the science-fictional element as colourful trimming.

A Time For Survival (1966)

R ★ ★ ★	I
C ★	L ★

MacDONALD, George (1824-1905) In *Phantastes* (1858), MacDonald combined his Calvinist heritage with anticipations of Jung and Kafka, to produce a surreal spiritual autobiography of Everyman: the long struggle of Anodos with his Shadow. In *Lilith* (1895), MacDonald's vision extended to encompass Civilization: the eponymous djinn princess embodies not just individual *gnosis*, but the Power Principle. Once Lilith reigns in the soul, salvation and damnation are at hand; once Lilith reigns over the city of Bulika – like Helen over Troy – so does the Shadow. Revolution comes, Lilith is taken; but now the riddle of Death confronts us nakedly. Finally, MacDonald suggests an answer in his usual surreal way.

Phantastes (1858)

R ★ ★ ★ ★ ★	I ★ ★ ★ ★ ★
C ★ ★	L ★ ★ ★ ★

Lilith (1895)

R ★ ★ ★ ★ ★	I ★ ★ ★ ★ ★
C ★ ★ ★	L ★ ★ ★ ★

"The Golden Key" (1871)

R ★ ★ ★ ★ ★	I ★ ★ ★ ★ ★
C ★ ★ ★	L ★ ★ ★ ★

MacDONALD, John D(ann) (1916) American writer who was prolific in the late 1940s and throughout the 1950s. Much of his work appeared in *Astounding*, and some of it appeared pseudonymously as by John Wade Farrell and Peter Reed. His novels are interesting and highly entertaining but all too often depend upon gimmick ideas and not solid extrapolated situations, as in *The Girl, The Gold Watch, And Everything* (1962), a power-fantasy about a man who has a watch that speeds up time for him.

Ballroom Of The Skies (1962)

R ★ ★ ★	I ★
C ★	L ★

McINTOSH, J. T. (1925) Pseudonym of Scottish writer James Murdoch MacGregor. He was prolifically active in the sf magazines of the 1950s and early 1960s, and published more than a dozen sf novels with paperback houses in the U.S.A. (a common pattern for British sf writers). His early work is probably his best; his novels and stories of the 1970s lack freshness. His concern with libertarian societies and for strong characters making sense of chaos is apparently unabated.

World Out Of Mind (1953)

R ★ ★ ★ ★	I ★ ★
C ★ ★	L ★ ★

This Is The Way The World Begins (1977)

R ★ ★ ★	I
C ★	L ★ ★

McINTYRE, Vonda N(eel) (1948) American writer whose first published story, "Of Mist, And Grass And Sand" (1973), won the Nebula Award. Her first novel, *The Exile Waiting*, was, however, a poor mixture of soap opera and space opera, an over-complex and rather garish

Vonda N. McIntyre

work which has derivative elements of Russ (q.v.), Delany (q.v.) and Sturgeon (q.v.), but attempts to show its super-normal heroine, Mischa's, initiation rite of passage. Whilst its sentimentality is for other values than male-dominated contemporary society's set, her work, with its strong feminist purpose, is sometimes archly sentimental. There is an almost adolescent quality to her work which, even at its best, as in the extended "Of Mist . . .", *Dreamsnake*, prevents it from being more than wish-fulfilment; as much power-fantasy as Robert E. Howard's (q.v.). Her male characters are emasculated, and her women – unattractive, disassociated and usually *different* in some crucial, alienating way – find ways and means of compensating for the unsatisfactory *now* in a wholly satisfactory far-future. This aspect of her work detracts from her fine story-telling abilities and her facility with prose which deservedly won her Hugo and Nebula awards for *Dreamsnake*.

The Exile Waiting (1975)

R ★ ★ ★	I ★
C ★	L ★ ★

Dreamsnake (1978)

R ★ ★ ★ ★ ★	I ★ ★
C ★ ★ ★	L ★ ★ ★

Fireflood And Other Stories (1979; coll.)

R ★ ★ ★ ★	I ★ ★
C ★	L ★ ★

McKENNA, Richard M(ilton) (1913-64) American writer whose science fiction and fantasy stories are few in quantity but high in quality. The relationship of world to imagination and language is a prime concern of his work; how the mind can change the nature of the landscape it inhabits.

Casey Agonistes And Other Science Fiction And Fantasy Stories (1973; coll.)

R ★ ★ ★ ★	I ★ ★ ★
C ★ ★	L ★ ★ ★

MacKENZIE, Compton (Edward Montague) (1883-1972) Scottish writer whose sf novel, *The Lunatic Republic*, is a lightweight humorous Utopian story, set on the Moon.

The Lunatic Republic (1959)

R ★ ★ ★	I ★
C ★	L ★ ★

McKILLIP, Patricia   American writer, whose children's novels, like *The Forgotten Beasts Of Eld* (1974) and *The Night Gift* (1976), are amongst the best juvenile fiction produced in the 1970s. However, her greatly underrated trilogy, *The Chronicles Of Morgon, Prince Of Hed* (1976-79), establishes her as one of the leading science fantasy writers. The trilogy, based loosely on the Welsh *Mabinogion* (myths and legends), is not a sub-Tolkein pastiche (despite the obligatory map) but a sophisticated and subtle study of its protagonist in a world where evil is loose and shape is plastic.

The Riddlemaster Of Hed (1976)

R ★ ★ ★ ★ ★	I ★ ★ ★
C ★ ★ ★ ★	L ★ ★ ★ ★

Heir Of Sea And Fire (1977)

R ★ ★ ★ ★ ★	I ★ ★ ★
C ★ ★ ★	L ★ ★ ★ ★

Harpist In The Wind (1979)

R ★ ★ ★ ★ ★	I ★ ★ ★
C ★ ★ ★ ★	L ★ ★ ★ ★

McLAUGHLIN, Dean (Benjamin) (1931) American writer of straightforward sf adventures, wherein a common man creates, through his actions, a world-changing situation. The exception to this is *Hawk Among The Sparrows*.

The Fury From Earth (1963)

R ★ ★ ★ ★	I ★
C ★ ★	L ★

Hawk Among The Sparrows (1976)

R ★ ★ ★	I ★ ★
C ★	L ★ ★

MacLEAN, Katherine (1925) American writer, mostly of short stories. She was most active in the 1950s, though her best

work is the novel *The Missing Man*, developed from a novelette which won a Nebula award in 1971. Her work is always competent and clever. "The Snowball Effect" (1952) is an amusing story in which a ladies' sewing circle takes over the world by using techniques later to be actualized as "pyramid selling." "Unhuman Sacrifice" is an excellent story in which missionaries on an alien world fail to come to terms with the peculiar biology of their would-be converts.

"Unhuman Sacrifice" (1958)

R ★ ★ ★	I ★ ★ ★
C ★ ★	L ★ ★ ★

The Missing Man (1975)

R ★ ★ ★	I ★ ★
C ★ ★ ★	L ★ ★ ★

MacLEOD, Sheila   Scottish writer whose *Xanthe And The Robots* describes the development of almost-human cyborgs, "Philophrenics," and *Circuit-Breaker* (1978) deals with a marooned astronaut who might be hallucinating his experience.

Xanthe And The Robots (1977)

R ★ ★ ★	I ★
C ★	L ★ ★

McLOUGHLIN, John C.   American scientist and writer (usually on zoology) whose *The Helix And The Sword* depicts a crowded solar system 5,700 years hence and a devastated Earth which is about to be re-opened. It is a remarkable and highly detailed picture of a different culture with its own language, religion and politics.

The Helix And The Sword (1983)

R ★ ★ ★	I ★ ★ ★
C ★ ★	L ★ ★

MACEY, Peter   English writer of light and amusing science fiction novels, splendidly entertaining but without any great speculative value. His scientific training makes the texture of the work highly convincing, as in *Alien Culture* (1977), but this is very much a satirical Wyndham (q.v.) without the teeth.

Stationary Orbit (1974)

R	★ ★ ★	I	★
C	★ ★	L	★ ★

MACHEN, Arthur (1863-1947) Welsh writer, whose lyrical anti-technological visions opposed the science-fictional trends of his time (Wells (q.v.), Verne (q.v.)), his richly gothic style more in the fantasy vein than anything, influencing H. P. Lovecraft (q.v.) amongst others. In his *The Terror: A Fantasy* (1917), mankind is turned upon by the animals, a wry symbolic comment, perhaps, on then contemporary events.

The Great God Pan And The Inmost Light (1894; coll.)

R	★ ★ ★	I	★ ★
C	★ ★	L	★ ★

MACKLEWORTH, R(onald) W(alter) (1930) English writer of fairly stock adventures in space which have a strong 1950s flavour to them, particularly in the weak and stereotyped female characters. His favourite theme seems to be the corruption of Power in all situations and at all times.

Starflight 3000 (1972)

R	★ ★ ★	I	★
C	★	L	★

The Year Of The Painted World (1975)

R	★ ★ ★ ★	I	★ ★ ★
C	★	L	★

MAHR, Kurt   West German writer, who authored or co-authored many of the prolific Perry Rhodan series, which ranged from mediocrity to plain awfulness, wallowing in the very tritest of space opera clichés without a great deal of imagination or style.

The Ghosts Of Gol: Perry Rhodan 10 (1971)

R	★ ★	I	
C		L	

MAINE, Charles Eric (1921) Pseudonym of English writer David McIlwain, who wrote a good deal of sf between 1953 and

1971. Three of his novels were filmed. Most of his novels are competent thrillers with sf ingredients or disaster stories in the John Wyndham (q.v.) vein. Among his more ambitious efforts were *World Without Men*, subsequently revised as *Alph*, about an all-female society of the future; and *The Mind Of Mr. Soames*, about a man who becomes conscious for the first time as an adult. He is prone to superficiality and sometimes seems to leave his ideas underdeveloped, but his later work is very competent and interesting.

The Tide Went Out (1958)

R	★ ★ ★	I	★
C	★ ★ ★	L	★ ★

The Mind Of Mr. Soames (1961)

R	★ ★ ★	I	★ ★
C	★ ★ ★	L	★ ★

The Darkest Of Nights (1962)

R	★ ★ ★	I	★
C	★ ★	L	★ ★

MALCOLM, Donald (1930) Scottish writer of several short story series for the British sf magazines in the 1950s and 1960s. His two sf novels are competent but unimaginative adventures.

The Unknown Shore (1976)

R	★ ★ ★	I	★
C	★	L	★

The Iron Rain (1976)

R	★ ★ ★	I	★
C	★	L	★

MALZBERG, Barry (1939) American writer who was amazingly prolific over a period of some seven years, following his début in 1967, but whose output has since declined to a trickle. His central characters tend to be alienated victims of circumstance trying hopelessly to come to terms with incomprehensible situations. Often the fate of the world hangs on their decisions, but things never work out right. This downbeat approach offended many readers, but it is easy to be captivated by the witty, relentless and claustrophobic stream-of-consciousness style in which he writes. He was the first winner of the John W. Campbell Memorial Award – a result considered inappropriate by some. His best work includes three novels about alienated astronauts, *The Falling Astronauts* (1971), *Revelations* and *Beyond Apollo* (1972); a fine study of the terminal disenchantment of an unappreciated sf writer, *Herovit's World* (1973); and his own version of a hard sf story, *Galaxies*. The two novels he has compiled since his partial retirement, *Chorale* (1978) and *Cross Of Fire*, are also exceptional. His phenomenal productivity suggested to some that he was not putting much effort into his work, but the rhetorical fervour and emotional intensity of his work is quite unparalleled, suggesting that the process of creation, however accelerated, was far from painless. He may well remain an acquired taste but he is one of the most impressive writers to have worked in the genre in recent years.

Revelations (1972)

R ★ ★ ★ ★	I ★ ★ ★
C ★ ★ ★	L ★ ★ ★ ★

Galaxies (1975)

R ★ ★ ★ ★	I ★ ★ ★
C ★ ★ ★	L ★ ★ ★ ★

Cross Of Fire (1982)

R ★ ★ ★ ★	I ★ ★ ★ ★
C ★ ★ ★ ★	L ★ ★ ★ ★

MANN, Philip (1942) English writer whose first sf novel, *The Eye Of The Queen*, is an impressive and original début. An anthropologist, Thorndyke, attempts to understand and penetrate an alien race, the Pe Ellians, a strictly disciplined telepathic culture who evolve through seven "changes" of skin to a final and perfected form. Contact with Thorndyke brings a new vitality into Pe Ellian culture, but is it for the good? Mann is undoubtedly a discovery for the field, writing intelligently, gracefully, humorously and entertainingly.

The Eye Of The Queen (1982)

R ★ ★ ★ ★	I ★ ★ ★ ★
C ★ ★ ★ ★	L ★ ★ ★ ★

MANNING, Laurence (Edward) (1899-1972) Canadian-born but American writer, most of whose work appeared in *Wonder Stories* in the early 1930s. He is best remembered, however, for his *The Man Who Awoke*, five connected stories involving Norman Winters, a man who wakes up every few thousand years to discover what humanity is doing and how it has progressed. It is still fascinating despite its garish pulp style.

The Man Who Awoke (1933; published in book form, 1975)

R ★ ★ ★ ★	I ★ ★ ★ ★
C ★ ★	L ★

MARGROFF, Robert E(rvien) (1930) American writer who collaborated with Piers Anthony (q.v.) on two novels, *The Ring* (1968) and *The E.S.P. Worm*.

The E.S.P. Worm (1970; with Piers Anthony)

R ★ ★ ★	I ★ ★
C ★	L ★

MARTIN, George R. R. (1948) American sf and fantasy writer. Martin rose to popularity in the 1970s with a distinguished body of glossy, traditional space operas characterized by coherently visualized settings and by overwhelming gloom.

George R. R. Martin

His principal sf novel, *Dying Of The Light*, shows the violent clash over matters ideological and amorous of several representatives of various human cultures who have stayed on a dying rogue world as it drifts out of the Galaxy. An important theme in his work is abhorrence of exploitation either of individuals by individuals or of other species: in the Hugo-winning "Sandkings" a sadist who likes watching combats between alien animals comes to a particularly sticky end. Recent work seems to indicate a growing interest in occult fantasy, though the historical vampire novel, *Fevre Dream*, is doggedly rationalistic in its view of vampirism, its picture of the workings of Mississippi riverboats and in the way it links vampirism with pre-Civil-War slavery.

Dying Of The Light (1977)

R ★ ★ ★ ★	I ★ ★
C ★ ★ ★ ★	L ★ ★ ★

"Sandkings" (1979)

R ★ ★ ★ ★ ★	I ★ ★
C ★ ★ ★	L ★ ★ ★

Fevre Dream (1982)

R ★ ★ ★ ★	I ★ ★
C ★ ★ ★ ★	L ★ ★ ★ ★

MARTINSON, Harry (Edmund) (1904-78) Swedish writer of *Aniara*, a 103-canto epic science fiction poem, depicting the voyage of a vast spacecraft out into deepest space. It has echoes in Aldiss's (q.v.) *Non-Stop*, with its theme of the inhumanity of unchecked technological progress and its philosophical defence of humanitarian values. It was turned into an opera in 1959.

Aniara (1956; trans. 1963; a poem)

R ★ ★ ★	I ★ ★ ★ ★
C ★	L ★ ★ ★ ★ ★

MASSON, David I(rvine) (1915) Scottish writer whose very limited sf output is nonetheless of the highest quality. One short story collection, *The Caltraps Of Time*, is a showcase of his undeniable talent, with only a few weak stories and no repetition of effects. "Traveller's Rest" (1965) is a classic study of distorted perception on a weird planet, and "Mouth Of Hell" (1968) is one of the most nightmarish and atmospheric tales outside of the horror genre.

The Caltraps Of Time (1968; coll.)

R ★ ★ ★ ★ ★	I ★ ★ ★
C ★ ★	L ★ ★ ★

MATHESON, Richard (1926) American writer who has worked extensively in films and TV, lately with Steven Spielberg. Most of his early work was sf but he is now better known as a writer of supernatural fiction. Most of his sf is horrific in tone, including the celebrated *I Am Legend*, in which a plague turns everyone into vampires, and *The Shrinking Man*, which includes an epic battle between the eponymous hero and a Black Widow spider. His best recent work is the rather uncharacteristic timeslip romance *Bid Time Return*, and he seems to have drifted away from the paranoid fantasies that made him famous, taking a strong interest in the possibility of life after death. Matheson is a slick writer with a good line in nasty twists, but his stories frequently lack depth.

I Am Legend (1954)

R ★ ★ ★	I ★ ★ ★
C ★ ★	L ★ ★

The Shrinking Man (1956)

R ★ ★ ★	I ★ ★
C ★ ★	L ★ ★

Bid Time Return (1975)

R ★ ★ ★	I ★ ★
C ★ ★ ★	L ★ ★ ★

MATURIN, Charles Robert (1782-1824) Irish novelist and playwright whose gothic romances were popular. He is probably best known for his *Melmoth The Wanderer*, a dark, rather Faustian story which has its echoes in much of the more sinister science fiction written.

Melmoth The Wanderer (1820)

R ★ ★ ★	I ★ ★ ★
C ★ ★ ★	L ★ ★

MAUROIS, André (1885-1967) French writer. A popular and prolific Gallic man of letters better remembered for his biographies, André Maurois often used the sf format for gentle, ironic philosophic tales. He tackled a surprising amount of classic themes ranging from alternate worlds to war in space, Utopia and telepathy.

Le Chapitre Suivant (1927; trans. as *The Next Chapter: War Against The Moon*, 1928)

R ★ ★ ★	I ★ ★
C ★ ★	L ★ ★

Voyage Aux Pays Des Articoles (1972; trans. as *Voyage To The Island Of The Articoles*, 1928)

R ★ ★ ★	I ★ ★ ★
C ★ ★ ★	L ★ ★ ★

Le Peseur D'Ames (1931; trans. as *The Weigher Of Souls*, 1931)

R ★ ★ ★	I ★ ★ ★ ★
C ★ ★	L ★ ★ ★

MAXWELL, Ann   American writer whose science fantasy novels are simply plotted and yet quite unusual in their atmospheric quality. Two early novels, *Change* (1975) and *The Singer Enigma* (1976), are somewhat flawed, but the recent *Dancer's Luck*, a humanistic tale of ex-slaves, is a marked improvement.

Dancer's Luck (1983)

R ★ ★ ★	I ★
C ★ ★	L ★ ★

MAY, Julian (1932) American writer whose first novel, *Dune Roller* (1951), was produced for cinema and television. She didn't publish sf again until the mid-1970s, when *The Many Coloured Land*, the first book in the highly popular Saga of Exiles series appeared. Two more volumes, *The Golden Torc* and *The Non-Born King*, have followed and a fourth, *The Adversary*, is projected. The Saga is a mixture of sf and fantasy, told initially as a time story – where a group from the twenty-second century are transported into the distant past of the Pleiocene Age and battle with two alien races struggling for supreme power over the Earth.

The Many Coloured Land (1982)

R ★ ★ ★	I ★ ★ ★ ★
C ★ ★ ★ ★	L ★ ★ ★

The Non-Born King (1983)

R ★ ★ ★	I ★ ★ ★
C ★ ★ ★	L ★ ★ ★

MAYHAR, Ardath   American writer who has come to the fore in the early 1980s, though with little real sign that he has anything original to offer the genre. *His Golden Dream: A Fuzzy Odyssey* (1982) merely capitalizes upon H. Beam Piper's (q.v.) sentimental books, whereas in books like *The Runes Of The Lyre* and *How The Gods Wove In Kyrannon* (1981) there is little more than a competent mixture of sf and fantasy.

The Runes Of The Lyre (1982)

R ★ ★ ★	I ★
C ★	L ★

MAYNE, William (1928) Prolific and popular English writer of children's fiction, whose *Earthfasts* is marginally science-fictional. In it an eighteenth-century drummer boy encounters a modern-day schoolboy.

Earthfasts (1966)

R ★ ★ ★	I ★ ★
C ★ ★	L ★ ★

MEAD, Harold (1910) English writer of two sf novels in the 1950s. His *The Bright Phoenix* is a post-holocaust story memorable for its fine characterization, if a little uninspired in its events. *Mary's Country* (1957) is again a post-catastrophe novel depicting an Utopian society, but this time for a group of children.

The Bright Phoenix (1955)

R ★ ★ ★	I ★
C ★ ★ ★	L ★ ★

MEAD, (Edward) Shepherd (1914) American writer whose sf work is usually of a satirical bent. Sometimes it is mild, with a sting in its tale, as in *The Carefully Con-*

sidered Rape Of The World (1966), where aliens artificially inseminate human females to advance our evolutionary development. In *The Big Ball Of Wax*, however, the satire is sharp and dark, portraying a totalitarian consumer state of the future and an empathy device subverted for ill uses.

The Big Ball Of Wax (1954)

R ★ ★ ★ ★	I ★ ★ ★
C ★ ★	L ★ ★

MEEK, Capt. S(terner St) P(aul) (1894-1972) American writer and army officer most of whose work was done for juveniles. He was prolific from 1929 to 1955, but wrote little science fiction, his short stories appearing in the pulps between 1929 and 1932 and his two novels in the 1960s. Neither *The Drums Of Tapajos* nor its sequel, *Troyana* (1962), have improved since they were serialized in the 1930s, and are essentially lost civilization tales in the mould of Burroughs (q.v.).

The Drums Of Tapajos (1961)

R ★	I
C	L

MELTZER, David (1937) American writer and poet. Better known for his seminal work in the San Francisco poetry movement of the 1960s and 1970s, David Meltzer's ventures into sf came through the fabled Essex House line of speculative erotica, of which he was a major supplier. A forceful author whose erotic tracts mined the fertile fields of political paranoia and urban decay, Meltzer's passage through the sf ranks was short, surprisingly uninfluential, but worthy of a major reassessment.

The Agency Trilogy (*The Agent, The Agency, How Many Blocks In The Pile*, all 1968)

R ★ ★ ★ ★	I ★ ★ ★
C ★ ★	L ★ ★ ★

The Brain-Plant Series (*Lovely, Healer, Out, Glue Factory*, all 1969)

R ★ ★ ★	I ★ ★ ★
C ★ ★ ★	L ★ ★ ★ ★

MENDELSON, Drew American writer whose *Pilgrimage* is an impressive début, describing The City, an almost-living massive organism, perpetually renewing itself and slowly edging its way across a degenerate Earth of the distant future.

Pilgrimage (1981)

R ★ ★ ★ ★	I ★ ★ ★
C ★ ★	L ★ ★ ★

MEREDITH, Richard C. (1937-79) American sf writer. Meredith's brief career produced a body of fast-moving intelligent commercial work, often more sombre than might be expected from the vigorous business of the plotting. *We All Died At Breakaway Station* is a moving multi-viewpoint tale of space battle; *At The Narrow Passage* and its two sequels, elegant and exciting tales of war across and through time.

We All Died At Breakaway Station (1969)

R ★ ★ ★	I ★ ★
C ★ ★ ★ ★	L ★ ★ ★

At The Narrow Passage (1973)

R ★ ★ ★ ★	I ★ ★ ★ ★
C ★ ★	L ★ ★ ★

MERLE, Robert (1908) French writer whose *The Day Of The Dolphin*, about the political use of the discovery of communication with dolphins, was filmed. His *Malevil* (1972; trans. 1974) about life at Castle Malevil after the Bomb has fallen, is a firmly constructed and more impressive work.

The Day Of The Dolphin (1967; *Un animal doué de raison*; trans. 1967)

R ★ ★ ★ ★	I ★ ★
C ★	L ★ ★

MERRIL, (Josephine) Judith (1923) American writer, primarily noted as an anthologist. She wrote two early novels in collaboration with Cyril Kornbluth (q.v.) as Cyril Judd, and was at one time married to Frederik Pohl (q.v.). Most of her work appeared in the 1950s. She was one of the few magazine sf writers to look at future technological changes from the viewpoint of bystanders – often women – rather than those actively involved. Her best stories focus on emotional and moral problems consequent upon involvement in various imaginary projects. She is occasionally prone to sentimentality but at her best is an effectively powerful writer. *Shadow On The Hearth* remains one of the classic stories of nuclear war, told from the viewpoint of a housewife. Her later works in novel length, including the fix-up novel *Daughters Of Earth* (1968), which takes the family saga into outer space, are nowhere near as impressive.

Shadow On The Hearth (1950)

R ★ ★ ★ ★	I ★ ★ ★
C ★ ★ ★ ★	L ★ ★ ★ ★

"Project Nursemaid" (1955)

R ★ ★ ★	I ★ ★
C ★ ★	L ★ ★ ★

The Tomorrow People (1960)

R ★ ★ ★	I ★ ★
C ★ ★	L ★ ★

Abraham Merritt

MERRITT, Abraham (1884-1943) American writer of lush fantasy novels. Although he was a top journalist the style of his novels is remarkably clotted and adjec-

tival; they presumably offered him a private means of escape into exotic fantasy worlds and work best when their emotional intensity is highest. Most of them feature beautiful *femmes fatales* and monsters. Although they bear little resemblance to sf, Merritt's fantasies were beloved by Hugo Gernsback (q.v.), who persuaded him to import some science-fictional ideas, not altogether successfully, into *The Metal Monster* (1946). As gorgeously decorated escapist fantasies *The Ship Of Ishtar* and *The Dwellers In The Mirage* have few equals, and Merritt was a significant influence on many early pulp sf writers, including Jack Williamson (q.v.) and Henry Kuttner (q.v.).

The Ship Of Ishtar (1924)

R ★ ★ ★	I ★ ★ ★
C ★	L ★ ★

The Dwellers In The Mirage (1932)

R ★ ★ ★	I ★ ★ ★
C ★	L ★ ★

Burn Witch Burn! (1932)

R ★ ★ ★	I ★ ★ ★
C ★	L ★ ★

MERWIN, Sam(uel Kimball) Jr (1910) American writer and editor of *Thrilling Wonder Stories* and *Startling Stories*. As might be expected, his own fiction is formularistic and characterized by wish-fulfilment fantasy, utilizing a pseudo-scientific framework, fast-paced and superficially highly enjoyable.

Three Faces Of Time (1955)

R ★ ★ ★	I ★
C ★	L ★

MEYERS, Roy (Lethebridge) (1910-74) English writer of three novels about the relationship between Man and the dolphins. As an exercise in contrast they are admirable, but elements of melodrama and overt preaching make them awkward reading.

Destiny And The Dolphins (1969)

R ★ ★	I ★ ★
C ★	L ★

MILLER, P(eter) Schuyler (1912-74) American writer and sf critic. He is best known for his reviews in *Astounding/Analog*, but did collaborate on one novel with L. Sprague De Camp – *Genus Homo* (1950) – and wrote several sf stories which were collected in *The Titan*.

The Titan (1952; coll.)

R ★ ★	I ★
C ★	L ★

MILLER, Walter M(ichael) (1922) American sf writer. Miller's short career in the 1950s culminated in the three novelettes collected as *A Canticle For Leibowitz*, perhaps the classic of post-atomic recovery stories and the favourite sf novel of a lot of people who do not like sf. Monks preserve literacy and scientific knowledge through a know-nothing Dark Age, a renaissance of power politics and self-serving scepticism and a second atomic war. Miller, himself a Catholic, is deeply and overtly optimistic about the role of faith and religious institutions in society, while making this palatable for the non-believer with touches of genial absurdity like the monk who spends a lifetime producing an illuminated copy of a circuit diagram. Notable among his shorter fiction is the Hugo-winning "The Darfsteller," in which an actor automated out of work fights back and comes to a more mature understanding of the nature of art and intelligence.

A Canticle For Leibowitz (1960)

R ★ ★ ★ ★	I ★ ★
C ★ ★ ★ ★	L ★ ★ ★ ★

"The Darfsteller" (1955)

R ★ ★ ★ ★	I ★ ★ ★
C ★ ★ ★ ★	L ★ ★ ★ ★

MITCHELL, Adrian (1932) English poet and novelist whose *The Bodyguard* describes a future totalitarian state in Britain through the deathbed reminiscences of a paramilitary bodyguard.

The Bodyguard (1970)

R ★ ★ ★	I ★
C ★ ★	L ★ ★ ★

MITCHELL, J. Leslie (1901-35) Scottish novelist, much better known for the novels he published as Lewis Grassic Gibbon than for those issued under his own name. Of the latter, two are striking sf stories in which female protagonists, with various companions, visit the prehistoric past and a post-holocaust future. Both stories contain near-hysterical criticisms of contemporary civilization, and make compelling reading.

Three Go Back (1932)

R ★ ★ ★	I ★ ★ ★
C ★ ★ ★	L ★ ★ ★ ★

Gay Hunter (1934)

R ★ ★ ★	I ★ ★ ★
C ★ ★ ★	L ★ ★ ★ ★

MITCHISON, Naomi (Margaret) (1897) Respected Scottish writer whose two sf novels are superior products of her maturity. *Solution Three* (1975) is the weaker work, with its picture of a conditioned future society which is non-aggressive. The book lacks fire purely because of its depicted situation. *Memoirs Of A Spacewoman*, on the other hand, is an imaginative firecracker, wherein a "communicator" journeys about meeting bizarre alien life-forms.

Memoirs Of A Spacewoman (1962)

R ★ ★ ★	I ★ ★ ★
C ★ ★	L ★ ★ ★

MODESITT, L. E. Jr American author of *The Fires Of Paratime*, a curious novel about Time Guards, Hell and becoming a God. Its mixture of myth and allegory makes it interesting, yet strangely old-fashioned; as if A. E. Van Vogt (q.v.) had merged with Samuel Delany (q.v.).

The Fires Of Paratime (1982)

R ★ ★ ★	I ★ ★
C ★	L ★ ★

MONTELEONE, Thomas F. (1946) American writer. His short stories began to appear in 1972 and since 1975 he has written a number of fast-paced adventures, many of which are set in vast cities of the future.

The Time-Swept City (1977)

R ★ ★ ★ ★	I ★
C ★	L ★

MOORCOCK, Michael (1939) English author and editor, hugely prolific, best known for his heroic fantasy and his radical editorial work on *New Worlds* from 1964 to 1974. Entering science fiction as an extremely precocious, energetic and idealistic young fan, Moorcock had the advantage over most of his contemporaries of having already read widely outside the genre. His inspiration and his models came as much from Dickens and Brecht as from Anderson (q.v.) and Bester (q.v.). Committed to the expression of literary values in popular fictional forms, he immediately won as many enemies as acolytes, and his work remains controversial. Detractors point to recurrent faults of hasty composition, irreverent and inconsistent use of sacred sf traditions, and a streak of obscurantism. Enthusiasts applaud his individuality, originality, compelling narration and strong sense of character. His *New Worlds* deliberately stirred up the much-misunderstood New Wave, with equally revolutionary, if quite separate, effects on sf both sides of the Atlantic. He published crucial work by Aldiss (q.v.), Ballard (q.v.), Disch (q.v.), Roberts (q.v.) and Sladek (q.v.), as well as many less famous but no less enterprising writers. For all its variety, Moorcock's own fiction is ambitiously interconnected, with abiding central themes and images. Multiplication has made them, if anything, more distinct. In his "multiverse" of parallel existences, every story recurs eternally, enacted over and over again. No battle is ever finally won, or lost. Ultimately all characters are the same character, or at least aspects of one, the Eternal Champion, doomed to quest forever for a balance between freedom and stability in the intractable flux of time and space. By giving his composite hero this Everyman role Moorcock subverted the customary escapism of heroic fantasy and exploited its latent symbolism.

Michael Moorcock

An offshoot of the Champion, Jerry Cornelius, became Moorcock's most distinctive creation, a beguiling, pathetic myth for the modern world.

The Sleeping Sorceress (1973)

R ★ ★ ★	I ★ ★
C ★ ★ ★	L ★

The Condition Of Muzak (1977)

R ★ ★ ★ ★	I ★ ★ ★ ★
C ★ ★ ★ ★ ★	L ★ ★ ★ ★ ★

Gloriana (1978)

R ★ ★ ★ ★ ★	I ★ ★ ★
C ★ ★ ★ ★ ★	L ★ ★ ★ ★

MOORE, Brian (1921) Irish-born Canadian writer, best known in sf circles for his play and novel of *Catholics*, about religious politics at the turn of the twentieth century. *The Great Victorian Collection* (1975) and *Fergus* (1971) contain elements which make them borderline sf and fantasy respectively.

Catholics (1972; play, 1980)

R ★ ★ ★	I ★
C ★ ★	L ★ ★ ★

MOORE, C. L. (1911) American writer whose first husband was Henry Kuttner (q.v.). Most of the stories they produced while together were collaborative to some degree, and Moore has written hardly any sf since his death. She began by writing highly coloured fantasies for *Weird Tales*, but produced much more mature work in the 1940s for *Astounding Science Fiction*. Her best stories are restrained psychological studies of people in extraordinary circumstances and her two solo novels do not show her at her best. "No Woman Born" is about the existential problems of a woman saved from death by means of an artificial body, and "Vintage Season" is a brilliantly atmospheric story about time tourists.

Judgment Night (1943)

R	★ ★ ★	I	★ ★
C	★	L	★ ★

"No Woman Born" (1944)

R	★ ★ ★	I	★ ★ ★
C	★ ★ ★	L	★ ★ ★

"Vintage Season" (1946)

R	★ ★ ★	I	★ ★ ★ ★
C	★ ★ ★	L	★ ★ ★ ★

MOORE, Patrick (Alfred) (1923) English astronomer, TV commentator and writer. He wrote 16 juvenile science fiction novels in the 1950s and early 1960s, the first series set on Mars, the second series, starring Scott Saunders, more wide-ranging. They are hackneyed but entertaining enough stories, where the young protagonist, armed with truth and a desire for knowledge, wins the day.

Wanderer In Space (1961)

R	★ ★	I	★
C	★	L	★

MOORE, Ward (1903-78) American writer whose ventures into the sf field were infrequent but always memorable. *Greener Than You Think* is a good ironic disaster story. *Bring The Jubilee* is a classic alternative history story in which the South won the Civil War. *Joyleg*, written in collabora-tion with Avram Davidson (q.v.), is an iconoclastic comic novel about an immortal mountain man. Although he usually gives the appearance of being a relaxed writer he can build up a remarkably tense atmosphere, as in his several nuclear war stories. He also wrote a remarkable surreal fantasy, "Transient" (1960).

Greener Than You Think (1947)

R	★ ★ ★	I	★ ★
C	★ ★ ★	L	★ ★ ★

Bring The Jubilee (1953)

R	★ ★ ★ ★	I	★ ★ ★
C	★ ★ ★	L	★ ★ ★ ★

Joyleg (1962; with Avram Davidson)

R	★ ★ ★	I	★ ★
C	★ ★	L	★ ★ ★

MORGAN, Dan (1925) English writer who, since his first short story appeared in the 1950s, has published steadily and regularly. Some of his work was done with John Kippax (q.v.), but his most interesting novels are in the Mind series, a competently told re-working of the telepathy theme.

The Mind Trap (1970)

R	★ ★ ★	I	★
C	★	L	★

MORLAND, Dick (1936) Pseudonym of English writer Reginald Hill. His two sf novels are both dystopian views of a future Britain. They are garish, exaggerated but darkly enjoyable reads, especially *Albion! Albion!* where the country is taken over by football hooligans.

Albion! Albion! (1974)

R	★ ★ ★ ★	I	★
C	★	L	★

MORRESSEY, John (1930) American writer whose books present a Hobbesian view of Mankind as a restrained beast. His novels are interlinked, but without a con-tinuous hero, and normally provide several levels of entertainment. His far-future galactic civilization is common to all but a few of his books and the space opera elements are skilfully dealt with.

Under A Calculating Star (1975)

R	★	★	★	★	I	★		
C	★	★			L	★	★	

MORRIS, Janet E(llen) (1946) American writer. Her four-part history of Silistra, which began with *High Couch On Silistra* (1977), is science fantasy within a science-fictional setting – a quest set in a future, barren world. A second series, more overtly science-fictional, has begun with two novels about the Kerrion Empire: *Cruiser Dreams* (1981), the follow-up to *The Dream Dancers*.

The Dream Dancers (1980)

R	★	★	★	★	I	★		
C	★	★			L	★	★	

MORRIS, William (1834-96) English artist, writer and designer of furniture. His Utopian novel *News From Nowhere* was a response to Edward Bellamy's (q.v.) best-selling *Looking Backward*, and champions the work of the individual craftsman against mechanical mass-production as the way to a rewarding life for all. In his last years he wrote several long romances set in

William Morris

imaginary quasi-medieval worlds, thus establishing himself at the head of the tradition of modern heroic fantasy.

News From Nowhere (1890)

R	★	★		I	★	★	★
C	★	★		L	★	★	★

The Well At The World's End (1896)

R	★	★		I	★	★	
C	★	★		L	★	★	★

The Water Of The Wondrous Isles (1897)

R	★	★		I	★	★	
C	★	★		L	★	★	

MORROW, James American writer whose first novel, *The Wine Of Violence*, is an impressive début. Its Utopian world, Quetzalia, is as much about the division in our selves between technology/progress and savagery/ritual as it is a fable about Mankind's future social schizophrenia. It is intelligent and well written and much more than simple allegory.

The Wine Of Violence (1982)

R	★	★	★	★	I	★	★	★
C	★	★			L	★	★	

MROZEK, Slawomir (1930) Polish writer. His *The Ugupu Bird* is a collection of his borderline sf, parables and stories written in an absurdist vein and incorporating myth.

The Ugupu Bird (1959; coll., trans. 1968)

R	★	★	★	I	★	★	
C	★			L	★	★	

NABOKOV, Vladimir (1899-1977) Russian-born American novelist and poet whose *Ada* is a borderline sf work only in that it depicts a Russian America and is, in that respect, an alternative world novel.

Ada: Or, Ardor: A Family Chronicle (1969)

R	★	★	★	★	★	I	★	★		
C	★	★	★			L	★	★	★	★

NATION, Terry (1930) English writer whose *Dr Who* series and *Survivors* display the comic and serious sides of his screenwriting. He wrote a novelization of the latter series, and has recently developed the *Blake's Seven* series for TV. His *Rebecca's World* is sf for the very young, a good and entertaining fable.

Rebecca's World (1975)

R ★ ★ ★	I ★
C ★ ★	L ★

NELSON, Ray (1931) American writer Radell Faraday Nelson whose first novel, *The Ganymede Takeover* (1967) was a collaboration with Philip K. Dick (q.v.). His own work is highly crafted as well as entertaining, as in *Blake's Progress* (1975) and *The Ecolog*. He has a fascination with time, sex and totalitarianism. Many of his sf ideas have an absurd basis, his writing a sharp satirical edge.

The Ecolog (1977)

R ★ ★ ★ ★	I ★ ★
C ★	L ★ ★

NESVADBA, Josef (1926) Czech writer rooted more in Wells (q.v.) and the adventure story than in mainstream science fiction. His work has a strangely self-conscious flavour, and achieves a rare complexity in its thematic resonance. His Continental background is at least as much responsible for his distinctive flavour as his use of sf imagery.

In The Footsteps Of The Abominable Snowman (1970; *The Lost Face* in U.S.A.)

R ★ ★ ★ ★	I ★ ★ ★ ★ ★
C ★ ★ ★	L ★ ★ ★ ★

NEVILLE, Kris (Otman) (1925) American writer of routine but carefully crafted sf and science fantasy stories and novels. He has published infrequently over the last 20 years, and is perhaps best known for "Bettyann" (1951), which tells of a crippled girl brought up in an orphanage who discovers she is of extra-terrestrial origin. Neville successfully extended it into a novel.

Bettyann (1970)

R ★ ★ ★ ★	I ★ ★
C ★ ★ ★	L ★ ★

NIVEN, Larry (1938) American writer noted as the leading contemporary writer of hard sf. His "Tales Of Known Space" presents a loosely knit future history in which men begin to explore the galaxy and meet several interestingly idiosyncratic alien species. Several of the Earthbound stories in this series deal with the exploits of law-enforcement agent Gil Hamilton, and represent the best recent exercises in the sf detective story. Niven likes to work in collaboration and has produced several successful novels with Jerry Pournelle (q.v.) as well as working with David Gerrold (q.v.) and Steve Barnes. His most famous work is *Ringworld*, about a massive and peculiar artifact based upon the Dyson sphere. The sequel, *Ringworld Engineers*, is not as good. He is a very good short story writer, but his longer works sometimes threaten to become tedious because he has rather a monotonous style. His great virtue is his ability to be inventive while keeping his ideas solidly based in contemporary astronomical knowledge and physical theory. No one is quicker than he to take up new ideas from contemporary scientific theory and build stories around them. He also delights in extrapolating logically the consequences of implausible premises, ranging from matter-transmission to magic. It could be argued that he is a little too much in love with the conventions of the genre, but he contrives to be playful and highly professional at the same time and his enthusiasm is infectious; despite his limitations he is rarely dull.

Ringworld (1970)

R ★ ★ ★	I ★ ★ ★ ★
C ★ ★	L ★ ★

Protector (1973)

R ★ ★ ★	I ★ ★ ★
C ★	L ★ ★

The Patchwork Girl (1980)

R ★ ★ ★	I ★ ★ ★
C ★ ★	L ★ ★ ★

NOLAN, William F(rancis) (1928) American writer best known for *Logan's Run*, a novel written in collaboration with George Clayton Johnson and filmed in 1976. His first short story was published in the sf magazines in 1954 and he is a fervid Ray Bradbury (q.v.) fan. His only other novel is a sequence to *Logan's Run*, *Logan's World* (1977). A few collections of his shorter work exist, among them the interesting *Wonderworlds* (1977).

Logan's Run (1967; with G. C. Johnson)

R ★ ★ ★ ★	I ★
C ★ ★	L ★ ★

NORMAN, Barry   English journalist, writer and TV presenter who wrote a near-future sf nasty, *End Product* (1975), in which the blacks are used as meat-produce for the Civilized West. Darkly satirical and allegorical.

NORMAN, John (1931) Pseudonym of philosophy teacher John F. Lange Jr, used primarily on a long series of novels set on the counter-Earth of Gor. The series began as orthodox Burroughsian fantasy but as it has developed through more than a dozen volumes has become obsessed with the idea of strong men taming wild women with the aid of ropes and whips. The stories are phenomenally popular with American adolescents, who have always found it difficult to conceive of women as people. Other people will find them simply distasteful – often acutely so.

Tarnsman Of Gor (1966)

R ★ ★	I ★
C ★	L ★

Marauders Of Gor (1975)

R ★	I
C	L

Slave Girl Of Gor (1977)

R ★	I
C	L

NORTON, Andre (1912) Pseudonym of American writer Alice Mary Norton who also writes as Andrew North and Allen Weston. Her earliest work was written for juveniles – fast-paced action/adventure for boys – but this overt power-fantasy (typified by *Sword In Sheath*, 1949) diminished in her writing when she began to produce adult sf. The adventure element remains, as does an emphasis upon character and an exotic blend of sf and fantasy. The Witch World books form a separate sequence in her writing, but all of her other adult work is interrelated (if only tenuously) by being set in the same vast future galaxy where alien races like the Zacathans exist. Many would consider her work to be no more than heroic fantasy utilizing science-fictional trappings, and the proliferation of jewels, swords and quests would seem to support this, yet her central theme – that of freeing Man from the limiting and dehumanizing effects of machines and bureaucracy and establishing a more natural relationship with things – is distinctly science-fictional. Her work forms, in effect, the boundary between the two distinct genres, blurring the devices and specific imagery of the two to form a highly readable, rich and occasionally powerful hybrid, as in *Merlin's Mirror* (1975) and *Star Ka'at World* (1978; with Dorothy Madlee). The lack of critical attention upon Norton's work – which has been prolific through three decades now – has not affected her great popularity, and her writing has certainly improved with the years.

Dark Piper (1968)

R ★ ★ ★ ★	I ★
C ★ ★	L ★ ★

Web Of The Witch World (1964)

R ★ ★ ★	I ★
C ★	L ★

Quag Keep (1978)

R ★ ★ ★ ★	I ★
C ★ ★	L ★ ★

NOURSE, Alan E. (1928) American writer and physician. He has recently become successful as a writer of novels about the medical profession, but was active in the 1950s as a writer of sf juveniles and magazine stories. Many of his sf stories

Flann O'Brien

O'BRIEN, Flann (1911-66) Pseudonym of Irish writer Brian O'Nolan, much of whose work uses a fantastic/absurdist framework. *The Third Policeman* depicts the adventures of its un-named protagonist in an afterworld shaped like a bicycle wheel and where the strange philosophy of De Selby (O'Brien's cranky Irish sage with, amongst other things, his theory of black air causing night) appears quite sane in the context of other events. O'Brien is one of the world's finest humorous writers and this borderline sf work one of his funniest.

The Third Policeman (1967)

R ★ ★ ★ ★ ★	I ★ ★ ★ ★
C ★ ★ ★	L ★ ★ ★ ★

have a medical background. His stories are usually straightforward accounts of individual courage, often in the face of stupid intolerance. His best sf novel for adults, *The Bladerunner*, has no connection with the film of that name.

A Man Obsessed (1955; later revised as *The Mercy Men*)

R ★ ★ ★	I ★ ★
C ★ ★	L ★ ★

Star Surgeon (1960)

R ★ ★ ★	I ★ ★
C ★ ★	L ★ ★

The Bladerunner (1974)

R ★ ★ ★	I ★ ★
C ★ ★	L ★ ★

NOWLAND, Philip Francis (1888-1940) American writer who collaborated with Dick Calkins on the Buck Rogers sf comic strip. His only novel, *Armageddon 2419 AD* introduced Buck Rogers when it was first serialized in *Amazing* in August 1928. Its mixture of the garishly exotic and the melodramatic is still fondly remembered and has influenced much of the genre's more adventure-oriented work.

Armageddon 2419 AD (1928; published in book form, 1962)

R ★ ★ ★	I
C ★	L

O'BRIEN, Robert C(arroll) (1922-73) American writer of two excellent juvenile sf novels, *Mrs Frisby And The Rats Of NIMH* (1971) and *Z For Zachariah*. The first is an intelligently written study of the escape and existence afterwards of a group of artificially enhanced intelligent rats from a laboratory. The second, upon which O'Brien's reputation in the field may rest, is a portrait of the Apocalypse through the eyes of a young farm girl, Ann Burden, which creates a genuinely mythic sense of archetypes.

Z For Zachariah (1975)

R ★ ★ ★ ★ ★	I ★ ★ ★
C ★ ★ ★ ★	L ★ ★ ★

OBRUCHEV, V(ladimir Afanas'evich) (1863-1956) Russian geologist and writer, two of whose novels have been translated. Both *Plutonia* (1924; trans. 1957) and *Sannikov's Land* are popularizations of scientific ideas in the manner of Jules Verne (q.v.); the first a hollow earth tale, the second a lost world story.

Sannikov's Land (1926; trans. 1955)

R ★ ★	I ★
C ★	L ★

ODLE, E. V.   English writer of *The Clockwork Man* – a delightful and idiosyncratic tale of a cyborg from the machine-regulated world of 8000 AD who returns to the England of the 1920s to describe his world and join in with their traditional game of cricket.

The Clockwork Man (1923)

R ★ ★ ★	I ★ ★ ★
C ★	L ★ ★

OFFUTT, Andrew J(efferson V.) (1934) American writer who also writes as John Cleve and Jeff Douglas. Since he became a full-time freelance writer in 1971 he has been one of the sf field's most prolific authors, producing a wide range of work of varying quality – from crude sword-and-sorcery to sophisticated sf, as in *The Castle Keeps*. Most of his work is slick, fast-moving adventure without depth.

The Castle Keeps (1972)

R ★ ★ ★ ★	I ★ ★
C ★ ★	L ★ ★

Chieftain Of Andor (1976; a.k.a. *Clansman Of Andor*)

R ★ ★ ★ ★	I
C ★	L ★

George Orwell

OLIVER, Chad (1928) American writer and anthropologist, noted for his skilful adaptation of anthropological data and perspectives in stories of confrontation between humans and aliens. His fiction is often nostalgic, and he has a tendency to glorify primitive ways of life, though he avoids the extreme ecological mysticism of some more recent writers. His best work was done in the 1950s but he has published occasional works since then. His best work is in his collections *Another Kind* (1955) and *Unearthly Neighbours* (1960), but his longer works tend to be a little bland.

Shadows In The Sun (1954)

R ★ ★ ★	I ★ ★ ★
C ★ ★ ★	L ★ ★

The Winds Of Time (1957)

R ★ ★ ★	I ★ ★
C ★ ★	L ★ ★

The Shores Of Another Sea (1971)

R ★ ★ ★	I ★ ★
C ★ ★	L ★ ★

O'NEILL, Joseph (1886-1953) Irish author of three sf novels in the 1930s which are thoughtful and quite literary works outside the pulp tradition. *Wind From The North* (1934) has a time-slip which sends its protagonist back to Viking Dublin. *Land Under England* depicts a lost race whose ancestors were the Roman Legion in Cumberland, living in a cave system and telepathically connected. *Day Of Wrath* (1936) describes a future-war in which Germany, Japan and China between them destroy civilization. All are articulate and memorable works.

Land Under England (1935)

R ★ ★ ★ ★	I ★ ★ ★
C ★ ★	L ★ ★ ★

ORWELL, George (1903-50) Pseudonym of Eric Arthur Blair, English novelist and essayist. Two of his works have been claimed by the sf field, although *Animal Farm* is better viewed as an extended fable or a Swiftian satire than as science fiction. *Nineteen Eighty-Four* however, is recognizably science-fictional, despite its overt political purpose (Orwell planned at one stage to call it *1948*). Its depiction of a future totalitarian world, divided into three super states, constantly at war, and ruled by political élites, is an image central to sf. Orwell's commentary on political manipulation (abuse of language, reduction of identity, constant observation of individuals, the rewriting of historical event: all undermining the truth of situations) has not been improved upon within the genre, and the story of Winston Smith's experiences under the régime of Big Brother remains the classic admonitory work on this subject.

Animal Farm (1949)

R ★ ★ ★ ★ ★	I ★ ★ ★ ★ ★
C ★ ★ ★	L ★ ★ ★ ★

Nineteen Eighty-Four (1949)

R ★ ★ ★ ★ ★	I ★ ★ ★ ★ ★
C ★ ★ ★	L ★ ★ ★ ★

OUSPENSKY, P. D. (1878) Russian-born philosopher, best known for his theory of "eternal recurrence," developed in his work, *A New Model Of The Universe.* His only novel, written in English, was *Strange Life Of Ivan Osokin*, an elegant story illustrating his theory. Osokin, a young student/soldier relives, without being able to affect, the 12 crucial years of his maturation.

Strange Life Of Ivan Osokin (1947)

R ★ ★ ★ ★	I ★ ★ ★ ★
C ★ ★ ★ ★	L ★ ★ ★ ★ ★

PANGBORN, Edgar (1909-76) American sf writer. Pangborn's deeply emotional work is characterized by a tension between an idealistic view of human potential and a realistic bitter knowledge that corruption and doom are more likely than transcendence. This was, perhaps, most effectively conveyed in *A Mirror For Observers*, in which two members of a secret Martian colony on Earth struggle for the allegiance and, by implication, the soul of a talented boy. Much of Pangborn's later work deals with a collapse of civilization in the early twenty-first century – most movingly in "The Music Master Of Babylon" – and with its eventual revival. Perhaps his most popular book, *Davy*, shows the brief success of an artistic and scholarly renaissance against religious tyranny.

"Angel's Egg" (1951)

R ★ ★ ★ ★	I ★ ★ ★
C ★ ★	L ★ ★ ★ ★

A Mirror For Observers (1954)

R ★ ★ ★ ★	I ★ ★ ★
C ★ ★ ★ ★	L ★ ★ ★ ★ ★

Davy (1964)

R ★ ★ ★ ★	I ★ ★
C ★ ★ ★	L ★ ★ ★ ★

PANSHIN, Alexei (1940) American writer and critic whose first novel, *Rite Of Passage*, won the Nebula Award. It is mainly set aboard a generation starship 150 years after Earth has been destroyed, and deals with the maturation of Mia Havero on the colony planet. It is a remarkable début, and the three novels that followed are lightweight spoofs of space opera; funny but forgettable. *Earth Magic* (1978), written with his wife Cory (with whom he also writes criticism) is heroic fantasy of an intelligent kind. His most recent work – published through his own press – is *Transmutations: A Book Of Personal Alchemy* (1983), which mixes criticism, verse and short fiction. As far as his critical work is concerned, Panshin is in the line of Blish (q.v.) and Amis (q.v.) in making sf criticism respectable. His own fiction shows something of the new self-consciousness of the genre, but his criticism is sharply focused and directly pertinent. His *Heinlein In Dimension* (1968) and *SF In Dimension* (1976; coll.) are showcases of his critical work.

Rite Of Passage (1968)

R ★ ★ ★ ★	I ★ ★ ★ ★
C ★ ★ ★	L ★ ★ ★ ★

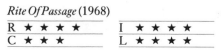

Farewell To Yesterday's Tomorrow (1975; coll.)

R ★ ★ ★	I ★ ★
C ★ ★	L ★ ★

PEAKE, Mervyn (1911-68) English author, poet, dramatist, illustrator and painter. Peake's zealous and particular approach to fantasy, in print as in paint, was less appreciated in his lifetime than it is now. His principal novels, the three Titus Groan books, are as vigorously romantic as all his work, a tale of spiritual and emotional revolt against a corrupt and decrepit order, portrayed as nonsensical, repressive and deadly. Anti-scientific, Peake was an apostle of the irrational, though not a Surrealist, and of beauty. His last book, *Titus Alone*, anticipates New Wave sf in its stricken landscapes and encounters with nameless catastrophes.

Titus Groan (1946)

R ★ ★ ★ ★	I ★ ★ ★
C ★ ★ ★ ★ ★	L ★ ★ ★ ★ ★

Titus Alone (1959)

R ★ ★	I ★ ★ ★
C ★ ★ ★	L ★ ★ ★ ★

Mervyn Peake (from a painting by Maeve Gilmore)

PEARCE, Brenda (1935) English writer of two fairly routine sf adventures in *Kidnapped Into Space* (1975) and *Worlds For The Grabbing*, which is interesting for its scientific ideas but uneven in its storytelling qualities.

Worlds For The Grabbing (1977)

R ★ ★ ★	I ★ ★
C ★ ★	L ★

PEARCE, Philippa   English writer, best known for her children's fantasy, *Tom's Midnight Garden*, one of the finest and most moving stories involving a time travel element.

Tom's Midnight Garden (1958)

R ★ ★ ★ ★ ★	I ★ ★
C ★ ★ ★	L ★ ★ ★

PECK, Richard E. (1936) American writer whose *Final Solution* is a humorous tale about an academic (rather like Peck himself) who is sent 50 years into the future where the universities have become part of a sealed-off ghetto system. A number of his short stories are also sf.

Final Solution (1973)

R ★ ★ ★	I ★
C ★	L ★ ★

PEDLER, Kit (1927) English writer and physician whose work on BBC's *Doomwatch* series led to a collaborated novel with Gerry Davis in *Mutant 59, The Plastic Eater* (1971) and a number of unrelated sf-oriented disaster novels. They have also worked on *Dr Who* material. In all of their work the hard science element is excellent, the characterization and plot weak.

The Dynostar Menace (1975)

R ★ ★ ★	I ★ ★
C	L ★

PENNY, David G.   English writer whose novels, whilst routine in their plot devices, have a charming lyricism that makes them more than standard sf adventures. *The Sunset People* (1975) depicts a jaded, de-populated future world, but *Sun-*

shine 43 is his best work, describing the return of violence to a post-war pastoral world.

Sunshine 43 (1978)

R ★ ★ ★ ★	I ★ ★
C ★ ★	L ★ ★ ★

PERCY, F. Walker (1916) American writer of two sf novels, *The Moviegoer* (1961) and *Love In The Ruins: The Adventures Of A Bad Catholic At A Time Near The End Of The World*, where the U.S.A., in decadent ruin in the 1980s, is the background for a psychiatrist's love story. Percy's work has a strong satiric purpose.

Love In The Ruins (1971)

R ★ ★ ★	I ★
C ★	L ★ ★

PERKINS, Michael (1942) American writer whose pornographic novels for Essex House were often borderline sf, particularly in *Terminus*, which depicts a savage urban situation in a future America.

Terminus (1969)

R ★ ★ ★	I ★ ★
C ★	L ★ ★ ★

PETAJA, Emil (Theodore) (1915) American writer who began publishing short sf in the magazines in the 1940s but was a prolific novel writer during the 1970s. His work is essentially formula sf adventure, but is notable for its basis in Finnish mythology (the *Kalevala*) in works like *The Star Mill* (1965) and *Time Twister* (1968); an early use of underpinning a saga with another older epic – more common in 1970s sf.

Alpha Yes, Terra No! (1965)

R ★ ★ ★ ★	I ★ ★
C ★	L ★ ★

Seed Of The Dreamers (1970)

R ★ ★ ★	I ★
C ★	L ★

PHILLIFENT, John T(homas) (1916-76) English writer best known for his sf adventure novels as John Rackham. They are competently written but unpretentious entertainments, attempting nothing beyond the simplest level of fast-action storytelling. This is not to say that Phillifent was a hack, simply that he created intelligent but undemanding fiction for an audience attuned to simplistic moral criteria: there is definable good and evil, wrongness and rightness in his work. Nothing, either in his own name or as Rackham, can be said to be outstanding.

Danger From Vega (1966; as John Rackham)

R ★ ★ ★	I
C ★	L ★

Genius Unlimited (1972)

R ★ ★ ★	I ★
C ★	L ★

PHILLIPS, Rog (1909-65) Pseudonym of Roger Phillips Graham, an American writer who was a prolific contributor of sf shorts to the magazines from 1945 until the early 1960s, with more than 120 to his credit. Four fairly mediocre sf novels can be added to this tally. His importance lies in his being one of those pulp writers who helped to create a vocabulary of standard sf ideas and devices.

World Of If (1951)

R ★ ★ ★ ★	I ★ ★
C ★	L ★

PHILLPOTTS, Eden (1862-1960) Prolific English writer, primarily noted for his tales of Dartmoor. His important scientific romance *Saurus* (1938) is the story of an alien visitor to Earth who comments on human follies and foibles. *Address Unknown* (1949) has a similar plot, but the author is much less sure of the legitimacy of the comments. Phillpotts also wrote some marginal sf thrillers as Harrington Hext, and produced a notable series of mythological fables promoting his own version of the Epicurean philosophy.

The Fall Of The House Of Heron (1948)

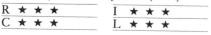

R ★ ★ ★	I ★ ★ ★
C ★ ★ ★	L ★ ★ ★

PIERCY, Marge (1936) American poet and novelist whose use of sf metaphors to accentuate her ideas about power, government manipulation and rigid role structures is wholly successful. *Dance The Eagle To Sleep* (1970) views the absurdities of late 1960s America by exaggerating its violent patterns of behaviour in an alternative universe. *Woman On The Edge Of Time* presents three different realities, one Utopian, one dystopian and the third our own present state of being. She is not so much strongly feminist – although the condition of women is essential to her work – as humanist, and her writing is rich in character and event without ever succumbing to dialectic.

Woman On The Edge Of Time (1976)

| R ★ ★ ★ ★ | I ★ ★ |
| C ★ ★ ★ | L ★ ★ ★ |

PIPER, H(enry) Beam (1904-64) American writer best known for his Fuzzy novels, *Little Fuzzy* and *Fuzzy Sapiens* (1964; a.k.a. *The Other Human Race*), set on the planet Zarathustra, where a peaceful, sentient non-human race is discovered: the books depict the attempts of sympathetic humans to have the fuzzies recognized as sentient and to protect them from less scrupulous humans. His other work shows a fascination with time, alternative worlds and the actions of heroes; fast-action adventures, many of them (including the Fuzzy novels) set in the Terran Federation series, and some of the shorter work in the Paratime Police series. His work is immensely enjoyable, even if occasionally overtly sentimental.

Little Fuzzy (1962)

| R ★ ★ ★ ★ ★ | I ★ ★ |
| C ★ ★ | L ★ ★ |

Space Viking (1963)

| R ★ ★ ★ ★ | I ★ |
| C ★ | L ★ ★ |

Gunpowder God (1965; a.k.a. *Lord Kalvan Of Otherwhen*)

| R ★ ★ ★ ★ ★ | I ★ ★ |
| C ★ ★ | L ★ ★ |

PISERCHIA, Doris (Elaine) (1928) American writer who emerged in the mid-1960s with well-crafted but often disconcerting and complex stories and novels. Disconcerting, that is, in their subject matter and scenarios, as in *Mister Justice*, a time travel vigilante tale and *A Billion Days Of Earth* (1976) with its vision of a brutal far-future Earth. Her writing, if often convoluted, is of the highest standard.

Mister Justice (1973)

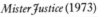

| R ★ ★ ★ ★ | I ★ ★ |
| C ★ ★ | L ★ ★ ★ |

PLATT, Charles (1944) English writer of the *New Worlds* school. His *The Garbage World* describes a garbage-dump asteroid and its population – messy but fun. *Planet Of The Voles* (1971) is straightforward space opera, but *Twilight Of The City* (a revision of the earlier *The City Dwellers*, 1970) is perhaps Platt's best work – a lurid vision of entropy at work upon the textures and inhabitants of a city.

The Garbage World (1967)

| R ★ ★ ★ ★ | I ★ ★ |
| C ★ | L ★ ★ |

Twilight Of The City (1977)

| R ★ ★ ★ ★ | I ★ ★ |
| C ★ | L ★ ★ |

PLAUGER, P. J. (1944) American writer who began publishing short stories in *Analog* in the 1970s. He has written one sf novel, *Fighting Madness*, and won the John W. Campbell Award for Best New SF Author in 1975.

Fighting Madness (1976)

| R ★ ★ ★ | I ★ |
| C ★ | L ★ |

POE, Edgar Allan (1809-49) American writer, generally credited as the founding father of American sf, though he wrote relatively little of it. He produced several stories in which mesmerism plays a crucial role, including "A Mesmeric Revelation" (1844), which encapsulates a cosmic vision elaborated in much more detail in his speculative essay, *Eureka* (1848). In a famous introduction to "The Unparalleled Adventure Of One Hans Pfaall" (1835) he is scathing about earlier Moon-voyage stories, criticizing them for lack of verisimilitude, but to modern readers this satirical account of a balloon trip to the moon seems hardly to be an improvement in that regard. Poe was, however, genuinely interested in scientific ideas and has few peers as a writer of intense psychological horror stories. His futuristic tales are mostly trivial, though there are some interesting points in "Mellonta Tauta" (1849), and his post-apocalyptic vignette "The Conversation of Eiros and Charmion" (1839) has a certain piquancy. Such stories as *The Narrative Of A. Gordon Pym* and "The Balloon Hoax" (1844) no longer look like sf today, but in their own time they could be counted serious speculative works. His real importance as a writer relevant to the tradition of imaginative fiction lies in his eccentric view of the relationship between appearance and reality, and his conviction that in moments of unusual intuitive insight the phenomenal veil could be penetrated to reveal the bizarre and spectacular hidden cosmos beyond the reach of ordinary perception.

Edgar Allan Poe

Frederik Pohl

"The Facts In The Case Of M. Valdemar" (1845)

R ★ ★ ★		I ★ ★ ★ ★
C ★		L ★ ★ ★ ★

The Narrative Of A. Gordon Pym (1837)

R ★ ★		I ★ ★ ★ ★
C ★ ★ ★		L ★ ★ ★ ★

POHL, Frederik (1919) American author, active in the sf field for the last 45 years. He began as editor of a pulp magazine at 19 and has since become one of sf's leading figures. His own fiction radically changed in the mid-1970s, winning him the genre's leading awards for his novels *Man Plus* (1976) and *Gateway*, both of which fused highly traditional science-fictional elements with a more literary concern for style and characterization. Most of Pohl's early work is of the slick adventure variety, especially at novel length (see *Slave Ship*, 1957, for instance), but there are a number of short stories which, in their stark, ironic view of American consumerism, are classics – "The Tunnel Under The World" (1955) is perhaps the best of these. There are many collaborations in this first period of Pohl's work, the most famous of which was with C. M. Kornbluth (q.v.), which produced *The Space Merchants* (1953), still the sf field's leading work of social satire. Another three novels were written with Kornbluth (including the marvellous *Wolfbane* (1959), which depicts aliens controlling human zombies). One collaborated novel with Lester del Rey (q.v.), *Preferred Risk* (1955), is his least successful joint effort, whilst the seven novels produced with Jack Williamson (q.v.) to date (including the three Jim Eden juveniles and the *Starchild* trilogy) are healthy adventures with few pretensions. The early solo novels seem rather lacklustre by comparison with what followed, but *The Age Of The Pussyfoot* (1969) and *A Plague Of Pythons* (1965) are, in their comic (*Pussyfoot*) and horrific (*Pythons*) manners, better than average sf. It is with *Man Plus*, however, that Pohl's solo work becomes respectable. The story retains all the scientific and extrapolative trappings of sf as it describes the U.S. government's attempts to establish a computer/machine-assisted colony on Mars, and the effect on one "cyborged" human, Roger Torraway, the first Martian. Pohl's re-evaluation of his writing in the previous seven years make this an outstanding work, and the same can be said of *Gateway*, which followed, and which depicts the discovery of alien (Heechee) artifacts and their technological exploitation. Its use of cut-in chapters showing its hero Robinette Broadbent's psychoanalytic treatment gives the work a considerable depth. One sequel, *Beyond The Blue Event Horizon* (1980), has been published, and the final unravelling of the Heechee mystery is promised in *Heechee Rendezvous*, to be published in the spring 1984. *Jem* presented an Utopian vision of sorts. Set on an alien planet, its essential message is "cooperate or else." Earth is destroyed to underline that point. Slightly less elegant, although no less eloquent or intelligent, are *The Cool War* (1980), a near-future eco-tragedy come spy thriller, and *Starburst*, a novelization of the earlier, excellent "The Gold At The Starbow's End" (1971), which best expresses Pohl's love of knowledge. With Asimov (q.v.) and Heinlein (q.v.) he could be said to be

Jerry Pournelle

exemplary of traditional science fiction. Unlike those two, however, his writing has embraced the increasingly literary concerns of the genre during the 1970s.

Gateway (1979)

R	★	★	★	★	★	I	★	★	★	★
C	★	★	★			L	★	★	★	

Jem (1979)

R	★	★	★	★		I	★	★	★	
C	★	★	★			L	★	★		

Starburst (1982)

R	★	★	★	★		I	★	★	★	
C	★	★	★			L	★	★		

"Day Million" (1966)

R	★	★	★	★	★	I	★	★	★	★
C	★	★				L	★	★	★	

PORGES, Arthur (1915) Prolific American writer of short stories for the sf magazines throughout the 1950s and 1960s. None of his work has been collected, perhaps because of its dependence upon gimmick twists and endings. Yet some of his work is impressive, for example "The Mirror" (1966), a vivid horror story, and "The Fly" (1952).

"The Ruum" (1953)

R	★	★	★	★	★	I	★	★	
C	★					L	★	★	

POURNELLE, Jerry (Eugene) (1933) American writer who has had greatest success with the three novels produced in collaboration with Larry Niven (q.v.), *Lucifer's Hammer* (1977), a comet-threatens-Earth disaster story, *Inferno* (1976), a re-working of Dante's epic in novel form with an sf writer as protagonist, and *The Mote In God's Eye*. This last is part of Pournelle's Co-Dominium series, depicting a Galactic civilization replete with exotic aliens and a militaristic hierarchical society. His work is marked by a strong political conservatism and a pro-technology, pro-expansionist attitude. His experience in the U.S. space programme is evident in the factual accuracy of the hard science in his work, but this specialist knowledge more often than not overbalances the softer, more human element, and characterization is generally weak throughout his fiction. The one exception is Falkenberg, the military hero of the CoDominium series, whose calm capability and certain strength make him an attractive, if sometimes unsympathetic, creation. Pournelle's emphasis on a fast-tempo adventure format usually suits his theme and, whilst little of his work is innovative, it is in the direct lineage of the field's development.

A Spaceship For The King (1973)

R	★ ★ ★ ★	I	★ ★
C	★	L	★

The Mote In God's Eye (1974; with Larry Niven)

R	★ ★ ★ ★ ★	I	★ ★ ★
C	★ ★	L	★ ★

Janissaries (1980)

R	★ ★ ★ ★	I	★ ★
C	★	L	★ ★

POWYS, John Cowper (1872-1963) English writer whose use of telepathy, astral travel and myth makes some of his work borderline sf, especially *Morwyn: Or The Vengeance Of God, All Or Nothing* (1960) and the collection *Up And Out* (1957). The apocalyptic merging of technological and mythological elements is peculiarly Powys's; a powerful hybrid and a potential direction for sf in the future.

Morwyn: Or The Vengeance Of God (1937)

R	★ ★ ★ ★	I	★ ★ ★
C	★ ★	L	★ ★ ★ ★

PRATCHETT, Terry English writer whose first few sf novels show a markedly irreverent attitude towards the sf field, particularly *Strata*, with its parody of Larry Niven's (q.v.) *Ringworld* and the underlying idea that future Man is planting fossils to shore up the ludicrous theory of Evolution.

Strata (1982)

R	★ ★ ★ ★ ★	I	★ ★
C	★	L	★ ★

PRATT, (Murray) Fletcher (1897-1956) American writer of hard science fiction as well as science fantasy. His work displays a fascination with American history (upon which he wrote numerous non-fiction works) and, under the influence of L. Sprague de Camp (q.v.), with creating alternative universes where our Myths are actualities. At his best his work can be spellbinding, at worst (as in most of his routine science fiction), unreadable.

Double Jeopardy (1952)

R	★ ★ ★	I	★
C	★	L	★

The Complete Enchanter: The Magical Adventures Of Harold Shea (1975)

R	★ ★ ★ ★	I	★ ★
C	★ ★	L	★ ★

PRIEST, Christopher (1943) English writer whose first novel, *Indoctrinaire* (1970), announced the split-reality theme that dominates his work. There are always two realities in his fiction between which the alienated protagonists fluctuate. At its starkest this schizophrenic state is depicted in "Double Consummation" (1970), and at its subtlest in his latest novel, *The Affirmation*, a beautifully crafted novel which demonstrates how far Priest's literary aspirations have led him. There is, throughout his work, a sense of coldness and distance which is perhaps at its greatest in his excellent novel, *Fugue For A Darken-*

ing Island (1972), in which a nuclear-devastated Africa dumps its refugees upon the shores of Britain and precipitates civil war. The catastrophe (which catalyses the division of reality) is always described in terms of its personal effects. Priest's anti-heroes define themselves in the face of the most radical challenges to their sense of continuous and whole existence. Sometimes this is described in traditional science-fictional ways, as in *Inverted World* (his most orthodox sf work) and *The Space Machine* (Priest's homage to Wells), but more often it is presented directly as "dream," as in *A Dream Of Wessex* (1977). With *The Affirmation*, however, Priest seems to have written himself out of the sf genre and it will be interesting to see what direction he will take. He seems, certainly, to have developed his theme to its ultimate expression.

Inverted World (1974)

R ★ ★ ★ ★	I ★ ★
C ★ ★	L ★ ★

The Space Machine (1976)

R ★ ★ ★	I ★ ★
C ★ ★	L ★ ★ ★

The Affirmation (1981)

R ★ ★ ★	I ★ ★
C ★ ★	L ★ ★ ★ ★

Christopher Priest

PRIESTLEY, J(ohn) B(oynton) (1894) English writer, several of whose works are borderline science fiction. The most overtly so is *The Magicians*, which involves drugs and the manipulation of time in its plot. Priestley generally uses his sf elements in an educational way, to create a moral change in his protagonists.

The Magicians (1954)

R ★ ★ ★ ★	I ★
C ★ ★	L ★ ★

PURDOM, Tom (1936) American writer whose continual reworking of the well-worn theme of overthrowing a tyrannous regime and establishing a new republic is more interesting than would appear possible. Novels like *The Tree Lord Of Imeten* (1966) and *The Barons Of Behaviour* are subtle variations on this theme.

The Barons Of Behaviour (1972)

R ★ ★ ★ ★	I ★
C ★	L ★

PYNCHON, Thomas (1937) American writer whose work shares the concerns and devices of science fiction, especially in its depiction of conspiracy theory (*The Crying Of Lot 49* (1966)) and of hidden purposes (both in *V*, 1963, and in *Gravity's Rainbow*, which is Pynchon's most science-fictional work).

Gravity's Rainbow (1973)

R ★ ★ ★	I ★ ★ ★ ★
C ★ ★	L ★ ★ ★ ★

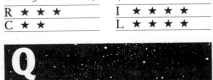

QUINN, Seabury G(randin) (1889-1969) American author best known for his numerous contributions to *Weird Tales* throughout its long history. His occult detective, Jules de Grandin, and his assistant Dr Trowbridge, were featured in almost 100 stories, and there are seven collections of these stories, including *The Adventures Of Jules de Grandin* (1976) and *The Casebook Of Jules de Grandin*.

The Casebook Of Jules de Grandin (1976; coll.)

R ★ ★ ★	I ★
C ★ ★	L ★ ★

RAND, Ayn (1905-82) American writer born in Russia, originator of a right-wing political philosophy which she called "objectivism" and which has much in common with the ideas of contemporary Libertarian movements. She became a bestseller with her non-sf novel of ideas, *The Fountainhead*. Her two sf novels are the very short anti-Communist polemic *Anthem* and the very long near-future novel of individualist entrepreneurs who withdraw their labour from an America which has succumbed to creeping socialism, *Atlas Shrugged*. She writes with great moral verve and a vividly dramatic style, and compels admiration even from readers who cannot share her views.

Anthem (1938)

R ★ ★ ★	I ★ ★ ★
C ★	L ★ ★ ★

Atlas Shrugged (1957)

R ★ ★ ★ ★	I ★ ★ ★
C ★ ★ ★	L ★ ★ ★ ★

RANDALL, Marta (1948) American writer whose work began to appear in the late 1970s. Much in the tradition of the women sf writers of this generation, her work tends towards a mixture of fantasy and sf, has strong female characters and focuses more on human predicament than scientific speculation. Several of her novels are linked in the Kennerin Saga, but most are set in varied exotic landscapes and show a fascination with the richly alien.

The Sword Of Winter (1980)

R ★ ★ ★ ★	I ★
C ★ ★	L ★ ★

RANKINE, John (1918) Pseudonym for English writer Douglas Rankine Mason, who also writes as Douglas R. Mason. His Rankine novels are slick adventures, well-told but basically entertainments. His Mason works are far more ambitious and possess a greater depth. Under both pen names he is prolific, a factor which has probably prevented him from producing anything of real originality or value. Some of his novels are set in the same future galaxy, including the Dag Fletcher series of space operas, of which *The Ring Of Garamas* (1972) is a typical example.

The Fingalnan Conspiracy (1973; as John Rankine)

R ★ ★ ★	I ★
C ★	L ★

Pitman's Progress (1976; as Douglas R. Mason)

R ★ ★	I
C	L

RAPHAEL, Rick (1919) American writer whose short stories are collected in *The Thirst Quenchers* (1965), and many of which deal with ecological concerns. His only sf novel, *Code Three*, is really three novellas linked to form the story of police life on a future super-highway, dealing with maniacs in cars which travel at 400 m.p.h.

Code Three (1965)

R ★ ★ ★	I ★ ★
C ★ ★	L ★ ★

RAYER, Francis G(eorge) (1921) English writer, most of whose work appeared in British magazines between 1947 and 1963. For the main part (as in his novels) he is a hack writer of unimaginative adventure stories, but he did transcend his limitations in *Tomorrow Sometimes Comes*, about a super-intelligent computer which takes over from Man in the event of a nuclear war.

Tomorrow Sometimes Comes (1951)

R ★ ★ ★	I ★ ★
C ★	L ★ ★

READ, Herbert (Edward) (1893-1968) English writer and expert on modern art whose *The Green Child* is a Utopian fantasy calling upon his own Yorkshire childhood and his absurdist/anarchist beliefs, weaving these into a fascinating and intelligent fantasy about the green-child, Siloën and his meeting with a former teacher, Oliver.

The Green Child (1935)

R ★ ★ ★ ★		I ★ ★ ★	
C ★ ★ ★		L ★ ★ ★ ★	

REAMY, Tom (1935-77) The sudden death of American writer Tom Reamy deprived the science fiction world of an immense talent. He had been awarded the Nebula Award, the year prior to his death, for his novelette "San Diego Lightfoot Sue," later published in a collection of his short fiction and completed his only novel *Blind Voices*, published posthumously. Reamy, a graphic designer, wrote in a style comparable to the Mid-Western voice of American literature, adding an almost callous degree of fantasy to an otherwise simple country setting which permeated all his fiction. *Blind Voices* tells the story of a travelling freak show, the wonderfully bizarre and bitter characters behind its façade, and the devastating effect it has on some of the younger inhabitants of a small Kansas town.

Mack Reynolds

"San Diego Lightfoot Sue" (1980)

R ★ ★ ★ ★		I ★ ★ ★ ★	
C ★ ★ ★ ★		L ★ ★ ★ ★ ★	

Blind Voices (1978)

R ★ ★ ★ ★		I ★ ★ ★ ★ ★	
C ★ ★ ★ ★ ★		L ★ ★ ★ ★ ★	

REED, Kit (1932) Writing name used by Lillian Reed, an American author who has been producing sf since the late 1950s but has published very little. Her writing is more fantasy-oriented than sf but is thoughtful, humanistic and firmly based upon characterization.

Armed Camps (1970)

R ★ ★ ★		I ★ ★	
C ★ ★ ★		L ★ ★	

RESNICK, Michael D. (1942) American writer whose first works were homages to Edgar Rice Burroughs (q.v.). His first novel, *Sideshow*, shows few signs of Resnick's hack activities in other genres, and though its subject matter seems trite (a carnival touring Earth, but containing real aliens), it is handled intelligently and memorably.

Sideshow (1982)

R ★ ★ ★ ★		I ★	
C ★ ★		L ★ ★	

REYNOLDS, Mack (1917-83) American writer notable for his attempts to import economic and political theory into magazine sf. His plots are deliberately crude and action-packed to sugar-coat discussions of sociological interest. As a radical socialist he was an unlikely recruit to John W. Campbell's *Analog*, but it was there that most of his work appeared in the 1960s. In the 1970s he embarked upon an ambitious series of books set in various versions of the year 2000, trying to establish blueprints for a better society based on high technology. His *Looking Backward From The Year 2000* is an updating of Edward Bellamy's (q.v.) classic Utopian novel. He always had great difficulty selling his more ambitious work and his published material does not do justice to his intelligence, wit and seriousness of purpose. His best novels of ideas are *The Rival Rigelians* and *Mercenary From Tomorrow* (1968), and he also wrote some good stories about attempts by Western nations to foster economic and social development in Africa, beginning with *Black Man's Burden* (1972). His potboilers are often awkward and certain recurrent formulae crop up with annoying regularity, but his best works are imaginatively lively and thought-provoking.

The Rival Rigelians (1967)

R ★ ★ ★	I ★ ★ ★ ★
C ★	L ★ ★

Looking Backward From The Year 2000 (1973)

R ★ ★	I ★ ★ ★ ★
C ★	L ★ ★

After Utopia (1977)

R ★ ★	I ★ ★ ★
C ★	L ★ ★

RICHMOND, Walt and Leigh American husband and wife collaborators (Walt; 1922-77) whose six sf novels are melodramatic and rather innocent – filled with amateur inventors whose discoveries rival the big secret establishments, one-handed defences of the Earth and other trappings of 1920s/1930s sf. They are delightful, unchallenging adventures.

The Lost Millenium (1967; a.k.a. *Siva!*)

R ★ ★ ★	I ★
C ★	L ★

RITCHIE, Paul (1923) Australian novelist and playwright whose experimental novel, *Confessions Of A People Lover*, is a dystopian view of a future Britain run by the degenerate and violent young.

Confessions Of A People Lover (1967)

R ★ ★ ★	I ★ ★
C ★ ★	L ★ ★ ★

ROBERTS, Jane (1929) American writer whose work is of a philosophical/metaphysical kind, examining sf themes like overpopulation and the nature of time, in works like *The Rebellers* (1963) and *The Education Of Oversoul Seven*.

The Education Of Oversoul Seven (1973)

R ★ ★ ★	I ★ ★
C ★	L ★ ★

ROBERTS, John Maddox American writer of *The Strayed Sheep Of Charun*, depicting a medieval society on an alien planet, violent and irreligious.

The Strayed Sheep Of Charun (1977)

R ★ ★ ★	I ★
C ★	L ★

ROBERTS, Keith (John Kingston) (1935) English writer, who has also acted as magazine editor and illustrator. His work taps the mythical depths of English culture and, in a manner reminiscent of Hardy, is concerned with the interaction of character and place. Most of his work is set in Hardy's Wessex and has the same intense visual sense. Roberts's artistic eye shapes his stories, and even the most overtly science-fictional focus upon how changes affect individuals and the places which they inhabit. *The Furies* (1966), his first novel, showed an England ravaged by giant mutated wasps: the story being less garish than its simple plot synopsis suggests. It was interesting, but with *Pavane* it could be seen that Roberts was a major sf writer. It is an alternative-world story, where Elizabeth I was assassinated and Catholicism never lost its grip on Europe. Scientific advancement has been checked; but the real focus of the book is on certain individuals and how they live in this changed world. The collections of Roberts's stories contain many of the finest pieces of writing in the sf field; "Weihnachtsabend" (1972), about a world in which Germany won World War II, and "Missa Privata" (1976), the study of an individual in a communist Britain of the future, are perfect examples of this. *The Chalk Giants* (like *Pavane*) is a collection of related stories set in a post-holocaust England which has reverted to ancient Druidical ways. The corn gods lie behind much of Roberts's work! His most recently published novel, *Molly Zero* (1980), again deals with a Britain torn apart by civil war and regressing. More contemporary than his other work, it is perhaps less successful, but its portrayal of Molly is excellent. Only his extreme Englishness can explain his lack of success in the U.S.A.; his talent is undoubted.

Pavane (1968)

R	★	★	★	★	★	I	★	★	★	
C	★	★	★	★		L	★	★	★	★	★

The Chalk Giants (1974)

R	★	★	★	★	I	★	★		
C	★	★	★		L	★	★	★	★

Ladies From Hell (1979; coll.)

R	★	★	★	★	I	★	★	★	
C	★	★	★		L	★	★	★	★

ROBINETT, Stephen (1941) American author, who sometimes writes under the name of Tak Hallus. His first novel, *Stargate* (1976), has as much to do with corporate finance, wheeler-dealing and murder as stargates. This interest in corruption, corporations and computers is also marked in *The Man Responsible*. His shorter fiction, collected in *Projections* (1979), is sharp, witty and occasionally ingenious.

The Man Responsible (1978)

R	★	★	★	★	I	★	★	
C	★	★		L	★			

ROBINSON, Frank M(alcolm) (1926) American writer. His first novel, *The Power* (1956), is about the Nazi experiments to create a superman. All of his other full-length work has been in collaboration with Thomas N. Scortia (q.v.), including the filmed *The Glass Inferno* (1974). These works are intelligent and well-researched disaster novels. *The Prometheus Crisis*, for example, is a story of corruption and the failure of a nuclear power plant.

The Prometheus Crisis (1975; with Thomas N. Scortia)

R	★	★	★	★	I	★	★	
C	★			L	★			

ROBINSON, Jeanne American writer, all of whose work has been in collaboration with her husband, Spider Robinson (q.v.), whom she married.

ROBINSON, SPIDER (1948) American writer most of whose work in the 1970s was produced for *Analog* magazine and has a hard science bias. "Stardance" (with Jeanne Robinson (q.v.)) won both the Hugo and Nebula awards and was later extended to novel length, though not with any great success. His work is rather garish and cluttered but nonetheless remains highly popular for its technological bias, its (often hideous) puns and its aura of "golden age" science fiction. *Telempath*, a post-holocaust story, again won awards at a shorter length (as "By Any Other Name" (1976)). His writing is occasionally awkward and is generally presented through a first-person narrative. If Robinson can be said to have a "theme" in his work, it is the depiction of the fragmentation of social cohesion and of the ultimate spiritual transcendence of that state (particularly in *Stardance* (1979)). Also of interest are the stories collected in *Callahans Crosstime Saloon* (1977).

Telempath (1976)

R	★	★	★	★	I	★	★	
C	★			L	★			

"Stardance" (1977; with Jeanne Robinson)

R	★	★	★	★	★	I	★	★	★
C	★	★			L	★	★		

ROCKLYNNE, Ross (1913) American writer Ross Louis Rocklin. Most of his short fiction appeared in the 1930s and 1940s. It consisted of ingenious science tales. Some of these were fixed-up to form two novels in the 1970s, *The Men And The Mirror* (1973) and *The Sun Destroyers*, telling of giant sentient star-like beings which live for millions of years. His work should not be judged by the standards of his pulp contemporaries.

The Sun Destroyers (1973)

R	★	★	★	I	★	★	★	
C	★			L	★	★		

ROGERS, Michael (Alan) (1951) American writer whose *Mindfogger* describes a hippy inventor's attempts to thwart the system with his "mindfogger" device. Can be read as a drop-out-take-drugs plea. The sf element is weak, as is the plot.

Mindfogger (1973)

R ★ ★	I ★
C	L ★

ROHMER, Richard (1924) Canadian writer of stereotyped, but nonetheless reasonably interesting, sf novels about power-games. They are generally near-future political scenarios with Canada crucially involved.

Exoneration (1974)

R ★ ★	I ★
C	L ★

ROMANO, Deane (Louis) (1927) American writer of *Flight From Time One*, a rather strained parapsychology tale with "astralnauts."

Flight From Time One (1972)

R ★ ★	I ★
C ★	L ★

ROSHWALD, Mordecai (Marceli) (1921) American writer. His *Level Seven* is a powerful warning about nuclear war, set at "level 7," 4,000 feet below ground at the heart of the anonymous defence centre. Its cold impersonality is convincing, even if its idea of irresponsible politicians is not so believable. *A Small Armageddon* (1962), where a nuclear submarine mutinies and makes piratical threats to cities, is wholly unconvincing in its premise, but makes a good adventure tale.

Level Seven (1959)

R ★ ★ ★ ★	I ★ ★
C ★	L ★ ★

ROSNY, J. H. (aîné) (1856-1940) Pseudonym of Belgian writer Joseph-Henri Boëx (shared sometimes with his brother Justin). Very little of his work has been translated, and none of his best. The

Giant Cat and a few other short fictions are available in English, but few of his pre-history tales, none of his lost world and end-of-world scenarios.

The Giant Cat (1918; trans. 1924; a.k.a. *Quest Of The Dawn Man*)

R ★ ★ ★	I ★
C ★	L ★

ROSSITER, Oscar (1918) Pseudonym of American writer Vernon H. Skeels, author of *Tetrasomy Two* – a rather crude superman fantasy with a humorous streak. Set in a mental hospital, its sf premises are unbelievable but fun.

Tetrasomy Two (1974)

R ★ ★ ★	I
C ★	L ★ ★

ROTH, Philip (1933) American novelist whose *The Breast* is a comic version of Kafka's "Metamorphosis" where a man is turned into a female breast. Its surreal humour and pointed satire is a delight.

The Breast (1972)

R ★ ★ ★ ★	I ★ ★
C ★	L ★ ★

ROTSLER, William (1926) American writer whose work began to appear in the 1970s. His first novel, *Patron Of The Arts*, was an impressive début, portraying a future synthesis of all the art forms and its effect on society. His more commercial work which followed is disappointing by comparison and is no more than fast-action formula space fiction.

Patron Of The Arts (1974)

R ★ ★ ★ ★	I ★ ★ ★ ★
C ★ ★	L ★ ★ ★

ROUSSEAU, Victor (1879-1960) English-born American writer Victor Rousseau Emanuel, who also wrote as H. M. Egbert. His work is generally in the fantastic vein with colourful large-screen effects which tend towards melodrama. Most of his shorter work appeared in *Weird Tales* and *Astounding Science Fiction* in the

1920s and early 1930s and there are also three novels (two as Egbert) from this period.

The Messiah Of The Cylinder (1917; a.k.a. *The Apostle Of The Cylinder*)

R ★ ★	I ★
C	L

RUCKER, Rudy (1946) American writer. A teacher of higher mathematics with various scientific titles to his credit, Rucker is both a surviving hippy in spirit, the worthy successor to Philip K. Dick (q.v.), and modern sf's latest major star. An irritatingly casual and undisciplined author, he is at his best juggling with dimensions and possibilities, attaining cartoon strip dimension lift-off while still retaining an affecting compassion for his characters. Almost too imaginative for his own sake, he is still an acquired taste, but the flavour is spreading fast.

White Light (1980)

R ★ ★ ★ ★	I ★ ★ ★ ★ ★
C ★ ★ ★	L ★ ★

Software (1981)

R ★ ★ ★	I ★ ★ ★
C ★ ★ ★	L ★ ★

The Sex Sphere (1983)

R ★ ★ ★ ★	I ★ ★ ★ ★
C ★ ★ ★	L ★ ★

RUNYON, Charles W. (1928) American thriller writer, some of whose work is borderline sf. *Pig World* depicts a near-future totalitarian America, and *Soulmate* (1974) portrays the possession of a young prostitute. Another novel, *I, Weapon* (1974), demonstrates Runyon's fast-paced all-action style.

Pig World (1971)

R ★ ★ ★ ★	I ★
C ★	L ★ ★

RUSHDIE, (Ahmed) Salman (1947) Indian writer educated and domiciled in England. His first novel, *Grimus*, is marginally sf in its use of myth and of an im-

Salman Rushdie

mortality theme, and his second, *Midnight's Children* – which won the prestigious Booker-McConnell Prize – tells of 1,001 children born on the hour of India's independence who are seen to have special talents. His use of sf metaphor is not the crucial factor in either book, but only an additional element in the rich texture of his work.

Grimus (1975)

R ★ ★ ★	I ★ ★
C ★ ★	L ★ ★ ★

Midnight's Children (1981)

R ★ ★ ★ ★	I ★ ★ ★
C ★ ★ ★	L ★ ★ ★ ★

RUSS, Joanna (1937) American author, dramatist and academic. Her former and most influential writings use the conventions of sf, heroic fantasy and Utopian fiction to conduct a powerful and uncompromising feminist critique, both of society and of sf itself. Later work appears to be moving in the direction of moderation. Russ specializes in strong, witty female protagonists whose understanding supersedes the status games and repressive obsessions that occupy the other characters, often representatives of far-future societies that parody our own. Her fragmented, allusive style can be hard to read, but amply rewards the effort it demands. One of the central concerns of all sf is power; Russ's sf is both an image and an actual case of power being wrested from patriarchal hands. Her most radical work – for example, the explosive *The Female Man* – seized sf as a medium for female anger and determination, but also opened it to less aggressive, less ambitious feminist visions, some of them her own.

The Female Man (1975)

R	★ ★ ★				I	★ ★ ★ ★			
C	★ ★ ★ ★ ★				L	★ ★ ★ ★ ★			

We Who Are About To . . . (1977)

R	★ ★ ★				I	★ ★ ★ ★ ★			
C	★ ★ ★ ★				L	★ ★ ★			

"The Second Inquisition" (1970)

R	★ ★ ★		I	★ ★ ★	
C	★ ★ ★ ★ ★		L	★ ★ ★ ★	

Joanna Russ

RUSSELL, Bertrand (Arthur William) (1872-1970) English philosopher who in his 80s wrote a number of stories in an sf idiom and some of a fabular nature. These were collected in three volumes, *Satan In The Suburbs* (1953), *Nightmares Of Eminent Persons* and *Fact And Fiction* (1961). The tales range from dystopias like "Eisenhower's Nightmare" to a vision of the robotic-machine age in "Dr Southport Vulpe's Nightmare: The Victory Of Mind Over Matter."

Nightmares Of Eminent Persons and Other Stories (1954; coll.)

R	★ ★ ★		I	★ ★ ★	
C	★		L	★ ★ ★	

RUSSELL, Eric Frank (1905-78) English writer who published most of his work in the American magazines. He was active from the late 1930s until the 1960s, adapting the manner of his work to changing market conditions. His Fortean fantasy, *Sinister Barrier*, was well-liked at the time, though its rough-hewn mock-American style grates on the ear. His best work was done for *Astounding Science Fiction* in the early 1950s, and includes a number of scathing attacks on militaristic philosophy, ranging in tone from the nightmarish "I Am Nothing" (1952) to the brilliant satire ". . . And Then There Were None" (1951) (later incorporated into *The Great Explosion*), in which the personnel of a naval spaceship are seduced away from the path of duty by colonists of an alien world who have borrowed a philosophy of life from Gandhi. His thrillers about invisible or super-human enemies in our midst seem routine by comparison. He also delighted in writing humorous stories about dim-witted aliens outwitted by human ingenuity, and these are fondly remembered by many readers.

Sinister Barrier (1939)

R	★ ★		I	★ ★ ★	
C	★		L	★ ★	

Three To Conquer (1956)

R	★ ★ ★		I	★ ★ ★	
C	★ ★		L	★ ★	

RUSSELL, John Robert   American author of *Cabu* (1974) and two other novels, *Sar* and *Ta* (1975), depicting strange and sometimes violent alien worlds and providing routine adventure.

Sar (1974)

R ★ ★ ★	I ★
C ★	L ★

RUSSELL, Ray (1924) American writer and Executive Editor of *Playboy*. His enthusiasm for sf occasionally spills over into his own novels, although more in a fantastic/horror vein than as straight sf.

Incubus (1976)

R ★ ★ ★	I ★
C	L ★

SABERHAGEN, Fred (1930) American writer who once worked as an editor on the *Encyclopedia Britannica*. He first attracted notice with a long series of stories about alien war machines called "Berserkers," and in recent years has begun to publish much more prolifically and with greater versatility. His interesting literary joke, *The Dracula Tape* (1975), which presents the events of Bram Stoker's novel from the point of view of the vampire (who thus becomes the hero, with van Helsing the villain), became the foundation stone for a series of novels capitalizing on the recent fashion for sympathetic vampire stories. His sf is less exciting than his vampire novels, but since he has begun to put more effort into the portrayal of human relationships than into his rather mechanical plotting his work has become more interesting and more popular.

Berserker (1967)

R ★ ★	I ★ ★
C ★	L ★

Specimens (1976)

R ★ ★	I ★ ★
C ★	L ★

ST CLAIR, Margaret (1911) American author who also writes as Idris Seabright. She has been writing science fiction since the mid-1940s and has written eight novels, one of which, *The Dolphins Of Altair*, is a moving ecology tale. Her earlier work is rather more subtle than the contemporary pulp fiction of the time, and is typified by *Agent Of The Unknown* (1956). She is still continuing to produce interesting sf.

The Dolphins Of Altair (1967)

R ★ ★ ★	I ★ ★ ★
C ★ ★	L ★ ★

SALLIS, James (1944) American writer of the *New Worlds* stable and editor. His collection, *A Few Last Words* (1970), is a good showcase of his tight, absurdist style.

A Few Last Words (1970; coll.)

R ★ ★ ★	I ★ ★
C	L ★ ★

SANDERS, Lawrence (1920) American writer of *The Anderson Tapes* (1970), a thriller. His one sf novel, *The Tomorrow File*, is a bleakly decadent tale of the near future, with more than a thematic nod at Orwell's (q.v.) *1984*. It is flawed but nonetheless works as an entertainment.

The Tomorrow File (1975)

R ★ ★ ★ ★	I ★ ★ ★
C ★ ★	L ★ ★

SAPIR, Richard Ben   American novelist, and co-author, with Warren Murphy, of *Created, The Destroyer* (1971), a long-running saga (now into more than 40 volumes). His solo work, *The Far Arena*, concerns the resuscitation of a Roman gladiator 2,000 years after his death.

The Far Arena (1978)

R ★ ★ ★	I ★ ★
C ★ ★	L ★

SARBAN (1910) Pseudonymous author of fantasies on themes of menace and enthralment. *The Sound Of His Horn* is a classic vision of Nazi rule in Britain.

Ringstones (1951)

R ★ ★ ★ ★ ★	I ★ ★
C ★ ★ ★	L ★ ★

The Sound Of His Horn (1952)

R ★ ★ ★ ★ ★	I ★ ★
C ★ ★	L ★ ★ ★

The Doll Maker (1953)

R ★ ★ ★ ★	I ★
C ★ ★ ★	L ★ ★ ★

SARGENT, Pamela (1948) American writer whose own work and edited anthologies reflect her concern with feminist issues. Her writing is varied in quality, and whilst her first novel *Cloned Lives* (1976) was extremely promising, she does not appear yet to have achieved her full potential. Likewise, an early collection, *Starshadows and Blue Roses,* has some excellent things in it. Her handling of genre materials is clumsy, however, and her novel about longevity, *The Golden Space,* manages only to be tedious. *The Alien Upstairs* (1983) is again strong on characterization but poor on basic storytelling. There are too many flaws in her work to see her as more than a minor talent in the genre.

Starshadows And Blue Roses (1977; coll.)

R ★ ★ ★	I ★ ★
C ★ ★	L ★ ★

The Golden Space (1982)

R ★ ★ ★	I ★ ★
C ★ ★ ★	L ★

SAUL, John   Best-selling American author, whose *The God Project* is a tale of genetic engineering. He is essentially a thriller writer working with genre themes, but demonstrates a reasonable mastery of sf's materials.

The God Project (1983)

R ★ ★ ★ ★ ★	I ★ ★ ★
C ★ ★	L ★ ★

SAVARIN, Julius Jay   West Indian (Dominican) writer, whose *Lemmus* trilogy is his contribution to sf. Uninspired and something like 30 years out of date, this is pure pulp space opera.

Lemmus Two: Beyond The Outer Mirr (1976)

R ★ ★	I
C	L

SAXON, Richard (1905) Pseudonym of American writer, Joseph Laurence Morrissey. His five sf novels are fairly routine reworkings of standard themes (time travel, Utopias, threatening comets, underground societies).

The Stars Came Down (1964)

R ★ ★ ★	I ★
C ★	L ★

SAXTON, Josephine (1935) Highly idiosyncratic, often anarchic, English writer who uses sf for symbols or enabling devices in her vivid fantasies. Frequently set in the psychologically vital landscapes of inner space, her stories are concerned with autonomy of the individual imagination and impulse. Her fiction embraces feminism rather than being committed to it. Energetic, comically bizarre, sometimes with a touch of self-mockery, Saxton's fiction stems from the 1960s vogue for free self-expression; her grasp of sf metaphors, no less than her optimistic extroversion, has enabled her work to endure. Even so, her published work is only a fraction of her actual output, currently regarded by publishers as uncommercial.

Group Feast (1971)

R ★ ★ ★ ★	I ★ ★
C ★ ★ ★	L ★ ★ ★

The Travails of Jane Saint (1980)

R ★ ★ ★ ★	I ★ ★ ★
C ★ ★ ★	L ★ ★

"The Power Of Time" (1971)

R ★ ★ ★ ★ ★	I ★ ★ ★
C ★ ★ ★ ★	L ★ ★ ★

SCHACHNER, Nat(han) (1895-1955) American writer for the pulp magazines throughout the 1930s. Most of his many sf short stories are unreadable now, and are simple *Astounding* fillers. One novel also exists.

Space Lawyer (1953)

R ★ ★	I ★
C ★	L

SCHEER, K(arl)-H(erbert) (1928) West German writer who collaborated with Walter Ernsting (Clark Darlton) on several Perry Rhodan titles – comic book-style space opera which has gone into countless volumes.

SCHENK, Hilbert American author whose first three novels are evidence of a major new talent in the sf field. Schenk seems to specialize in sea stories with a science-fictional difference, and his novel *At The Eye Of The Ocean* (1981) is notable for that. His latest work, *A Rose For Armageddon*, is a science fiction love story through time, and quite superbly told.

A Rose For Armageddon (1982)

R ★ ★ ★ ★ ★	I ★ ★
C ★ ★ ★	L ★ ★ ★ ★

SCHMIDT, Stanley (Albert) (1944) American writer with a Ph.D. in physics. His sf novels are hard science stories which, as with most technophilic writers in the genre, begin to collapse when the human element is introduced. Nonetheless, both *Newton And The Quasi-Apple* (1975) and *The Sins Of The Fathers* (1976) possess a symbolic depth unexpected in such writing. *Lifeboat Earth* is a sequel to the latter.

Lifeboat Earth (1978)

R ★ ★ ★	I ★ ★ ★
C ★	L ★ ★

SCHMITZ James (1911-81) American sf writer. Schmitz's fast-moving space operas, unusually for the 1950s and early 1960s, mostly featured strong female protagonists and a degree of sympathy for the alien menaces which they overcame. Perhaps his most appealing work is *The Witches Of Karres*, in which a pair of psionically gifted adolescent women and an older but more naïve space captain (unwittingly acquiring powers of his own) succeed against the odds in driving alien menaces back to their own universe. The early *Agent Of Vega* is a less tongue-in-cheek space opera but goes even further over the top with its protagonists' and their opponents' powers.

Agent Of Vega (1960)

R ★ ★ ★ ★	I ★ ★ ★
C ★ ★ ★	L ★ ★ ★

The Demon Breed (1968)

R ★ ★ ★ ★	I ★ ★ ★
C ★ ★ ★ ★	L ★ ★ ★

The Witches Of Karres (1966)

R ★ ★ ★ ★	I ★ ★ ★
C ★ ★ ★ ★	L ★ ★ ★ ★

SCHUTZ, J(oseph) W(illard) (1912) American writer of two sf adventure novels, *People Of The Rings* (1975) and *The Moon Microbe*.

The Moon Microbe (1976)

R ★ ★	I
C ★	L

SCORTIA, Thomas N(icholas) (1926) American writer who often collaborates with Frank M. Robinson (q.v.). Although he has been writing sf since the 1950s, he is best known for his disaster novels, including *The Glass Inferno* (1974) – part of the inspiration for the film *Towering Inferno*. He utilizes his scientific knowledge to produce slick marketable fiction.

Earthwreck! (1974)

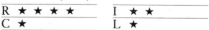

R ★ ★ ★ ★	I ★ ★
C ★	L ★

SEARLS, Hank (1922) American writer Henry Hunt Searls. Most of his fiction is obsessively concerned with space projects. Unfortunately, most of his novels were therefore out of date almost as soon as they were written: a case of fact being more exciting than Searls's fiction, especially in cases like *The Big X* (1959) and *The Astronaut* (1960).

Overboard (1977)

R	★ ★	I	★
C	★	L	★

SELLINGS, Arthur (1921-68) Pseudonym of English writer Robert A. Ley. His early short stories were mostly conventional, but his novels, published at regular intervals through the 1960s, showed steady improvement. His early novels deal with E.S.P., and *The Silent Speakers* is one of the better speculative accounts of a man coming to terms with such an ability. *Junk Day* is an unusual post-holocaust story. It is a pity that the career of such a promising writer was interrupted by sudden and premature death. He was underrated while alive and would surely have enhanced his reputation had he lived.

The Silent Speakers (1962)

R	★ ★ ★	I	★ ★
C	★ ★ ★	L	★ ★ ★

The Power Of X (1968)

R	★ ★ ★	I	★ ★ ★
C	★ ★	L	★ ★ ★

Junk Day (1970)

R	★ ★ ★	I	★ ★ ★
C	★ ★ ★ ★	L	★ ★ ★

SENARENS, Luis Philip (1965-1939) American writer whose two series of books based on the characters Frank Reade and Jack Wright were amazingly popular at the turn of the century. They are almost wholly unreadable now, even though Senarens was the Verne of America at his time. One hundred and seventy-eight titles exist of Frank Reade's exploits, and 103 of Jack Wright's. They even have one adventure together. Simplistic use of scientific fact and invention makes them vaguely sf. A militaristic and chauvinistic streak is also very marked.

The Electric Horse; or, Frank Reade, Jr. and His Father In Search Of The Lost Treasure Of The Peruvians (1888)

R	★	I	★
C		L	

Rod Serling

SERLING, Rod (1924-75) American writer best known for his *The Twilight Zone*. Several collections of stories written by Serling for the programme exist. They are better in a visual rather than a literary, format.

Stories From The Twilight Zone (1960; coll.)

R	★ ★ ★	I	★
C	★	L	★

SERVISS, Garett P(utnam) (1851-1929) American writer of popular science, some of which he framed in a fictional form. Much dated now, they were popular in their time.

Edison's Conquest Of Mars (1898; republished 1947 in book form)

R	★ ★ ★	I	★
C	★	L	★

SEVERN, David (1918) Pseudonym of David Storr Unwin, used for his children's fiction. *The Future Took Us* is an interesting juvenile in which two boys are caught in a time-slip and carried forward to 3000 A.D., where a power struggle is going on.

The Future Took Us (1957)

R	★ ★ ★	I	★ ★
C	★	L	★

SEYMOUR, Alan (1927) English author of *The Coming Self-Destruction Of The United States*, one of several intelligent studies of a possible black/white civil war in America following Vietnam and the race riots. It is more personal than other works of its time and, in a way, more convincing than the accounts written by American writers.

The Coming Self-Destruction Of The United States (1969)

R ★ ★ ★ ★	I ★ ★
C ★	L ★ ★ ★

SHARKEY, Jack (1931) American writer John Michael Sharkey. Prolific in the early 1960s, he produced good adventure fiction which used sf gimmicry and themes. Two novels, *The Secret Martians* and *Ultimatum In 2050 AD* (1965), are good-humoured romps. His series of Jerry Norcriss, Space Zoologist stories is also quite memorable.

The Secret Martians (1960)

R ★ ★ ★	I ★
C ★	L ★

SHAVER, Richard S(harpe) (1907-75) American writer, whose Shaver Mystery stories, ostensibly "non-fiction" but actually pure invention, are still fondly remembered by sf readers of the 1940s. They are collected in *I Remember Lemuria*.

I Remember Lemuria And The Return Of Sathanas (1948; coll.)

R ★ ★	I ★ ★
C	L ★

SHAW, Bob (1931) Until the mid-1970s, Shaw combined a prolific literary career with engineering and journalism, and the compromise involved makes, at best, for a rare combination of depth and lucidity. It also explains Shaw's concern with communication in highly advanced societies, whether through shared eyesight (*Night Walk*), time travel (*The Two-timers*, 1968), pan-psychism (*The Palace Of Eternity*, 1969), neutron resonation (*Ground Zero Man*, 1971), light-retentive glass (*Other Days, Other Eyes*), neutrino-sensitive glasses (*A Wreath Of Stars*), or gestalt minds (*Medusa's Children*, 1977). These devices can be seen as metaphors for Shaw's own art, though self-reflexiveness only really surfaces in his later work: the Space Legion in the delightfully comic *Who Goes Here?* (1977), the Cartographic Service in *Ship Of Strangers* (1978), the "anti-gravity harness" in *Vertigo* (1978). This last, a "psychological" novel, suggests that Shaw is still growing, unsatisfied with compromise; as, indeed, does the relative scrappiness of *Dagger Of The Mind* (1979), and *The Ceres Solution* (1981), obviously written to a deadline. Of Shaw's many short stories, the best are the longest. The Dysonian decentralization of *Orbitsville* (1975) remains his most sustained – and pessimistic – vision. Since then, his orbit has been interestingly irregular.

Other Days, Other Eyes (1972)

R ★ ★ ★ ★ ★	I ★ ★ ★ ★ ★
C ★ ★	L ★ ★ ★

A Wreath Of Stars (1976)

R ★ ★ ★ ★ ★	I ★ ★ ★ ★ ★
C ★ ★ ★	L ★ ★ ★

Night Walk (1967)

R ★ ★ ★ ★ ★	I ★ ★ ★ ★ ★
C ★ ★ ★	L ★ ★ ★

Robert Shaw

SHAW, George Bernard (1856-1950)
Irish writer, whose play *Back To Methuselah*
is wide-screen sf in its scope and effects,
tracing five stages of Man's evolutionary
process, from the distant past to the far
future. He also published a collection of
fables which are vaguely sf-oriented,
Buoyant Billions (1950; coll.)

*Back To Methuselah: A Metabiological
Pentateuch* (1921; revised 1945)

R ★ ★	I ★ ★
C ★	L ★ ★

SHEA, Michael   American writer
whose work is on the borderline of sf and is
more often fantasy or horror. An early
novel, *Quest For Simbilis* (1974), is a far-
future fantasy, a sequel to Vance's *The Eyes
Of The Overworld*. A recent novel, *Nifft The
Lean*, is in a similar vein, a fix-up of four
novelettes about a thief in a horrific future
world. It is a dark, hallucinatory and
strangely impressive work.

Nifft The Lean (1982)

R ★ ★ ★ ★	I ★ ★
C ★ ★	L ★ ★

SHEA, Robert   American editor and
writer, collaborator with Robert Anton
Wilson (q.v.) on the three volumes of the
Illuminatus! series: *The Eye In The Pyramid*,
The Golden Apple and *Leviathan*.

The Golden Apple (1975; with Robert Anton
Wilson)

R ★ ★ ★ ★	I ★ ★
C ★ ★	L ★ ★

SHECKLEY, Robert (1928) American
writer who emerged in the early 1950s as
one of the leading satirists in science
fiction. Whilst he has won no awards for his
work, his short fiction and novels are some
of the finest and funniest things produced
in the genre. His deep philosophical concerns – and especially his notion that life is
an essentially tragic state – underlie his
hilarious tales, which use absurd and surrealist techniques to achieve their effects.
His humour masks the fact that he is one of
the most literate writers to have come out of

the magazines of the 1950s. Most of his
early fiction has been collected, and there
are nine sf novels available, which vary in
quality from the brilliant to the competent.
Options is the former, a space non-opera
which ostensibly is the tale of Mishkin's
search for a spare part for his spaceship,
but which is in fact an intellectual and
literary conundrum. *Mindswap* is another
excellent work, taking us through a whole
series of alien minds and into alien environments. At the other end of the spectrum there is *The Tenth Victim* (1965), a
mediocre thriller based on a far better short
story, and *Immortality Inc.* (1958), which,
whilst not bad is neither as funny nor as
fascinating as his later work. Sheckley's
protagonists are usually idealists who have
to undergo a moral education via extraordinary events. Thomas Carmody in
Dimension Of Miracles (1968) mistakenly
wins a prize in the Intergalactic Sweep-
stakes, then discovers not only that the
prize is sentient and can talk and eat, but
that he is the victim of a specially adapted
predator. This novel, like most of
Sheckley's, is in the picaresque form, each
episode bizarrely different. The latest in
this line is *Dramocles* (1983), wherein
Sheckley parodies standard science fantasy
metaphors to create what is more a soap
opera than a space opera. Greatly under-

Robert Sheckley

rated by the field's academics, Sheckley is one of a handful of unique talents who could not have thrived in any other field than sf.

Mindswap (1966)

R	★ ★ ★ ★ ★	I	★ ★ ★ ★ ★
C	★ ★	L	★ ★ ★

Options (1975)

R	★ ★ ★ ★ ★	I	★ ★ ★ ★ ★
C	★ ★	L	★ ★ ★ ★

The Alchemical Marriage Of Alistair Crompton (1978; a.k.a., *Crompton Divided*)

R	★ ★ ★ ★ ★	I	★ ★ ★ ★ ★
C	★ ★	L	★ ★ ★

Citizen In Space (1955; coll.)

R	★ ★ ★ ★ ★	I	★ ★ ★ ★
C	★	L	★ ★

SHEFFIELD, Charles English-born author and physicist now living in the U.S.A., who began writing hard sf in the mid-1970s. Also Vice-President of the Earth Satellite Corporation, under whose auspices he has produced two large format books showing Earth from space. He is a prolific short story writer, and in an initial burst of writing produced two novels, *Sight Of Proteus* and *The Web Between The Worlds*. The latter, about the construction of a bridge between the Earth and the Moon, is remarkably similar to Arthur C. Clarke's (q.v.) *Fountains Of Paradise*, published the same year. The début novel, which describes a scientist's obsession with form-change, is an excellent work. Of his short fiction "The Man Who Sold The Moon" shows his talent for characterization and storytelling.

Sight Of Proteus (1978)

R	★ ★ ★ ★ ★	I	★ ★ ★ ★
C	★ ★ ★ ★	L	★ ★ ★

The Web Between The Worlds (1979)

R	★ ★ ★ ★ ★	I	★ ★ ★ ★ ★
C	★ ★ ★ ★	L	★ ★ ★ ★ ★

"The Man Who Sold The Moon"

R	★ ★ ★ ★	I	★ ★ ★
C	★ ★ ★ ★	L	★ ★

SHELLEY, Mary (1797-1851) Only recently has Mary Shelley received critical attention, although her novel *Frankenstein; or The Modern Prometheus* has been celebrated ever since it was published anonymously in 1818. While continental Utopianists were projecting the Enlightenment into later centuries, this young girl was introducing the unexpected and irrational into the future, an innovation which many sf writers have followed since. *Frankenstein,* with its horrific story of life created from the dismembered dead, is now generally accepted as the first modern science fiction novel. True, it is not generically pure, but impurities have been the strength of sf throughout its history. Mary Shelley's later novel, *The Last Man,* portrays the collapse of civilization, until only one man is left. This theme also has been widely imitated. But it is as the creator of the monster, malicious because it is miserable, bound to its luckless maker, Victor Frankenstein, that Mary is always – and rightly – remembered.

Frankenstein (1818)

R	★ ★ ★ ★ ★	I	★ ★ ★ ★ ★
C	★ ★ ★	L	★ ★ ★ ★

The Last Man (1826)

R	★ ★ ★	I	★ ★ ★
C	★ ★	L	★ ★ ★

SHERRED, T(homas) L. (1915) American writer of limited output. His four stories written in the late 1940s and early 1950s are collected in *First Person Peculiar* (1972), a graceful, humorous, but ultimately pessimistic, book. His only novel, *Alien Island,* is an aliens-amongst-us tale.

Alien Island (1970)

R	★ ★ ★	I	★
C	★ ★	L	★

SHERRIFF, R(obert) C(edric) (1896-1975) English author of *The Hopkins Manuscript,* a catastrophe story about the collision of Earth and Moon and a subsequent war over plundering the Moon's resources. An early and typical English catastrophe novel.

Mary Shelley

extravagant speculative fictions. He is an acquired taste, but is an intellectually stimulating writer who delights in violating the expectations of his readers, and can be a joy to read.

The Lord Of The Sea (1901)

R ★ ★ ★	I ★ ★ ★
C ★ ★ ★	L ★ ★ ★ ★

The Purple Cloud (1901)

R ★ ★	I ★ ★ ★
C ★ ★ ★	L ★ ★ ★ ★ ★

The Young Men Are Coming (1937)

R ★ ★ ★	I ★ ★ ★ ★
C ★ ★ ★	L ★ ★ ★ ★

SHIRAS, Wilmar H(ouse) (1908) American author known for her collection of short fiction, *Children Of The Atom* — connected stories about the development of 30 super-intelligent children after a radioactive accident. The super-kids eventually give moral leadership to the world. Naïve entertainment.

Children Of The Atom (1953)

R ★ ★ ★	I ★ ★
C ★	L ★

SHIRLEY, John   American author, mainly of sf shorts, whose first novel, *City Come A-Walkin'*, is a near future story of the San Francisco underworld, rich in incident but worth reading for its well-observed characterization.

City Come A-Walkin' (1980)

R ★ ★ ★ ★	I ★ ★
C ★ ★ ★	L ★ ★

SHUTE, Nevil (1899-1960) English writer, several of whose thriller-oriented novels are science-fictional. His *On The Beach,* upon which the film of the same title was based, is a tense piece of drama, but the sf element is secondary. *In The Wet* (1953) is a better piece of fiction, with its picture of Australia dominating the Commonwealth after a rapid rise in its population. Another five novels, including *No Highway* (1948), must be considered as sf, although science

The Hopkins Manuscript (1939; a.k.a., *The Cataclysm*)

R ★ ★	I ★
C ★	L ★

SHERWOOD, Martin (1942) English writer of two science thrillers, *Survival* (1975) and *Maxwell's Demon*, the latter of which is a fairly run-of-the-mill alien invasion story, where a mysterious sleeping sickness takes over people. Scientist has to solve. Traditionally English in its conception.

Maxwell's Demon (1976)

R ★ ★	I ★
C ★	L ★

SHIEL, M. P. (1865-1947) English writer of some importance in the development of scientific romance. He began by writing future-war novels but rapidly diversified. His most famous book, *The Purple Cloud*, is a remarkable disaster story but stands somewhat aside from the main current of his thought, which was dominated by a peculiar evolutionism borrowed from Herbert Spencer and a socialist economic theory borrowed from Henry George. Most critics call attention to his unorthodox style, but this is well-suited to his more has overtaken much of their speculative content.

On The Beach (1957)

R ★ ★ ★	I ★
C ★ ★	L ★ ★

SIEGEL, Martin (1941-72) American writer who published two sf novels, *Agent Of Entropy* (1969), a satirical space opera, and *The Unreal People*, a post-holocaust story.

The Unreal People (1973)

R ★ ★	I ★
C ★	L ★

SILLITOE, Alan (1928) English novelist and playwright, who has published two sf novels, *The General* (1960), and the manic and often hilarious dystopia *Travels In Nihilon*, which depicts a totally corrupt and authoritarian state engaged in quasi-mafiosi activities: a delightful satire on Western society.

Travels In Nihilon (1971)

R ★ ★ ★ ★	I ★ ★ ★
C ★	L ★ ★ ★

SILVERBERG, Robert (1936) An amazingly prolific American writer of over 75 sf books and over 60 non-fiction books, whose career has to be judged in three different stages. Silverberg the sf writer first emerged during the 1950s, encouraged by the Hugo Award for Most Promising New Author in 1956. Within ten years he had written, sometimes in collaboration or in pseudonym, 19 novels, more easily placed in the pulp sf category. From this period, three novels highlight his potential, if not his ability to regurgitate sf stories at will. However, *Master Of Life And Death*, *Invaders From Earth* (1958) and *Recalled To Life* (1962) do emerge as good novels. During the mid-1960s Silverberg eased his sf writing to concentrate on non-fiction books, about ancient civilizations, exotic races and wonders of the world. When he returned to sf his writing was more serious and it reflected in the novels and short stories he produced. The premier sf

Robert Silverberg

awards – the Hugo and Nebula – were showered on him for the best of his fiction. The novella "Nightwings" winning the Hugo, and the novel *A Time Of Changes* (1971) and the short fiction "Passengers" (1968), "Good News From "The Vatican" (1970) and "Born With The Dead (1974) winning Nebulas. "Nightwings" was later expanded into a novel and the story of future Earth's fall from grace into regimented beings controlled by an elaborate Guild structure of Dominators, Rememberers, Defenders, Fliers and Watchers awaiting the imminent alien invasion shows Silverberg using the complete range of his literary talents. His vivid imagination and clever characterization was further demonstrated in *The Time Hoppers* (1967), *Hawksbill Station* (1968), *To Live Again* (1969) and *Downward To The Earth* (1970), as he entered the 1970s with a string of almost flawlessly brilliant novels. Although Silverberg had begun editing sf anthologies in the 1960s, it wasn't until the New Dimensions series, which began in 1971, that this extra talent was recognized. This success seemed to prompt him into retirement from sf in 1976, but the urge to write returned and in 1979 *Lord Valentine's Castle*, a new fantasy novel, was serialized in *Fantasy And Science Fiction*, his considerable talent for characterization being exaggerated as he described the journey of a usurped King – suffering from amnesia – attempting to retain his throne on a world of wonderfully exotic aliens.

Master Of Life And Death (1957)

R	★ ★ ★ ★	I	★ ★ ★
C	★ ★ ★	L	★ ★ ★

"Nightwings" (1968)

R	★ ★ ★ ★	I	★ ★ ★ ★ ★ ★
C	★ ★ ★ ★ ★	L	★ ★ ★ ★

Lord Valentine's Castle (1979)

R	★ ★ ★ ★ ★	I	★ ★ ★
C	★ ★ ★ ★ ★	L	★ ★ ★

SIMAK, Clifford D. (1904) American writer who began publishing sf in 1931 and remains active. He wrote some good short fiction for John W. Campbell's *Astounding Science Fiction* in the 1940s, showing greater imaginative range than most of the other writers of the day. His most striking product of the time was a series of stories collected as *City* (1952), in which dogs and robots inherit the Earth after the exodus of Mankind. Robots feature prominently in his work, always depicted sympathetically as kindly and dignified beings harshly treated by unthinking men. *Time And Again* is a classic novel championing android rights, with metaphysical overtones that were to become increasingly common in his work. Simak is fond of rural environments and many of his stories are heavily nostalgic after a pattern first set in *Ring Around The Sun* (1953), where a child's toy becomes the means of unlocking a gateway into an infinite array of unspoiled alternative Earths. Many of his recent works are quest stories set in post-technological *milieux*, often dabbling in a quiet mysticism that comes to the forefront in novels where theology becomes a real issue of debate, including *A Choice Of Gods* and *Project Pope* (1981). Simak is a very likeable writer; the underlying philosophy in his work is a passionate advocacy of neighbourliness and the spirit of fellowship. Even as he approaches his eightieth year he remains a highly imaginative writer and, though some of his recent novels are basically self-pastiche, the best are still readable and stimulating. Although his output is variable in quality his best works set a very high standard.

Time And Again (1951)

R	★ ★ ★ ★	I	★ ★ ★ ★
C	★ ★ ★	L	★ ★ ★ ★

A Choice Of Gods (1972)

R	★ ★ ★	I	★ ★ ★
C	★ ★ ★	L	★ ★ ★

A Heritage Of Stars (1977)

R	★ ★ ★	I	★ ★
C	★ ★	L	★ ★ ★

City (1982)

R	★ ★ ★ ★ ★	I	★ ★ ★
C	★ ★	L	★ ★

Clifford D. Simak

SINCLAIR, Upton (1878-1968) Respected American novelist, playwright and political commentator, whose sf is mainly social satire, predicating future Utopias, or using reality-switches (as in *Roman Holiday*, 1931) to contrast American consumer society with other ages and societies. *The Millennium* is his most interesting sf work, where the survivors of a catastrophe fight to control a food-making machine. Sinclair's exposition of Marxism is quite overt in the book.

The Millennium: A Comedy Of The Year 2000 (1924)

R	★ ★ ★	I	★ ★
C	★	L	★ ★

SIODMAK, Curt (1902) German-born American writer and film-maker. His most notable sf work is *Donovan's Brain* (with its sequel, *Hauser's Memory*, 1968). Its use of telepathy and pseudo-science is quite powerful, emphasizing Siodmak's mistrust of unchecked technological development; an update and variation upon the Franken-stein theme. Siodmak's other work utilizes a thriller format influenced by his screen-writing activities.

Donovan's Brain (1943)

R	★	★	★	★	★	I	★		
C	★	★				L	★	★	

SKINNER, B(urrhus) F(rederick) (1904) American author of *Walden Two*, which depicts a scientific experiment – a functioning Utopia. Whilst it is rather a didactic work (Skinner is a behavioural psychologist) it is nonetheless an excitingly speculative work, cleverly and lucidly written.

Walden Two (1948)

R	★	★	★			I	★	★	★	★	★
C	★	★				L	★	★			

SKY, Kathleen (1943) American writer (wife of Stephen Goldin (q.v.)), whose works contain strong female characters, presented in lucid, stimulating and highly visual prose. Her Star Trek novel, *Vulcan!* (1978) is perhaps exceptional, in that it is a study of Spock's character and not a straightforward adventure. Her adventures are always inward, charting experience rather than event.

Birthright (1975)

R	★	★	★	★	I	★	
C	★	★	★		L	★	★

SLADEK, John (1937) American writer resident in England from 1966 to 1983. Sladek exploits the surrealistic and satirical potential of sf. All his novels use the image of the robot to examine the insecure dis-tinction between humans and machines, usually to the discredit of humanity, seen as comparatively irrational, greedy, short-

sighted, and too self-preoccupied for any genuine communication. A conspicuous feature of Sladek's prose is his fondness for word-games, palindromes, bizarre ciphers and improbable cryptographic interpreta-tions of innocent texts. Like many satirists his tone grows gradually more bitter, but his intellectual playfulness never ceases.

The Müller-Fokker Effect (1970)

R	★	★	★	★	I	★	★	★	★
C	★	★	★	★	L	★	★	★	★

Roderick (1980)

R	★	★	★	★		I	★	★	★
C	★	★	★	★	★	L	★	★	★

"The Secret Of The Old Custard" (1966)

R	★	★	★	★	I	★	★	★	
C	★	★	★		L	★	★	★	★

SLESAR, Henry (1927) American writer, mainly of thrillers, but some of whose work is borderline sf. His science fiction short stories are, for the most part, no more than clever entertainments, utilizing sf as a colouring or as gimmickry. *The Bridge Of Lions* is his only novel-length dalliance with sf.

The Bridge Of Lions (1963)

R	★	★	★	I	★	★
C	★	★		L	★	

SLOANE, William M(illigan) (1906-74) American writer of two novels which blended science fiction and horror tech-niques in a fascinating and successful way. *To Walk The Night* depicts the possession by an alien of a widow. His other work, *The Edge Of Running Water* (1939), is even more involved in the occult/supernatural end of the sf spectrum, telling of a machine that can communicate with the dead.

To Walk The Night (1937)

R	★	★	★	I	★	★
C	★			L	★	★

SMITH, Clarke Ashton (1893-1961) American writer whose work, like that of H. P. Lovecraft (q.v.), blends elements of sf, horror and fantasy. His prose style is less garish than Lovecraft's yet still retains something of the gothic flavour one expects from contributors to *Weird Tales* in the 1920s and 1930s. Much of his fiction is highly evocative, however, bringing vividly to life lost worlds (Atlantis and its culture, particularly), graveyard planets and ancient civilizations with Necromancers and other dimensions. "The City Of The Singing Flame" (1931), whilst it has the stylistic trappings of its time (letters left by a traveller into alien and distant parts), nevertheless transcends its pulp constituents, as does much of Smith's better work. On the other hand, Smith at his worst is purest purple and his effects as stereotyped as any pulp hack. Generally, however, the strange flavouring of his work – idiosyncratically Smith's – and his sense of undiscovered areas of existence make him still a writer worth encountering.

Out Of Space And Time (1942; coll.)

R ★ ★ ★ ★	I ★ ★ ★
C ★	L ★ ★

Lost Worlds (1944; coll.)

R ★ ★ ★	I ★ ★
C ★	L ★ ★

SMITH, Cordwainer (1913-66) Pseudonym of Paul Linebarger, American sf writer and expert on psychological warfare and Chinese affairs. Smith achieved a modest fame in the field with his first few stories, notably "Scanners Live In Vain" (1950) and "The Game of Rat and Dragon," and was enticed into regular production by editor Frederic Pohl (q.v.), producing a small but memorable body of novelettes and one novel *Norstrilia*. Almost all of his work deals with a Future History in which, under the guidance of a bureaucratic and military élite, the "Instrumentality" Mankind arrives at a dull and static pseudo-Utopia from which it is evicted by fiat into a revival of fertile irrationalities. Smith did not live to write the implied stories in which social evolution produces some higher state of spiritual awareness along the lines envisaged by Teilhard de Chardin. Important in these stories and the

process they describe was to have been the liberation from slavery, and the old-time religion of the Underpeople, intelligent races evolved from animals. Smith's social attitudes included a fair measure of high-toned Christian paternalism towards women and towards other races. His narratice strategies owe much to Chinese models – he is fond of telling a tale by discussing the alternative ways in which posterity recapitulated it as legend or art. Smith is a writer in whom poetically expressed sentiment often drifts towards sentimentality, particularly when he is writing about cats.

Norstrilia (1975)

R ★ ★ ★ ★	I ★ ★ ★
C ★ ★ ★	L ★ ★ ★

"The Game Of Rat And Dragon" (1955)

R ★ ★ ★ ★ ★	I ★ ★ ★
C ★ ★ ★	L ★ ★ ★ ★

"A Planet Named Shayol" (1961)

R ★ ★ ★ ★	I ★ ★ ★
C ★ ★	L ★ ★ ★

SMITH, Edward E. (1890-1965) American writer, affectionately known as "Doc Smith," celebrated as the founding father and greatest exponent of space opera. *The Skylark Of Space* was one of the first stories to take its adventurous heroes outside the solar system. In the sequels to this novel and in his more famous Lensman series, Smith turned the galaxy into a gigantic back yard where his heroes (existentially becalmed at nine years of age, despite their apparent maturity) could play an endless game of super-cops and super-robbers with fantastic rayguns and magnificent spaceships. He made his appeal directly to the capacity which we all have (or once had) for projecting ourselves into such ambitious games of make-believe. His prose style was dreadful and his imagination (despite all claims to the contrary) woefully limited, but he was a great naïve writer in much the same way that Edgar Rice Burroughs (q.v.) and Abraham Merritt (q.v.) were. Many people now cannot read him at all, but young readers and older ones who can put themselves under the spell of nostalgia can still extract thrills from his juvenile extravanganzas. He continued wirting into the 1950s, and added the last Skylark sequel just before he died, but his work looked increasingly out of place as magazine sf slowly became sophisticated.

The Skylark Of Space (1928)

R ★ ★ ★	I ★
C	L ★

Gray Lensman (1939-40)

R ★ ★ ★	I ★
C	L ★

Children Of The Lens (1947-48)

R ★ ★ ★	I ★
C	L ★

SMITH, Evelyn E. (1927) American sf writer and crossword compiler. Smith's career as the "other" E. E. Smith produced a body of work mainly for Galaxy in the 1950s characterized by a delicacy which tends towards the fey and an ironic wit which often drifts towards the heavy-handed. Her two later novels have the same occasional charm but are rather looser in structure; *The Perfect Planet* (1962) is a satire on body-building while *Unpopular Planet* is an all-purpose satiric jamboree.

"Baxbr/Daxbr" (1954)

R ★ ★ ★	I ★ ★
C ★ ★	L ★ ★

"The Vilbar Party" (1957)

R ★ ★ ★	I ★
C ★ ★	L ★ ★ ★

Unpopular Planet (1975)

R ★ ★ ★	I ★
C ★ ★ ★	L ★ ★ ★

SMITH, George H(enry) (1922) American writer, most of whose work is slick action-adventure with a strong emphasis on sex and violence. He wrote much shorter fiction for the magazines in the 1950s and a dozen novels for small pub-

lishers in the 1960s, none of which has anything exceptional to offer. His alternative worlds books are colourful fantasy, for the main part, and, as Diana Summers, he has had more success in writing romantic fiction with a sexual *frisson*.

The Unending Night (1964)

R ★ ★ ★	I ★
C ★	L ★

SMITH, George O. (1911-82) American writer. An engineer by profession, he briefly became important when John W. Campbell attempted to import a certain kind of realism into *Astounding Science Fiction*, for which he wrote the Venus Equilateral stories about a community of engineers whose crucial series of problem-solving inventions transform the future. His later works tend to be conventional space operas with little to recommend them, but *The Fourth R* is an interesting novel about a boy with super-human powers who has to get by in a corrupt world until he grows to adulthood. He virtually abandoned sf after 1960.

Venus Equilateral (1947)

R ★ ★ ★	I ★ ★ ★
C ★	L ★ ★

Highways In Hiding (1956)

R ★ ★ ★	I ★ ★
C ★	L ★ ★

The Fourth R (1959)

R ★ ★ ★	I ★ ★
C ★ ★ ★	L ★ ★ ★

SMITH, L. Neil   American author of *The Nagasaki Vector*, a complex time travel/ aliens story with alternative worlds, medieval Japan and libertarian politcs as elements.

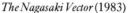

The Nagasaki Vector (1983)

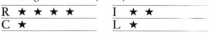

R ★ ★ ★ ★	I ★ ★
C ★	L ★

SOHL, Jerry (1913) American writer Gerald Allen Sohl, most active in the 1950s. He has written for the TV series

Norman Spinrad

Star Trek, Twilight Zone and *The Outer Limits*, and all of his work is polished entertainment of a none too deep variety.

The Altered Ego (1954)

R ★ ★ ★ ★	I ★
C ★	L ★

SOLDATI, Mario (1906) Italian novelist whose *The Emerald* (Lo Smeraldo), which uses a post-atomic war scenario, with Italy divided between North and South (a division mirrored in the World). Love and Wealth are sought in the ruins. Soldati's conclusion is darkly pessimistic.

The Emerald (1974; trans. 1977)

R ★ ★ ★ ★	I ★
C ★ ★	L ★ ★

SPENCER, John   English writer of *The Electronic Lullaby Meat Market*, a colourful and bizarre picaresque which blends space opera and sexual odyssey.

The Electronic Lullaby Meat Market (1975)

R ★ ★ ★	I ★
C ★	L ★

SPIELBERG, Steven (1947) American Wunderkind film director/producer, whose novelization of his own film, *Close Encounters Of The Third Kind*, provides some of the background that the film omits.

Close Encounters Of The Third Kind (1977)

R ★ ★ ★ ★	I ★ ★
C ★ ★	L ★ ★

SPINRAD, Norman (1940) American writer. He began writing in the late 1960s and became identified with the sf *avant garde* of the period thanks to his controversial novel *Bug Jack Barron*. He had an interest in many themes topical at that time: the Vietnam war, the use of the media, and the counter-culture; these interests have remained central to his work to such an extent that his recent novels, *A World Between* (1979) and *Songs From The Stars*, have a curious nostalgic appeal, although their 1960s-style enthusiasm and reformist fervour are rather refreshing. Spinrad's best novel is *The Iron Dream*, which includes a novel supposedly written by one Adolf Hitler, a German immigrant into America who became a writer of visionary pulp sf. This novel, *Lord Of The Swastika*, is readily recognizable both as a typical pulp sf adventure and a symbolic transformation of Hitler's rise to power in Germany. The irony of the novel is lost on some readers and the implied criticism of the ideology of pulp sf resented by others, but the case is compelling. Spinrad writes in a strangely aggressive manner, grabbing the reader's attention with dramatic scenes and muscular prose. His iconoclastic manner and oratorical fervour are appealing, though they sometimes make it a little difficult to take him seriously. His attacks on contemporary American culture and its values alienate him from some readers but endear him to others (especially outside the U.S.A.) and he has a large following. His reputation is likely to increase as his writing matures.

Bug Jack Barron (1969)

R ★ ★ ★ ★	I ★ ★
C ★ ★	L ★ ★ ★

Songs From The Stars (1980)

R ★ ★ ★ ★	I ★ ★ ★
C ★ ★	L ★ ★ ★

SPRINGER, Nancy   Popular American author of fantasy novels which seem to form a hybrid with the best-selling romance genre. At least four of her novels are set in the magic land of Isle (map provided!), and mix traditional fantasy and myth elements together. Easily accessible and highly readable, she is nonetheless far from original and her style is archaic. *The Silver Sun* and *The Golden Swan* (1983) are perfect introductions to her work. *The Black Beast* (1982) utilizes another setting, that of Vale (map provided!), but with little difference in style or content.

The Silver Sun (1977)

R ★ ★ ★	I ★
C ★ ★	L ★

The White Hart (1979)

R ★ ★ ★ ★	I ★ ★
C ★ ★ ★	L ★

SPRUILL, Steven G. (1946) American writer whose first novel, *Keepers Of The Gate* (1977), typifies his complex adventure stories, the latest of which, *The Imperator Plot*, uses the same hero as in the earlier *The Psychopath Plague* (1978) and is a thriller/mystery in the Sherlock Holmes vein, with an alien side-kick Pendrake.

The Imperator Plot (1983)

R ★ ★ ★	I ★
C ★	L ★

STABLEFORD, Brian M. (1948) An English writer who has managed to combine a university career with a prolific output, and fuse the two with much fascinating work on the sociology and history of sf. His early work was marked by reliance on myth-based plots featuring characters with "poetic" names such as Mark Chaos (*Dies Irae* trilogy, 1971) and Craig Star Gazer (*To Challenge Chaos*). Later work saw him turn to altogether tougher influences for, perhaps his best series, the Hooded Swan tales, featuring the hard-bitten space pilot Grainger, and veer towards actual *science* fiction, using his training in biology to provide solid substance for his tales. Stableford's gifts are often underrated because he

is largely a formula writer. Certainly, although he may use the most hackneyed of plots such as a mysterious treasure (*Halcyon Drift*) and a threat to colonists (*Critical Threshold*, 1977), he brings to the conventions he employs a welcome shrewdness and scientific intelligence.

To Challenge Chaos (1972)

R ★ ★ ★	I ★ ★
C ★	L ★ ★

Halcyon Drift (1972)

R ★ ★ ★ ★	I ★ ★ ★
C ★ ★ ★	L ★ ★ ★

The Realms Of Tartarus (1977)

R ★ ★ ★	I ★ ★ ★
C ★ ★	L ★ ★

STAPLEDON, Olaf (1886-1950) English philospher who used sf as a vehicle for his ideas, constructing cool commentaries on human affairs. *Last And First Men* is a history of Man from beginning to end, detailing the careers of many human species descended from *Homo sapiens*. In *Star Maker* the career of Man becomes a part of a great cosmic scheme through which an experimentally minded God is getting practice at the difficult business of Creation. The imaginative scope of this

Olaf Stapledon

work is unparalleled. His superman story, *Odd John* (1935) is untypically caustic, but there is much more warmth and human interest in *Sirius*, an excellent story of a dog with artificially augmented intelligence. His later works are mostly semi-fictional exercises in social philosophy, but include an interesting novella, "The Flames," which features strange alien beings who once inhabited the sun and now seek a home on Earth. Some posthumous publications have been added to the canon, including a discarded introductory section written for an early draft of *Star Maker*, now titled *Nebula Maker*, and a volume of short stories. No one else has used sf as ambitiously as Stapledon, and admiration for this ambition has caused some critics to overlook the fact that he did not understand evolutionary theory and the fact that as a philosopher he was something of a dilettante. His best work, though, displays an intelligence found almost nowhere else and there is a grandeur in his visionary essays that is quite breathtaking. Bertrand Russell (q.v.), who was a much greater philosopher, could not hold a candle to him as an imaginative writer. He has achieved more in the genre than any other writer except Wells (q.v.).

Last And First Men (1930)

R ★ ★	I ★ ★ ★ ★ ★
C ★ ★	L ★ ★ ★ ★

Star Maker (1937)

R ★ ★ ★	I ★ ★ ★ ★ ★
C ★	L ★ ★ ★ ★ ★

Sirius (1944)

R ★ ★ ★ ★	I ★ ★ ★ ★
C ★ ★ ★ ★	L ★ ★ ★ ★ ★

STASHEFF, Christopher (1944) American writer whose three novels are mixtures of sf and science fantasy with a strong humorous undercurrent. The juxtaposition of sophisticated and backward cultures allows Stasheff to revel in colourful adventures, as in *A Wizard In Bedlam* (1979). His *The Warlock In Spite Of Himself* is considered his minor classic (with a sequel in *King Kobold*, 1971), with a

delightfully clumsy robot and a general sense of linguistic playfulness.

The Warlock In Spite Of Himself (1969)

R ★ ★ ★ ★ ★	I ★ ★ ★
C ★	L ★ ★ ★

STEPHENSON, Andrew M(ichael) (1946) Venezuelan-born English writer. *Nightwatch* (1977), his first novel, is a hard science story of semi-sentient machines and alien intruders. His second work, *The Wall Of Years*, is both better written and of greater interest. Experiments in parallel worlds allow Jerlan Nissen to go back to the ninth century to ensure history is not changed. The atmosphere and details of the Dark Ages are beautifully evoked.

The Wall Of Years (1979)

R ★ ★ ★ ★	I ★ ★
C ★ ★	L ★ ★ ★

STERLING, Bruce   American writer whose two novels show evidence of a potentially good sf talent. *Involution Ocean* (1977) is unfortunately too literary in its allusions and too cluttered to be more than an average alien sea-yarn. *The Artificial Kid*, about a combat artist's adventures, is simpler and better written.

The Artificial Kid (1981)

R ★ ★ ★ ★	I ★ ★
C ★	L ★ ★

STERNBERG, Jacques (1923) Belgian author of *Future Without Future (Futurs sans Avenir)*, a collection of five sf stories ranging from the dystopian "Fin de Siècle" to time-riddles like "Ephemera."

Future Without Future (1971; trans. 1974)

R ★ ★ ★	I ★ ★
C	L ★

STEVENS, Francis (1884-1939) Pseudonym of Gertrude Barrows Bennett, an American writer for the pulp magazines from 1917 to 1923. Her best work is perhaps *The Heads Of Cerberus*, which is set in the dystopian land of Ulithia and in a Philadelphia of 2118. It is a good satire and quite possibly the first alternate/parallel worlds tale.

The Heads Of Cerberus (serialized 1919; book form, 1952)

R ★ ★ ★	I ★ ★
C ★	L ★ ★ ★

STEVENSON, Robert Louis (Balfour) (1850-94) Scottish author of the classic split-personality tale, *The Strange Case Of Dr. Jekyll And Mr. Hyde*, which can be read in several ways: as the repression and revenge of the Freudian id, as a study of drug dependency or – at its primary level – as a murder mystery. Its influence upon the sf field is considerable.

The Strange Case Of Dr. Jekyll And Mr. Hyde (1886)

R ★ ★ ★	I ★ ★
C ★ ★	L ★ ★

STEWART, George R(ippey) (1895) American writer whose only sf work, the novel *Earth Abides*, is one of the field's classics. A plague sweeps the Earth and only hundreds survive. Stewart's story tells how Ish (and his woman, Em) witness the last days of civilization and begin to reform a new race of Man with their "tribe." It is a beautifully written work without the normal science-fictional hyperbole.

Earth Abides (1949)

R ★ ★ ★ ★ ★	I ★ ★
C ★ ★ ★	L ★ ★ ★ ★

STINE, Hank (1945) Pen-name of Henry Eugene Stein, American writer and editor. Three sf novels exist, two of which involve a heavy pornographic element. His *Season Of The Witch* (1968) describes how a rapist is punished by having his brain put into his victim's body – and learns to live harmoniously.

Thrill City (1969)

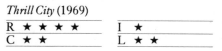

R ★ ★ ★ ★	I ★
C ★ ★	L ★ ★

STOCKTON, Frank R(ichard) (1834-1902) American writer some of whose vast output was science fiction of a fantastic and humorous nature. His shorter work depends upon gimmicks and inventions, but his longer work is more serious and more important. *The Great War Syndicate* describes a war between England and the U.S.A. featuring a large U.S. "disintegrator" weapon. His *The Great Stone Of Sardis* (1898) is less notable, depicting the whole Earth as a vast diamond.

The Great War Syndicate (1889)

R ★ ★	I ★ ★
C	L ★

STORY, Jack Trevor (1917) English writer whose novels sometimes involve a mild science-fictional element in depicting entropy at work upon the fabric of English society. He was published in *New Worlds* magazine and a strong surrealism is evident in some of his work.

The Wind In The Snottygobble Tree (1971)

R ★ ★ ★	I ★
C ★ ★	L ★ ★ ★

STOVER, Leon E(ugene) (1929) American writer and anthropologist. Better known as a critic and teacher of sf, Stover has produced a handful of sf short stories and one novel, in collaboration with Harry Harrison (q.v.), *Stonehenge* (upon which he has also written a factual study).

Stonehenge (1972; with Harry Harrison)

R ★ ★ ★	I ★ ★
C ★	L ★ ★

STOW, Randolph (1935) Australian writer whose novel *Visitants* won the 1979 Patrick White Award. Told from five different viewpoints it is an ambiguous U.F.O.-mystery set in Papua in 1959. The clash of rational and mystical explanations for the events is powerfully captured.

Visitants (1979)

R ★ ★ ★ ★	I ★ ★ ★
C ★ ★	L ★ ★ ★ ★

STRAUB, Peter   American bestselling author whose work is generally in the horror vein but has sf trappings, especially in *Floating Dragon*, which describes a sentient cloud of bacteria. Its premises are those of 1920s scientifiction but its writing is thoroughly modern (slick, fast-paced, contemporary); which rather makes it a derivative muddle held together only by Straub's prose facility.

Floating Dragon (1983)

R ★ ★ ★	I
C	L ★ ★

STRETE, Craig American writer. Of American Indian descent, Craig Strete is unique in incorporating into his sf tales religious allegories and imagery of the Indian traditions. A strongly obsessive writer more at ease in the art of fables, his sf is punctuated by a poetic affection for the beat years and the influence of Borges and music. He has written an autobiographical novel about days spent with Jim Morrison, the charismatic musician.

If All Else Fails (1976; coll.)

R ★ ★ ★	I ★ ★
C ★ ★	L ★ ★ ★

The Bleeding Man (1977; coll.)

R ★ ★	I ★ ★ ★
C ★ ★ ★	L ★ ★ ★

Dreams That Burn In The Night (1982; coll.)

R ★ ★ ★	I ★ ★
C ★ ★	L ★ ★

STRUGATSKY, Boris (1933) and **Arkadi** (1925) Russian brothers, most of whose work has not been translated into English. Their earliest work formed a future history series composed of three novels and two collections of shorter work. The most interesting of these is the collection *Noon: 22nd Century* (1962; trans. 1978), where the mixture of adventure and moral concern is strongest. The masterful satirical element of their later work is barely evident, but in their work of the early 1960s they began to produce works of the first order, including *Hard To Be A God*, depicting a regressed society on an alien world. Its rich detail and complex story are impressive, as is the underlying sense of

Boris Strugatsky

mythopoeic depths. Alienated protagonists making their way through increasingly senseless social landscapes – this description typifies the Strugatsky novels of the mid- and late-1960s, *Monday Begins On Saturday* (1965; trans. 1977) and the superb *The Snail On The Slope*, which reads like a mixture of Kafka and Voltaire given a distinctively Russian colouring. These works are fabular and powerfully enigmatic

Arkadi Strugatsky

at the same time, the science-fictional element used to create a sense of inexplicable otherness – an otherness scientific method cannot contain. This otherness lies – literally – at the heart of *Roadside Picnic* (1972; trans. 1977) and in the country described in *Tale Of The Troika* (1968; trans. 1977), a novel which utilizes Russian folk-tales, modern Utopian thought and the Strugatskys' own brand of dark humour. *Definitely Maybe* (1976; trans. 1978) again deals with the realm of inexplicable event – metaphorically rendered as alien intrusion, as is the case so often in their work. Their writing, which stems from a wholly different tradition than the American pulps, is perhaps the most important addition to the field of sf in the late 1970s, suggesting possibilities for sf's development not glimpsed by Western sf writers.

Hard To Be A God (1964; trans. 1973)

R ★ ★ ★ ★	I ★ ★ ★ ★
C ★ ★	L ★ ★ ★

The Snail On The Slope (1968; trans. 1980)

R ★ ★ ★ ★	I ★ ★ ★ ★ ★
C ★ ★ ★	L ★ ★ ★ ★

Prisoners Of Power (1971; trans. 1978)

R ★ ★ ★ ★	I ★ ★ ★
C ★ ★	L ★ ★ ★

STUART, L. T.   American author of the post-apocalypse work, *The House Of The Lions*, which describes a barbaric New York and its inhabitants, religion and monsters; a promising début novel.

The House Of The Lions (1983)

R ★ ★ ★ ★	I ★ ★
C ★ ★	L ★ ★

STURGEON, Theodore (1918) American sf writer. Sturgeon is a good example of the sf writer who has done the greater part of his successful work in short forms. His most famous book, *More Than Human*, is a compilation of linked short stories in which a number of psionically gifted individuals form themselves into a gestalt; the gestalt proves to need an ordinary human to act as its conscience. His work has tended to

centre on a quest for new ways in which the love of individuals for each other and for humanity can be expressed; interventions by alien intelligences, new social systems, marvellous inventions and mutations all turn up in his stories as pegs on which attractive and rarely boring sermonettes can be hung. Part of Sturgeon's importance – certainly the root of his influence on the American New Wave – derives from the fearlessness with which, from an early date, he tore into taboos both political (the ultimate refusal of the hero to retaliate for the nuclear destruction of America in "Thunder and Roses" (1947), or sexual (his satirical treatments of homophobia in "The World Well Lost" and "Affair With The Green Monkey"). Much of his fiction, particularly Utopian works like *Venus Plus X*, was ahead of its time in its questioning of conventional wisdom about sex roles. The typical Sturgeon protagonist, like the typical Heinlein (q.v.) one, is a Man Who Learns Better; but in Sturgeon earlier ignorance is a corrective to the arrogance that might infect purer wisdom. Even in his early work, Sturgeon often adopts narrative methods which operate at a diagonal to what the standard pulp treatment of his plot would dictate. He has made something of a specialty of the depiction from the inside of abnormal psychology; much of his fiction is effective and original in its use of terror.

More Than Human (1953)

R ★ ★ ★ ★	I ★ ★ ★
C ★ ★ ★	L ★ ★ ★ ★

"The World Well Lost" (1953)

R ★ ★ ★ ★	I ★ ★
C ★ ★ ★ ★	L ★ ★ ★ ★

Venus Plus X (1960)

R ★ ★ ★	I ★ ★ ★
C ★ ★ ★	L ★ ★ ★

SUCHARITKUL, Somtow   American (?) writer who won the John W. Campbell Award for Best New SF Writer. His *Light On The Sound* (first in a trilogy) is a rich space opera, a myth, a power fantasy, a vision of Utopias and many other things. Sucharitkul is one of a new generation of

Theodore Sturgeon

writers who are breaking down the barriers between distinct genres.

Light On The Sound (1982)

R	★ ★ ★ ★	I	★ ★
C	★ ★	L	★ ★

SUSANN, Jacqueline (1925-76) American best-selling novelist whose post-humously published *Yargo* is a strange love story – a God-like father-figure from an alien Utopia meets a human woman, allowing a rather tame satirical comparison.

Yargo (1979)

R	★ ★ ★	I	★
C	★	L	★ ★

SUTTON, Jeff(erson Howard) (1913-79) American writer of fairly routine sf melodramas and, with his wife Jean (1916), a series of unexceptional juveniles. The work which is, perhaps, an exception, is *Whisper From The Stars*, about human transcendence and cosmology.

Whisper From The Stars (1970)

R	★ ★ ★	I	★ ★
C	★	L	★

SWANN, Thomas Burnett (1928-76) American writer who first found a home for his delicate fantasies set in the classical world in the British magazine *Science-Fantasy*. His stories are a sentimental re-working of Graeco-Roman myth which champion the non-human folk – centaurs, dryads, etc. – against the crassness and frequent brutality of the humans who are hounding them to extinction. His earliest works are economical and affectively powerful novelettes; when he began working at novel length his stories tended to become wordy and rather languid. He was unappreciated until his death, but now commands something of a cult following.

"Where Is The Bird Of Fire?" (1962)

R	★ ★ ★	I	★ ★ ★
C	★ ★ ★	L	★ ★ ★ ★

Day Of The Minotaur (1966)

R	★ ★ ★	I	★ ★ ★
C	★ ★ ★	L	★ ★ ★

Will-O-The-Wisp (1976)

R	★ ★ ★	I	★ ★
C	★ ★ ★	L	★ ★ ★

SWIFT, Jonathan (1667-1745) Irish writer whose satirical work, *Gulliver's Travels*, is considered by many to be one of the most important examples of proto-sf, with its four books depicting different alien cultures which can be viewed as variations on dystopia, satirizing government, science, humanism and ultra-intellectualism through exaggerated metaphor.

Travels Into Several Remote Nations Of The World By Lemuel Gulliver, First A Surgeon, And Then A Captain Of Several Ships (1726; revised 1735)

R	★ ★ ★ ★ ★	I	★ ★ ★ ★ ★
C	★ ★	L	★ ★ ★ ★

SZILARD, Leo (1898-1964) Hungarian-born American physicist and writer, whose collection *The Voice Of The Dolphins* is stylistically outmoded but nonetheless interesting for its title story – an early hypothesis concerning cetian sentience.

The Voice Of The Dolphins And Other Stories (1961; coll.)

R	★ ★	I	★ ★
C		L	

TABORI, Paul (1908-74) Hungarian writer, living in Britain. His first sf novel, *The Green Rain* (1961), was a delightful and sharp-cutting satire. His other sf novels deal with sex, the occult and political machinations.

The Cleft (1969)

R ★ ★ ★	I ★ ★
C ★	L ★

TAINE, John (1883-1960) Pseudonym of American writer and research mathematician Eric Temple Bell (born in Scotland). He began publishing in the pulps of the 1920s and kept writing into the 1950s producing 13 novels under his pseudonym and the same number of mathematical works as Bell. Little of his work has more than a colourful interest now, especially those works which tell of super-civilizations in our distant past. For their time, however, they were educative adventures with a bent for disaster.

Before The Dawn (1934)

R ★	I ★ ★
C	L

TALL, Stephen (1908) Pseudonym of American writer Compton Newby Crook. Much of his work concerns the adventures of Stardust, an interstellar exploration craft, and its crew. The novel, *The Ramsgate Paradox* (1976) is part of this. They are all good, fast-action stories with not too great a depth of characterization. *The People Beyond The Wall* is something different; a Utopian tale set in the Antarctic.

The People Beyond The Wall (1980)

R ★ ★ ★	I ★
C ★	L ★

TATE, Peter   Welsh writer much influenced by Bradbury (q.v.), but with a journalistic grasp of science and politics that strengthens his work. Primarily concerned with environmentalism.

Faces In The Flames (1976)

R ★ ★ ★	I ★ ★ ★
C ★ ★ ★	L ★ ★

Greencomber (1979)

R ★ ★ ★	I ★ ★
C ★ ★	L ★

"Daylength Talking Blues" (1975)

R ★ ★ ★ ★	I ★ ★ ★
C ★ ★ ★	L ★ ★ ★

TEMPLE, William F. (1914) English writer who began publishing in the 1930s, when he wrote the novelette on which his novel *Four-Sided Triangle* is based. This is a love story in which a matter-duplicator allows both men to get the girl. In the 1950s and 1960s his works were mostly routine, including a series of juvenile space operas, but he won praise with his near-future novel *Shoot At The Moon*, which combines – uneasily – realism and parody. His fiction varies greatly in quality, but at his best he is an interesting, if idiosyncratic, writer.

Four-Sided Triangle (1949)

R ★ ★ ★	I ★ ★ ★
C ★ ★	L ★ ★

The Three Suns Of Amara (1962)

R ★ ★ ★	I ★ ★ ★
C ★	L ★ ★

Shoot At The Moon (1966)

R ★ ★ ★	I ★ ★
C ★ ★	L ★ ★ ★

TENN, William (1920) Pseudonym of American writer Philip Klass, who published a good deal of sf in the 1950s and early 1960s but has done almost nothing since. He wrote one novel but his best work is in shorter lengths, most of it humorous. His humour ranges from the slapstick of "Venus And The Seven Sexes" to the bitterly sarcastic "The Liberation Of Earth" (1953), in which warring alien races liberate and re-liberate Earth, devastating it completely, somewhat after the fashion of certain American adventures in post-colonial aid. He tends to be polemical in speaking out against Man's inhumanity to Man, but much of his work was written in a spirit of pure fun. He has been missed since he stopped writing.

"Firewater" (1952)

R ★ ★ ★	I ★ ★ ★
C ★ ★	L ★ ★

"Time Waits For Winthrop" (1957)

R ★ ★ ★	I ★ ★ ★
C ★ ★	L ★ ★ ★

Of Men And Monsters (1968)

R ★ ★ ★	I ★ ★ ★
C ★ ★	L ★ ★

TENNANT, Emma (1937) Scottish writer first noted for her editorship of *Bananas* (1975-79), a speculative quarterly. Her own work tends to the fantastic, but self-consciously avoids treating fantasy imagery as an end unto itself: as well as *being* fantasies, her stories are about the *way* we fantasize. *The Bad Sister* was recently filmed.

Hotel de Dream (1976)

R ★ ★ ★ ★	I ★ ★ ★ ★ ★
C ★ ★ ★	L ★ ★ ★ ★

The Bad Sister (1978)

R ★ ★ ★ ★	I ★ ★ ★
C ★ ★ ★	L ★ ★ ★

Wild Nights (1979)

R ★ ★ ★ ★	I ★ ★ ★ ★
C ★ ★ ★ ★	L ★ ★ ★ ★

TEVIS, Walter (1928) American academic and general writer, best known for his sf. In a subdued, meditative, often melancholy style Tevis considers the limitations of the human and the humane. *The Man Who Fell To Earth*, made famous by Nicolas Roeg's film of it, is a sombre inversion of the hostile alien theme, the story of a hopeful visitor to Earth rendered powerless by the sheer weight of individual and organized indifference. Tevis's only other sf novel, *Mockingbird* (1980), is less successful because more derivative. His short stories can be divided into unambitious commercial exercises and more challenging, uneasy, introspective pieces.

The Man Who Fell To Earth (1963)

R ★ ★ ★ ★ ★	I ★ ★ ★ ★
C ★ ★ ★ ★ ★	L ★ ★ ★ ★

"Far From Home" (1958)

R ★ ★ ★ ★	I ★
C ★ ★ ★ ★	L ★ ★ ★

"Out Of Luck" (1980)

R ★ ★ ★ ★	I ★ ★ ★
C ★ ★ ★ ★	L ★ ★ ★

Far From Home (1983; coll.)

R ★ ★ ★ ★	I ★ ★ ★
C ★ ★	L ★ ★

THOMAS, D(onald) M(ichael) (1935) English writer, best known, until 1979, as a poet. Since then he has published four novels, one of which, *The White Hotel*, was an international bestseller. His first two novels, *The Flute-Player* (1979) and *Birthstone* (1980), were labelled fantasies when they were first published, but are better described as prose poems. They possess certain science-fictional elements common to the *New Worlds* school of sf (wherein Thomas published much of his overtly science-fictional poetry): characters come back from the dead, information given by the author proves untrustworthy, and even the sex of a character (like the multi-schizophrenic protagonist of *Birthstone*) is dubious. *The White Hotel* is Thomas's *tour de force*, and deserves mention here for its final segment where the characters transcend the atrocity at Babi Yar. There are also a number of uncollected short stories, some of which, like "Seeking A Suitable Donor," are borderline sf.

The White Hotel (1981)

R ★ ★ ★ ★ ★	I ★ ★ ★ ★ ★
C ★ ★ ★	L ★ ★ ★ ★ ★

"Seeking A Suitable Donor" (1969)

R ★ ★	I ★ ★
C ★	L ★ ★ ★

THOMAS, Theodore L. (1920) American writer, who sometimes wrote as Leonard Lockhart. Much of his work appeared in the sf magazines of the 1950s and early 1960s, and he wrote two novels in collaboration with Kate Wilhelm, *The Clone* and *The Year Of The Cloud* (1970). Both are rather realistic works using sf disaster elements.

The Clone (1965)

R ★ ★	I ★
C ★	L ★

THURSTON, Robert (Donald) (1936) American writer who has produced three volumes of the Battlestar Galactica series and one interesting but highly flawed novel, *Alicia II*, where an old man's mind is transferred into a young man's body. He is perhaps better in the numerous short stories that appeared throughout the 1970s.

Alicia II (1978)

R ★ ★	I ★ ★
C ★	L ★

TILLEY, Patrick (1928) English writer, two of whose thrillers are borderline sf. In *Fade-Out*, the U.S. Government has to deal with an alien spacecraft, whilst in *Mission* we are given Jesus Christ, trapped in the wrong time, and revealing a few truths.

James Tiptree Jr (Alice Hastings Sheldon)

Both are good, fast-paced and intelligent dramas which use their sf ideas well.

Fade-Out (1975)

R ★ ★ ★ ★	I ★ ★
C ★	L ★ ★

Mission (1982)

R ★ ★ ★ ★ ★	I ★ ★
C ★ ★ ★	L ★ ★

TIMLETT, Peter Valentine (1933) English writer of a fantasy trilogy about Atlantis and its fall, focusing upon the survivors – our forefathers. The first in the sequence, *The Seedbearers* (1974), is probably the best, though all three are interestingly written.

Twilight Of The Serpent (1977)

R ★ ★ ★	I ★
C ★	L ★

TIPTREE, James Jr (1916) Pseudonym of American writer Alice Hastings Sheldon, who revealed her true identity only in 1977, after winning Hugo and Nebula awards for her shorter fiction. Her emergence in the 1970s was sudden and impressive, and her (or, as it was then thought, *his*) lyrical treatment of human themes (inclusive of what it was to be alien) produced some of the finest and most memorable stories of the decade, including "And I Awoke And Found Me Here On The Cold Hill's Side" (1971), "Love Is The Plan, The Plan Is Death", which won a Nebula, and "The Girl Who Was Plugged In" (1973), a Hugo winner. A deeply poetic sensibility underlies most of her better work, together with a strong sense of compassion. Her first novel, *Up The Walls Of The World*, was less impressive stylistically than her shorter work but nonetheless had a powerfully humane quality in dealing with its stunted E.S.P.-experimentees, the skate-like creatures of an alien world and the Star-destroyer, the interstellar being of vast age and size. It is one of the most impressive space operas, transcending its simple elements, and, as in her best shorter work, the reader is forced to re-evaluate their reading experience. It is this ability of Tiptree's to transform sf clichés into memorable new visions which may ultimately prove to have been her greatest gift to the field, much more than the sexual politics of "Houston, Houston, Do You Read?" (1976; Hugo and Nebula winner) or the delightful clarity of her prose. She has published little since her self-revelation, yet her work is still influential five years on.

Up The Walls Of The World (1978)

R ★ ★ ★ ★	I ★ ★ ★
C ★ ★ ★	L ★ ★ ★ ★

Warm Worlds And Otherwise (1975; coll.)

R ★ ★ ★ ★ ★	I ★ ★ ★ ★
C ★ ★	L ★ ★ ★ ★

"Love Is The Plan, The Plan Is Death" (1973)

R ★ ★ ★ ★ ★	I ★ ★ ★ ★
C ★ ★ ★	L ★ ★ ★ ★ ★

TOLKIEN, J(ohn) R(onald) R(euel) (1892-1973) South African born English writer, whose *The Lord Of The Rings* has been the most influential fantasy novel of this century, attaining cult status. Tolkien's thorough knowledge of Northern European root languages – an interest which was both the starting-point for and the original purpose of his epic trilogy – and his creation of a credible world for his fantasy, Middle Earth, have formulated the parameters for the whole modern genre of science fantasy. The work is viewed by some as allegory, although Tolkien strongly denied this, but its portrait of a world sharply and starkly divided between the powers of Good and Evil, and where the actions of small, seemingly insignificant creatures (the hobbits Frodo Baggins and Sam Gamgee) can affect the moral outcome for that world, is greatly appealing on an allegorical level. It is more complex than that, however, and the dark and potent undercurrents – focused upon the ring of power itself – make it also a realistic psychological study of "possession". On other "realist" grounds it might be criticized – for its lack of sex, sexual jealousy, interim moral shades, economic structure,

J. R. R. Tolkien

etc. – but Tolkien's heroic purpose and Teutonic models must be borne in mind. It remains one of the most readable lengthy books written. *The Hobbit* (1937), is a prequel and much more in a juvenile vein, with its quest for treasure and its conquest of the dragon. *The Silmarillion*, unfinished when Tolkien died, traces various threads of the fictional history mentioned in the trilogy.

The Lord Of The Rings (1954/5; revised 1966)

R ★ ★ ★ ★ ★	I ★ ★ ★ ★ ★
C ★ ★ ★ ★	L ★ ★ ★ ★

The Silmarillion (1976; edited by Christopher Tolkein)

R ★ ★	I ★ ★ ★
C ★	L ★ ★

TOOMEY, Robert E. Jr (1945) American author of *A World Of Trouble* which, as in Herbert's (q.v.) work, has a galactic agent land on an alien planet. Unlike Herbert's agents, Toomey's encounter rather trivial adventures.

A World Of Trouble (1973)

R ★ ★	I
C ★	L ★

TOWNSEND, John Rowe (1922) English writer of children's fiction. Some of his work strays upon sf themes, as in the excellent *Noah's Castle*, which depicts a dystopian future through the eyes of a young boy trying to cope.

Noah's Castle (1975)

R ★ ★ ★ ★	I ★ ★ ★
C ★ ★ ★	L ★ ★ ★

TRAIN, Arthur (Cheney) (1875-1945) American writer, most of whose work was outside of the sf field. Two novels and a collection of stories can be considered sf, though of a very crude, Verne-inspired kind. *The Man Who Rocked The Earth* (1915; with Robert William Wood) is interesting for its future vision of exploding the atom to gain strategic control over the world; its development of this theme, however, is uninspired. Its sequel, *The Moon Maker*, adds little but a romantic interest.

The Moon Maker (1916/17; in book form, 1958)

R ★	I ★
C	L ★

TREVOR, Elleston (1920) English writer, mainly of thrillers. He has written a number of fast-paced sf novels, ranging from time travel stories to holocaust-warning tales and disaster scenarios (in *The Pillars Of Midnight*, 1957). None of them are particularly memorable, but they are enjoyable reads.

The Mind Of Max Duvine (1960)

R ★ ★ ★	I ★
C ★ ★	L ★

TRIMBLE, Louis (Preston) (1917) American writer of Westerns and sf, whose work in the sf field is generally more entertaining than interesting. Like most writers prolific in both genres, his work is profoundly gothic and its settings prone to become garishly exotic, his characters violent loners with a romantic streak. Poor plotting and a limited imagination undermines much that he attempts.

The City Machine (1972)

R ★ ★ ★ ★	I ★
C ★	L ★

TROLLOPE, Anthony (1815-82) English writer who produced one sf novel, *The Fixed Period*, a rather weak Utopian tale incorporating a scheme for euthenasia.

The Fixed Period (1882)

R ★	I ★
C ★	L ★

TSIOLKOVSKY, Konstantin (Eduardovich) (1857-1935) Russian scientist and writer, whose early speculations about space flight are memorable. His fictionalizing of his ideas proved popular.

Beyond The Planet Earth (1920; trans. 1960)

R ★ ★	I ★ ★ ★
C ★	L ★

TUBB, E. C. (1919) English writer who published a large number of very undistinguished sf novels (mostly pseudonymous) in the early 1950s. Occasionally he showed that he was capable of better work, and went on to produce several unpretentious but effective novels, including *Alien Dust*, about the colonization of Mars, and *The Space-Born* (1956), a generation-ship story. In 1967 he began a series of novels starring Earl Dumarest, who wanders through a vast galactic civilization looking for his lost homeworld (Earth). The early volumes were excellent adventure stories set on exotic worlds, but as the series now moves inexorably towards its thirtieth volume it is becoming increasingly harder for Tubb to be convincing in fleshing out his formularistic bones. He remains a thoroughly competent writer of entertainments, but seems to have become stuck in a rut. On the rare occasions when he has tried to add some food for thought to his literary confections, as in *Dead Is A Dream*, he has left the impression that he could have achieved rather more than he has had he not been so committed to action-adventure material.

Alien Dust (1955)

R ★ ★ ★	I ★ ★ ★
C ★ ★	L ★ ★

The Winds Of Gath (1967)

R ★ ★ ★ ★	I ★ ★
C ★ ★	L ★ ★

TUCKER, (Arthur) Wilson (1914) American writer who began publishing sf in the 1940s. His thematic interests are more historical and archaeological than scientific, and, as in his time travel story, *The Lincoln Hunters* (1958), his focus is on the effect of historical event on the lives of certain individuals. There is a simplicity of style in Tucker's work which nonetheless creates a lucid picture of the changed worlds he creates, exemplified by the post-holocaust world of *The Year Of The Quiet Sun*, a novel which also exhibits the darker, seemingly pessimistic side of Tucker's writing. In *The Long Loud Silence* (1952; revised 1962) he examines the moral questions involved in survival after the holocaust and comes to very brutal conclusions (which involve cannibalism). *The Time Masters*, again, deals with time travel, perhaps Tucker's favourite theme, but throws in a stranded extra-terrestrial, the Gilgamesh of Sumer's ancient civilization. His unchecked enthusiasm for time machines is, however, his undoing in *Ice And Iron*, where a rather clumsy piece of scientific detection is set amidst a fascinating after-the-next-Ice Age scenario. There, as in places elsewhere in his other science fiction works his experience of mystery/thriller writing gives both shape and pace to his entertainments.

The Time Masters (1953; revised 1971)

R ★ ★ ★ ★	I ★ ★
C ★ ★	L ★ ★

The Year Of The Quiet Sun (1970)

R ★ ★ ★ ★	I ★ ★ ★
C ★ ★ ★	L ★ ★ ★

Ice And Iron (1974; revised 1975)

R ★ ★ ★	I ★ ★ ★
C ★ ★	L ★ ★

TUNG, Lee   Indian author of *The Wind Obeys Lama Toru*, which describes the disastrous see-saw effect on life and death rates when artificial fertility and sterility drugs are tried out on vast populations. An allegorical condemnation of human illogic, well written and memorably told.

The Wind Obeys Lama Toru (1967)

R ★ ★ ★ ★	I ★ ★
C ★	L ★ ★ ★

TURNER, Frederick   English writer whose first novel, *A Double Shadow*, is a rich vision of a Mars where the imaginative faculty in Man appears to have been made concrete in the landscape. An extreme and esoteric work, more metaphysical than scientific.

A Double Shadow (1978)

R ★ ★ ★	I ★ ★ ★
C ★	L ★ ★

TURNER, George (1916) Australian writer and critic, who has published three novels in a sequence, beginning with *Beloved Son* (1978). All are set in a reconstructed 21st-century world, after the Catastrophe (a mixture of causes), and involve a number of sf devices – cloning, immortality, high-technology – but are ultimately unconvincing. *Vaneglory* (1981) typifies Turner's poor characterization and illogical socio-ecological structure, whereas *Yesterday's Men* is simply recollections of his World War II experiences as a soldier in the jungle, revamped in an sf framework. On the evidence of these works Turner has little which is new or interesting to add to the genre.

Yesterday's Men (1983)

R ★ ★	I ★
C ★	L ★

TUTTLE, Lisa (1952) American writer whose short stories first appeared in the sf magazines in the 1970s. "Changelings" is a good example of her lucid and effective style, where characterization and ideative content are closely interconnected in a tale of betrayal in a future conformist régime.

Lisa Tuttle   *Mark Twain*

Her collaboration with George R. R. Martin (q.v.), *Windhaven*, deserved to win the Nebula Award. However, her first novel, *Familiar Spirit*, is not by any means her best work and demonstrates her predilection for horror stories in recent years.

"Changelings" (1975)

R ★ ★ ★ ★	I ★ ★ ★
C ★ ★	L ★ ★ ★

Windhaven (1980; with George R. R. Martin)

R ★ ★ ★ ★	I ★ ★ ★
C ★ ★ ★	L ★ ★ ★ ★

Familiar Spirit (1983)

R ★ ★ ★	I ★ ★
C ★ ★	L ★ ★

TWAIN, Mark (135-1910) Pseudonym of American writer Samuel Langhorne Clemens, whose one sf work is the delightful *A Connecticut Yankee In King Arthur's Court*. Twain's portrait of the Yankee coming to terms with medieval beliefs, social justice (or lack of it) and brutality is not merely a perfect satire on élitist power systems but also on the materialism of America in the late years of the nineteenth century. The device of time travel via a blow to the head with a crowbar is, perhaps, somewhat crude, but effective, and the final Apocalpytic scene with machine guns, minefields and barbed wire against the flower of medieval knighthood is darkly memorable if wholly anti-romantic. A number of his shorter fictions are overtly science-fictional, like "Letters From The Earth" (1909) and "The Secret History Of Eddypus, The World-Empire" (1902). His *Mysterious Stranger* work is also of note to the sf enthusiast.

A Connecticut Yankee in King Arthur's Court (1889)

R ★ ★ ★ ★ ★	I ★ ★ ★ ★
C ★ ★ ★	L ★ ★ ★

The Mysterious Stranger: A Romance (1916)

R ★ ★ ★ ★	I ★ ★ ★
C ★ ★	L ★ ★ ★

URICK, Kevin   American author who has only recently appeared in the genre. His *Snow World* is a competent but unimpressive post-holocaust story.

Snow World (1983)

R ★ ★ ★	I ★
C ★ ★	L ★

UTLEY, Steven (1948) Prolific American writer of short stories, who was published widely in the sf magazines of the 1970s. His work covers a wide variety of styles but is marked by an impressive literary ability throughout. His collaborations with Howard Waldrop (q.v.) and Lisa Tuttle (q.v.) have also been most successful.

"Ghost Seas" (1976)

R ★ ★ ★ ★	I ★ ★ ★
C ★ ★	L ★ ★ ★

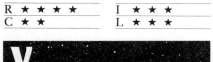

VANCE, Jack (1920) One of the most accomplished and meticulous American sf writers. Author of nearly 50 sf books and a dozen mystery novels, whose work engulfs fantasy, science fiction and mystery/detective writing. It could be accepted that all his stories are set in one large future universe, whose history and culture Vance has researched; then placed his characters, whose adventures are chronicled in his novels, many of which are in series form. Vance has five series running or completed: Demon Princes, Tschai, Planet of Adventure, Alastor and Durdane. These comprise slightly under half of his total of novels. In all these series, the early novels are the strongest, giving the impression that once he has completed the hard work of establishing backgrounds and characters he becomes bored with the initial concept. The exception here seems to be the Alastor series, *Trullion: Alastor 2262, Marune: Alastor 993* (1975) and *Wyst: Alastor 1716* (1978), where he describes a portion of history from individual planets in the Alastor Cluster system. These novels reveal Vance's fiction as adventurous, fast-flowing and exciting, his characters bizarre but believable, his worlds exotic and cosmopolitan. *The Dying Earth* has all the above qualities, yet it was his first published book, a collection of six related stories set

on Earth of the far future, suggesting he developed a definitive style at an early stage. Although Vance has written very little short fiction, two of his short works achieved awards. The short novel "The Dragon Masters" (1963) winning a Hugo, and the novella "The Last Castle" lifting both Hugo and Nebula. Both pieces of fiction diversify from his usual style enough to suggest he can be a writer of many moods. His present work is also moving away from his traditional style, particularly in *Lyonesse* (1983), a long, epic fantasy.

The Dying Earth (1950; coll.)

R ★ ★ ★ ★	I ★ ★ ★
C ★ ★ ★ ★	L ★ ★ ★ ★

"The Last Castle" (1967)

R ★ ★ ★ ★	I ★ ★ ★ ★ ★
C ★ ★ ★ ★ ★	L ★ ★ ★ ★ ★

Trullion: Alastor 2262 (1973)

R ★ ★ ★ ★	I ★ ★ ★ ★
C ★ ★ ★ ★	L ★ ★ ★ ★

VAN GREENAWAY, Peter (1929) English writer of several sf novels. *The Crucified City* (1962) depicts a post-holocaust London, and *Manrissa Man* is a rather unimaginative satire on Mankind, as seen through the eyes of super-intelligent apes.

Manrissa Man (1982)

R ★ ★ ★	I ★
C ★	L ★

VAN HERCK, Paul (1938) Belgian author of *Where Were You Last Pluterday*, wherein the upper classes have eight days to their week. A tame satire, but with high points.

Where Were You Last Pluterday? (1968; trans. 1973)

R ★ ★ ★	I ★
C ★ ★	L ★ ★

VAN SCYOC, Sydney J(oyce) (1939) American writer of *Salt Flower, Assignment Nor' Dyren* (1973), *Starmother, Cloudcry* (1977) and *Sunwaifs* (1982). All of these show a considerable sense of wonder and evoke alien landscapes rather beautifully. A flawed style can be forgiven for the richness of her vision.

Salt Flower (1971)

R	★	★	★	★		I	★		
C	★	★				L	★		

Starmother (1976)

R	★	★	★	★		I	★	★	
C	★	★				L	★	★	

VANSITTART, Peter (1920) English writer whose *The Story Teller* uses the longevity of its viewpoint character to give an overview of the last 500 years of European history.

The Story Teller (1968)

R	★	★	★	★		I	★	★	★
C	★	★				L	★	★	

VAN VOGT, A. E. (1912) Canadian-born American writer. He is one of the most distinctive writers of sf, specializing in plots which are intricate and marginally incoherent, usually involving super-human heroes and spectacular climaxes. If subjected to rational analysis his stories are absurd, but they have a curious mesmeric

A. E. van Vogt

power which thrusts all questions of rationality aside. (Often, indeed, they are openly scornful of the puny pretensions of rationality, as in *The World Of Null-A* and its sequel, whose miracles are vaguely attributed to the capabilities of "non-Aristotelian logic".) His novel *Slan* was the most striking superman story published in the sf pulps, describing the adventures of the young Jommy Cross – his super-humanity still latent and undeveloped – as he struggles to survive in a cruel world whose mysteries and conspiracies are impenetrable. His space operas have a grandiose sweep, seen to good advantage in *The Mixed Men* (1952), and he wrote some fine suspense stories about alien monsters, including those in *The Voyage Of The Space Beagle* (1950). This was the first of his many fix-up novels (he coined the term), and he has relentlessly cannibalized his own works, making patchwork novels out of stories which sometimes seem to be ill-fitted for combination. Van Vogt is something of a literary enigma. It is not at all obvious why his odd methods and melodramatic flourishes should work so well, but they do. Other writers have been heavily influenced by him, including Charles Harness (q.v.) and Ian Wallace (q.v.), but there remains a certain inimitable craziness which franks his work and makes it, in its own strange way, quite brilliant.

Slan (1940)

R	★	★	★		I	★	★	★	★
C	★	★			L	★	★	★	

The World Of Null-A (1945)

R	★	★	★		I	★	★	★	★
C	★				L	★	★	★	

The Battle Of Forever (1971)

R	★	★	★		I	★	★	★	★
C	★	★			L	★	★	★	

VARLEY, John (1947) American writer who attracted instant attention when he began publishing clever and innovative short stories in the mid-1970s. He arrived at a time when magazine sf seemed imaginatively enervated, showing refreshing in-

ventiveness, but in his most recent work he has often become involved with sententious and sometimes sickly commentaries on the nature of human relationships. His award-winning novella "The Persistence Of Vision" was widely admired, although it is at heart rather a sick story. His novels so far have been a little shapeless, but when he has mastered the form he will undoubtedly be able to put his fecund imagination to good use.

The Ophiuchi Hotline (1977)

R ★ ★ ★	I ★ ★ ★
C ★ ★	L ★ ★

"The Persistence Of Vision" (1977)

R ★ ★ ★	I ★ ★
C ★ ★	L ★ ★

Titan (1979)

R ★ ★ ★	I ★ ★ ★
C ★ ★	L ★ ★ ★

VERCORS (1902) Pseudonym of French author Jean Bruller. Two of his works are worthy of mention. *You Shall Know Them* (1952; a.k.a., *Borderline* and *The Murder Of The Missing Link*) is an anthropological mystery story, attempting to define what is human. *Sylva* tells of a vixen who is changed into a woman and educated, but eventually returns to savagery. It is a marvellous fable of exceptional power.

You Shall Know Them (1952)

R ★ ★ ★ ★	I ★ ★ ★ ★
C ★ ★ ★	L ★ ★ ★

Sylva (1961)

R ★ ★ ★ ★	I ★ ★ ★
C ★ ★ ★	L ★ ★ ★ ★

VERNE, Jules (1828-1905) French writer. Although only a small fraction of his work is sf he is universally recognized as one of the founding fathers of the genre. Most of his novels are accounts of voyages to the remote corners of the world (and beyond); he was the imaginary tourist *par excellence*, and his work only became science-fictional when he was compelled to invent new means of transport to get his characters to otherwise-inaccessible places. In his second novel, *Journey To The Centre Of The Earth*, he created an imaginary world deep beneath the Earth's crust, populating it with creatures borrowed from the fossil record, but he rarely went in for imaginary destinations. His lunar voyagers in *From The Earth To The Moon* (1865) and *Round The Moon* (1870) merely observe our heavenly companion at close quarters – they could not land because he had no way to bring them back. *Twenty Thousand Leagues Under The Sea* introduced one of his few memorable characters, Captain Nemo, and provided nineteenth-century readers with a glimpse of a world about which almost nothing was known. Modern undersea photography has now taken us all into the ocean depths via our TV screens, and Verne's novel has therefore dated badly, but in its day it was a *tour de force*. Verne's later novels become repetitive and rather flaccid, and his airship novel *The Clipper Of The Clouds* is unimpressive, but even his last work, "The Eternal Adam" (1915), reveals that he never lost the spirit of imaginative adventure. He has been very badly served by his English translators, but his best works retain something of their excitement even in butchered form. Nowadays, he has to be read with a certain antiquarian insight, but he is still worth reading.

Journey To The Centre Of The Earth (1864)

R ★ ★ ★	I ★ ★ ★ ★
C ★ ★	L ★ ★ ★ ★

Twenty Thousand Leagues Under The Sea (1870)

R ★ ★ ★	I ★ ★ ★
C ★ ★ ★	L ★ ★ ★ ★

The Clipper Of The Clouds (1887)

R ★ ★ ★	I ★ ★
C ★	L ★ ★ ★

VIAN, Boris (1920-59) French writer who blended sf and surrealism. *Froth On the Daydream* (1947; trans. 1966) and *Red Grass* have been translated.

Red Grass (1950; *L'herbe rouge*)

R ★ ★ ★	I ★ ★
C ★ ★	L ★ ★

VIDAL, Gore (1925) Popular American writer who has often dabbled with sf themes whilst maintaining a Mainstream following (in the manner of Vonnegut (q.v.), though without the talent and optimism). Most of his work is satiric in intent and is dark if not overtly bitter. *Messiah* particularly shows this streak of Vidal's nature, where the Christ-like figure

Gore Vidal

teaches America to worship Death. *Myra Breckinridge* (1968) and *Myron* (1974), its sequel, utilizes the Frankenstein theme satirically through the sex-change of its hero/heroine. *Kalki* is the blackest of his visions, however, where most of the world's population dies when an ex-GI poses as the Hindu god Kalki.

Messiah (1954)

R ★ ★ ★ ★	I ★
C ★ ★	L ★ ★ ★

Kalki (1978)

R ★ ★ ★ ★	I ★ ★
C ★ ★ ★	L ★ ★ ★

VILLIERS DE L'ISLE, Adam (Jean Marie Mathias August) (1840-89) French writer whose *Axel* is one of the foremost "decadent" novels. He often toyed with borderline sf themes, as in "The Future Eve" (1886), but will be probably best remembered for his hero's comment "We have just exhausted the future." – the statement of an extreme fantasist and symbolist.

Axel (1890)

R ★ ★ ★	I ★ ★ ★
C ★ ★	L ★ ★ ★ ★

VINGE, Joan (1948) American sf writer. Vinge achieved early notice through novelettes like "Tin Soldier," in which standard sf topics like cyborging and time dilation are made the motive force of stories in which sentiment is more important than more standard sf narrative topics. This had been done before, but Vinge did it with the sensibility of a woman of the 1970s. Her large space opera *The Snow Queen*, like "Tin Soldier," engages from a mildly feminist standpoint in a dialogue with a Hans Christian Anderson fairytale with effects that vary from the elegant and witty to the slightly fatuous. It is a notable example of the obsession in modern sf with city life and has some strong characterization.

"Tin Soldier" (1974)

R ★ ★ ★ ★	I ★ ★ ★
C ★ ★ ★ ★	L ★ ★ ★ ★

The Outcasts Of Heaven Belt (1978)

R ★ ★ ★ ★	I ★ ★
C ★ ★ ★	L ★ ★ ★

The Snow Queen (1980)

R ★ ★ ★ ★	I ★ ★ ★
C ★ ★ ★ ★	L ★ ★ ★ ★

VINGE, Vernor (Steffen) (1944) American writer whose novels are competent space adventures. *Grimm's World* (1969) is a somewhat crude exploitation story; *The Witling* is slightly more subtle. He is the husband of Joan Vinge (q.v.).

The Witling (1976)

R ★ ★ ★	I ★
C ★	L ★

VOLTAIRE (1694-1778) Pseudonym of French writer/philosopher François Marie Arouet. His *Micromegas* is considered as a precursor of science fiction, describing the visit to Earth of two giants from Sirius. It is satirical and prefigures much similar sf as accomplished by Sheckley (q.v.), Sladek (q.v.) and Vonnegut (q.v.).

Micromegas (1750)

R ★ ★ ★	I ★ ★ ★
C ★	L ★ ★ ★

Voltaire

Kurt Vonnegut

VONNEGUT, Kurt (1922) American writer of idiosyncratic fictions, many wholly or partly sf. Uncommitted to anything save a cheerfully nihilistic egalitarianism, Vonnegut was swift to object to being classified as a science fiction writer once he had attracted literary and academic attention. He also, temporarily, attempted to disown his equally formative years as a journalist. All his fiction is dogmatic, imaginatively ingenious and morally reassuring. He evidently regards stories as the most pleasant way of making observations, and science fiction as the most palatable sort of story, though he admires Sinclair Lewis and John Dos Passos more. His original and eclectic blend of everyting from Zen to New Journalism is charmingly iconoclastic. It was enormously popular at the end of the 1960s. Vonnegut describes a perfectly random universe devoid of meaning, except in a few places where intelligence sits trying to make sense of it. Meaning is therefore entirely local and temporary. In *The Sirens Of Titan* the inhabitants of the planet Tralfamadore have engineered the whole history of Earth to transmit five brief signals to a castaway. Time, and therefore space, are illusory; objectively there *is* no history, so no progress, but no decline either, nothing to regret. Vonnegut's prose is episodic, his storylines erratic or fragmented, his associations comically or pathetically incongruous. His deliberate lack of perspective enables him to decorate a profound concern for modern humanity with the arbitrary wonders of pulp sf: *Slaughterhouse 5* presents a disorientated time traveller's experience of the fire-bombing of Dresden.

The Sirens Of Titan (1959)

| R ★ ★ ★ ★ | I ★ ★ ★ ★ ★ |
| C ★ ★ ★ | L ★ ★ ★ ★ |

Slaughterhouse 5 (1969)

| R ★ ★ ★ ★ ★ | I ★ ★ ★ |
| C ★ ★ ★ ★ | L ★ ★ ★ ★ |

"Harrison Bergeron" (1961)

| R ★ ★ ★ ★ | I ★ ★ |
| C ★ ★ ★ | L ★ ★ ★ |

VYSE, Michael   English author of several rather disappointing sf books. *The Outer Reaches* (1980) is a collection of tired and reworked traditional themes. *Overworld* is, similarly, an uninspired rendition of the crowded future city theme.

Overworld (1981)

| R ★ ★ | I |
| C ★ | L ★ |

WALTERS, Hugh (1910) English writer of juveniles of no great originality or scope. They are essentially old-fashioned space operas for boys.

The Last Disaster (1978)

| R ★ ★ | I |
| C ★ | L ★ |

WAGNER, Karl Edward (1945) American writer, whose work is essentially sword-and-sorcery of a particularly blood-thirsty kind.

Bloodstone (1975)

| R ★ ★ ★ | I |
| C ★ | L ★ |

WAHLÖÖ, Per (1926-75) Swedish author of *Murder On The 31st Floor*, an sf/detective novel, which had a sequel featuring the same character, Inspector Jensen, *The Steel Spring* (1968; trans. 1970).

Murder On The 31st Floor (1966; trans. 1967)

| R ★ ★ ★ | I ★ ★ |
| C ★ ★ | L ★ |

WALDROP, Howard   American author of several short stories and one collaborated novel, *The Texas-Israeli War: 1999* (with Jake Saunders).

The Texas-Israeli War: 1999 (1974)

| R ★ ★ | I ★ |
| C ★ | L ★ |

WALLACE, (Richard Horatio) Edgar (1875-1932) English writer of detective fiction who also wrote two future-war novels, *Private Selby* (1909) and *The Story Of A Fatal Peace* (1915) and several border-line sf novels, like *The Green Rust* and *Planetoid 127* (1929). Prolific elsewhere, his science fiction lacks depth or originality despite the relatively small quantity of speculative work.

The Green Rust (1919)

| R ★ ★ ★ | I ★ |
| C ★ | L ★ |

WALLACE, Ian (1912) Pseudonym used by American psychologist John W. Pritchard for his novels. His first sf novel was the VanVogtian (q.v.) superman story *Croyd*; he has published more regularly since his retirement in 1974 and his recent work is not stamped so obviously with VanVogtian influence. He is a melodramatic writer with a fondness for ideative flourishes. Some of his works are afflicted with an odd kind of playful pomposity, but there is an imaginative vigour about his stories which is attractive. He has a tendency to prolixity, and is overfond of saving the world from total destruction at the last possible moment, but his mystery stories featuring the sexy detective Claudine St Cyr are excellent examples of their kind and his books are always enjoyable if one can enter into the spirit of the games he plays.

Croyd (1967)

R ★ ★ ★	I ★ ★ ★
C ★ ★	L ★ ★ ★

The Purloined Prince (1971)

R ★ ★ ★	I ★ ★ ★
C ★ ★	L ★ ★ ★

The Rape Of The Sun (1982)

R ★ ★ ★	I ★ ★ ★ ★
C ★ ★	L ★ ★ ★

WANDREI, Donald (1908) American writer and founder with H. P. Lovecraft (q.v.) of Arkham House. He has continued Lovecraft's tradition for gothic horror of the *Weird Tales* variety.

The Web Of Easter Island (1948)

R ★ ★ ★	I ★ ★
C ★	L ★

WATERS, Thomas A.   American writer of *The Probability Pad* (1970), the final third of a trilogy began with Chester Anderson's *Butterfly Kid* and Michael Kurland's *The Unicorn Girl*. His second novel, *Centerforce*, is an apocalyptic vision of a future America divided between police-storm troopers and rebel bikers.

Centerforce (1974)

R ★ ★ ★	I
C ★	L ★

WATKINS, William Jon (1942) American writer and academic whose sf novels are simple sf adventures utilizing a wide range of devices; mindpowers, future totalitarian states, future galactic empires, extra-terrestrials muddling in our affairs, etc. There is nothing to suggest that Watkins will develop beyond being a competent storyteller.

What Rough Beast (1980)

R ★ ★ ★	I ★
C ★ ★	L ★

WATSON, Ian (1943) English writer whose interest in and investigation of the interrelationship between reality and human consciousness is the predominant theme of his work. An acutely cerebral writer, his first novel, *The Embedding*, was an intellectual *tour de force*, displaying a fertility of imagination that immediately marked him as a major writer. In that, and in later works, he is asking how perception and language are related, and whether what we can see is all there is. Accompanying this is a sense that Man is in a neotenous form (i.e., undeveloped in evolutionary terms) and can transcend his present state. This was behind both *The Martian Inca* (1977) and the beautifully written *Alien Embassy*, both of which were impressive advances on his first novel. From *Miracle Visitors* (1978) onwards, however, there is a certain intellectual coldness to the novels, though no diminishing of ideative energy and imaginative verve. This culminated in *The Gardens Of Delight* (1980), a fascinating but static game with reality inspired by a Hieronymus Bosch painting. *Under Heaven's Bridge* (1980), a collaboration with Michael Bishop, seems to have marked a change in Watson's direction and his recent work, whilst not neglecting or omitting his intellectual concerns, has an outward

Ian Watson

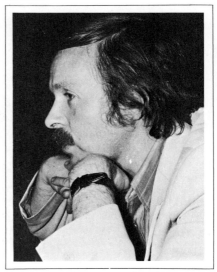

direction, being rather more (though not too greatly) adventure stories with the idea as hero. *Deathhunter* (1981) is an example of this; almost a thriller. Watson seems to be losing some depth with this new emphasis, even though *Chekhov's Journey* (1983) is as rich in ideas as any of his previous work. One constant factor in his work is the fine use of exotic international settings, meticulously described; colour to his occasionally monochrome metaphysics. A new novel, *The Book Of The River*, is due in 1984.

The Embedding (1973)

R ★ ★ ★	I ★ ★ ★ ★ ★
C ★ ★	L ★ ★ ★

Alien Embassy (1977)

R ★ ★ ★ ★ ★	I ★ ★ ★ ★ ★
C ★ ★ ★	L ★ ★ ★ ★

God's World (1979)

R ★ ★ ★	I ★ ★ ★
C ★ ★	L ★ ★

WATSON, Simon   English writer of juveniles, whose *No Man's Land* is an interesting yet flawed dystopia.

No Man's Land (1975)

R ★ ★	I ★
C ★	L ★

WAUGH, Evelyn (1903-66) English writer whose black satires occasionally utilized sf themes. *Scott-King's Modern Europe* (1947) created Neutralia, a postwar totalitarian state. *Love Among The Ruins: A Romance Of The Near Future* is a masterful piece of satire on Welfare State England, with a particularly dark pessimistic streak.

Love Among The Ruins (1953)

R ★ ★ ★ ★ ★	I ★ ★ ★
C ★ ★	L ★ ★ ★

WEBB, Sharon   American author of two entertaining and thoughtful books, *Earthchild* (1982) and *Earth Song*, its sequel. In the first novel a medical discovery in the future has allowed eternal youth and immortality of sorts. The de-

velopment of the idea (stasis, boredom, lack of creativity) in the second book is predictable but nonetheless well handled. These are very intelligent juveniles with a certain adult appeal also.

Earth Song (1983)

R ★ ★ ★	I ★ ★
C ★ ★	L ★ ★

WEINBAUM, Stanley G. (1900-35) American writer. Although he died within two years of the appearance of his first pulp story, "A Martian Odyssey," Weinbaum established a reputation as one of the most inventive and able of the early pulp writers. He wrote several lively stories set in bizarre alien environments, and tried to transform pulp romance with his two stories of *The Black Flame*, although these were only published posthumously. He had already written several novels before writing for the pulps; two of these were sf, including the magnificent *The New Adam*, a thoughtful story about the career of a superman.

"A Martian Odyssey" (1934)

R ★ ★ ★ ★	I ★ ★ ★ ★
C ★	L ★ ★

The Black Flame (1939)

R ★ ★ ★	I ★ ★
C ★ ★	L ★ ★

The New Adam (1939)

R ★ ★ ★	I ★ ★ ★
C ★ ★ ★	L ★ ★ ★ ★

WELLMAN, Manley Wade (1903) American writer who has been publishing sf and fantasy for more than 50 years. He has been more prolific in the latter genre and has written relatively little sf since the days of the pulps, though he collaborated recently with his son on *Sherlock Holmes's War Of The Worlds*. He wrote a good series of stories in the 1950s and 1960s about a wandering guitar-player's encounters with the demons of Appalachian folklore, and has recently been writing novels in the same series. His sf is quite undistinguished, save, perhaps, for the timeslip story, *Twice In Time*.

Twice In Time (1940)

R ★ ★ ★	I ★ ★
C ★	L ★

Sherlock Holmes's War Of The Worlds (1975; with Wade Wellman)

R ★ ★	I ★
C ★	L ★

H. G. Wells

WELLS, H. G. (1866-1946) English writer who played many roles in a long writing life, from teacher to journalist, pedagogue to historian, but is best remembered for his novels, of which the most remarkable are the early "scientific romances." Such novels as *The Time Machine*, *The Island Of Dr Moreau*, and *War Of The Worlds* found a world audience. Here, invention, knowledge of science, and a unifying imagination create sf of a high order, praised by such critics as T. S. Eliot and Vladimir Nabokov (q.v.). At the same time, Wells poured out short stories, among which "The Country Of The Blind" and "The Door In The Wall" should not be forgotten. After *The First Men In The Moon* (1901), Wells's mythopoeic gift seems to weaken. His novels become more like arguments, less like dreams. *A Modern Utopia* (1905) is still essential reading for anyone interested in the genre. He wrote ordinary novels, histories of the world, and surveys of science.

An evolutionary view of mankind continued to inform his thinking. One of his sprawling Utopian monologues of the 1930s became the Korda film, *Things To Come* (1935), a classic of the sf cinema. He died despairingly just after the dropping of the atomic bomb he had predicted, and his *Mind At The End Of Its Tether* (1945) is unfairly remembered against him. Better to read his splendid *Experiment in Autobiography* (1934), a memoir of a full and exuberant life. From humble beginnings, Wells rose to become a world figure, but somewhere along the way lost his claim to being a great writer. He always inspired affection, not least in women. He gave to sf many of its greatest themes; few who followed him have come near to rivalling his best work – or his second best, come to that.

The Time Machine (1895)

R ★ ★ ★ ★ ★	I ★ ★ ★ ★ ★
C ★ ★	L ★ ★ ★

War Of The Worlds (1898)

R ★ ★ ★ ★ ★	I ★ ★ ★ ★ ★
C ★ ★	L ★ ★ ★ ★

The Island Of Dr Moreau (1896)

R ★ ★ ★ ★ ★	I ★ ★ ★ ★
C ★ ★ ★	L ★ ★ ★

"A Story Of The Stone Age" (1897)

R ★ ★ ★ ★	I ★ ★ ★
C ★	L ★ ★

WELLS, Robert   American writer of fairly simplistic space adventures, like the inspid, not to say trite *The Spacejacks* (1975) and the earlier but no less flawed *The Parasaurians*. There are other sf novels from Wells (q.v.), but none show more than a competent use of sf gimmicry.

The Parasaurians (1969)

R ★	I ★
C ★	L

WERFEL, Franz (1890-1945) Austrian poet and novelist whose *Star Of The Unborn* was published posthumously. It depicts a far future Earth and a vast underground city-Utopia filled with long-lived beautiful, decadent people. Werfel's *persona*, FW, visits this future world and observes its philosophical tapestry.

Star Of The Unborn (1946)

R ★ ★ ★	I ★ ★ ★ ★
C ★ ★	L ★ ★ ★

WEST, Wallace (George) (1900) American writer who first published in *Amazing Stories* in 1929. His short stories are collected in *The Bird Of Time* (1959) and *Lords Of Atlantis* (1960), and his novels – simple but fast-paced and entertaining space adventures – were written in the 1930s but published only in book form in the 1960s. They have lasted the intervening years.

River Of Time (1963)

R ★ ★ ★	I ★
C ★	L ★

The Everlasting Exiles (1967)

R ★ ★ ★	I ★ ★
C ★	L ★

WHEATLEY, Dennis (Yates) (1897-1977) English writer of macabre and other novels. A fantastic streak runs throughout his more popular work, but only a few use science-fictional devices. One is *Black August*, which describes a future England undergoing a communist revolution. *Star Of Ill Omen* (1952) is a flying-saucer mystery, whilst *Sixty Days To Live* (1939) is a fairly standard comet-threatens-Earth story.

Black August (1934)

R ★ ★ ★	I ★ ★
C ★	L ★

WHITE, James (1928) Belfast-born writer of traditional science fiction who has always been more popular in the U.S.A. than in the U.K. He is known as the man who successfully introduced medicine into sf with his Sector General stories. A 384 level space-station-hospital "far out on the galactic rim," introduces the multi-species in "Hospital Station", a collection of linked stories, and the novel *Star Surgeon* (1963). The novels *The Watch Below* (1966), *All*

Judgement Fled (1968) and *The Dream Millennium* highlight his propensity for conventional sf with a strong moral. His *The Secret Visitors* (1957) is an above average first novel.

"Hospital Station" (1962)

R ★ ★ ★ ★	I ★ ★ ★ ★ ★
C ★ ★ ★ ★ ★	L ★ ★ ★ ★ ★

The Secret Visitors (1957)

R ★ ★ ★	I ★ ★
C ★ ★ ★	L ★ ★ ★

The Dream Millennium (1974)

R ★ ★ ★ ★	I ★ ★ ★
C ★ ★ ★ ★	L ★ ★ ★

WHITE, Ted (1938) American writer Theodore Edward White, best known as an editor in the field. Much of his early work was in collaboration and under pseudonyms, but in the late 1960s a number of sf fantasies appeared under his own name, like *Android Avenger* (1965), *Sorceress Of Qar* (1966) and *The Spawn Of The Death Machine* (1968). All are readable, enjoyable adventures with little depth. His best work remains, however, *By Furies Possessed*, where the alien parasites actually make Man a better creature. He has published very little since 1971: one novel with David

James White

Bischoff, *Forbidden World* (1978) and about a dozen stories being the sum total.

By Furies Possessed (1970)

R ★ ★ ★	I ★ ★
C ★ ★	L ★

WIBBERLEY, Leonard (Francis) (1915) Irish-born American writer whose *The Mouse That Roared* (1955) was filmed. He wrote several sequels, but his only other sf work is straightforward adventure, utilizing science-fictional gimmicry and, in *Encounter Near Venus*, an exotic setting. He is essentially a writer for juveniles.

Encounter Near Venus (1967)

R ★ ★ ★	I ★
C ★	L ★

WILDER, Cherry (1930) Australian writer who has yet to produce her best work. Her short story, "The Ark of James Carlyle" (1974) was an impressive début, and a juvenile novel, *The Luck Of Brin's Five*, whilst entertaining, lacked any real depth or significance. Much more promising is *The Nearest Fire* (1980). She seems fascinated in all her work by the interaction of human and alien.

The Luck Of Brin's Five (1977)

R ★ ★ ★ ★	I ★
C ★ ★	L ★

"Double Summer Time" (1976)

R ★ ★ ★ ★	I ★ ★ ★
C ★ ★	L ★ ★

WILHELM, Kate (1928) American writer, wife of Damon Knight. She began publishing in the 1950s but her career developed slowly. Her early novels were uninspiring, save for two collaborations with Theodore L. Thomas (q.v.), but in the 1970s she developed into a fine and careful writer of near-future stories describing the impact of extraordinary events on ordinary people. Although she won an award with *Where Late The Sweet Birds Sang* this is in fact the least convincing of her mature novels. *The Clewiston Test* is one of the outstanding studies of scientists at work. She

has written several mainstream novels, including mystery stories and a fine psychological novel *Fault Lines* (1977). She is at her best describing women under stress, detailing the strategies with which they cope (or fail to cope) with threatening circumstances. Her two collections *The Infinity Box* (1975) and *Somerset Dreams* (1978) contain some outstanding short fiction.

Where Late The Sweet Birds Sang (1976)

R ★ ★ ★	I ★ ★
C ★ ★	L ★ ★ ★

The Clewiston Test (1976)

R ★ ★ ★	I ★ ★ ★
C ★ ★ ★ ★	L ★ ★ ★ ★

Juniper Time (1979)

R ★ ★ ★	I ★ ★
C ★ ★ ★	L ★ ★ ★

WILLIAMS, Charles (1886-1945) English writer whose long association with C. S. Lewis (q.v.) and J. R. R. Tolkien (q.v.) is significant. His fantasy works use multidimensions and time travel in their essentially quest formats. Williams's Anglican beliefs do not overly intrude in his fiction, but there is a theological depth to works like *War In Heaven* (1930) and *The Place Of The Lion* (1931).

Descent Into Hell (1937)

R ★ ★ ★ ★	I ★ ★
C ★ ★	L ★ ★ ★

WILLIAMS, Eric C. (1918) English writer of undistinguished space adventures like *The Time Injection* (1968) and *The Call Of Utopia* (1971); work which has not really progressed since the 1950s.

The Drop In (1977)

R ★	I
C ★	L

WILLIAMS, Jay English writer of an interesting juvenile, *The Time Of The Kraken*, which has a strong mythical atmosphere and uses telepathy, spacecraft and anti-gravity devices. It is a startlingly effective mixture of fantasy and sf genres and is memorable for its vivid Icelandic landscapes.

The Time Of The Kraken (1978)

R ★ ★ ★ ★	I ★ ★ ★
C ★ ★	L ★ ★

WILLIAMS, John A(lfred) (1925) Black American writer whose *The Man Who Cried I Am* (1967) is a powerful future-oriented thriller which exposes the U.S. Government's plan to wipe out all blacks if they revolt. Two other novels are overtly science-fictional but again deal with black oppression. *Sons Of Darkness, Sons Of Light* (1969) is a frightening vision of racial war, whilst *Captain Blackman* tells of a black soldier who is jolted back in time and experiences 200 years of American history as a black soldier. Williams is one of the contemporary writers and these novels demonstrate the fact.

Captain Blackman (1972)

R ★ ★ ★ ★	I ★ ★
C ★ ★ ★	L ★ ★ ★

WILLIAMS, Robert Moore (1907-78) American writer of numerous pulp adventures in the 1950s and 1960s. His Zanthar series is popular but, like most of his work, has no real depths. His books are all-action "yarns" with no probing of the surface icing. A fair idea of science fiction's range of themes can be had from his work, but nothing of its potentiality.

Zanthar Of The Many Worlds (1967)

R ★ ★ ★ ★	I ★
C ★ ★	L ★

Beachhead Planet (1970)

R ★ ★ ★	I ★
C ★	L ★

WILLIAMSON, Jack (1908) American writer who began publishing in the early days of the sf pulp. His early work was influenced by A. Merritt (q.v.) and consisted of extravagant adventure stories. *The Legion Of Space* (1947) is a swashbuckling space opera to which he added several

sequels, the latest quite recently. His most striking early work is *The Legion Of Time* (1952), in which armies from two parallel futures fight to control the event on which their reality depends. In the 1940s he wrote a good series of stories as Will Stewart about "seetee," or contraterrene matter (now usually called anti-matter). A good deal of his work in the 1950s and 1960s was in collaboration with Frederik Pohl (q.v.). His best works are the classic story rationalizing lycanthropy, *Darker Than You Think*, and the novelette "With Folded Hands" (1947), about the invention of a race of robots who take their mission ("to serve Man and protect him from harm") rather too seriously. The sequel to the latter work, originally called ". . . And Searching Mind" (1948) is more familiar as *The Humanoids*; is it weak by comparison with the first story, but not as weak as the recent continuation of the series, *The Humanoid Touch* (1980). Williamson is at times an infuriating writer, who seems unable to handle the products of his fertile imagination. His best works are excellent, but much of the time he produces stale and routine material that hardly seems worthy of him. He has been actively involved in teaching sf and promoting it within the academic world but even his most recent books are for the most part determinedly unambitious. He still shows flair and imagination in his work, though, and is always readable.

The Legion Of Time (1938)

R ★ ★ ★ ★	I ★ ★ ★ ★
C ★	L ★ ★

Darker Than You Think (1940)

R ★ ★ ★ ★	I ★ ★ ★
C ★ ★	L ★ ★ ★

Seetee Ship (1951)

R ★ ★ ★	I ★ ★ ★ ★
C ★ ★	L ★ ★ ★

WILSON, Angus (1913) English writer of considerable literary reputation. He was an early supporter of sf in Britain and published one sf novel, *The Old Men At The Zoo*, now outdated, a future view of England's

Jack Williamson

political situation in the 1970s.

The Old Men At The Zoo (1961)

R ★ ★ ★	I ★
C ★ ★	L ★ ★

WILSON, Colin (Henry) (1931) English writer noted for his intelligent interest in psychology and the paranormal. His three sf novels are erudite but colourful thought-adventures with a final transcendent streak. Wilson's message is that Man is only at an undeveloped mental state at present (see Ian Watson also). Some sf readers find his work *too* crammed with his obvious learning, as in *The Philosopher's Stone* (1969).

The Mind Parasites (1967)

R ★ ★ ★ ★	I ★ ★ ★
C ★	L ★ ★

WILSON, F. Paul (1946) American writer who has set his first two novels in the same framework, the LaNague Federation. The aspects of symbiosis, telepathy and alien landscapes are poorly handled, in what are essentially power-fantasies. *Healer* (1976) is confused, whereas *Wheels Within Wheels* is simply rather hollow and unsatisfying.

Wheels Within Wheels (1980)

R ★ ★	I
C ★	L

WILSON, Richard (1920) American writer whose work first appeared in the 1950s. He is not a prolific writer and some of his earliest work was rather awkward, but he has developed into quite a stylist. Humour and satire have always been elements of his work, as in the early novels, *The Girls From Planet 5* (1955) and *And Then The Town Took Off* (1960). However, it is for his later short fiction that he is best noted. The Nebula Award-winning "Mother To The World," a last Man/last Woman scenario, is justly praised.

30-Day Wonder (1960)

R ★ ★ ★ ★	I ★
C ★ ★	L ★

"Mother To The World" (1968)

R ★ ★ ★ ★ ★	I ★ ★
C ★ ★ ★	L ★ ★ ★ ★

WILSON, Robert Anton American writer, who constructs fast-moving, humorous, polemical, stylistically mildly adventurous narratives of post-psychedelic anarchism. His writing blends heady cocktails of polymorphous sex, drugs, cryogenics, alternate worlds, the improvement of human intelligence, and complex international conspiracies of all kinds and times: Wilson's message is that all these are intrinsically connected.

The Eye In The Pyramid (1975; with Robert Shea)

R ★ ★ ★	I ★ ★ ★ ★
C ★	L ★

Masks Of The Illuminati (1981)

R ★ ★ ★	I ★ ★ ★
C ★ ★ ★	L ★ ★

The Earth Will Shake (1983)

R ★ ★ ★	I ★ ★
C ★ ★	L ★ ★

WILSON, Robert Hendrie English writer of thoughtful but not wholly successful sf works, peculiarly English in their atmosphere but with a sharp analytical/philosophical bent. *Ring Of Rings* (1976) is the less ambitious work, whereas *A Blank*

Card is a novel which utilizes sf devices as metaphors for artistic creation.

A Blank Card (1977)

R ★ ★ ★	I ★ ★ ★
C ★ ★	L ★ ★

WILSON, Steve (1943) English author whose *The Lost Traveller* is a post-holocaust motorcycle grail quest, romanticizing the Hell's Angel ethos.

The Lost Traveller (1976)

R ★ ★ ★ ★	I ★
C ★ ★	L ★

WINTERBOTHAM, Russ(ell) R(obert) (1904-71) American writer whose love of gothic led him to write both sf and Westerns, the sf under the pseudonyms J. Harvey Bond and Franklin Hadley as well as his own name. They are routine, enjoyable adventures, like *The Space Egg* (1958), *The Men From Arcturus* (1963) and *Planet Big Zero*.

Planet Big Zero (1964)

R ★ ★	I ★
C ★	L ★

WODHAMS, Jack (1931) English-born Australian writer, active in the late 1960s and throughout the 1970s. His work is speculative, dependent upon scientific or sociological ideas and is intelligently presented. He writes mainly for *Analog*, the most traditional of the genre's magazines, and his fiction tends towards masculine problem-solving as a result.

The Authentic Touch (1971)

R ★ ★ ★	I ★ ★
C ★	L ★

"There Was A Crooked Man" (1967)

R ★ ★ ★ ★	I ★ ★ ★
C ★	L ★ ★

WOLF, Gary K. American author of sharply drawn and often violent novels set in a near future which is always barbarous and corrupt. His shorter fiction is much better, moving between the lyrical and the hilarious, typical of which is "Dr. Rivet and Supercon Sal" (1976).

Killerbowl (1975)

R ★ ★ ★ ★	I ★
C ★	L ★

The Resurrectionist (1979)

R ★ ★ ★	I ★ ★
C ★ ★	L ★

WOLFE, Bernard (1915) American author of *Limbo*, a clever dystopian novel which is as much a literary experiment as a portrayal of a future Utopia and its ills. *Limbo* is impressive in ways in which Wolfe's shorter fiction in the sf genre is not. Lacking a background in science fiction, like many mainstream novelists he utilizes trite themes in fairly mundane ways: "The Girl With The Rapid Eye Movements" (1972) is a good example of that.

Limbo (1952)

R ★ ★ ★	I ★ ★ ★
C ★ ★	L ★ ★ ★

WOLFE, Gene (1931) American writer, something of a cult in the 1970s, now winning acclaim as the most impressive writer to emerge from that decade. A versatile stylist, Wolfe nevertheless has a characteristic voice which is urbane, controlled and exact, though never direct. There is usually a puzzle in his work, an unpredictable significance or overlooked implication, inexplicit but crucial to the story and perfectly possible to deduce from its telling. He customarily achieves this by rearranging conventional sf material with a different emphasis, to provoke a more thoughtful conclusion; this is the key to his importance. Most recently he has broken new ground in an unexpected area of science fantasy. Innumerable writers have set arbitrary tales in a new Dark Age centuries after the collapse of our own civilization. Wolfe has called this milieu "posthistoric" and reclaimed it for science fiction by means of rigorous logic of imagination. His series *The Book Of The New Sun* is better considered as a four-volume novel than a tetralogy. Wolfe, a Catholic, is primarily interested in questions of identity and purpose, the location of the individual in a satisfactory moral and philosophical system. *The Fifth Head Of Cerberus*, a collection of three novellas, is a compellingly elusive investigation of the enigmas raised by cloning and by beings who can imitate the forms of alien races so perfectly they deceive themselves. Wolfe's metaphysical pursuits fortunately involve adventures of the most dramatic and engaging kind, often with adolescent protagonists in no danger of getting lost in abstraction. Wolfe's non-generic novels, *Peace* (1975) and *The Devil In A Forest* (1976), are of more than secondary interest for sf readers. The first employs fantasy as a mode of experience, rather than an alternative to experience; the second is a naturalistic narrative set in medieval terrain usually reserved for folkloric fantasy.

The Fifth Head Of Cerberus (1972)

R ★ ★ ★ ★	I ★ ★ ★ ★
C ★ ★ ★ ★ ★	L ★ ★ ★ ★ ★

The Sword Of The Lictor (1982)

R ★ ★ ★ ★ ★	I ★ ★ ★ ★
C ★ ★ ★ ★	L ★ ★ ★ ★

"The Hero As Werewolf" (1975)

R ★ ★ ★ ★ ★	I ★ ★ ★ ★
C ★ ★ ★ ★	L ★ ★ ★ ★

Gene Wolfe

WOLLHEIM, Donald A(llen) (1914) American writer, editor and founder of DAW Books. He sometimes writes as David Grinnell. Active since the early 1930s, Wollheim is one of the genre's most influential figures not through what he has written (which is basically adventure stories set in space and time) but through what he has caused to be written. One of the Futurians (which include Pohl (q.v.), Asimov (q.v.), Blish (q.v.) and Knight (q.v.) amongst others) he also helped create Ace Books in 1952. Without his efforts sf would have taken much longer to develop as a novel form.

The Men From Ariel (1982; coll.)

R ★ ★ ★	I ★
C ★	L ★

Across Time (1957)

R ★ ★ ★	I ★
C ★ ★	L ★

WOOLF, Virginia (1882-1941) English novelist, one of whose novels, *Orlando: A Biography*, uses an sf device. Ostensibly the story of a character who is immortal and can change sex, the book is a glance at life and literature from Shakespeare's time to 1928, when it was published. It is rather an artificial delicacy, where everything is seen through a bohemian eye. Extremely mannered and limited in its tastes, it is not convincingly real in any respect, the work of a dilettante, which Woolf generally was not.

Orlando (1928)

R ★ ★ ★ ★	I ★
C ★ ★	L ★ ★ ★

WOUK, Herman (1915) Best-selling American author, whose *The "Lomokome" Papers* is his only sf work, a satire of sorts wherein an Utopia, Lomokome, is discovered on the Moon. It is a rather stilted allegory.

The "Lomokome" Papers (1956)

R ★ ★	I ★ ★
C ★	L ★

WRIGHT, Austin Tappan (1883-1931) American author of *Islandia*, one of the finest and most exhaustive alternative cultures ever depicted. The story is of Islandia's decision to join the rest of the world after centuries of isolation. Its meticulous detail is admirable.

Islandia (1942)

R ★ ★ ★	I ★ ★ ★ ★ ★ ★
C ★ ★	L ★ ★

WRIGHT, S. Fowler (1874-1965) British writer, who first made a career as an accountant but began writing when he was a leading member of the Empire Poetry League. His earliest novels were self-published but he shot to fame with the spectacular success of *Deluge*, which became a bestseller in America and was filmed. He produced a great many detective stories but always put more effort into his historical novels and his scientific romances, of which the most famous are the lurid far-future fantasy, *The World Below*, and the lost race novel, *The Island Of Captain Sparrow*. He was a determined enemy of technological progress and produced in his collection *The New Gods Lead* (1932) some of the most striking images of a future dehumanized by technocratic rule.

The World Below (1929)

R ★ ★ ★	I ★ ★ ★ ★
C ★	L ★ ★ ★ ★

Deluge (1928)

R ★ ★ ★	I ★ ★ ★
C ★ ★ ★	L ★ ★ ★ ★

The Island Of Captain Sparrow (1929)

R ★ ★ ★	I ★ ★ ★
C ★ ★	L ★ ★ ★

WUL, Stefan (1922) French author of a dozen finely crafted sf novels, only one of which has been translated so far. The *Temple Of The Past* uses pulp elements (18-foot tall men from Atlantis, 300-ft sea-monsters, alien planets and human space exploration teams) unashamedly but intelligently.

The Temple Of The Past (1958; trans. 1973)

R ★ ★ ★ ★	I ★ ★
C ★	L ★ ★

WYATT, Patrick   English novelist of *Irish Rose*, part farce, part satire on a future England where most of the white women have died and where the Pill Wars are raging. Illogical as it is, it is a fascinating adventure story with a certain whimsical charm.

Irish Rose (1975)

R ★ ★ ★	I ★ ★
C ★	L ★

WYLIE, Philip (1902-71) American writer, best known for his scathing work of social criticism, *Generation of Vipers* (1942). He wrote the early superman story, *Gladiator*, and a popular cosmic disaster story, *After Worlds Collide* (1934) (the latter, a sequel to *When Worlds Collide*, written in collaboration with Edwin Balmer) in the 1930s, thus becoming one of the few American writers of the day publishing sf outside the pulps. He wrote screenplays for several sf films, including one for *The Invisible Man*, which owed as much to his own *The Murderer Invisible* as to Wells. He wrote two novels about nuclear civil defence, *Tomorrow!* (1954) and *Triumph* (1963), in the post-war years, and left for posthumous publication one of the fiercest anti-pollution novels, *The End Of The Dream*. None of his sf matches his superb mainstream novel *Finnley Wren* (1934) but it is always lively and intelligent in spite of its didactic undertones.

Gladiator (1930)

R ★ ★ ★ ★	I ★ ★ ★
C ★ ★ ★	L ★ ★ ★

The Disappearance (1951)

R ★ ★ ★ ★	I ★ ★ ★
C ★ ★ ★ ★	L ★ ★ ★ ★

The End Of The Dream (1972)

R ★ ★ ★	I ★ ★ ★ ★
C ★ ★	L ★ ★ ★

WYNDHAM, John (1903-69) Pseudonym used by English writer John Wyndham Parkes Lucas Beynon Harris, who also used several other combinations of those names at various points in his career. As John Beynon Harris he wrote lurid stories for the early sf pulps. His first novels, as John Beynon, were mediocre but he began a whole new career as Wyndham following the success of *The Day Of The Triffids*, initially as a newspaper serial. He followed this up with several other disaster stories, and carved himself a niche in the marketplace. His books were not labelled sf and built up a large following of readers who were otherwise not attracted by the genre. His best novel is probably the post-holocaust story *The Chrysalids*, but his most famous after *Day Of The Triffids* is *The Midwich Cuckoos* (filmed as *Village Of The Damned*), in which the inhabitants of a small village are mysteriously impregnated with super-human children. It could be argued that Wyndham simply adapted sf ideas for people who would not normally read sf, placing them in homely stories of ordinary folk, but this would be to underestimate his real achievement. His main characters are usually models of decency –

John Wyndham

the English as they like to think of themselves – and his stories have the same obsession with matters of propriety and loyalty that characterizes much archetypally English fiction, from the public school story to the middle-class domestic drama. To blend this with the amazing and the apocalyptic, as he did with style and panache, was no mean achievement. He helped by example to make sf respectable in Britain, and influenced several other writers – most notably John Christopher (q.v.).

The Day Of The Triffids (1951)

R ★ ★ ★ ★	I ★ ★
C ★ ★ ★	L ★ ★

The Chrysalids (1955)

R ★ ★ ★ ★	I ★ ★ ★
C ★ ★	L ★ ★ ★

The Midwich Cuckoos (1957)

R ★ ★ ★ ★	I ★ ★
C ★ ★ ★	L ★ ★ ★

Y

YARBRO, Chelsea Quinn (1942) American writer of sf, fantasy, horror and detective fiction. So far Yarbro's sf novels have been notably less successful, either artistically or commercially, than her other work, notably the St Germain books in which in various periods of history the forces of human evil in general, and oppressors of women in particular, are combated by a charming and resourceful male vampire. The theme of the possibility of the Good Male – Yarbro is in an implied debate with other feminist writers like Charnas (q.v.) – is present in her sf novels *Time Of The Fourth Horseman* (1976), in which eugenicists' attempts to reduce the population by plague get out of hand even by their standards and a woman doctor fails to stop it all, and *False Dawn*, a downbeat post-ecodoom odyssey by a mutant woman and a reformed bandit. Her feisty smartness perhaps shows up to its best advantage in *Ariosto*, an alternative world story whose hero is writing a fantasy and being betrayed by the genre he has picked.

False Dawn (1978)

R	★ ★ ★		I	★ ★	
C	★ ★ ★		L	★ ★ ★	

Hotel Transylvania (1978)

R	★ ★ ★ ★		I	★ ★ ★	
C	★ ★ ★ ★		L	★ ★ ★ ★	

Ariosto (1980)

R	★ ★ ★ ★		I	★ ★ ★	
C	★ ★ ★ ★		L	★ ★ ★ ★	

YEFREMOV, Ivan Antonovich (1907-72) Russian writer who was a leading figure in Soviet sf in the 1950s. An Utopian novel, *Andromeda*, and an historical fantasy, *The Land Of Foam* (1957), are available in English, as are a number of his short stories. Whilst much of his work now seems dated, he was a pioneer, liberating Russian sf from authoritarian restrictions.

Andromeda (1959)

R	★ ★ ★		I	★ ★ ★	
C	★		L	★ ★	

YEP, Laurence (Michael) (1948) American children's writer and novelist. A highly talented Chinese-American, Yep's first novel in the genre was a juvenile, *Sweetwater*, and his second an adult colony-planet story, *Seademons* (1977), a hauntingly evocative work which vividly captures the alien planet, Fancyfree. *Dragon Of The Lost Sea* (1982) is a colourful fantasy novel based on Chinese mythology and is again a juvenile. However, he might yet produce a major work within the genre.

Sweetwater (1976)

R	★ ★ ★ ★		I	★ ★ ★	
C	★ ★ ★		L	★ ★ ★	

YERMAKOV, Nicholas   American author whose work shows evidence of the influence of Samuel Delany (q.v.), but has yet to master the techniques of the genre. Two novels, *Journey From Flesh* and *Clique* (1982), are interesting but badly flawed.

Journey From Flesh (1981)

R	★ ★ ★		I	★ ★	
C	★		L	★ ★	

YOLEN, Jane (1939) American writer and editor best known for her juvenile fantasies, such as *The Wizard Of Washington Square* (1969). She has published a number of science fiction stories in magazines, some of which are collected in *Dream Weaver* (1979). A comic space adventure, *Commander Toad And The Planet Of The Grapes* (1982), is a juvenile.

"Brother Hart" (1978)

R	★ ★ ★ ★		I	★	
C	★ ★		L	★ ★	

"Sule Skerry" (1982)

R	★ ★ ★ ★ ★		I	★	
C	★ ★ ★		L	★ ★ ★	

YOUNG, Robert F(ranklin) (1915) American writer of science fiction since 1935. Two collections of his stories appeared in the 1960s, the best of which is *The Worlds Of Robert F. Young* (1965), but much remains uncollected. His humanistic style of science fiction is displayed in a recent novel, *Eridahn* (1983), and in its predecessor, *The Last Yggdrasil*, which, if not unduly original or intelligent, are moving and, in the first case, unashamedly romantic.

The Last Yggdrasil (1982)

R	★ ★ ★		I	★ ★	
C	★		L	★ ★	

ZAMYATIN, Yevgeny (Ivanovich) (1884-1937) Russian author of *We*, a dystopian novel which is a precursor of Huxley's *Brave New World* and Orwell's *1984*. It can be read as a fantasy but is most rewardingly seen as a satiric attack upon the repressive centralized State and its standards of conformity. Its bleak ending – the "fantasiectomy" which erases the creative life of the protagonist – foreshadows much of the speculative, drug-oriented fiction of the 1970s. (See also the short story, "A Story About The Most Important Thing.")

We (1920)

R ★ ★ ★ ★		I ★ ★ ★ ★ ★	
C ★ ★		L ★ ★ ★ ★	

ZEBROWSKI, George (1945) American writer. He has a strong interest in metaphysics, and is also devoted to exercises in hypothetical sociology – two tendencies which do not fit in well with the space opera plots of his early novels. By far his most successful work to date is *Macrolife*, a sprawling and uneven account of Man's forced exodus from Earth. So far he seems to be a writer with big ideas but little control of form, but he is a very promising writer who may well produce first-class sf in the future.

The Omega Point (1972)

R ★ ★		I ★ ★ ★	
C ★ ★		L ★ ★	

Macrolife (1979)

R ★ ★ ★		I ★ ★ ★ ★	
C ★ ★		L ★ ★ ★ ★	

ZELAZNY, Roger (1937) At his best, Roger Zelazny is a writer of true quality, emphasizing not ideas but *style* – especially literary style – though there is always a danger of such writing becoming excessively mannered. Some may think that his early potential has not quite been fulfilled, but there can be no doubting the lauded excellence of the early work. "A Rose For Ecclesiastes" (1963), "The Doors Of His Face, The Lamps Of His Mouth" (1965), and the underrated (perhaps because it lacks any kind of traditionally heroic or romantic protaganist) "The Graveyard Heart" are some of the finest stories in science fiction. The first two novels, too, are notable for their stylistic qualities: overwhelming verve in the case of *This Immortal*, and a richly poetic (if somewhat stilted) evocativeness in *The Dream Master*. As always, Zelazny's interest in myth, miracles, local colour and theatricality is evident. After these books, Zelazny's career has remained near the heart of our essentially conservative genre, and there is progressively less concentration on character and more concentration on colourful caricature, and less rigour and seriousness altogether. On first encounter, the Hugo Award-winning novel *Lord Of Light* (1967) appears to be a considerable work. This impressive long narrative is based on Hindu mythology, but is built out of traditional sf materials – heroes and villains, clever gimmicks, superfluous spectacle – like a kind of impressive comic-book in prose. There have been a number of novels since then, but no great novels. There is some genuine experimentation in *Creatures Of Light And Darkness* (1969), and some good writing in the five-volume Amber series. This sequence of sword-and-sorcery novels shows signs of hasty writing, and the books are notably under-visualized, even though the scenes of transformation are sometimes impressive. Overall, Zelazny is perhaps a writer who has not yet given us all he might. Nevertheless, his love of language and the striking gesture, his flashes of genuine poetry, allow us to read even the lesser works with pleasure.

This Immortal (1966)

R ★ ★ ★ ★ ★		I ★ ★ ★	
C ★ ★ ★ ★		L ★ ★ ★ ★	

The Dream Master (1966)

R ★ ★ ★ ★		I ★ ★ ★ ★	
C ★ ★ ★ ★		L ★ ★ ★ ★ ★	

Nine Princes In Amber (1970)

R ★ ★ ★ ★		I ★ ★	
C ★ ★ ★ ★		L ★ ★ ★	

ZOLINE, Pamela (1941) American writer, resident in the U.K., known principally for her excellent short story, "The Heat Death Of The Universe" (1967). She also illustrated Disch's (q.v.) *Camp Concentration*.

"The Heat Death Of The Universe" (1967)

R ★ ★ ★ ★		I ★ ★ ★	
C ★ ★ ★ ★		L ★ ★	

First Magazine Publication of Leading Authors

1927
Manly Wade Wellman — *Weird Tales*
1928
E. E. "Doc" Smith — *Amazing*
Jack Williamson — *Amazing*
1930
John W. Campbell Jr — *Amazing*
Clark Ashton Smith — *Wonder Stories*
John Taine — *Amazing*
1931
Clifford D. Simak — *Wonder Stories*
John Wyndham
(as *John Beynon-Harris*) — *Wonder Stories*
1933
John Russell Fearn — *Amazing*
C. L. Moore — *Weird Tales*
1934
Stanley G. Weinbaum — *Wonder Stories*
Donald A. Wollheim — *Wonder Stories*
1936
Henry Kuttner — *Weird Tales*
1937
L. Sprague de Camp — *Astounding*
Frederik Pohl — *Amazing*
Eric Frank Russell — *Astounding*
1938
Lester del Rey — *Astounding*
L. Ron Hubbard — *Astounding*
William F. Temple — *Astounding*
1939
Isaac Asimov — *Astounding*
Robert A. Heinlein — *Astounding*
Fritz Leiber — *Unknown*
Theodore Sturgeon — *Astounding*
A. E. Van Vogt — *Astounding*
1940
James Blish — *Super-Science Stories*
Leigh Brackett — *Astounding*
C. M. Kornbluth — *Astounding*
1941
Ray Bradbury — *Super-Science Stories*
Fredric Brown — *Captain Future*
Damon Knight — *Stirring Science Stories*
Wilson Tucker — *Super-Science Stories*
1942
Hal Clement — *Astounding*
George O. Smith — *Astounding*
1945
Jack Vance — *Thrilling Wonder Stories*
1946
Arthur C. Clarke — *Astounding*
1947
Poul Anderson — *Astounding*
H. Beam Piper — *Astounding*

1948
Charles L. Harness — *Astounding*
Judith Merrill — *Astounding*
1949
John Christopher — *Astounding*
(as *Christopher Youd*)
Katherine McLean — *Astounding*
1950
Gordon R. Dickson — *Fantastic Stories Quarterly*
Richard Matheson — *F&SF*
Mack Reynolds — *Fantastic Adventures*
Cordwainer Smith — *Fantasy Book*
1951
Harry Harrison — *Worlds Beyond*
Walter M. Miller Jr — *Amazing*
E. C. Tubb — *New Worlds*
1952
Algis Budrys — *Space SF*
Philip K. Dick — *Planet Stories*
Philip Jose Farmer — *Startling Stories*
Frank Herbert — *Startling Stories*
Daniel Keyes — *Marvel SF*
Robert Sheckley — *Imagination*
1953
Marion Zimmer Bradley — *Vortex*
John Brunner — *Astounding*
(as *John Loxmith*)
Anne McCaffrey — *SF Plus*
Kurt Vonnegut Jr — *Galaxy*
James White — *New Worlds*
1954
Brian W. Aldiss — *Science Fantasy*
Barrington J. Bayley — *Vargo Statten SF Magazine*
Avram Davidson — *F&SF*
Robert Silverberg — *Nebula*
Roger Zelazny — *Literary Cavalcade*
1955
Stephen Tall — *Galaxy*
1956
J. G. Ballard — *New Worlds/Science Fantasy*
Lloyd Biggle Jr. — *Galaxy*
Harlan Ellison — *Infinity Science Fiction*
1957
David R. Bunch — *If*
1958
Richard McKenna — *F&SF*
Thomas Burnett Swann — *Fantastic Universe*
1959
Keith Laumer — *Amazing*
Michael Moorcock — *New Worlds*
Joanna Russ — *F&SF*

1960
Ben Bova — *Amazin[g]*
R. A. Lafferty — *Science Fictio[n]*
1961
Fred Saberhagen — *Galax[y]*
1962
Terry Carr — *F&S[F]*
Thomas M. Disch — *Fantasti[c]*
Ursula K. LeGuin — *Fantast[ic]*
1963
Piers Anthony — *Fantast[ic]*
Hilary Bailey — *New Worl[d]*
Alexei Panshin — *[…]*
Norman Spinrad — *Analo[g]*
Ted White — *Amazin[g]*
1964
Larry Niven — *[…]*
Keith Roberts — *Science Fantas[y]*
1965
Greg Benford — *F&S[F]*
David I. Masson — *New Worl[d]*
Brian Stableford — *Science Fantas[y]*
1966
Gardner R. Dozois — *[…]*
Christopher Priest — *Impuls[e]*
John Sladek — *New Worl[d]*
Gene Wolfe — *[…]*
1967
Dean R. Koontz — *F&S[F]*
Barry Malzberg — *Galax[y]*
(as *K. M. O'Donnell*)
1968
Michael Coney — *New World[s]*
Robert P. Holdstock — *New World[s]*
James Tiptree Jr. — *Analo[g]*
1969
David Gerrold — *Galax[y]*
Joe Haldeman — *Galax[y]*
Ian Watson — *New World[s]*
1970
Michael Bishop — *Galax[y]*
Ed Bryant — *New World[s]*
Gordon Eklund — *Fantasti[c]*
1971
Geo. Alec Effinger — *Amazin[g]*
George R. R. Martin — *Galax[y]*
1974
Tom Reamy — *F&S[F]*
John Varley — *F&S[F]*
1975
Richard Cowper — *F&S[F]*

The Science-Fiction Magazines
David Wingrove

SCIENCE FICTION IS ESSENTIALLY A SHORT STORY FORM and it is a fairly recent phenomenon to find science-fiction writers cutting their teeth at novel length. Samuel Delany, John Crowley, and C. J. Cherryh all won acclaim for their novels long before their shorter fiction appeared in the SF magazines, but it is still more common for writers entering the SF field to do so through the pages of one of the current specialist magazines – *Analog, F & S F, Omni, Amazing, Fantastic,* or *Isaac Asimov's Science Fiction Magazine.* These, and many others now defunct have always been the best guide to what is happening in the genre at any instant.

Between them the magazines have always covered a wide range of themes and treatments, displaying in the stories they published a vast disparity of achievement in terms of literary talent and imaginative flair. Some, more consistent in their quality and more persistent in their regularity, have survived decade after decade. Others, cashing in on periodic booms, have suffered the magazine equivalent of sudden death for their ephemeral bad taste. Even so, the quality they have all shared is *immediacy*: while they talked of vast expanses of space and time, they reflected, in their thematic and stylistic preoccupations, a constant obsession with the real-time *Now* of the ongoing science-fiction field. The science articles, the readers' letters, the newest stories – all echoed the latest state of the speculative art, so that anyone reading science fiction of the 1950s, for example, can hear echoes of the Cold War fears, the paranoia of McCarthyism and fears of nuclear escalation. Science fiction is – and sometimes it would like to deny the fact – more time-bound than it first appears.

However, this aspect of immediacy – a sense of "work in progress" lost in all but, perhaps, the most literary of modern magazines – has been one of the SF magazine's greatest strengths and is the main reason for its survival into the 1980s as a thriving form: immediacy . . . and a sense of continual feedback.

Stories have always spawned other stories in the same way that ex-fans who became writers and editors encouraged other, younger fans to write and edit in their turn. In several cases those same young fans became influential figures or editors in the field. John W. Campbell Jr, Fred Pohl, Harry Harrison, Isaac Asimov, and Damon Knight are all examples of this syndrome, which dates back as far as the appearance of the first specialist "scientifiction" magazine, *Amazing Stories*, in April 1926 under the editorship of Hugo Gernsback.

There were outlets for science-fiction stories long before *Amazing* was conceived. Magazines like *The Argosy* and *All-Story Weekly*, both run by the Frank A. Munsey Corporation, published a substantial amount of early science fiction in the opening decades of this century, including the work of Ray Cummings, A. Merritt, Murray Leinster, and Edgar Rice Burroughs. But they were general fiction magazines with a bias towards adventure. Gernsback's *Amazing* was something different, something if not quite new then innovatory. It contained nothing but the sort of fictional material previously published in smaller doses in Gernsback's factual magazine *Science And Invention* and was, at the outset, a reflection of Gernsback's belief in science and technology. Its stories were supposedly (though not in actuality) true to extant scientific knowledge – a factor which hardcore SF writers (of the *Analog* variety, in particular) still maintain is a necessary ingredient of good science fiction. This "educational"/"extrapolative" bias took a firm grip on the field from the start – particularly as Gernsback also founded the next two science-fiction magazines, *Science Wonder Stories* and *Air Wonder Stories*, in 1929. Fantasy and horror stories, which until then had co-existed with science fiction in the more general magazines, found a home in places like *Weird Tales* (founded in 1923). Cross-pollination between these genres continues to this day; yet it was Gernsback, in the late 1920s, who created an artificial schism between the forms with his emphasis on scientific fidelity.

Amazing was a bedsheet-sized magazine; that is, it was 8½ by 11½ inches and was printed on newspaper presses from reclaimed pulp paper which often had signs of the previous print mingled with the new text. Its covers were of the most garish, eye-catching kind, competing on the news-stands with other covers that displayed a riot of primary colours to match the purple contents. But *Amazing* was not strictly a "pulp", which were much smaller magazines at 7 by 10 inches. Nonetheless it held its own, and by 1928 Gernsback was claiming a circulation of 150,000 copies per month.

Amazing proved the success of this special category and when, in 1929, Harry Bates spotted a gap in a sheet of cover proofs for the Clayton chain's magazines and suggested a science-fiction title, Clayton agreed at once. *Astounding Stories of Super-Science* was born. It offered two cents a word to its contributors – four times what Gernsback offered – and stressed a bias towards space adventure. Through its connection with the Clayton chain it had two advantages over its competitor; a cheaper cover price (20 cents against *Amazing*'s 25) and better distribution. Bates, the editor, was openly scathing of the low fictional standards of *Amazing* which, under the octogenarian editor, T. O'Conor Sloane, had grown drab and tedious. Bates downgraded the scientific content of his magazine and sought to entertain his readers more than to educate them.

Science Fiction's longest-running magazines. *Astounding* (October 1941) and *Amazing* (July 1939). Each has spanned six decades.

In size and production *Astounding* was the first true pulp science-fiction magazine. It was a success from the word go and even survived the collapse of the Clayton chain in 1933 and a six-month hiatus before the title was bought by Street & Smith. Even then, its golden years lay ahead of it. A new editor, F. Orlin Tremaine, took over with the first Street & Smith issue in October 1933. Instantly he introduced a new policy which he termed "thought variant" – at least one story per issue which would look at an old idea from a new standpoint. This has remained one of SF's characteristic modes and produced some of its finest stories. Tremaine edited 50 issues of *Astounding* before handing over to John W. Campbell Jr in September 1937.

During the 1930s Campbell had established himself as a popular writer of space opera and scientific tales. The rich inventiveness apparent in his fiction was carried through into his editorial role, and within three years he had created a stable of writers who, between them, were to dominate science fiction for the next decade and more – Asimov, Heinlein, Sturgeon, and Van Vogt amongst them.

Harry Harrison and Brian Aldiss in their retrospective essay on *Astounding/ Analog* (in *The Astounding Analog Reader, Volume One*; 1972) conclude of Campbell, "It might be said that he had a literary feel for stories yet was hostile to literature." This dynamic tension sometimes led him astray (as in his championing of L. Ron Hubbard's "dianetics", later to become scientology) but more often it brought its rewards. He had a deliberate policy of seeking a more mature and more intelligent audience – an adult audience for what had, until that time, been essentially a juvenile form. He took his role seriously and that seriousness was reflected in the contents and appearance of *Astounding* from the late 1930s onward. He also changed the emphasis of the magazine, replacing Tremaine's "thought variant" policy with his own "nova" policy, similar in its aims but with a greater stress on how new developments affected people. Although this was by no means as sociological as the new SF of the 1950s it was more humanistic than its rival magazines. Under Gernsback and Tremaine machines and ideas had dominated the pages; now the focus was upon the men who made the machines and had the ideas – competent engineers and inventors, scientists and savants. With this change of emphasis came the idea of "series" stories, of interconnected long-running stories: future histories like Heinlein's, Asimov's Foundation and Robot stories (which began in *Astounding*'s pages in 1940-41), and so forth.

Campbell shaped his young writers – gave them ideas, story-lines, critical feedback. He was continually bouncing ideas off them and then using their combined responses to launch an editorial. *Astounding* was, in a very real sense, an early example of a "think-tank" and, from the early 1940s onward, it had a very definite character. Not only that, but in the space of three to four years it can be said to have laid the foundations of modern science fiction as a genre. As well as this, Campbell can also take credit for founding the most colourful of the magazines to evolve in the 1939-41 magazine "boom" – *Unknown*.

Unknown catered for the fantastic and attracted writers like L. Sprague de Camp, Henry Kuttner, Fritz Leiber (with his Fafhrd/Gray Mouser stories), Fletcher Pratt, Theodore Sturgeon, and Jack Williamson. It lasted only four years but seemed every bit as important as *Astounding* while it lasted.

Other magazine chains, seeing the sudden popularity of science fiction,

Galaxy (August 1974)   *F & S F* (July 1982)

launched their own titles – *Startling Stories, Marvel Science Stories, Fantastic Adventures, Planet Stories, Super-Science Stories.* This boom, begun in 1939, reached its peak in 1941 when more than 20 magazines were being published. Many of them were bi-monthly "companion" magazines, a device by which each title got space on the newsrack and remained on sale for two months rather than one. It was therefore more attractive to launch two bi-monthlies than one monthly title. Nonetheless, many of the major titles folded during 1941 and the coming of the Second World War to America in December of that year killed off others. For the rest of the 1940s seven magazines were to dominate the racks – *Amazing, Astounding, Famous Fantastic Mysteries, Fantastic Adventures, Planet Stories, Startling Stories,* and *Thrilling Wonder Stories.*

Among that temporary glut of magazines was one, founded in 1940, which is of more than passing interest: *Super-Science Stories.* At its helm was a 19-year-old fan turned writer turned editor named Fred Pohl, and in his first few years his fledgling magazine (which, with its companion *Astonishing Stories,* died in 1943) published the first stories of James Blish, Ray Bradbury, and Wilson Tucker. It was Pohl's first spell of editorship but, as we shall see, not the last, and he drew a lot of his stories from members of the New York "Futurian" group, many of Asimov's earliest amongst them.

The Second World War brought smaller issues, irregularity of appearance, and the absence of key writers and editors. Things quietened down and, in America at least, stayed fairly quiet until the end of the 1940s. In Britain it was a different story. A post-war boom began in 1946 when seven magazines were launched. They were mainly reprints of American material (as much British and Australian magazine fiction has been until recently) and folded quickly. One important title survived – E. J. Carnell's *New Worlds,* which published its first issue in April 1946.

British magazine science fiction has always tended to fall into two categories; that which emulates and sometimes seeks a home in the American magazines; and the more pastoral and somewhat more pessimistic (some say humanistic) home-grown strain. Amongst *New Worlds*' early contributors were names like Arthur C. Clarke, A. Bertram Chandler, John Wyndham, and John Christopher. With the exception of Clarke they seemed less obsessed with winning the stars than with depicting a leisurely drift into social chaos following some natural or man-made catastrophe. Between 1949 and 1964 *New Worlds* contained much more of the latter category than of the mock-American variety. A companion magazine, *Science Fantasy*, was launched in 1950, edited at first by Walter Gillings (who had run the first British pulp, *Tales Of Wonder*, before the War), then, from 1954, by Carnell.

In America the late 1940s saw the beginning of hardcover re-publication of magazine material (short stories and serialized novels), first by the specialist publishers such as Fantasy Press and Gnome Press, and then by established houses like Doubleday. Throughout the 1940s and early 1950s there was a constant movement towards a more adult form of science fiction in the majority of the magazines (*Planet Stories*, with its emphasis on Space Opera might be seen as an enjoyable exception), but permeating it all was still the strict scientific heritage of Gernsback. The birth of *The Magazine of Fantasy and Science Fiction* (*F & SF*, as it is better known) towards the end of 1949 and *Galaxy* in October 1950 changed that dramatically.

Both of the new magazines were "digest" size (5½ by 7½ inches) and both, from the outset, aimed for an adult audience similar to that reached by *Astounding*. *F & SF* was more literary in its emphasis than any of its predecessors, while *Galaxy* sponsored a type of science fiction which was sociologically oriented and often sharply satirical. The 1940s had seen steady changes in the publishing industry and the pulps were effectively dead even before *Thrilling Wonder* and *Startling* folded in 1955. Paperbacks were appearing for the first time and encroaching upon the traditional magazine market – as indeed was television. Yet at the same time people were becoming more affluent. Another boom was on its way. *F & SF* and *Galaxy*, appearing regularly and publishing the most exciting new names in the field, won large, regular readerships. It was like the early 1940s again, with what seemed like an unending well of new talent to be tapped. Algis Budrys, Philip K. Dick, Philip Jose Farmer, Frank Herbert, and Bob Sheckley were all published for the first time in 1952, John Brunner, Anne McCaffrey, and Kurt Vonnegut Jr in 1953, Brian Aldiss, Robert Silverberg, and Roger Zelazny in 1954, to name but a few. The two new magazines drew these names to them and, when *If* appeared in 1952, it could truly be said that the field had never been so richly endowed. More than 50 different science-fiction magazines were published in America alone in the 1950s, including *Science Fiction Plus*, which, under editor Sam Moskowitz, was Hugo Gernsback's last dalliance with the SF field.

Despite the proliferation of material, science fiction was dominated by the "Big Three" throughout the 1950s. *Astounding*, under Campbell's continued editorship, still kept the lion's share of the audience, but often at the expense of being rather dour and uninventive. *F & SF*, first under the editorship of Anthony Boucher (with J. Francis McComas) and then, from April 1958, under Robert P. Mills, had a policy of publishing "respectable", mainstream authors like James

New Worlds in its heyday, issue 191, June 1969.
The cover depicts British science fiction's most
popular anti-hero, Jerry Cornelius.

Thurber, P. G. Wodehouse, C. S. Lewis, and Kingsley Amis. *Galaxy*'s editor, Horace L. Gold, was again very strict in his selection of material – a policy which has *always* worked in the science-fiction market – and seemed to inherit that same "school" of writers Pohl had first encouraged in *Super-Science Stories* and *Astonishing*. Damon Knight, James Blish, Theodore Sturgeon, Pohl and C. M. Kornbluth, Alfred Bester, Leiber, Asimov, Heinlein, Dick, and Sheckley were all regular contributors. When Gold finally retired through ill-health in 1961 it was no surprise that Fred Pohl should take over his editorial chair.

Astounding changed its name to *Analog* in October 1960 and, throughout the 1960s was the market leader in sales if not always in quality. *Amazing* and *Fantastic*, under the editorship of Cele Goldsmith, took on a new lease of life and in the early 1960s began to publish exciting new work from such as Aldiss, J. G. Ballard, and Philip Jose Farmer. These three, together with *F & SF*, *Galaxy*, and *If*, formed the core of magazine science fiction in the 1960s, providing a broad spectrum of genre writing. *F & SF* was recognized as the "quality" magazine and won four of the 1960s Hugo Awards for best magazine (*Analog* won three and *If* the remaining three). However, the 1960s were notable for two dramatic developments in SF; the rise of the original anthology and the "New Wave".

The first original anthology series had been Fred Pohl's *Star Science Fiction Stories*, six volumes of which were published by Ballantine Books between 1953 and 1959. In the 1960s others followed, becoming more and more popular throughout the decade, Damon Knight's *Orbit* series perhaps the field leader among them. They had advantages over the SF magazines (payment, distribution, cost, timing) and flourished until they too suffered a glut in the mid-1970s (a glut which affects publishers' attitudes to them even now). The 1960s saw the beginning of their influence on the field. They attracted some of the finest writing and – much more important – some of the most experimental. Coincidental was the rise, both in America and Britain, of a movement against traditional forms of science fiction; the "New Wave".

When Michael Moorcock took over *New Worlds* in 1964 he did so with an editorial manifesto which promised more adventurous and experimental writing. Indeed, the adventure was very often to be in the writing itself rather than in the stories produced. Despite various financial problems *New Worlds* managed to live up to its promises and, under various formats, utterly changed the kind of fiction being produced under the SF label. Moorcock and his writers claimed that SF stood for "speculative fiction" and were much influenced by the modernist writers of the mainstream – William Burroughs, Jorge Luis Borges, Franz Kafka, and Albert Camus. They championed expressionist and surrealist art, valued the idea of literature more than the idea of story and generally antagonized the traditional science-fiction writers who were to be found in the American magazines. Some of them did find an occasional and sympathetic home in *F & SF*, but most of the new writers – among them the best new American writers, like Tom Disch, Samuel R. Delany, and Harlan Ellison – were attracted to *New Worlds* where they published stories which could not have found a home elsewhere.

In America the effect of the "New Wave" was muted by the strong influence of the six major magazines. Changes could be seen, especially towards the end of the 1970s, but they were effected by a new generation of writers who had assimilated both new and old traditions – writers like Michael Bishop, George R.

R. Martin, and John Crowley – as well as by established writers who had re-assessed their approach to science fiction, Robert Silverberg and Fred Pohl amongst them. Throughout the 1960s and 1970s the taboos against sexual explicitness and various other subjects slowly disappeared (though not altogether) from the magazines, and the field became truly adult for the first time. These changes took place against a background of diminishing circulations and a slow depletion of the number of titles. *Worlds Of Tomorrow*, which had first appeared in 1963, was absorbed by *If* in 1967, and, after various fluctuations in its regularity, *If* was swallowed up by *Galaxy* in 1975, despite *If*'s larger circulation. Throughout this period *Analog* kept its share of the market and at the death of John Campbell in 1971 its circulation was estimated at 110,000, compared to *F & SF*'s 50,000 and *Amazing* and *Fantastic*'s approximate 20,000 each.

Ben Bova took over at *Analog*, maintaining rather than changing Campbell's scientific emphasis. And when *Omni* was formed in October 1978, Bova quickly took over from Frank Kendig as editor, controlling a magazine which, even more than Gernsback's original *Science and Invention*, straddled the two fields of science fact and science fiction. There had been several attempts to publish "slick" or "glossy" magazines of the *Playboy/Penthouse* variety throughout the late 1960s and early 1970s, but most folded very quickly – *Cosmos* and *Vertex* amongst them – without gaining the necessary circulation. *Omni* was different. It was launched by the *Penthouse* group and had a rumoured early circulation of one million copies worldwide – a figure which settled to 800,000. It was (and currently is) better produced and better distributed than any of its competitors and it paid better ($1500 to $2000 for a short story!). Yet it has not really affected the traditional science fiction "digests" which have been added to by *Isaac Asimov's Science Fiction Magazine*. *Asimov's*, under the author's patronage and George Scithers' editorship, has ousted *Analog* as the "digest" market leader. *Omni* sees itself as competing more with *National Geographic* than with the "digests" and must be seen as an anomaly in this history and not an indicator of the shape of things to come. *Asimov's*, with its emphasis on pure science-fiction stories, seems much more to indicate the way ahead.

In Britain the end of *New Worlds* as a regular magazine in January 1971 left a gap which has only partially been filled. There was no British SF magazine between 1971 and 1974 when *Science Fiction Monthly*, developed from the publisher New English Library's wish to have a poster-magazine, was momentarily successful and claimed a circulation of 100,000 copies. A series of small magazines have followed, the latest of which, *Interzone*, is, after five issues, facing the age-old problem of finding satisfactory distribution and a sufficiently large circulation to survive on more than a subscription basis.

Publishing advances, technological changes, and shifts in taste have all affected the science-fiction magazines in the past. The best magazines have adjusted and survived, as they will doubtlessly adjust and survive the coming microcomputer revolution and other changes that are sure to follow. What will not change – at least, not in the near future – is the fact that science fiction remains one of the last homes of the short story and novella – one of the last places where the writers of the future can be seen working out their apprenticeships. Its *immediacy* remains, as does its sense of community. And, for someone seeking what is happening now in SF, there is no better place to start.

Magazine Checklist

It is impossible to draw any clear line of distinction between SF *and fantasy magazines, so both are included here. Periodicals entirely or substantially devoted to horror fiction are, however, omitted (e.g.* WEIRD TALES, TWILIGHT ZONE).

Titles marked * still published (November 1983).

A MERRITT'S FANTASY MAGAZINE. (USA). Pulp magazine. 5 issues, December 1949-October 1950. Editor Mary Gnaedinger. Companion to FAMOUS FANTASTIC MYSTERIES and FANTASTIC NOVELS.

AIR WONDER STORIES. (USA). Bedsheet magazine. 11 issues, July 1929-May 1930. Editor Hugo Gernsback. Companion to SCIENCE WONDER STORIES, with which it merged from June 1930 as WONDER STORIES. Devoted to stories of futuristic aviation, etc.

AMAZING STORIES.* (USA). Bedsheet magazine April 1926-August 1933; pulp October 1933-March 1953; digest April/May 1953 to date. Editors Hugo Gernsback (April 1926-April 1929); Arthur Lynch (May 1929-October 1929); T. O'Conor Sloane (November 1929-April 1938); Ray Palmer (June 1938-December 1949); Howard Browne (January 1950-August 1956); Paul W. Fairman (September 1956-November 1958); Cele Goldsmith (later Cele Lalli) (December 1958-June 1965); Joseph Ross (August 1965-October 1967); Harry Harrison (December 1967-September 1968); Barry Malzberg (December 1968-January 1969); Ted White (March 1969-December 1978); Elinor Mavor (March 1979-September 1982); George Scithers (December 1982-date). The first English language science-fiction magazine. Now incorporates FANTASTIC STORIES.

AMAZING STORIES QUARTERLY. (USA). Bedsheet magazine. 22 issues, Winter 1928-Fall 1934. Editors Hugo

Gernsback (Winter 1928-Winter 1929); Arthur Lynch (Spring 1929-Summer 1929); T. O'Conor Sloane (Fall 1929-Fall 1934). Companion to AMAZING STORIES.

ANALOG SCIENCE FICTION/SCIENCE FACT* (USA). Pulp magazine January 1930-December 1941; bedsheet January 1942-April 1943; pulp May 1943-October 1943; digest November 1943-February 1963; bedsheet March 1963-March 1965; digest April 1965-date. Editors Harry Bates (January 1930-March 1933); F. Orlin Tremaine (October 1933-October 1937); John W. Campbell (November 1937-December 1971); Ben Bova (January 1972-November 1978); Stanley Schmidt (December 1978-date). Originally ASTOUNDING STORIES; became ASTOUNDING SCIENCE FICTION in March 1938 and ANALOG in February 1960. Continuous monthly publication since October 1933 – a record no other SF magazine comes near matching.

ASTONISHING STORIES. (USA). Pulp magazine. 16 issues, February 1940-April 1943. Editors Frederik Pohl

(February 1940-September 1941); Alden H. Norton (November 1941-April 1943). Companion to SUPER SCIENCE STORIES.

ASTOUNDING STORIES. *see* ANALOG.

AUTHENTIC SCIENCE FICTION. (UK). Paperback size magazine. 85 issues, January 1951-October 1957. Editors L. G. Holmes (1-27); H. J. Campbell (28-65); E. C. Tubb (66-85). Various title revisions. Nos. 3-8 were titled SCIENCE FICTION FORTNIGHTLY and nos. 9-12 SCIENCE FICTION MONTHLY. Began as a paperback novel series and evolved into a magazine.

AVON FANTASY READER. (USA). Digest magazine. 18 numbered but undated issues, 1947-1952. Editor Donald A. Wollheim. Reprint magazine. Short-lived companions were AVON SCIENCE FICTION READER (3 issues) and AVON SCIENCE FICTION AND FANTASY READER (2 issues).

BEYOND. (USA). Digest. 10 issues, July 1953-1955. Editor H. L. Gold. Fantasy companion to GALAXY.

BRITISH SPACE FICTION MAGAZINE. (UK). 19 issues, various formats, mostly undated, January 1954-February 1956. Editor Vargo Statten (i.e. John Russell Fearn). Originally VARGO STATTEN SCIENCE FICTION MAGAZINE.

CAPTAIN FUTURE. (USA). Pulp magazine. 17 issues, Winter 1940-Spring 1944. Editors Leo Margulies with Mort Weisinger (1940-1941); Oscar J. Friend (1941-1944). Companion magazine to STARTLING STORIES and THRILLING WONDER STORIES; featured a "Captain Future" novel each issue.

COMET STORIES. (USA). Pulp magazine. 5 issues, December 1940-July 1941. Editor F. Orlin Tremaine.

DYNAMIC SCIENCE FICTION. (USA). Pulp magazine. 6 issues, December 1952-January 1954. Editor Robert A. W. Lowndes. Companion to FUTURE SCIENCE FICTION and SCIENCE FICTION QUARTERLY.

FAMOUS FANTASTIC MYSTERIES. (USA). Pulp magazine. 81 issues, September/October 1939-June 1953. Editor Mary Gnaedinger. Almost entirely devoted to reprints.

FANTASTIC. (USA). Digest magazine. 210 issues, Summer 1952-October 1980. Editors Howard Browne (Summer 1952-August 1956); Paul W. Fairman (October 1956-November 1958); Cele Goldsmith (later Cele Lalli) (December 1958-June 1965); Joseph Ross (September 1965-November 1967); Harry Harrison (January 1968-October 1968); Barry Malzberg (December 1968-February 1969); Ted White (April 1969-January 1979); Elinor Mavor (April 1979-October 1980). Various minor title variants: FANTASTIC SCIENCE FICTION, FANTASTIC STORIES, etc. Companion magazine to AMAZING STORIES, and merged with it in 1980.

FANTASTIC ADVENTURES. (USA). Pulp magazine. 129 issues, May 1939-March 1953. Editors Ray Palmer (May 1939-December 1949); Howard Browne (January 1950-March 1953). Also a companion of AMAZING STORIES, but quite different from FANTASTIC.

FANTASTIC NOVELS. (USA). Pulp magazine. 25 issues in two series: 5 issues July 1940-April 1941; 20 issues March 1948-June 1951. Editor Mary Gnaedinger. Companion to FAMOUS FANTASTIC MYSTERIES.

FANTASTIC STORY MAGAZINE. (USA). Pulp magazine. 23 issues, Spring 1950-Spring 1955. Editors Sam Merwin (Spring 1950-Fall 1951); Sam Mines (Winter 1951-Fall 1954); Alexander Samalman (Winter 1954-Spring 1955). The first four issues were titled FANTASTIC STORY QUARTERLY. Reprint magazine, companion to STARTLING STORIES and THRILLING WONDER STORIES.

FANTASTIC UNIVERSE. (USA). Digest magazine (last six issues intermediate digest/pulp size). 69 issues, June/July 1953-March 1960. Editors Sam Merwin (June 1953-October 1953); Beatrice Jones (January 1954-March 1954); Leo Margulies (May 1954-August 1956); Hans Stefan Santesson (September 1956-March 1960).

FANTASY. (UK). Pulp magazine. 3 issues numbered and not dated, 1938-1939. Editor T. Stanhope Sprigg. Britain's first adult science-fiction magazine.

FANTASY AND SCIENCE FICTION.* (USA). Digest magazine. First issue Fall 1949. Editors Anthony Boucher and J. Francis McComas (Fall 1949-August 1954); Boucher (September 1954-August 1958); Robert P. Mills (September 1958-March 1962); Avram Davidson (April 1962-November 1964); Edward L. Ferman (December 1964-date). Full title is THE MAGAZINE OF FANTASY AND SCIENCE FICTION.

FANTASY BOOK (1). (USA). Various formats. 8 issues, numbered, 1947-1971. Editor Garret Ford (i.e. William H. Crawford plus helpers).

FANTASY BOOK (2).* (USA). Bedsheet magazine. First issue October 1981. Editor Nick Smith.

FUTURE FICTION. (USA). Pulp magazine until March 1954; then digest. 65 issues in two series: 17 issues November 1939-March 1943; 48 issues May/June 1950-April 1960. Editors Charles D. Hornig (November 1939-April 1941); Robert A. W. Lowndes (August 1941-April 1960). Several minor title variants; was retitled SCIENCE FICTION STORIES for the last two issues of the first series (April and July 1943).

GALAXY. (USA). Digest magazine (last issue in larger format). 201 issues, October 1950-mid 1980. Editors H. L. Gold (October 1950-October 1961); Frederik Pohl (December 1961-May 1969); Ejler Jakobsson (July 1969-May 1974); James Baen (June 1974-October 1977); Hank Stine (1978-1979); Floyd Kemske (final issue).

GALILEO. (USA). Bedsheet magazine. 16 issues, numbered and not dated, 1976-1980. Editor Charles C. Ryan.

GAMMA. (USA). Digest magazine. 5 issues, 1963-September 1965. Editor Charles E. Fritch.

IF. (USA). Digest magazine. 175 issues,

March 1952-December 1974. Editors Paul W. Fairman (March 1952-September 1952); James L. Quinn (November 1952-August 1958); Damon Knight (October 1958-February 1959); H. L. Gold (July 1959-September 1961); Frederik Pohl (November 1961-June 1969); Ejler Jakobsson (July 1969-February 1974); James Baen (April 1974-December 1974). IF – whose full title was, first, IF: WORLDS OF SCIENCE FICTION and, later, WORLDS OF IF SCIENCE FICTION – became a companion magazine to GALAXY in 1961. In 1967 it absorbed another stablemate, WORLDS OF TOMORROW. It was itself absorbed by GALAXY at the end of 1974.

IMAGINATION. (USA). Digest magazine. 63 issues, October 1950-October 1958. Editors Ray Palmer (October-December 1950); W. L. Hamling (February 1951-October 1958). Companion to IMAGINATIVE TALES.

IMAGINATIVE TALES. (USA). Digest magazine. 26 issues, September 1954-November 1958. Editor W. L. Hamling. The last three issues (July-November 1958) were retitled SPACE TRAVEL. Companion to IMAGINATION.

IMPULSE. *see* SCIENCE FANTASY

INFINITY SCIENCE FICTION. (USA). Digest magazine. 20 issues, November 1955-November 1958. Editor Larry T. Shaw.

INTERZONE.* (UK). A4 size magazine. First issue Spring 1982. Editorial collective of 6-8 people.

ISAAC ASIMOV'S SCIENCE FICTION MAGAZINE.* (USA). Digest magazine. First issue Spring 1977. Editors George Scithers (Spring 1977-1981); Kathleen Moloney (1982); Shawna McCarthy (1982-date).

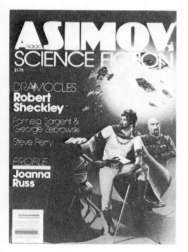

MAGAZINE OF FANTASY AND SCIENCE FICTION *see* FANTASY AND SCIENCE FICTION

MARVEL SCIENCE STORIES. (USA). Pulp magazine, with three digest issues (May-November 1951). 15 issues in two series: 9 issues August 1938-April 1941; 6 issues November 1950-May 1952. Editor Robert O. Erisman.

MARVEL TALES. (USA). Various formats. 5 issues, May 1934-Summer 1935. Editor William L. Crawford. The first semi-professional science-fiction magazine.

NEBULA. (UK). Intermediate digest/pulp size magazine. 41 issues, Autumn 1952-June 1959. Editor Peter Hamilton.

NEW WORLDS. (UK). Intermediate digest/pulp size 1946-March 1953; digest June 1953-April 1964; paperback size May/June 1964-April 1967; A4 size July 1967-March 1971. 201 issues, 1946-March 1971. Editors E. J. Carnell (1946-April 1964); Michael Moorcock (May/June 1964-1970); Charles Platt (1970-1971); various guest editors on later issues. Was followed by a paperback, NEW WORLDS QUARTERLY, which saw 10 issues, and then by further small circulation issues, which resumed the numbering (212-215).

ORBIT SCIENCE FICTION. (USA). Digest magazine. 5 issues, 1953-November/December 1954. Editor Donald A. Wollheim (Jules Saltman listed on masthead).

ORIGINAL SCIENCE FICTION STORIES. (USA). Digest magazine. 38 issues, 1953-May 1960. Editor Robert A. W. Lowndes. Companion to FUTURE and SCIENCE FICTION QUARTERLY.

OTHER WORLDS. (USA). Digest magazine. 55 issues, November 1949-October 1957. Editor Ray Palmer. The magazine has a tortuous history. After 31 issues it suspended publication in July 1953. Editor Palmer had then taken over UNIVERSE SCIENCE FICTION, whose first two issues (July and September 1953) were credited to editor George Bell. After 10 issues UNIVERSE ceased and OTHER WORLDS resumed, continuing with UNIVERSE's numbering (OTHER WORLDS 11 appearing in May 1955). After no. 22 (May 1957) the title changed to FLYING SAUCERS FROM OTHER WORLDS, and it became a UFO magazine, except that two further issues (July and October 1957) were filled with science fiction, possibly to use up inventory.

PLANET STORIES. (USA). Pulp magazine. 71 issues, Winter 1939-Summer 1955. Editors Malcolm Reiss (Winter 1939-Summer 1942); Wilbur S. Peacock (Fall 1942-Fall 1945); Chester Whitehorne (Winter 1945-Summer 1946); Paul L. Payne (Fall 1946-Spring 1950); Jerome Bixby (Summer 1950-July 1951); Malcolm Reiss (September 1951-January 1952); Jack O'Sullivan (March 1952-Summer 1955).

RIGEL.* (USA). Bedsheet magazine. First issue Summer 1981. Editor Eric Vinicoff.

SATELLITE SCIENCE FICTION. (USA). Digest (October 1956-December 1958); bedsheet (February-May 1959). 18 issues, October 1956-May 1959. Editors Samuel Merwin (October-December 1956); Cylvia Kleinman (February 1957-May 1959). Some copies of the June 1959 issue were printed, and four are still known to exist.

SATURN SCIENCE FICTION AND FANTASY. (USA). Digest magazine. 5 issues, March 1957-March 1958. Editor Donald A. Wollheim.

SCIENCE FANTASY. (UK). Intermediate digest/pulp size Summer 1950-March 1953; digest March 1954 (no. 7)-April 1964; paperback size June/July 1964-February 1967. 93 issues, Summer 1950-February 1967. Editors Walter Gillings (1950); E. J. Carnell (1951-April 1964); Kyril Bonfiglioli (June/July 1964-September 1966); Harry Harrison and Keith Roberts (October 1966-February 1967). Retitled IMPULSE in March 1966, with the numbering beginning again from no. 1 (thus there are SCIENCE FANTASY 1-81 and IMPULSE 1-12).

SCIENCE FICTION. (USA). Pulp magazine. 12 issues, March 1939-September 1941. Editors Charles D. Hornig (March 1939-March 1941); Robert A. W. Lowndes (June-September 1941). Companion to FUTURE FICTION.

SCIENCE FICTION ADVENTURES (1). (USA). Digest magazine. 9 issues, November 1952-May 1954. Editors Philip St. John (Lester del Rey) (November 1952-September 1953); Harry Harrison (December 1953-May 1954).

SCIENCE FICTION ADVENTURES (2), (USA). Digest magazine. 12 issues, December 1956-June 1958. Editor Larry T. Shaw.

SCIENCE FICTION ADVENTURES (3). (UK). Digest magazine. 32 issues, March 1958-May 1963. Editor E. J. Carnell. For the first five issues this was a British edition of SFA (2); then, when the American counterpart folded, it continued, publishing original material, as a companion to NEW WORLDS and SCIENCE FANTASY.

SCIENCE FICTION MONTHLY. (UK). Poster-size magazine. 28 issues, February 1974-May 1976. Editors Pat Hornsey (February 1974-January 1975); Julie Davis (February 1975-May 1976).

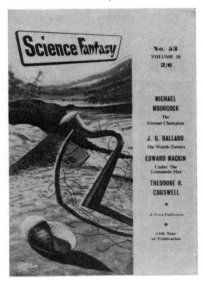

SCIENCE FICTION PLUS. (USA).
Bedsheet magazine. 7 issues, March-
December 1953. Editor Hugo Gernsback
(with Sam Moskowitz).

SCIENCE FICTION QUARTERLY.
(USA). Pulp magazine. 38 issues in two
series: 10 issues Summer 1940-Spring
1943; 28 issues May 1951-February 1958.
Editors Charles D. Hornig (Summer-Fall
1940); Robert A. W. Lowdes (Spring
1941-February 1958). Companion to
FUTURE FICTION.

SCIENCE FICTION STORIES. *see*
FUTURE FICTION

SCIENCE WONDER STORIES. *see*
WONDER STORIES

SCIENCE WONDER QUARTERLY.
see WONDER STORIES QUARTERLY

SCOOPS. (UK). Tabloid-size magazine.
20 issues, February-June 1934. Editor
Haydn Dimmock. Weekly "boy's paper";
Britain's first SF periodical.

SPACE SCIENCE FICTION. (USA).
Digest magazine. 8 issues, May 1952-
September 1953. Editor Lester del Rey.

SPACE STORIES. (USA). Pulp
magazine. 5 issues, October 1952-June
1953. Editor Sam Mines. Companion to
STARTLING STORIES and THRILLING
WONDER STORIES.

SPACE TRAVEL. *see* IMAGINATIVE TALES

SPACEWAY. (USA). Digest magazine. 12
issues in two series: 8 issues December
1953-June 1955; 4 issues January 1969-
June 1970. Editor William L. Crawford.

STARTLING STORIES. (USA). Pulp
magazine. 99 issues, January 1939-Fall
1955. Editors Mort Weisinger (January
1939-May 1941); Oscar J. Friend (July
1941-Fall 1944); Sam Merwin (Winter
1945-September 1951); Sam Mines
(November 1951-Fall 1954); Alexander
Samalman (1955). Companion to
THRILLING WONDER STORIES and various
lesser titles.

SUPER-SCIENCE FICTION. (USA).
Digest magazine. 18 issues, December
1956-October 1959. Editor W. W. Scott.

SUPER SCIENCE STORIES. (USA).
Pulp magazine. 31 issues in two series: 16
issues March 1940-May 1943; 15 issues
January 1949-August 1951. Editors
Frederik Pohl (March 1940-August 1941);
Alden H. Norton (November 1941-May
1943); Ejler Jakobsson (January 1949-
August 1951). The first series was a
companion to ASTONISHING STORIES; the
second series was a companion to FAMOUS
FANTASTIC MYSTERIES and FANTASTIC
NOVELS. A Canadian edition also appeared
in two series. The first (21 issues, August
1942-December 1945) reprinted stories
from various US sources, but also
published some original fiction. The
second simply reprinted the second US
series.

TALES OF WONDER. (UK). Pulp
magazine. 16 issues, 1937-Spring 1942.
Editor Walter S. Gillings.

THRILLING WONDER STORIES. *see*
WONDER STORIES

**TWO COMPLETE SCIENCE
ADVENTURE BOOKS.** (USA). Pulp
magazine. 11 issues, Winter 1950-Spring
1954. Editors Jerome Bixby (Winter 1950-
Summer 1951); Malcolm Reiss (Winter
1951-Summer 1953); Katherine Daffron
(Winter 1953-Spring 1954). Companion
to PLANET STORIES.

UNEARTH. (USA). Digest magazine. 7
issues, Winter 1977-Summer 1978.
Editors Jonathan Ostrowsky-Lantz and
John M. Landsberg.

UNIVERSE. *see* OTHER WORLDS

UNKNOWN. (USA). Pulp magazine. 39
issues, March 1939-October 1943. Editor
John W. Campbell. Title changed to
UNKNOWN WORLDS in 1941. Fantasy
companion to ASTOUNDING SCIENCE
FICTION.

**VARGO STATTEN SCIENCE
FICTION MAGAZINE.** *see* BRITISH
SPACE FICTION MAGAZINE

VENTURE SCIENCE FICTION.
(USA). Digest magazine. 16 issues in two
series: 10 issues January 1957-July 1958; 6
issues May 1969-August 1970. Editors

Robert P. Mills (first series); Edward L. Ferman (second series). Companion to FANTASY AND SCIENCE FICTION. The title was also used for a British magazine (28 issues September 1963-December 1965) which reprinted stories from F&SF and the American VENTURE.

VERTEX. (USA). Bedsheet (later folded-tabloid) magazine. 16 issues, April 1973-October 1975. Editor Donald J. Pfeil.

VISION OF TOMORROW. (UK). Bedsheet magazine. 12 issues, August 1969-September 1970. Editor Philip Harbottle.

VORTEX. (UK). Small bedsheet magazine. 5 issues, January-May 1977. Editor Keith Seddon.

WONDER STORIES. (USA). Bedsheet magazine June 1929-October 1930; pulp November 1930-Winter 1955. 189 issues, June 1929-Winter 1955. Editors Hugo Gernsback (June 1929-April 1936, with David Lasser and Charles D. Hornig as Managing Editors from June 1930-October 1933 and November 1933-April 1936 respectively); Mort Weisinger (August 1936-June 1941); Oscar J. Friend (August 1941-Fall 1944); Sam Merwin (Winter 1945-October 1951); Sam Mines (December 1951-Summer 1954); Alexander Samalman (Fall 1954-Winter 1955). Started life as SCIENCE WONDER STORIES, then absorbed AIR WONDER

STORIES in June 1930 to become plain WONDER STORIES. In August 1936 it changed publishers and for the rest of its life was THRILLING WONDER STORIES. STARTLING STORIES was a later companion.

WONDER STORIES QUARTERLY. (USA). Bedsheet magazine. 14 issues, Fall 1929-Winter 1933. Editor Hugo Gernsback (David Lasser Managing Editor). The first three issues were titled SCIENCE WONDER QUARTERLY.

WORLDS OF TOMORROW. (USA). Digest magazine. 26 issues in two series: 23 issues April 1963-May 1967; 3 issues 1970-71. Editors Frederik Pohl (first series); Ejler Jakobsson (second series). Absorbed by IF when the first series ceased publication.

Note on terminology:
Bedsheet: term used originally for larger format pulp magazines, measuring approx 8½ by 11½ inches and often printed on better quality paper. Used here to denote all larger format magazines of similar dimensions.
Digest: term used for magazines measuring approx 5½ by 7½ inches: the size of the *Reader's Digest*.
Pulp: term used for magazine measuring approx 7 by 10 inches. Pulp magazines were usually printed on very low grade, bulky paper, but the term as used here denotes only size.

SF Publishing: The Economics
Malcolm Edwards

SCIENCE-FICTION MAGAZINE PUBLISHING IS A COTTAGE INDUSTRY. The four titles appearing regularly in the 1980s (*Amazing, Analog, F & SF,* and *Isaac Asimov's Magazine*) have very small staffs – typically, an editor, one or two assistants, someone to run the subscriptions, and perhaps an art director. It seems that the ceiling circulation for an SF magazine published in the USA is a little over 100,000 copies: with the exception of a brief period in the mid-1940s, when *Amazing* claimed a circulation of 200,000, this has apparently always been the ceiling. The magazines rely on money from sales for survival. This may seem an obvious thing to say, yet it is not the case with most news-stand magazines. The bulk of *their* income comes from advertising rather than sales. SF magazines, however, do not attract lucrative advertising (tobacco, alcohol, cars, perfume, and so on) and have to make do with occasional ads from book publishers, plus a page or two of classifieds. (Curiously enough, none of the magazines has been able to attract advertising from the booming home computer market; one would think that for once their audience profile was the correct one for the product.) Sales produce the vast majority of the SF magazines' income, and here there has recently been an important change in the balance between news-stand sales and subscription sales. Edward Ferman, editor and publisher of *F & SF* describes the change thus:

"We always used to be distributed by the American News Company. But they went out of business, which left nothing but a series of independent whole-salers, who essentially found themselves with a monopoly of each area of the country. If you wanted to distribute your magazine in Chicago, say, there was only one wholesaler.

Meanwhile, at the same time, the small news-stands and stationery stores across the country have been going out of business, and their place has been taken by big drug stores and supermarket chains. That's where most magazines are sold now, and these big chains have what they call 'restricted lists'; they only want magazines that sell a lot of copies. They want teenage romances or men's magazines or women's magazines. They don't want small magazines, so it's hard to get in.

We used to sell seventy-five percent of our copies by news-stand, the rest by subscription, and now it's completely reversed itself. It hasn't killed us, because we've concentrated more on subscription promotion . . . but having a big subscription list requires a lot more effort on our part than selling copies on the news-stand, where the national distributor takes care of collecting the money and sends us one big check every month. The one big check is now a very small check."

Similar distribution problems affect the UK, where the big newsagent chains – W.H. Smith and John Menzies – have now got together with big local distributors to pool their warehousing and distribution arrangements. But in the UK there was no living news-stand magazine, and while it is possible (at least in theory) to switch from news-stand to subscription sales, it is not easy to build up a large subscription base without news-stand distribution to bring the magazine to people's attention. Thus new publications – both in the UK and the USA – tend to have far smaller circulations, and do not generally pay wages to their editorial staff, who do the job purely out of dedication.

The change in sales pattern can readily be verified by means of the circulation information which American magazines are obliged to publish each year. Take *F&SF*'s sales figures for alternate years in the period 1973-83:

Year	News-stand sales	Subscriptions	Total sales
1973	25,582	16,612	42,194
1975	25,995	26,360	52,355
1977	23,206	28,526	51,732
1979	23,224	34,676	57,900
1981	21,799	40,272	62,071
1983	16,719	49,400	66,119

These figures seem to indicate that the magazine has very successfully overcome the trend. However, subscriptions are not necessarily all good. A lot depends on what proportion are cut-price introductory subscriptions, which do not begin to make money for the magazine until they are renewed at the full rate. *Galileo* magazine, which began as a successful small-scale semi-professional magazine, expanded enormously by launching a huge subscription drive, but found very quickly that it had actually created for itself a cash-flow problem which helped cause its demise within a matter of months.

BOOK PUBLISHING OF SCIENCE FICTION IS A VERY DIFFERENT KIND OF INDUSTRY. With a few notable exceptions companies on both sides of the Atlantic are parts of very large conglomerates, and SF fantasy publishing forms only a part of their output, typically accounting for somewhere between seven and fifteen percent of their turnover, depending on the size and success of their particular list. The SF bestseller is still a recent phenomenon. Although many of the SF "classics" have achieved very high total sales over the years these have been as a result of steady sales, unspectacular in any given year, rather than as a result of a huge initial sale. Only recently have such authors as Asimov, Clarke, Heinlein, Herbert, and McCaffrey achieved genuine bestseller status; and when several of these are in the hands of a single publisher (in the USA all except Herbert are published in paperback by Del Rey Books, which also has fantasy bestsellers Piers Anthony and Stephen Donaldson) the implications for SF's market share and profitability are considerable.

The economics of publishing vary greatly between paperback and hardcover houses, and between bestsellers and less popular books; there is little of the month-to-month consistency to be found in a magazine operation. But the principles are common to all publishers; a simple balancing of revenue against expenditure.

Expenditure divides into three sections: manufacturing costs, royalties, and overhead costs. Manufacturing costs are obvious: the book has to be typeset, cover art has to be bought, paper and printing and binding must be paid for (there are other, lesser costs which we need not look at here). Some of these costs – such as typesetting and art – are incurred equally whether you print a thousand books or a million. Others – printing and binding – diminish proportionately as the print run increases: in any printing the "run-on" costs, for extra copies, is small compared with the initial cost of getting the piece of work on the machine and ready to run. The net result of this is that the manufacturing cost per book diminishes substantially the longer the print run is.

Royalties are a matter of negotiation. Generally speaking, on a hardback book the royalty is 10% of the published price, though after a certain number of copies have been sold this may rise to 12.5%, 15%, and even 17.5%. A few authors – assured bestsellers – can command higher starting royalties. In virtually all cases a different provision is made for copies sold at very large discounts – e.g. to overseas distributors or to large wholesalers. Here, typically, an author might receive 15% of the proceeds (which, on a 50% discount means a 7.5% royalty; on 60% means 6%; and so forth). In paperback a standard royalty in Britain is 7.5% on home sales and 6% on overseas sales, rising to 10% and 8% after a certain number of copies sold. Again, major authors can command a 10% and 8% starting royalty. In the USA the figure may sometimes be lower – e.g. 6% and 4.5%.

Overheads vary from company to company. These are the costs of running the business: office space, salaries, electricity, telephone bills, stationery, and so on. Overheads also include some provision for gross profit without which the company will make a loss after tax. In smaller companies the total figure for overheads might be 45% or so; in larger ones 55% or even more.

Revenue consists of the money received from selling the book. All sales (or virtually all) are made at substantial discounts to booksellers, wholesalers, and overseas distributors – discounts ranging from 35% to 60%.

Thus, the cost of physically *making* a book is a very small element of its final selling price. If the average discount is 45%, then the publisher has 55% of the book's gross income (price times copies sold) with which to cover costs. Half of this might go in overheads, and a further 10% on royalties – leaving a mere 17.5% to pay for producing the book. If often puzzles people to learn that a book on sale for $12.00 only cost $2.00 actually to make. Surely someone somewhere is making a huge profit? Not necessarily, as I have shown.

Where profits *do* start to come in, however, is when the print run is very large. Then the cost of production starts to fall to a much lower figure per copy, and while this is partly taken up in many cases by increased royalties, there is still more left over for the publisher to call his own.

There are still other ways in which a publisher makes money. There are book clubs, which rely on huge promotion campaigns to sell vast numbers of books at much reduced margins. They pay a royalty which is split between publisher and author, usually 50/50 (the reasoning behind this is that the publisher has to sell the book to the club, which may also use the publisher's typesetting, jacket artwork, and so forth, making a division of the spoils equitable). In Britain the publisher may also manufacture for the book club, making some profit on the transaction. This is less usual in the USA, where the SF Book Club is a very large organization which prints its own editions.

There are also subsidiary rights. If a publisher sells these on behalf of the author, the publisher takes some percentage of the proceeds. In the case of a hardcover publisher selling rights to a paperback company wishing to reprint the book, the split may be a basic 50/50, though in Britain 60/40 is more common (in the author's favour). The split may rise as high as 80/20 to the author. There are also overseas rights where the publisher – acting as the author's agent – may take up to 25% of the income. Many authors' agents prefer to keep these rights themselves, but some publishers counter by increasing the author's advance to take account of projected earnings, so that the author gets the money all in one lump, in advance, rather than in small quantities paid over years. One American SF writer of reasonable – though not bestseller – prominence quoted recently a figure of $30,000 which his American publisher had added to his advance in order to handle British and translation rights on a new novel. That may mean that in the long run the publisher expects to make $40,000 on the sale of these rights, keeping $10,000 as commission and setting the rest against the advance already paid. (This may not be quite as profitable as it seems, of course, as there are small matters like interest payments on that $30,000 to be considered if the rights take years to sell.)

All in all, though, science-fiction publishing has never been more profitable, at the top end of the market. A few writers can now command advances measured in hundreds of thousands of dollars, even millions in a few cases; and these advances are covered by multi-million sales (and even if the advance is *not* covered, the book may still be profitable: by the time you get to your millionth copy the cost of printing a paperback is only a few pennies). But for most writers the prospect is of advances more like $5,000 in the USA and £1,500 in the UK. A gulf has developed between the superstars and the rest which many publishers find hard to bridge; and that "rest" represents marginally profitable publishing, in which the more serious and demanding works are increasingly pushed aside in favour of simple-minded fantasy. How far this trend will continue is hard to foresee. Yet at the same time there are publishers – notably Del Rey, Bantam, Berkley, and DAW in the USA; Futura, Gollancz, Granada, and NEL in the UK – with proven commitment to SF and, apparently, a continuing ability to sell books.

SF CRITICISM
David Wingrove

IF WE ARE TO GIVE any descriptive label to the state of science fiction up to 1945 it must be *naïve*. Its first 20 years are quite clearly the childhood of the genre, and the only sign of critical activity exists in the letter-columns of the pulp magazines and in the fanzines, those small, hand-produced magazines put out by science fiction fans for other science-fiction fans. Both forms of "criticism" still exist and are still almost as partisan as they were in the late 1920s and throughout the 1930s. But between then and now something happened in the genre: like a child waking to the greater world science fiction slowly grew self-conscious.

The last clear sign of the absence of self-awareness in the genre is to be found in a symposium collected in volume form in 1947, *Of Worlds Beyond* (edited by Lloyd Arthur Eschbach). It is the genre's first how-to-write-science-fiction guide, by seven of the genre's then leading writers, and is, perhaps, the perfect summation of the attitudes of the category's first 20 years. Between them, Robert Heinlein, John W. Campbell Jr., L. Sprague de Camp, Jack Williamson, John Taine, A. E. VanVogt and Edward "Doc" Smith set down a series of "market rules" for the production of that commodity called a science-fiction story: don't re-write unless the editor asks you to; sell everything you write; tell a good "yarn" always, and if the plot-line grows anaemic throw in a few sub-plots to spice it up; only ever use one idea per story. All the false rules of writing which have since plagued the field are to be found here, in one slim book, and this, more than any later, supposedly impartial study of the period, provides an insight into the true state of science fiction in its infant years.

A more impartial critical voice was added with the publication in 1960 of *New Maps of Hell*, Kingsley Amis's fond but intelligent and subtle investigation of science fiction. Amis wrote more as a fan than as a practitioner and tended to limit his considered successes in science fiction to those works of social satire, neglecting the more visionary and apocalyptic element in the genre. This flaw, however, is small by comparison with the earlier partisan view, and the attempt to utilize the normal criteria of literary criticism and to give the study a shape (*New Maps* is, in part, a history) make up for it. His conclusion – that science fiction was, in general, inferior to the mainstream – was a justifiable assertion in 1959; yet Amis saw also that science fiction possessed great potential. C. S. Lewis and Edmund Crispin, of the literary fraternity, were to add their voices to Amis's in claiming this potential and in trying to legitimize the genre in academic circles. Yet before that potential could be turned into solid literary achievement the genre had first to suffer an internal revolution.

Between 1947 and 1960 there were small but sure signs of change even within the magazines. The pulps had gone with the War's end, but a whole series of digest-sized magazines proliferated in the 1950s, bringing with them a new generation of writers. That new generation, bred on the pulps but dependent upon them neither for their livelihood nor their complete reading matter, gave the genre a new liveliness and a greater thoughtfulness. The market limitations remained – sex was unmentionable and characterization was always secondary to the ideas – but the range of inventiveness (the ways of circumventing the old criteria) was vastly extended. Satire, as Amis noted, was *in*, but so too were more complex philosophical, theological, and moral explorations (Aldiss, Blish, Dick, and Sheckley were all masters of this kind of witty-yet-poignant short story). Inside the magazines there was a growing need to debate these new forms and new questions. It was no longer a matter of staunchly defending your own favourite adventure writer in the letter columns whilst attacking others: the ideas themselves merited discussion. Book review columns sprang up, and in the fanzines a more serious tone developed. In 1959, *Extrapolation*, a critical journal purely about science fiction, was established, and critics like James Blish (as William Atheling Jr), Damon Knight, and Anthony Boucher – all of whom were also writers of science fiction – began to do inside the genre what Amis had attempted from without. By the mid-1960s this movement towards self-consciousness was almost complete and the fruits of an increased literary awareness began to be plucked. The third generation of science-fiction writers were also critics. Of the winners of the major science-fiction awards in the 1960s many were the foremost critics of the genre – Alexei Panshin, Ursula LeGuin, Samuel Delany, Thomas M. Disch, Michael Moorcock, Brian Aldiss, and James Gunn. For some of them science fiction became the abbreviated SF, which, more often than not, stood for *speculative* fiction. The hard science bias was dropped and the softer social sciences were in. The nature of the criticism changed accordingly. It became valid (if not always interesting) to bring a Marxist or Taoist or Sociological viewpoint to bear on SF criticism. *Science Fiction Studies* in the U.S.A., for instance, often adopted a Marxist ideological approach which, if usually misguided, had an academic thoroughness hitherto absent.

One important and transitional work of this period was Alexei Panshin's *Heinlein In Dimension*, which, more than any other volume, illustrates the radical change of emphasis in the genre. Its subject, Heinlein, was of the old partisan, market-oriented school of "Yarn"-tellers. Its writer, Panshin, was of the new school, conscious of normal literary criteria, academically trained, yet at the same time a creative writer in his own right and within the same field as Heinlein. What the book sets out to do, therefore, is to examine both what was excellent and what poor in Heinlein's work. It did so with a clear eye and a refreshing sense of method. For the first time a coherent and non-partisan, indeed, almost objective view was set out, not in the least defensive. The book stressed Heinlein's importance as the greatest influence on other genre writers and praised his early works, but was justly critical of the poor art of the later, more didactic novels, where the central characters tended to be simple mouthpieces for Heinlein's ideology. Overall it had the analytical depth which, ten years before, would have seemed impossible in the genre, bringing the full range of the mainstream's literary criteria to bear, more often than not to Heinlein's detriment. More important, however, is the sense we have now that Panshin was not providing an overview simply of Heinlein's opus, but of the whole of the emergent science-fiction field. "In a sense, Heinlein may be said to have offered science fiction a road to adulthood," Panshin wrote, but he leaves us with the implication that Heinlein and his generation never took that road themselves.

The growth of self-awareness necessitates a loss – and not merely the shedding of *naïveté*. Not surprisingly, much of the work produced in the genre in the late 1960s and early 1970s became introspective and experimental, aware more of the art-form than of the story-teller's art. The *New Worlds* experiment in England and the New Wave in the States (typical of which was Harlan Ellison's *Dangerous Visions* anthologies) were symptomatic of this. Sex was at last dealt with openly, and often explicitly and obsessively, and there was a far greater emphasis upon character. But although this period was undoubtedly liberating, it also produced many art-for-art's-sake excesses and bred an extreme reaction from those who preferred the old pulp criteria of "yarn" first, literature second. The genre divided markedly during these years into "old" and "new" camps, each of which had their critical adherents. One who bridged both camps, however, both in his fiction and his criticism, was Brian Aldiss, whose *Billion Year Spree* (1973) was the first full-length historical study of the genre.

The single pertinent criticism one can make of *Billion Year Spree* is that more than half of its 320 pages deal with the origins of the genre, rather than with its development from a simple category fiction into the subtle and diverse form it now has. Despite this literary bias Aldiss is highly partisan and a deal less critical of science fiction's excesses than many contemporary critics; which is not to say that his critical standards are lower than theirs, simply that his fondness for extravagance and for the childish traits of the genre is far greater. Aldiss's work is, perhaps, the watershed between two radically different responses to the science-fiction field – between that earliest defensiveness and the most recent scathing disparagement of anything that aims simply to tell an unadorned adventure. *Billion Year Spree* is as articulate and self-aware as the most stringent and supposedly objective essay in *Foundation* (the foremost English critical magazine) or *Science Fiction Studies*, but it also recognizes that science fiction (or SF) *needs* what Aldiss calls elsewhere "the secret schlock ingredient".

Another writer who embraces both "old" and "new" is Fred Pohl. In his 1978 volume of autobiography, *The Way The Future Was*, he provides an inside view of the development of the genre from the late 1920s through to the present day. Pohl, who was editing a science-fiction magazine at the age of 19, during the first years of the Second World War, has also been a literary agent, a publisher's editor, and one of the genre's leading practitioners for the last 40 years, and his comments carry an authority similar to Aldiss's. Pulp-fiction publishing, he asserts, was a matter of simple economics: it allowed no literary thrills. Pages had to be filled for very little reward. But, like the genre, Pohl developed from that, and transformed his art accordingly. Indeed, if I had to recommend one single volume to illustrate the true history of the science-fiction field, I would recommend this immensely readable and thoroughly entertaining book. Pohl's love of knowledge and his evocation of the much disparaged yet all-important "sense of wonder" in the genre are beautifully captured.

Science fiction *has* developed, has become the subtle and varied "SF", and that subtlety is reflected in the new criticism which possesses not merely an under-standing and love of the genre, but a matching academic authority and strin-gency. One such work is Colin Greenland's *The Entropy Exhibition* (1983), which is a study of the *New Worlds* experiment of the late 1960s and early 1970s. There is a sense both of what is good writing and what good SF, and any failing on either part is seen as a failing in the whole work. This is a sensible and healthy approach. Greenland is clearly an admirer of the *New Worlds* school, as the three long studies of Aldiss, Ballard, and Moorcock demonstrate, yet he is far from blindly partisan. Here, at the far end of the genre's development, we have a clear perspective – a sense not merely of achievement and potential, but of limitations and failings, and of the context of the greater literary world of which science fiction is, and must be, a part.

Criticism Checklist
David Wingrove

General Essays and Thematic Studies by SF Writers and Critics

by SF writers

SCIENCE FICTION AS SCIENCE FICTION
Brian W. Aldiss; 1978 (Pamphlet)

THIS WORLD AND NEARER ONES
Brian W. Aldiss; 1979

THE ISSUE AT HAND: STUDIES IN CONTEMPORARY MAGAZINE SCIENCE FICTION
William Atheling Jr (James Blish); 1964

MORE ISSUES AT HAND: CRITICAL STUDIES IN CONTEMPORARY SCIENCE FICTION
William Atheling Jr; 1970

NOTES TO A SCIENCE FICTION WRITER
Ben Bova; 1975

THROUGH EYES OF WONDER: SCIENCE FICTION AND SCIENCE
Ben Bova; 1975

SCIENCE FICTION HANDBOOK
L. Sprague de Camp; 1953

SCIENCE FICTION HANDBOOK, REVISED
L. Sprague de Camp & Catherine Crook de Camp; 1975

THE JEWEL-HINGED JAW: ESSAYS ON SCIENCE FICTION
Samuel R. Delany; 1977

IN SEARCH OF WONDER: ESSAYS ON MODERN SCIENCE FICTION
Damon Knight; 1956

IN SEARCH OF WONDER: ESSAYS ON MODERN SCIENCE FICTION (Revised/Enlarged)
Damon Knight; 1967

TURNING POINTS: ESSAYS ON THE ART OF SCIENCE FICTION
Damon Knight; 1977

FROM ELFLAND TO POUGHKEEPSIE
Ursula K. LeGuin; 1973 (Pamphlet)

DREAMS MUST EXPLAIN THEMSELVES
Ursula K. LeGuin; 1975 (Pamphlet)

THE LANGUAGE OF THE NIGHT: ESSAYS ON FANTASY AND SCIENCE FICTION
Ursula K. LeGuin; 1979

SCIENCE FICTION: WHAT IT'S ALL ABOUT
Sam J. Lundwall; 1971

SF IN DIMENSION: A BOOK OF EXPLORATIONS
Alexei and Cory Panshin; 1976

THE STRENGTH TO DREAM: LITERATURE AND THE IMAGINATION
Colin Wilson; 1962

SCIENCE FICTION AS EXISTENTIALISM
Colin Wilson; 1978 (Pamphlet)

by critics

SCIENCE FICTION: THE FUTURE
Dick Allen; 1971

SCIENCE FICTION READER'S GUIDE
L. David Allen; 1974

FANTASY LITERATURE
T. E. Apter; 1982

LINGUISTICS AND LANGUAGE IN SCIENCE FICTION-FANTASY
Myra Barnes; 1974

SCIENCE FICTION AND THE NEW DARK AGE
Harold L. Berger; 1976

MODERN SCIENCE FICTION: ITS MEANING AND FUTURE
(Ed.) Reginald Bretnor; 1953 (2nd Edition; 1979)

SCIENCE FICTION, TODAY AND TOMORROW
(Ed.) Reginald Bretnor; 1974

A RHETORIC OF THE UNREAL: STUDIES IN NARRATIVE AND STRUCTURE, ESPECIALLY IN THE FANTASTIC
Christine Brooke-Rose; 1981

A MULTITUDE OF VISIONS
Cy Chauvin; 1975

SF: THE OTHER SIDE OF REALISM: ESSAYS ON MODERN FANTASY AND SCIENCE FICTION
(Ed.) Thomas D. Clareson; 1971

SF: A DREAM OF OTHER WORLDS
Thomas D. Clareson; 1973

VOICES FOR THE FUTURE: ESSAYS ON
MAJOR SCIENCE FICTION
WRITERS
(Ed.) Thomas D. Clareson; 1976

MANY FUTURES, MANY WORLDS:
THEME AND FORM IN SCIENCE
FICTION
(Ed.) Thomas D. Clareson; 1977

EXTRAPOLATION: A SCIENCE FICTION
NEWSLETTER, 1959-1969
(Ed.) Thomas D. Clareson; 1978

THE SCIENCE FICTION NOVEL:
IMAGINATION AND SOCIAL
CRITICISM
(Ed.) Basil Davenport; 1959/64

THE SCIENCE FICTION HANDBOOK
FOR READERS AND WRITERS
George S. Elrick; 1978

SCIENCE IN UTOPIA: A MIGHTY
DESIGN
Nell Eurich; 1967

ALTERNATIVE PERSONS: THE
ENTITIES OF SCIENCE FICTION AND
MYTH
Stan Gooch; 1979

THE ENTROPY EXHIBITION:
MICHAEL MOORCOCK AND THE
BRITISH 'NEW WAVE' IN SCIENCE
FICTION
Colin Greenland; 1983

THREE TOMORROWS: AMERICAN,
BRITISH AND SOVIET SCIENCE
FICTION
John Griffiths; 1980

DARWIN TO DOUBLE HELIX: THE
BIOLOGICAL THEME IN SCIENCE
FICTION
Leonard Isaacs; 1977

FANTASY: THE LITERATURE OF
SUBVERSION
Rosemary Jackson; 1981

INTRODUCTORY PSYCHOLOGY
THROUGH SCIENCE FICTION
(Eds) Harvey A. Katz, Patricia Warrick & Martin
H. Greenberg; 1974

UTOPIA AND REVOLUTION
Melvin J. Lasky; 1976

APPROACHES TO SCIENCE FICTION
Donald L. Lawler; 1978

THREE FACES OF SCIENCE FICTION
Robert A. W. Lowndes; 1973

SCIENCE FICTION AS
FUTUROLOGY
Richard L. McKinney; 1976

SCIENCE FICTION: THE ACADEMIC
AWAKENING
Willis E. McNelly; 1974

MODERN FANTASY: FIVE STUDIES
C. N. Manlove; 1975

THE IMPULSE OF FANTASY
LITERATURE
C. N. Manlove; 1982

ALIENS AND LINGUISTICS:
LANGUAGE STUDY AND SCIENCE
FICTION
Walter E. Meyers; 1980

SCIENCE FICTION STUDIES:
SELECTED ARTICLES ON SCIENCE
FICTION, 1973-1975
(Eds) R. D. Mullen & Darko Suvin; 1976

FOUNDATION: THE REVIEW OF
SCIENCE FICTION, MARCH 1972-
MARCH 1975
(Ed.) Peter Nicholls; 1978

THE SCIENCE IN SCIENCE FICTION
Peter Nicholls; 1983

VOYAGES TO THE MOON
Marjorie Hope Nicolson; 1948

SCIENCE FICTION: A CRITICAL GUIDE
Patrick Parrinder; 1979

FANTASY AND SCIENCE FICTION: A
CRITICAL GUIDE
John R. Pfeiffer; 1971

EXPERIMENT PERILOUS: THREE
ESSAYS ON SCIENCE FICTION
(Ed.) Andrew Porter; 1976

THE FANTASTIC IN LITERATURE
Eric S. Rabkin; 1976

WORLD'S END: THE IMAGINATION OF
CATASTROPHE
Eric S. Rabkin & Martin H. Greenberg; 1982

CRITICAL ENCOUNTERS: WRITERS
AND THEMES IN SCIENCE
FICTION
(Ed.) Dick Riley; 1979

THE SHATTERED RING: SCIENCE
FICTION AND THE QUEST FOR
MEANING
Lois Rose & Stephen Rose; 1970

TWENTIETH CENTURY VIEWS:
SCIENCE FICTION
(Ed.) Mark Rose; 1976

VISIONS OF TOMORROW: SIX
JOURNEYS FROM OUTER TO INNER
SPACE
(Ed.) David Samuelson; 1974

A READER'S GUIDE TO SCIENCE
FICTION
Baird Searles, Martin Last, Beth Meacham &
Michael Franklin; 1979

A READER'S GUIDE TO FANTASY
Baird Searles, Beth Meacham & Michael
Franklin; 1982

BRIDGES TO FANTASY
George Slusser, Eric S. Rabkin & Robert
Scholes; 1980

CRITICAL ENCOUNTERS II: WRITERS
AND THEMES IN SCIENCE FICTION
(Ed.) Tom Staicar; 1982

THE FEMININE EYE: SCIENCE FICTION
AND THE WOMEN WHO WRITE IT
(Ed.) Tom Staicar; 1982

TERMINAL VISIONS: THE
LITERATURE OF LAST THINGS
W. Warren Wagar; 1982

THE CYBERNETIC IMAGINATION IN
SCIENCE FICTION
Patricia S. Warrick; 1980

THE KNOWN AND THE UNKNOWN:
THE ICONOGRAPHY OF SCIENCE
FICTION
Gary K. Wolfe; 1979

INTERSECTIONS: THE ELEMENTS OF
FICTION IN SCIENCE FICTION
Thomas L. Wymer; 1978

Critical Histories/Histories

BILLION YEAR SPREE: THE HISTORY
OF SCIENCE FICTION
Brian W. Aldiss; 1973

NEW MAPS OF HELL
Kingsley Amis; 1960

YESTERDAY'S TOMORROWS
W. H. G. Armytage; 1968

FACES OF THE FUTURE: THE LESSONS
OF SCIENCE FICTION
Brian Ash; 1975

THE FANTASTIC TRADITION IN
AMERICAN LITERATURE – FROM
IRVING TO LEGUIN
Brian Attebery; 1980

PILGRIMS THROUGH SPACE AND
TIME: TRENDS AND PATTERNS IN
SCIENTIFIC AND UTOPIAN FICTION
J. O. Bailey; 1947

BRAVE NEW WORLD, 1984 AND WE:
ESSAYS ON ANTI-UTOPIA
E. J. Brown; 1976

IMAGINARY WORLDS
Lin Carter; 1973

THE CREATION OF TOMORROW:
FIFTY YEARS OF MAGAZINE SCIENCE
FICTION
Paul A. Carter; 1977

THE PATTERN OF EXPECTATION:
1644-2001
I. F. Clarke; 1979

VOICES PROPHESYING WAR, 1763-1984
I. F. Clarke; 1966

INQUIRY INTO SCIENCE FICTION
Basil Davenport; 1955/1959

THE WORLD OF SCIENCE FICTION,
1926-1976: THE HISTORY OF A
SUBCULTURE
Lester del Rey; 1979

THIRTY YEARS OF ARKHAM HOUSE
August Derleth; 1970

THE SHAPE OF UTOPIA: STUDIES IN A
LITERARY GENRE
Robert C. Elliot; 1970

FUTURE PERFECT: AMERICAN
SCIENCE FICTION OF THE
NINETEENTH CENTURY
(Ed.) H. Bruce Franklin; 1968

A HISTORY OF THE HUGO, NEBULA
AND INTERNATIONAL FANTASY
AWARDS
Donald Franson & Howard DeVore; 1975
(Revised 1980)

UTOPIAN FANTASY: A STUDY OF THE
ENGLISH UTOPIAN FANTASY SINCE
THE END OF THE NINETEENTH
CENTURY (2nd Edition)
Richard Gerber; 1973

CHEAP THRILLS: AN INFORMAL
HISTORY OF THE PULP
MAGAZINES
Ron Goulart; 1972

THE IMAGINARY VOYAGE IN PROSE
FICTION: A HISTORY OF ITS
CRITICISM AND A GUIDE FOR ITS
STUDY, WITH AN ANNOTATED CHECK
LIST OF 215 IMAGINARY VOYAGES
FROM 1700 TO 1800
Philip Babcock Gove; 1941/1975

INTO OTHER WORLDS: SPACE FLIGHT
IN FICTION FROM LUCIAN
TO LEWIS
Roger Lancelyn Green; 1957

ALTERNATE WORLDS: THE
ILLUSTRATED HISTORY OF SCIENCE
FICTION
James Gunn; 1975

THE DISCOVERY OF THE FUTURE:
THE WAYS SCIENCE FICTION
DEVELOPED
James E. Gunn; 1975

NEW WORLDS FOR OLD: THE
APOCALYPTIC IMAGINATION:
SCIENCE FICTION AND AMERICAN
LITERATURE
David Ketterer; 1971/74

THE ILLUSTRATED BOOK OF SCIENCE
FICTION IDEAS AND DREAMS
David Kyle, 1977

A PICTORIAL HISTORY OF SCIENCE
FICTION
David Kyle; 1976

MOON TRAVELLERS: A DREAM THAT
IS BECOMING A REALITY
Peter Leighton; 1960

SCIENCE FICTION: AN ILLUSTRATED
HISTORY
Sam J. Lundwall; 1978

THE SHAPE OF FUTURE PAST
Chris Morgan; 1980

INTO THE UNKOWN: THE EVOLUTION
OF SCIENCE FICTION FROM FRANCIS
GODWIN TO H. G. WELLS
Robert M. Philmus; 1970

A REQUIEM FOR ASTOUNDING
Alva Rogers; 1964

STRUCTURAL FABULATION: AN
ESSAY ON FICTION OF THE
FUTURE
Robert Scholes; 1975

SCIENCE FICTION: HISTORY,
SCIENCE, VISION
Robert Scholes, Eric S. Rabkin; 1977

METAMORPHOSES OF SCIENCE
FICTION: ON THE POETICS AND
HISTORY OF A LITERARY GENRE
Darko Suvin; 1979

OTHER WORLDS – FANTASY AND
SCIENCE FICTION SINCE 1939
John J. Teunissen; 1980

THE FANTASTIC: A STRUCTURAL
APPROACH TO A LITERARY GENRE
Tzvetan Todorov; 1973

ALL OUR YESTERDAYS: AN INFORMAL
HISTORY OF SCIENCE FICTION IN
THE FORTIES
Harry Warner Jr; 1969

A WEALTH OF FABLE: THE HISTORY
OF SCIENCE FICTION FANDOM IN THE
1950s
Harry Warner Jr; 1977

THE WEIRD TALES STORY
Robert Weinberg; 1977

THE UNIVERSE MAKERS: SCIENCE
FICTION TODAY
Donald A. Wollheim; 1971

Bibliographies/Listings

ITEM EIGHTY-THREE BRIAN W.
ALDISS, A BIBLIOGRAPHY
Margaret Aldiss; 1972

BRACKETT, BRADLEY, McCAFFREY:
A PRIMARY AND SECONDARY
BIBLIOGRAPHY
Rosemarie Arbur; 1982

THE ILLUSTRATED BOOK OF SF LISTS
(Ed.) Mike Ashley; 1982

CLIFFORD D. SIMAK: A PRIMARY AND
SECONDARY BIBLIOGRAPHY
Muriel R. Becker; 1980

SCIENCE FICTION BOOKS PUBLISHED
IN BRITAIN 1974-1978
Gerald Bishop; 1979

THE CHECKLIST OF SCIENCE FICTION
AND SUPERNATURAL FICTION
Everett F. Bleiler; 1978

SF BIBLIOGRAPHIES: AN
ANNOTATED BIBLIOGRAPHY OF
BIBLIOGRAPHICAL WORKS ON
SCIENCE FICTION AND FANTASY
FICTION
Robert E. Briney & Edward Wood; 1972

SCIENCE FICTION CRITICISM: AN
ANNOTATED CHECKLIST
Thomas D. Clareson; 1972

THE TALE OF THE FUTURE FROM THE
BEGINNING TO THE PRESENT DAY: AN
ANNOTATED BIBLIOGRAPHY
I. F. Clarke; 1978 (3rd Edition)

INDEX TO THE WEIRD FICTION
MAGAZINES (Two volumes)
T. G. L. Cockcroft; 1962/64

A CHECKLIST OF SCIENCE FICTION
ANTHOLOGIES
Walter L. Cole; 1964

CDN SF & F: A BIBLIOGRAPHY OF
CANADIAN SCIENCE FICTION AND
FANTASY
John Robert Colombo, Michael Richardson,
John Bell & Alexandre L. Amprimoz; 1979

INDEX TO THE SCIENCE FICTION
ANTHOLOGIES AND COLLECTIONS
William Contento; 1978

'333': A BIBLIOGRAPHY OF THE
SCIENCE FANTASY NOVEL
Joseph H. Crawford; 1953

SCIENCE FICTION AND FANTASY
AUTHORS: A BIBLIOGRAPHY OF FIRST
PRINTINGS OF THEIR FICTION AND
SELECTED NONFICTION
L. W. Currey; 1979

THE SUPPLEMENTAL CHECKLIST OF
FANTASTIC LITERATURE
Bradford M. Day; 1963

THE COMPLETE CHECKLIST OF
SCIENCE FICTION MAGAZINES
Bradford M. Day; 1961

INDEX TO THE SCIENCE FICTION
MAGAZINES, 1926-1950
Donald B. Day; 1952 (Revised 1982)

THEODORE STURGEON: A PRIMARY
AND SECONDARY BIBLIOGRAPHY
Lahna F. Diskin; 1980

SCIENCE FICTION BOOK REVIEW
INDEX, 1923-1973
(Ed.) H. W. Hall; 1975

SCIENCE FICTION BOOK REVIEW
INDEX, 1974-1979
(Ed.) H. W. Hall; 1981

AN INDEX TO "UNKNOWN" AND
"UNKNOWN WORLDS" BY AUTHOR
AND BY TITLE
Stuart Hoffman; 1955

THE SF BOOK OF LISTS
Maxim Jakubowski & Malcolm Edwards; 1983

FANTASMS: A BIBLIOGRAPHY OF THE
LITERATURE OF JACK VANCE
Daniel J. H. Levack & Tim Underwood; 1978

PKD: A PHILIP K. DICK BIBLIOGRAPHY
Daniel J. H. Levack; 1981

SCIENCE FICTION FIRST EDITIONS
George Locke; 1978

VOYAGES IN SPACE: A BIBLIOGRAPHY
OF INTERPLANETARY FICTION,
1801-1914
George Locke; 1975

SCIENCE FICTION AND FANTASY
PSEUDONYMS
Barry McGhan; 1979

AN INDEX AND SHORT HISTORY OF
UNKNOWN
Arthur Metzger; 1976

JACK WILLIAMSON: A PRIMARY AND
SECONDARY BIBLIOGRAPHY
Robert E. Meyers; 1980

FRITZ LEIBER: A BIBLIOGRAPHY,
1934-1979
Chris Morgan; 1979

UTOPIAN LITERATURE:
A BIBLIOGRAPHY WITH A
SUPPLEMENTARY LISTING OF WORKS
INFLUENTIAL IN UTOPIAN THOUGHT
Glenn Negley; 1978

INDEX TO THE SCIENCE FICTION
MAGAZINES, 1966-1970
New England Science Fiction Association; 1971

INDEX TO THE SF PUBLISHERS
(aka. THE INDEX TO SCIENCE FANTASY
PUBLISHERS)
Mark Owings & Jack L. Chalker; 1966 (Revised,
1979)

STELLA NOVA: THE CONTEMPORARY
SCIENCE FICTION AUTHORS
R. Reginald; 1970

CONTEMPORARY SCIENCE FICTION
AUTHORS (1st Edition)
R. Reginald; 1974

SCIENCE FICTION AND FANTASY
LITERATURE; 1: INDEXES TO THE
LITERATURE (A CHECKLIST, 1700-1974)
R. Reginald; 1979

SCIENCE FICTION AND FANTASY
LITERATURE; 2: CONTEMPORARY
SCIENCE FICTION AUTHORS II
(AUTHOR BIOGRAPHIES)
R. Reginald; 1979

BY ANY OTHER NAME:
A COMPREHENSIVE CHECKLIST OF
SCIENCE FICTION AND FANTASY
PSEUDONYMS
R. Reginald; 1980

TO BE CONTINUED: AN ANNOTATED
BIBLIOGRAPHY OF SCIENCE FICTION
AND FANTASY SERIES AND SEQUELS
R. Reginald; 1980

WHO GOES THERE? A BIBLIOGRAPHIC
DICTIONARY
James A. Rock; 1979

BRITISH AND AMERICAN UTOPIAN
LITERATURE, 1516-1975: AN
ANNOTATED BIBLIOGRAPHY
Lyman Tower Sargent; 1979

ANDRE NORTON: A PRIMARY AND
SECONDARY BIBLIOGRAPHY
Roger C. Schlobin; 1980

SF STORY INDEX, 1950-1968
Frederick Siemon; 1971

AUSTRALIAN SCIENCE FICTION
INDEX, 1925-1967
Graham Stone; 1976

THE M.I.T. SF SOCIETY'S INDEX TO
THE SF MAGAZINES, 1951-1965
(Ed.) Eerwin S. Strauss; 1965

RUSSIAN SCIENCE FICTION: 1956-1974;
A BIBLIOGRAPHY
Darko Suvin; 1971/76

HARLAN ELLISON:
A BIBLIOGRAPHICAL CHECKLIST
Leslie Kay Swigart; 1982

THE SCIENCE FICTION COLLECTOR:
1: ACE BOOK INDEX
J. Grant Thiessen; 1976

AMERICAN FANTASTY AND SCIENCE
FICTION: TOWARD A BIBLIOGRAPHY
OF WORKS PUBLISHED IN THE
UNITED STATES, 1948-1973
Marshall B. Tymm (1979)

INDEX TO STORIES IN THEMATIC
ANTHOLOGIES OF SCIENCE FICTION
Marshall B. Tymm, Martin H. Greenberg,
L. W. Currey & Joseph D. Olander; 1978

A RESEARCH GUIDE TO SCIENCE
FICTION STUDIES: AN ANNOTATED
CHECKLIST OF PRIMARY AND
SECONDARY SOURCES FOR FANTASY
AND SCIENCE FICTION
Marshall B. Tymm, Roger C. Schlobin & L. W.
Currey; 1977

THE YEAR'S SCHOLARSHIP IN
SCIENCE FICTION AND FANTASY,
1972-1975
Marshall B. Tymm, Roger C. Schlobin; 1979

THE SCIENCE FICTION REFERENCE
BOOK: A COMPREHENSIVE
HANDBOOK AND GUIDE TO THE
HISTORY, LITERATURE,
SCHOLARSHIP, AND RELATED
ACTIVITIES OF THE SCIENCE
FICTION AND FANTASY FIELDS
Marshall B. Tymm; 1981

THE SCIENCE FICTION AND HEROIC
FANTASY INDEX
Stuart W. Wells III; 1978

TOLKIEN CRITICISM: AN
ANNOTATED CHECKLIST
Richard C. West; 1970

Autobiographies, Biographies, and
Interview Collections

THE SHAPE OF FURTHER THINGS
Brian W. Aldiss; 1970

HELL'S CARTOGRAPHERS: SOME
PERSONAL HISTORIES OF SCIENCE
FICTION WRITERS
(Ed.) Brian W. Aldiss & Harry Harrison; 1975

BIOGRAPHY OF LORD DUNSANY
Mark Amory; 1972

WHO'S WHO IN SCIENCE FICTION
Brian Ash; 1976

IN MEMORY YET GREEN: THE
AUTOBIOGRAPHY OF ISAAC ASIMOV,
1920-1954
Isaac Asimov; 1979

IN JOY STILL FELT: THE
AUTOBIOGRAPHY OF ISAAC ASIMOV,
1954-1978
Isaac Asimov; 1980

H. G. WELLS: AUTHOR IN AGONY
Alfred Borrello; 1972

J. R. R. TOLKIEN: A BIOGRAPHY
Humphrey Carpenter; 1977

THE INKLINGS (Lewis, Williams & Tolkien)
Humphrey Carpenter; 1978

G. K. CHESTERTON
Lawrence J. Clipper; 1974

H. G. WELLS
Richard Hauer Costa; 1967

LOVECRAFT: A BIOGRAPHY
L. Sprague de Camp; 1975

H. G. WELLS: HIS TURBULENT LIFE
AND TIMES
Lovat Dickson; 1969

SF VOICES No. 2
Jeffrey M. Elliot; 1979

J. R. R. TOLKIEN
Robley Evans; 1973

C. S. LEWIS: A BIOGRAPHY
Roger Lancelyn Green & Walter Hooper; 1974

FANTASTIC LIVES:
AUTOBIOGRAPHICAL ESSAYS BY
NOTABLE SCIENCE FICTION
WRITERS
(Ed.) Martin H. Greenberg, 1981

JULES VERNE: A BIOGRAPHY
Jean Jules-Verne; 1976

THE FUTURIANS: THE STORY OF THE
SCIENCE FICTION "FAMILY" OF THE
30s THAT PRODUCED TODAY'S TOP SF
WRITERS AND EDITORS
Damon Knight; 1977

THE TIME TRAVELLER: THE LIFE OF
H. G. WELLS (aka. H. G. WELLS:
A BIOGRAPHY)
Norman & Jeanne Mackenzie; 1973

EXPLORERS OF THE INFINITE: SHAPES
OF SCIENCE FICTION
Sam Moskowitz; 1963

SEEKERS OF TOMORROW: MASTERS
OF MODERN SCIENCE FICTION
Sam Moskowitz; 1965

HUGO GERNSBACK
Sam Moskowitz; 1959

H. G. WELLS
Patrick Parrinder; 1970

WHO WRITES SCIENCE FICTION
(aka. THE DREAM MAKERS)
Charles Platt; 1980

THE WAY THE FUTURE WAS
Frederik Pohl; 1980

EDGAR RICE BURROUGHS: THE MAN
WHO CREATED TARZAN
Irwin Porges; 1976

SF VOICES No. 1
Darrell Schweitzer; 1976

SPEAKING OF SCIENCE FICTION
Paul Walker; 1978

Single Author Criticisms

Brian W. Aldiss
ALDISS UNBOUND: THE SCIENCE
FICTION OF BRIAN W. ALDISS
Richard Mathews; 1977

APERTURES: A STUDY OF THE
WRITINGS OF BRIAN W. ALDISS
Brian Griffin & David Wingrove; 1984

Poul Anderson
THE COLLECTOR'S POUL
ANDERSON
David Stever & Andrew Adams Whyte; 1976

AGAINST TIME'S ARROW: THE HIGH
CRUSADE OF POUL ANDERSON
Sandra Miesel; 1978

Isaac Asimov
ASIMOV ANALYSED
Neil Goble; 1972

ASIMOV'S FOUNDATION TRILOGY
AND OTHER WORKS
L. David Allen; 1977

ISAAC ASIMOV
(Ed.) Joseph D. Olander & Martin Harry
Greenberg; 1977

ISAAC ASIMOV: THE FOUNDATIONS
OF SCIENCE FICTION
James Gunn; 1982

ISAAC ASIMOV
Jean Fiedler & Jim Mele; 1983

J. G. Ballard
J. G. BALLARD: THE FIRST TWENTY
YEARS
(Eds) James Goddard & David Pringle; 1976

EARTH IS THE ALIEN PLANET:
J. G. BALLARD
David Pringle; 1979

Alfred Bester
ALFRED BESTER
Carolyn Wendell; 1980

James Blish
A CLASH OF SYMBOLS: THE TRIUMPH
OF JAMES BLISH
Brian Stableford; 1979

Marion Zimmer Bradley
THE GEMINI PROBLEM: A STUDY IN
DARKOVER
Walter Breen; 1973

THE DARKOVER DILEMMA:
PROBLEMS OF THE DARKOVER SERIES
S. Wise; 1976

Ray Bradbury
THE RAY BRADBURY COMPANION:
A LIFE AND CAREER HISTORY,
PHOTOLOG, AND COMPREHENSIVE
CHECKLIST OF WRITINGS WITH
FACSIMILES FROM RAY BRADBURY'S
UNPUBLISHED AND UNCOLLECTED
WORK IN ALL MEDIA
William F. Nolan; 1975

THE DRAMA OF RAY BRADBURY
Benjamin P. Indick; 1977

BRADBURY'S WORKS
Audrey Smoak Manning; 1977

THE BRADBURY CHRONICLES
George Edgar Slusser; 1977

RAY BRADBURY
(Eds) Joseph D. Olander & Martin H.
Greenberg; 1979

RAY BRADBURY
Wayne L. Johnson; 1981

John Brunner
THE HAPPENING WORLDS OF JOHN
BRUNNER: CRITICAL EXPLORATIONS
IN SCIENCE FICTION
(Ed.) Joseph W. De Bolt; 1975

Edgar Rice Burroughs
EDGAR RICE BURROUGHS: MASTER
OF ADVENTURE (2nd Revised Edition)
Richard A. Lupoff; 1975

EDGAR RICE BURROUGHS AND THE
MARTIAN VISION
Richard A. Lupoff; 1976

A GUIDE TO BARSOOM: ELEVEN
SECTIONS OF REFERENCES IN ONE
VOLUME DEALING WITH THE
MARTIAN STORIES BY EDGAR RICE
BURROUGHS
John Flint Roy; 1976

G. K. Chesterton
G. K. CHESTERTON: A CENTENARY
APPRAISAL
(Ed.) John Sullivan; 1974

THE NOVELS OF G. K. CHESTERTON:
A STUDY IN ART AND PROPAGANDA
Ian Boyd; 1975

Arthur C. Clarke
ARTHUR C. CLARKE
(Eds) Joseph D. Olander & Martin H.
Greenberg; 1977

THE SPACE ODYSSEYS OF ARTHUR C.
CLARKE
George Edgar Slusser; 1978

ARTHUR C. CLARKE
Eric S. Rabkin; 1979 (Revised 2nd Edition,
1980)

Samuel R. Delany
THE DELANY INTERSECTION:
SAMUEL R. DELANY CONSIDERED AS A
WRITER OF SEMI-PRECIOUS WORDS
George Edgar Slusser; 1977

WORLDS OUT OF WORDS: THE SF
NOVELS OF SAMUEL R. DELANY
Douglas Barbour; 1979

Philip K. Dick
PHILIP K. DICK: ELECTRIC
SHEPHERD
(Ed.) Bruce Gillespie; 1975

PHILIP K. DICK AND THE UMBRELLA
OF LIGHT
Angus Taylor; 1975

PHILIP K. DICK
(Eds) Joseph D. Olander & Martin H.
Greenberg; 1983

Thomas M. Disch
THE AMERICAN SHORE:
MEDITATIONS ON A TALE OF SCIENCE
FICTION BY THOMAS M. DISCH –
ANGOULEME
Samuel R. Delany; 1978

Harlan Ellison
HARLAN ELLISON: UNREPENTANT
HARLEQUIN
George Edgar Slusser; 1977

Philip Jose Farmer
PHILIP JOSE FARMER
Mary T. Brizzi; 1980

John Russell Fearn
THE MULTI-MAN: A BIOGRAPHIC
STUDY OF JOHN RUSSELL FEARN
Philip Harbottle; 1968

Alan Garner
A FINE ANGER: A CRITICAL
INTRODUCTION TO THE WORK OF
ALAN GARNER
Neil Philip; 1981

H. Rider Haggard
RIDER HAGGARD: HIS LIFE AND WO
Morton N. Cohen; 1960

H. RIDER HAGGARD: A VOICE FROM
THE INFINITE
Peter Beresford Ellis; 1978

Joe Haldeman
JOE HALDEMAN
Joan Gordon; 1980

Robert A. Heinlein
HEINLEIN IN DIMENSION: A CRITICAL ANALYSIS
Alexei Panshin; 1968

STRANGER IN A STRANGE LAND AND OTHER WORKS
Baird Searles; 1975

THE CLASSIC YEARS OF ROBERT A. HEINLEIN
George Edgar Slusser; 1977

ROBERT A. HEINLEIN: STRANGER IN HIS OWN LAND
George Edgar Slusser; 1977 (2nd Edition)

ROBERT A. HEINLEIN
(Eds) Joseph D. Olander & Martin H. Greenberg; 1978

ROBERT A. HEINLEIN: AMERICA AS SCIENCE FICTION
H. Bruce Franklin; 1980

Frank Herbert
HERBERT'S "DUNE" AND OTHER WORKS
L. David Allen; 1975

FRANK HERBERT
David M. Miller; 1980

FRANK HERBERT
Timothy O'Reilly; 1981

Aldous Huxley
ALDOUS HUXLEY: THE CRITICAL HERITAGE
(Ed.) Donald Watt; 1975

Ursula K. LeGuin
THE FARTHEST SHORES OF URSULA K. LeGUIN
George Edgar Slusser; 1976

URSULA K. LeGUIN: VOYAGER TO INNER LANDS AND TO OUTER SPACE
(Ed.) Joe de Bolt; 1979

URSULA K. LeGUIN
(Eds) Joseph D. Olander & Martin H. Greenberg; 1979

URSULA K. LeGUIN
Barbara J. Bucknall; 1981

Fritz Leiber
FRITZ LEIBER
Jeff Frane; 1980

FRITZ LEIBER
Tom Staicar; 1982

C. S. Lewis
SURPRISED BY JOY
C. S. Lewis; 1955

LIGHT ON C. S. LEWIS
(Ed.) Jocelyn Gibb; 1965

David Lindsay
THE STRANGE GENIUS OF DAVID LINDSAY (*aka* THE HAUNTED MAN)
J. B. Pick, Colin Wilson & E. H. Visiak; 1970

THE LIFE AND WORKS OF DAVID LINDSAY
Bernard Sellin; 1981

Jack London
THE ALIEN WORLDS OF JACK LONDON
Dale L. Walker; 1973

H. P. Lovecraft
SOME NOTES ON H. P. LOVECRAFT
August Derleth; 1959

LOVECRAFT: A LOOK BEHIND THE CTHULHU MYTHOS
Lin Carter; 1972

READER'S GUIDE TO THE CTHULHU MYTHOS
Robert Weinberg & Edward P. Berglund; 1973

HOWARD PHILLIPS LOVECRAFT: DREAMER ON THE NIGHTSIDE
Frank Belnap Long; 1975

ESSAYS LOVECRAFTIAN
Darrell Schweitzer; 1976

THE H. P. LOVECRAFT COMPANION
Philip A. Schreffler; 1977

THE DREAM QUEST OF H. P. LOVECRAFT
Darrell Schweitzer; 1977

George Orwell
GEORGE ORWELL: A LITERARY STUDY
John Atkins; 1954

THE LAST MAN IN EUROPE: AN ESSAY ON GEORGE ORWELL
Alan Sandison; 1974

GEORGE ORWELL: A COLLECTION OF CRITICAL ESSAYS
(Ed.) Raymond Williams; 1974

THE ROAD TO MINILUV: GEORGE ORWELL, THE STATE AND GOD
Christopher Small; 1975

GEORGE ORWELL AND THE ORIGINS OF 1984 (*aka.* THE ROAD TO 1984)
William Steinhoff; 1975

GEORGE ORWELL: A LIFE
Bernard Crick; 1980

Mervyn Peake
MERVYN PEAKE: A BIOGRAPHICAL
AND CRITICAL EXPLORATION
John Batchelor; 1974

A GUIDE TO THE GORMENGHAST
TRILOGY
Arthur Metzger; 1976

MERVYN PEAKE
John Watney; 1976

Keith Roberts
BRITISH SCIENCE FICTION WRITERS
VOL 2: KEITH ROBERTS
(Eds) Paul Kinkaid & Geoff Rippington; 1983

Bob Shaw
BRITISH SCIENCE FICTION WRITERS
VOL 1: BOB SHAW
(Eds) Paul Kinkaid & Geoff Rippington; 1982

Mary Shelley
MARY SHELLEY'S "FRANKENSTEIN":
TRACING THE MYTH (*aka.* ARIEL LIKE A
HARPY: SHELLEY, MARY AND
FRANKENSTEIN)
Christopher Small; 1972

THE FRANKENSTEIN LEGEND
Donald F. Glut; 1973

MARY SHELLEY'S MONSTER: THE
STORY OF
FRANKENSTEIN
Martin Tropp; 1976

FRANKENSTEIN'S CREATION: THE
BOOK, THE MONSTER, AND HUMAN
REALITY
David Ketterer; 1979

THE ENDURANCE OF FRANKENSTEIN:
ESSAYS ON MARY SHELLEY'S
NOVEL
(Eds) George Levine & V. C. Knoepflmacher;
1979

Clarke Ashton Smith
IN MEMORIAM CLARK ASHTON
SMITH
(Ed.) Jack L. Chalker; 1963

THE LAST OF THE GREAT ROMANTIC
POETS
Donald Sidney-Fryer; 1973

PLANETS AND DIMENSIONS:
COLLECTED ESSAYS OF CLARK
ASHTON SMITH
(Ed.) Charles K. Wolfe; 1973

Cordwainer Smith
EXPLORING CORDWAINER SMITH
(Ed.) Andrew Porter; 1975

E. E. "Doc" Smith
THE UNIVERSES OF E. E. SMITH
Ron Ellik & Bill Evans; 1966

Frank Stockton
FRANK R. STOCKTON
Henry L. Golemba; 1981

Theodore Sturgeon
THEODORE STURGEON
Lahna Diskin; 1980

THEODORE STURGEON
Lucy Menger; 1982

James Tiptree Jr
THE FICTION OF JAMES TIPTREE JR
Gardner Dozois; 1977

J. R. R. Tolkien
TOLKIEN: A LOOK BEHIND LORD OF
THE RINGS
Lin Carter; 1969

MASTER OF MIDDLE EARTH: THE
FICTION OF J. R. R. TOLKIEN
Paul Kocher; 1972

TOLKIEN'S WORLD
Randel Helms; 1974

A TOLKIEN COMPASS
(Ed.) Robert E. Kuehn; 1975

J. R. R. TOLKIEN: ARCHITECT OF
MIDDLE EARTH
Daniel Grotta-Kurska; 1976

TOLKIEN AND THE SILMARILLION
Clyde S. Kilby; 1976

OF ORC RAGS, PHIALS AND A FAR
SHORE: VISIONS OF PARADISE IN
LORD OF THE RINGS
Bruce Palmer; 1976

THE TOLKIEN COMPANION
J. E. A. Tyler; 1976

THE MYTHOLOGY OF MIDDLE EARTH
Ruth S. Noel; 1977

THE COMPLETE GUIDE TO MIDDLE
EARTH (Revised Edition of A GUIDE TO
MIDDLE EARTH)
Robert Foster; 1978

MIDDLE EARTH: A WORLD IN
CONFLICT
Stephen O. Miller; 1978

AN INTRODUCTION TO ELVISH
Jim Allan 1979

THE NEW TOLKIEN COMPANION
J. E. A. Tyler; 1979

Jack Vance
JACK VANCE: SCIENCE FICTION
STYLIST
Richard Tiedman; 1965

JACK VANCE
(Eds) Tim Underwood & Chuck Miller;
1980

Jules Verne
JULES VERNE: INVENTOR OF SCIENCE
FICTION
Peter Costello; 1978

Kurt Vonnegut Jr
KURT VONNEGUT: FANTASIST OF
FIRE AND ICE
David H. Goldsmith; 1972

KURT VONNEGUT JR
Peter J. Reed; 1972

KURT VONNEGUT JR
Stanley Schatt; 1976

VONNEGUT: A PREFACE TO HIS
NOVELS
Richard Giannone; 1977

VONNEGUT IN AMERICA: AN
INTRODUCTION TO THE LIFE AND
WORK OF KURT VONNEGUT
(Eds) Jerome Klinkowitz & Donald L. Lawler;
1977

KURT VONNEGUT
James Lundquist; 1977

KURT VONNEGUT: THE GOSPEL FROM
OUTER SPACE (OR, YES, WE HAVE NO
NIRVANAS)
Clark Mayo; 1977

H. G. Wells
EXPERIMENT IN AUTOBIOGRAPHY
H. G. Wells; 1934 (In Two Volumes)

THE EARLY H. G. WELLS: A STUDY OF
THE SCIENTIFIC ROMANCES
Bernard Bergonzi; 1961

H. G. WELLS AND THE WORLD STATE
W. Warren Wagar; 1961

THE LIFE AND THOUGHT OF
H. G. WELLS
Julius Kagarlitsky; 1966

THE FUTURE AS NIGHTMARE:
H. G. WELLS AND THE
ANTI-UTOPIAS
Mark R. Hillegas; 1967

H. G. WELLS: THE CRITICAL
HERITAGE
(Ed.) Patrick Parrinder; 1972

H. G. WELLS AT THE TURN OF THE
CENTURY
J. P. Vernier; 1973 (Pamphlet)

H. G. WELLS: CRITIC OF PROGRESS
Jack Williamson; 1973

H. G. WELLS: A COLLECTION OF
CRITICAL ESSAYS
Bernard Bergonzi; 1976

H. G. WELLS AND MODERN SCIENCE
FICTION
(Eds) Darko Suvin & Robert M. Philmus; 1977

WHO'S WHO IN H. G. WELLS
Brian Ash; 1982

Austin Tappan Wright
AN INTRODUCTION TO ISLANDIA
Basil Davenport; 1942

THE ISLANDIAN WORLD OF
AUSTIN WRIGHT
Lawrence Clark Powell; 1957

Philip Wylie
PHILIP WYLIE
Truman Frederick Keefer; 1977

Ivan Yefremov
IVAN YEFREMOV'S THEORY OF SOVIET
SCIENCE FICTION
G. V. Grebens; 1978

Yevgeny Zamyatin
A SOVIET HERETIC: ESSAYS
Yevgeny Zamyatin; 1970

Roger Zelazny
A READER'S GUIDE TO
ROGER ZELAZNY
Carl B. Yoke; 1979

General
SHADOWS OF HEAVEN: RELIGION AND
FANTASY IN THE WRITINGS OF
C. S. LEWIS, CHARLES WILLIAMS AND
J. R. R. TOLKIEN
Gunnar Urang; 1971

SHADOWS OF IMAGINATION: THE
FANTASIES OF C. S. LEWIS,
J. R. R. TOLKIEN AND CHARLES
WILLIAMS
Mark R. Hillegas; 1976

Encylopaedias

THE VISUAL ENCYCLOPEDIA OF
SCIENCE FICTION
(Ed.) Brian Ash; 1977

THE ANATOMY OF WONDER
(Ed.) Neil Barron; 1976

THE ANATOMY OF WONDER: SECOND
EDITION
(Ed.) Neil Barron; 1981

SF WRITERS
(Ed.) Everett F. Bleiler; 1984

ENCYCLOPEDIA OF SCIENCE
FICTION
(Ed.) Robert Holdstock; 1978

THE INTERNATIONAL SCIENCE
FICTION YEARBOOK
(Ed.) Colin Lester; 1978

SURVEY OF SCIENCE FICTION (Five
Volumes)
(Ed.) Frank N. Magill; 1979

THE ENCYCLOPEDIA OF SCIENCE
FICTION
(Ed.) Peter Nicholls; 1979

THE SCIENCE FICTION BOOK: AN
ILLUSTRATED HISTORY
Franz Rottensteiner

TWENTIETH CENTURY SCIENCE
FICTION WRITERS
(Ed.) Curtis S. Smith; 1981

THE ENCYCLOPEDIA OF SCIENCE
FICTION AND FANTASY: VOLUME 1:
WHO'S WHO, A-L
Donald H. Tuck; 1974

THE ENCYCLOPEDIA OF SCIENCE
FICTION AND FANTASY: VOLUME 2:
WHO'S WHO, M-Z
Donald H. Tuck; 1978

ENCYCLOPEDIE DE L'UTOPIE ET DE
LA SCIENCE FICTION (in French)
Pierre Versins; 1972

SF Workshopping, Symposiums and
Teaching Aids

SF HORIZONS (2 Volumes in 1)
(Eds) Brian W. Aldiss & Harry Harrison; 1965

THE CRAFT OF SCIENCE FICTION
(Ed.) Reginald Bretnor; 1976

TEACHING TOMORROW:
A HANDBOOK OF SCIENCE FICTION
FOR TEACHERS
Elizabeth Calkins & Barry McGhan; 1972

SCIENCE FICTION IN THE ENGLISH
CLASS
(Ed.) Kenneth Donelson; 1972

OF WORLDS BEYOND: A SYMPOSIUM
(Ed.) Lloyd Arthur Eshbach; 1947

SCIENCE FICTION: THE CLASSROOM
IN ORBIT
Beverley Friend; 1974

WRITING AND SELLING SCIENCE
FICTION
(Ed.) Charles L. Grant; 1977

THE ALTERED I
(Ed.) Lee Harding; 1976

BACKDROP OF STARS: THE CRAFT OF
SCIENCE FICTION
(Ed.) Harry Harrison; 1968

GROKKING THE FUTURE: SCIENCE
FICTION IN THE CLASSROOM
Bernard C. Hollister & Deane C. Thompson;
1973

SCIENCE FICTION PRIMER FOR
TEACHERS
Susan Millies; 1975

SCIENCE FICTION AT LARGE
(aka. EXPLORATIONS OF THE
MARVELLOUS)
(Ed.) Peter Nicholls; 1976

SCIENCE FICTION: ITS CRITICISM
AND TEACHING
Patrick Parrinder; 1981

THOSE WHO CAN: A SCIENCE FICTION
READER
(Ed.) Robin Scott Wilson; 1973

THE VIEW FROM THE EDGE
(Ed.) George Turner; 1977

TEACHING SCIENCE FICTION:
EDUCATION FOR TOMORROW
(Ed.) Jack Williamson; 1972 (revised 1980)

Afterword
Kingsley Amis

Near the end of *New Maps of Hell* I wrote that science fiction was as inferior "in subtlety and importance" to mainstream literature as popular music was to what I rather pompously called "the whole classical corpus". I added that I should like to be offered the chance of disputing the analogy "round about the year 1984". Well, here comes 1984, and here is the chance, but where is the dispute to come from?

Alas! The reader will see that I was hoping, even expecting, to have to revise upwards my opinion of science fiction and its status. Those last pages of my book are free of all doubt, of the least suspicion that the star-cluster of talent I so much admired would soon be afflicted by galloping entropy. When in 1980 I came to choose the stories for my anthology, *The Golden Age of Science Fiction* – not my choice of title, but fair enough – I found nothing published later than 1962 that seemed to me too good to leave out. (Nothing earlier than 1949, either, but that is another question.)

In my Introduction to the anthology I tried to argue out what had gone wrong. Four main reasons for the calamity suggested themselves. One of these concerned the readership, which soon became less specialized, increasingly composed of youngsters who saw science fiction as just part of the Sixties scene, and so in a sense less demanding than the old fans. Another reason had to do with the "breaking-down of the barriers" between science fiction and general fiction, which brought among other things dilution and de-flavouring. I summed up a lot of what I felt when I wrote:

"Science fiction could never enrich orthodox fiction by merging the one with the other anywhere near as much as it has enriched literature as a whole by staying separate."

In *New Maps* I had put the point rather differently, but it was essentially the same point:

"It is not by capturing more territory that science fiction will improve itself, but by consolidating what it already has."

– about the only decently prophetic remark in the whole book, and even then it was unconscious and back-to-front. True, I did foresee an increasing number of forays into the genre by mainstream writers, but fondly supposed that this would be a good thing.

To resume: a third reason for the sudden decline of science fiction was (I suggested in the later book) an increase in self-consciousness, an unwonted concern to do things other than tell a story as effectively as possible, a farewell for ever to primal innocence and – vulgarity? Call it want of refinement. And fourthly, and I now think chiefly, the supply of new ideas, on which the science-fiction writer had always depended much more intimately than his general-fiction colleague, simply gave out, or looked like doing so, which was just as bad. New things to go wrong with a time-machine or in a space-ship had disappeared down the same hole as new methods of murder and new ways of faking an alibi longer ago in another genre.

Since *Golden Age*, the science fiction that has come my way – these days it has to do that; I don't go to it any more – might have been specially written to reinforce my conclusions. At this point I find myself in something of a difficulty. It would be poor fun for both me and the reader if I were to take a select handful of recent books and give them a drubbing on what would mostly be insufficient evidence – insufficient for any sort of public appraisal, that is to say, however sufficient (and to spare) it might be to make up my mind for me that this or that was not worth going on with. Flat generalization would be objectionable for a different reason. Looked at in one way, science fiction is still, or more than ever before, too various for one set of cavils to be generally relevant. On the other hand, its shortcomings can be considered no different from those of any other kind of writing – being silly, being predictable, being illiterate, being dull (especially that).

Having said that, I propose to relax my rule in favour of *Riddley Walker*, a novel by a writer of children's books called Russell Hoban. As all too many readers will know, this is a post-cataclysmic tale of folk-myth and spiritual regeneration among tribal-feudal villagers who hunt wild dogs and smoke hash. The prose is a synthetic kind of semi-phonetic patois with an American accent, though the setting is south-east England. There seems no good reason for this linguistic invention, unless as a way (a rather lazy one) of suggesting barbarism. And on a second look, the language turns out to be not so very different from our own, except for the spelling and a few easily-understood special phrases. So what was the point of Mr Hoban's laborious exercise in transliteration? Its result is not at all interesting in itself.

There were two related benefits. (I don't suggest that they were consciously planned.) The odd look of the words helped to cover up the banality of the author's imagination and the tawdriness of his emotional appeal, and also, positively, it reinforced the general suggestion that something genuinely strange was being said, something mysterious and important. Anyway, the operation was a success – an assorted crew of distinguished dupes found *Riddley* stunning, dizzying, a masterpiece, a real achievement, what literature is meant to be. Most critics and reviewers, of course, have no idea whether what they may have just finished reading is any good or not. They need guidance, and this time, as often happens, they got it from the book itself, which slipped them the message that it was extraordinary and significant by talking about "conkreat" instead of concrete and "fents" when you or I would have put fence. No special blame attaches to the reviewers I have in mind; they were mainstreamers to a man and so doubly at a loss, most of them no doubt under the impression that writing about a society after the holocaust was a jolly original idea.

I notice finally that neither the British nor the American paperback of *Riddley* says anything on its outside or inside about science fiction. Is it possible that the label is still thought to be the turn-off it undoubtedly was at the time of *New Maps*, even now that it means hardly anything? More likely "science fiction" has gone through a period of relative respectability before entering upon a second and, this time, richly deserved state of exclusion from the concerns of civilized people.

In *Golden Age* I said (not as the first or last to do so) that I thought the future of the genre looked more hopeful in the cinema than on the page. Still my view, even with the latest works of Arthur C. Clarke, Isaac Asimov, and Marion Zimmer Bradley on the April 1983 general list of US best-sellers in hardback (that's what I call barrier-breaking) and the screening of *Return of the Jedi* and *ET*. Reactions to the latter were interesting. The general public (including me) and the critics were united for once in enthusiasm; some SF fans were sniffy, resentful that a piece of their private property (SF as a whole) had been thrown open to all regardless of qualification, fearful too, perhaps that the centre of gravity of SF was indeed swinging away from print, where they felt they had some control, and towards film, where anything could happen. In one sense they need not have worried; only the excellent, evocative opening had any recognizable SF feel.

Blade Runner inevitably comes next, a masterpiece according to me, though the script lurched into the language of melodrama here and there – I wept at Rutget Hauer's valedictory speech, but I knew it was hokum all the same. The film as a whole scored by making no concessions and by its thoroughness, every detail lovingly used to fill in the picture of a city and a society of the future. Above all, perhaps, this was done as if casually, seemingly at random – *of course* the shops and stalls of this American megalopolis are full of Orientals, *of course* the skyscrapers carry huge video-screens. All the best literary representations of imaginary places go about their business in that way.

I noticed intramural restiveness here too. "Hollywood," wrote Brian Aldiss in the tone of one mentioning Nuremberg or Pyongyang – "Hollywood has made what from the trailers looks like a rotten film from a lovely book, and called it by a crummy old Alan Nourse title, *Blade Runner*." Not quite such a crummy old title, you may think, as that of the Philip K. Dick novel on which the film was based, *Do Androids Dream of Electric Sheep?*, which the film company wisely kept out of sight until the end-titles. And not quite such a lovely book as his great work of five years earlier, *The Man in the High Castle* (1963), but lovelier far than the sad farrago of the last novel of his to have come my way, *The Divine Invasion* (1981). His death in the following year was the final event in what seems to have been an unusually harrowing personal decline, but the decline in his work was, alas again, no more than representative. The excellence of *Blade Runner* has a melancholy appropriateness.

PS: All may be well. *Battlefield Earth*, by L. Ron Hubbard, 819 pp., $24.00, 3 lb. approx., has just come thumping on to my table, and could be the harbinger of a new dawn. But somehow . . .